The Missing Monument Murders

Judy Stove

W WATERSIDE PRESS

The Missing Monument Murders
Judy Stove

ISBN 978-1-909976-24-5 (Paperback)
ISBN 978-1-910979-08-2 (Epub ebook)
ISBN 978-1-910979-09-9 (Adobe ebook)

Copyright © 2016 This work is the copyright of Judy Stove. All intellectual property and associated rights are hereby asserted and reserved by her in full compliance with UK, European and international law. No part of this book may be copied, reproduced, stored in any retrieval system or transmitted in any form or by any means, or in any language, including in hard copy or via the internet, without the prior written permission of the publishers to whom all such rights have been assigned worldwide.

Cover design © 2016 Waterside Press. Back cover images used by permission: print of Chandos Leigh © National Portrait Gallery, London; photograph of Charles Griffin © Leamington Spa Art Gallery & Museum; painting of Christopher Leigh © The Trustees of Lamport Hall.

Main UK distributor Gardners Books, 1 Whittle Drive, Eastbourne, East Sussex, BN23 6QH. Tel: +44 (0)1323 521777; sales@gardners.com; www.gardners.com

North American distribution Ingram Book Company, One Ingram Blvd, La Vergne, TN 37086, USA. Tel: (+1) 615 793 5000; inquiry@ingramcontent.com

Cataloguing-In-Publication Data A catalogue record for this book can be obtained from the British Library.

Printed by Lightning Source.

e-book *The Missing Monument Murders* is available as an ebook and also to subscribers of Myilibrary, Dawsonera, ebrary, and Ebscohost.

Published 2016 by
Waterside Press
Sherfield Gables
Sherfield-on-Loddon
Hook, Hampshire
United Kingdom RG27 0JG

Telephone +44(0)1256 882250
E-mail enquiries@watersidepress.co.uk

Table of Contents

About the Author *iv*
Acknowledgements *v*
Image details *vii*
Who's Who in the Stoneleigh Story *ix*

	Introduction..19	
1	**Inheritance** 21	
2	**Julia-Judith** 35	
3	**Rivals** 47	
4	**Witness** 61	
5	**Denial** 81	
6	**Not Far From Here**..101	
7	**Chandos: The Severest Satire on Lord Byron**...........115	
8	**A Death's Head**... 141	
9	**"Let go!"** 161	
10	**Drink to the Dead Men** 183	
11	**The Billinges Problem**... 203	
12	**A Mock Funeral**.. 219	
13	**The White Powder**...241	
14	**Coffin Plates** 257	
15	**The Book Transaction**... 273	
16	**A Soul for the Structure**.. 289	

Afterword *305*
Family Tree *307*
Select Bibliography *310*
Index *320*

About the Author

Judy Stove is an academic based at the University of New South Wales, a role she balances with working in school administration. After studying classics at the University of Sydney, she worked for the Australian Commonwealth Departments of Defence and Finance. She is married with two adult sons, and is an active member of the Jane Austen Society of Australia.

Acknowledgements

The following friends have had faith in this project from when I first began it. To them, sincere thanks. The first group are all members of the Jane Austen Society of Australia (JASA), the best literary society in the world, to which it has been my pleasure to belong for many years.
- Adrienne Bradney-Smith
- Elizabeth Budge
- Susannah Fullerton
- Tracey Pearce
- Joanna Penglase

Part of the material in this book first appeared in the JASA journal *Sensibilities* for June 2015, and I thank JASA for permission to use it in this work.

Many friends encouraged me during the drafting, including:
- Jennifer Crockart and Andrew Macdonald
- James Franklin
- Michaela James and David Hickling
- Claire Hogan, Claire Moore, Margaret North, and Kathy Sapsford, and their families
- Carolyn Chapple and Debra Mullen, colleagues and friends in my day job

I also thank the following:
- Victoria Slade, Leamington Spa Art Gallery and Museum
- Staff of the National Archives, London
- Staff of the National Portrait Gallery, London
- Staff of the Shakespeare's Birthplace Trust Record Office (SBTRO), Stratford-upon-Avon

- Garry Strachan, who provided me with transcriptions of documents from the SBTRO.

Special thanks to Bryan Gibson, Alex Gibson, and everyone at Waterside Press for making this book a reality.

The final group is my family, who have always supported my writing. They are my husband Stuart Wilson, sons James Wilson and Hugh Wilson, my brother R J Stove, and my mother-in-law Margaret Wilson. Thank you all.

Any errors in this work are mine alone.

Judy Stove
Mulgoa, New South Wales
Australia

May 2016

Image details

Front cover

Stoneleigh Abbey and Bridge, 1849 engraved print in the possession of Waterside Press.

Back cover (left to right)

Chandos Leigh, 1st Baron Leigh, stipple engraving by unknown artist, early 19th century, from the collection, and reproduced by permission, of the National Portrait Gallery, London.

Charles Griffin, photograph (undated but probably 1860s) from the collection, and reproduced by permission of Leamington Spa Art Gallery and Museum, Leamington Spa, Warwickshire.

Christopher Leigh, portrait by unknown artist, probably 1640s, from the collection at Lamport Hall, and reproduced by permission of the Trustees of Lamport Hall, Northamptonshire.

Judy Stove, copyright of the author.

The Missing Monument Murders

Who's Who in the Stoneleigh Story

Note: Some people appear in more than one section, e.g. as perpetrator and as witness.

The alleged murder victims

Billinge(s), Joseph Stonemason, worked on the new Stoneleigh Abbey bridge; alleged victim of murder, c.1814.

Blissett, William (c.1791–c.1815) Labourer on bridge; alleged victim of shooting.

Dingley, Daniel Alleged victim of murder, c.1815.

Forbes, William Stonemason, alleged victim of murder, c.1814.

Leigh, John (I) Claimant to Stoneleigh, alleged victim of murder, 1823.

Proud, Thomas Stonemason, alleged victim of murder, c.1814.

Smith, Joseph Stonemason, alleged victim of murder, c.1814.

Sprawson, John (c.1741–buried 1815) Stoneleigh village carrier; alleged to have assisted in the removal of the Christopher stone from Stoneleigh village church, and bodies of murdered stonemasons to Adlestrop; alleged to have been murdered by order of Julia-Judith Leigh.

Thomas, John Black man alleged to have been brought by Thomas Hill Mortimer from London to assist in conspiracy to murder Billinge(s) and Forbes; alleged to have been murdered by George Shaw and others.

Four, possibly five unnamed stonemasons Who worked on the Stoneleigh Abbey cellars.

The alleged perpetrators of fraud and/or murder

Barnett, Richard (c.1796–1848) Stonemason, admitted to removing coffin plates from Stoneleigh village church vault, 1811; witness of bridge murders, c.1814.

Hay (Hayward/Haywood), John (fl. 1810–1825) Stoneleigh gamekeeper; featured in sporting literature of period; implicated in murders, in particular that of William Blissett.

Hill Mortimer, Thomas Worked for Stoneleigh agent Joseph Hill, 1798–1811; solicitor and agent for Leigh family, 1811–1849.

Jones, George (Senior, d. by 1848) Engineer; engaged by John Rennie in 1811 to supervise construction of the new bridge; accused of taking part in murders, c.1814.

Kirkland, Samuel Valet to James Henry Leigh, c.1820; accused of taking part in murder of John Leigh (I) and in faked death of James Henry Leigh 1823; Stoneleigh house steward 1844.

Leigh, Chandos (1791–1850) Romantic poet, first Lord Leigh of the second creation (1839); charged with murder of Billinge(s) and Forbes, 1848.

Leigh, Julia-Judith Twisleton (1765–1843) Wife of James Henry Leigh and mother of Chandos Leigh; effectively mistress of Stoneleigh Abbey from c.1811 until her death; accused after her death of having orchestrated several murders, and the fake funeral of her husband.

Who's Who in the Stoneleigh Story

Shaw, George (d. January 1847) Stonemason; claimed that he had taken money as payment for removing monuments from Stoneleigh village church, c.1812; claimed that he had been sworn to taking part in bridge murders, and that he had taken money from Leigh family afterwards.

Smallbone, Sarah (née Silk; d. December 1846) Cook at Stoneleigh Abbey c.1815–1826; claimed that under orders from Julia-Judith Leigh, she had taken part in poisoning stonemasons, and in fake funeral for James Henry Leigh, 1823.

Wilcox (or Wilcooks), John (b.c.1800) Stoneleigh post-boy; witness to monument removal and participant in alleged murders, 1811–1815; possibly blackmailer of Chandos Leigh, 1812–1818.

Wood, William Stoneleigh employee; alleged to have assisted in murders of Billinge(s), Forbes, Dingley, and Sprawson; charged in 1848 but charges withdrawn; did not testify, 1848; denied involvement, 1849.

Selected witnesses attesting existence of Christopher stone prior to 1811 (in 1828–1829 case), and/or murder (1812–1849)

Barnett, Richard (c.1796–1848) Stonemason, admitted to removing coffin plates from Stoneleigh village church vault, 1811; witness of bridge murders, c. 1814.

Baylis, Edward (b.c.1764) Stoneleigh employee and witness to monument removal, c.1812.

Burford, Ann Stoneleigh still room maid, c.1819–1821/2; witness for destruction of records ordered by Julia-Judith Leigh.

Draper, Mary Kenilworth resident; witness on behalf of Charles Griffin, 1849; claimed to have heard confessions from Sarah Smallbone and John Wilcox.

xi

Faxon, William Bone-collector at Ashow, witness for bridge murders and concealment of monuments, c.1814.

Gumley/Gumbley, Hannah Widow of Stoneleigh tenant farmer; evicted 1821; in prison 1824; witness for Reverend James Roberts having discussed Christopher stone.

Iorns/Irons/Hiorns, Mary (b.c.1774) Stoneleigh pensioner; recalled cleaning Christopher stone in 1811.

Palfrey, Jasper Farmer, parish committee member 1810–1811, recalled Christopher stone; resigned from committee in protest at interference by Julia-Judith Leigh.

Perks, Ann née Whitmore Wife of John Perks, witness in 1828–1829 case recalling Christopher stone in place at marriage in 1806.

Perks, John Plumber and gas engineer, witness in 1828–1829 case recalling Christopher stone in place at marriage in 1806.

Perks, Richard Plumber, brother of John Perks, worked on alterations to church in 1811; recalled Christopher stone removed from wall and placed within church (put his tools behind it).

Place, Lionel (1766–1838) Landowner at Weddington, northern Warwickshire; witness for Reverend James Roberts having attested existence of Christopher stone, prior to denying it.

Roberts, Gregory Brother of Reverend James Roberts; witness for existence of Christopher stone, 1829.

Shaw, George (d. January 1847) Stonemason; claimed that he had taken money as payment for removing monuments from Stoneleigh village church, c. 1812; claimed that he had been sworn to taking part in bridge murders, and that he had taken money from Leigh family afterwards.

Who's Who in the Stoneleigh Story

Smallbone, Sarah (née Silk; d. December 1846) Cook at Stoneleigh Abbey c. 1815–1826; claimed that under orders from Julia-Judith Leigh, had taken part in poisoning stonemasons, and in fake funeral for James Henry Leigh, 1823.

Wilcox (or Wilcooks), John (b.c.1800) Stoneleigh post-boy; witness to monument removal and alleged murders, 1811–1815; possibly blackmailer of Chandos Leigh, 1812–1818.

Selected witnesses denying existence of Christopher stone prior to 1811 (in 1828–1829 case), and/or murder (1812–1849)

Alcott, John Master stonemason of Coventry; worked on Stoneleigh village church south wall 1811; witness against existence of Christopher stone, but admitted not looking at the wall prior to starting work.

Darley, Richard Stoneleigh steward, c.1811–1822; alleged agent for removal of Christopher stone from church; later fell out with Leigh family.

Ilett, John (b.c.1754) Stoneleigh bailiff c.1812, witness against monument removal; alleged by other witnesses to have known of its existence and suppression.

Jeacock, Job Name of several generations of Stoneleigh parish clerks; including as witness against existence of Christopher stone 1828, 1849.

Jones, George (Snr) (d. by 1848) Engineer; engaged by John Rennie in 1811 to supervise construction of new bridge; accused of taking part in murders, c. 1814.

Mason, Captain Francis (b.1779) Royal Navy captain; served in Peninsular War; ally in 1828–1829 of Reverend James Roberts; friend of James Roberts and (formerly) of Lionel Place.

Hill Mortimer, Thomas Worked for Stoneleigh agent Joseph Hill, 1798–1811; solicitor and agent for Leigh family, 1811–1849.

Roberts, Reverend James Stoneleigh curate; witness against Christopher stone's existence (and, *a priori*, its removal), 1828–1829.

Soden, Jonathan Witness against existence of Christopher stone, 1828–1829; later admitted conviction that it must have existed (many members of his own family maintained that it had); witness against murders, 1849.

Thomas, Reverend Vaughan (1775–1858) Absentee vicar of Stoneleigh and other livings; antiquarian author; unsatisfactory witness against existence of Christopher stone; benefactor of medical facilities in Birmingham.

Wake, Dr Officiated at reported death of James Henry Leigh (1823); denied inquest necessary.

The claimants to Stoneleigh

Leigh Perrot, James (1735–1817) Brother of Mrs Cassandra Leigh Austen; claimant to part of Stoneleigh estate, 1806–1808.

Leigh Perrot, Jane (1744–1836) Wife of above; recipient of extensive Stoneleigh largesse, 1808–1836.

Leigh, George (d. 1834) Of Blackrod, Lancashire; son of tanner from Wigan; claimant to Stoneleigh estate, c. 1817–1829.

Leigh, James Claimant, 1844; sentenced to imprisonment with hard labour for breaking into Stoneleigh Abbey.

Leigh, John (I), (d. 1823), Claimant c. 1820–1823.

Leigh, John (II), Claimant, 1844.

Who's Who in the Stoneleigh Story

The lawyers

Adam, William Lawyer for claimant George Leigh, 1828–1829.

Brougham, Henry (1778–1868) Whig celebrity, scientist, journalist, lawyer, politician; raised to peerage as Lord Brougham and Vaux and Lord Chancellor, 1830.

Copley, Sir John Singleton (1772–1863) Whig lawyer and politician; as Attorney-General, recommended Leigh claim to House of Lords Committee, 1825/6; as Lord Chancellor (Lord Lyndhurst), judged claim to have been fraudulent, 1829.

Denman, Thomas (1779–1854) Celebrity Whig lawyer, acted for Chandos Leigh in 1828–1829; raised to peerage 1834; Lord Chief Justice, 1832–1850.

Grey, Lord George (1799–1882) Whig politician; Home Secretary 1846–1852 and 1855–1858; took no action on Stoneleigh allegations.

Griffin, Charles (c1805–1874) Solicitor, scientist, lawyer for Stoneleigh claimants 1844; author of book about case 1848; charged with and convicted of libel 1849; sentenced to gaol.

Jones, George (Jnr) Lawyer, son of George Senior; acted for Chandos Leigh at murder trial 1848.

Kelly, Fitzroy (1796–1880) Lawyer for claimant George Leigh 1828–1829; Lord Chief Baron of Exchequer, 1866–1880.

Pollock, (William Frederick?) Lawyer prosecuting Chandos Leigh, 1848.

Roberts, William Prowting (1806–1871) "The miners' attorney-general", lawyer for working people 1840s to 1860s; advised on charging Chandos Leigh with murder, 1848.

Scarlett, Sir James (1769–1844) Celebrity Whig lawyer, acted for Chandos Leigh 1828–1829; in 1835 raised to peerage as Lord Abinger; Lord Chief Baron of Exchequer, 1835.

Wilde, Thomas (1782–1855) Whig lawyer and politician; judge at trial of Griffin, 1849; Lord Chancellor and Baron Truro, 1850.

The Austens, Leighs, and Twisletons

Austen, Jane (1775–1817) Author; visitor to Stoneleigh Abbey 1806.

Austen, Mrs Cassandra Leigh (1739–1827) Mother of Jane Austen, first cousin of the Reverend Thomas Leigh; visitor to Stoneleigh Abbey 1806.

Leigh, Chandos (1791–1850) Romantic poet, first Lord Leigh of the second creation (1839); charged with murder of Billinge(s) and Forbes, 1848.

Leigh, Christopher (1626–1672) Claimed ancestor of claimants George Leigh, James Leigh, John Leigh (I, II); with alleged first marriage and children, subject of purported Christopher stone in Stoneleigh village church.

Leigh, Edward (Fifth Lord) (d. 1786) Certified insane; named heirs sisters Mary Leigh and Anne Hackett; then 'first and nearest [male] of my name and blood;' barony of Stoneleigh extinct upon his death (revived in 1839 when Chandos Leigh attained the title).

Leigh, James Henry (1765–disappeared 1823) Second cousin of Jane Austen; father of Chandos Leigh and husband of Julia-Judith Twisleton Leigh, nephew and heir of Reverend Thomas Leigh; MP for Winchester, 1802–1822.

Leigh, Julia-Judith Twisleton (1765–1843) Wife of James Henry Leigh and mother of Chandos Leigh; effectively mistress of Stoneleigh Abbey from c.1811 until her death; accused after her death of having orchestrated several murders, and the fake funeral of her husband.

Leigh, Mrs Mary (d. 1806) Inherited Stoneleigh Abbey and estates on death of brother Edward, fifth Lord Leigh (1786).

Leigh, Robert (mid-18th century) Grandfather of claimant George Leigh.

Leigh, Robert Holt (1762–1843) Distant relative and admirer of Jane Austen; MP for Wigan 1802–1820; created baronet 1814.

Leigh, Roger (17th century) Putative son of Christopher Leigh; alleged ancestor of claimant/s.

Leigh, Reverend Thomas (1734–1813) First cousin of Mrs Cassandra Leigh Austen; inherited Stoneleigh Abbey and estates 1806.

Leigh Perrot, James (1735–1817) Brother of Mrs Cassandra Leigh Austen; claimant to part of Stoneleigh estate, 1806–1808.

Leigh Perrot, Jane (1744–1836) Wife of above; recipient of extensive Stoneleigh largesse, 1808–1836.

Twisleton, Colonel Thomas (c. 1735–1788) Hero in suppression of Gordon Riots, 1780; successful claimant to title and raised to peerage as Lord Saye and Sele, 1781; took own life, 1788; father of Julia-Judith Twisleton Leigh.

Other participants and commentators

Billinge(s), Matthew Stonemason, worked on new bridge; father of Joseph Billinge(s).

Billinge(s), William Stonemason, alleged brother of victim.

Byron, Lord George Gordon (1788–1824) Poet, alumnus of Harrow School, inspiration for a generation of writers including Chandos Leigh.

Causton, Henry Kent London printer, creditor of George Leigh (claimant) and chronicler of 1828–1829 Lords Privileges Committee case.

Hunt, James Henry Leigh (1784–1859) Radical author and critic; champion in his autobiography of James Henry Leigh and Chandos Leigh.

Murray, Adam Scottish estate agent and agriculture consultant; prepared *Agricultural Report for Warwickshire,* 1813, including unfavourable comment on Leigh stewardship at Stoneleigh.

Parr, Reverend Samuel (1747–1825) Master at Harrow School; Whig celebrity, author, friend of Chandos Leigh.

Rennie, John (1761–1821) Engineer, architect; designer and contractor for construction of new bridge at Stoneleigh Abbey, 1812–1818.

Rhodes, Jane (b.c.1800) Sex worker, in relationship with Chandos Leigh in period 1814–1817; later blackmailed him.

Smith, Reverend Sydney (1771–1854) Whig celebrity, wit, critic and author.

Introduction

I first encountered the matters described in this book during 2011, while I was researching Stoneleigh Abbey, Warwickshire, in relation to Jane Austen's *Northanger Abbey* (1817). Stoneleigh Abbey, the home of the Leigh family for many centuries, has in the last ten years become an important site of Jane Austen scholarship. Jane Austen's mother was born Cassandra Leigh. Jane and her mother, in 1806, visited Stoneleigh when Mrs Austen's cousin, the Reverend Thomas Leigh, inherited the magnificent estate.

At that time, I mentally put the topic aside for another year. When I was ready, there were the primary sources, freely available online. The Google Books which nobody, it seemed, had bothered to read: long out of print, the seemingly endless reports of the House of Lords Privileges Committee proceedings from 1828–29. They were in small print, closely spaced, and apparently deeply uninteresting to most people. But I immediately found them fascinating. To me, there is nothing more exciting than an inscription in stone. And this, it turned out, was at the very centre of the Leigh peerage case: the existence and fate of a particular funerary monument to Christopher Leigh (1626–1672), which many people attested had existed in the village church of Stoneleigh, before disappearing in about 1811. I soon discovered that this missing monument was only the start of a mysterious, even bizarre, courtroom drama.

In 1848, murder charges were added to the tale. The sources for this period were two books: Charles Griffin's, *Stoneleigh Abbey Thirty-four Years Ago* (1848), and the *Report* of Griffin's trial for libel (then a criminal offence punishable by imprisonment as well as a civil wrong) in 1849. Jane Austen's relative, Chandos Lord Leigh (1791–1850), was charged with the murder of several workmen on the Stoneleigh estate, alleged to have occurred around the same time as the disappearance of the monument.

Griffin, the local lawyer who pursued the allegations, was in his turn prosecuted in 1849 and sentenced to gaol for libel.

Griffin's claims were sensational. In the spring of 1848, when social unrest was in the air and establishments in England feared a revolution along European lines, he reported statements made by a middle-aged stonemason called Richard Barnett. Barnett claimed that in about 1814, as a teenager, part of a shift of stonemasons working on a new bridge at Stoneleigh Abbey, he had witnessed a double murder of two of the masons. He named the two men as Billinges and Proud.

The claims of Barnett were supported by evidence from two other witnesses (both deceased), George Shaw—who had also been in the working party—and Sarah Smallbone, who had been a cook for several years at Stoneleigh Abbey. Smallbone had never made a formal statement, fearing for her own life if she were implicated in the crimes she described, which included carrying out poisonings under the direction of Julia-Judith Leigh, the mother of Chandos. A further witness, John Wilcox, was still living, and had played an ambiguous role, at times corroborating, at others denying, the sensational allegations. Were these bizarre events linked with the disappearance of the monument?

The case swiftly disappeared into the stuff of legend. Yet the mystery of Stoneleigh remains. What lies beneath the fine bridge at Stoneleigh, designed by the great Scottish engineer John Rennie and completed in 1818? What became of a monumental stone in Stoneleigh parish church, which 40 parishioners remembered seeing, and which probably disappeared in 1811?

This book seeks to explore these questions, which have rested largely unasked for a century and a half. It is clear that part of the reason for this lack of inquiry is that reports of these events were, for decades it seems, as described in later chapters, suppressed.

One of the most important aspects of this case is that it preserves the testimony of the servants, tradesmen, and village people of Stoneleigh, classes of people who are generally silent in the literary tradition. This strange case allowed many of them to be heard. I have not solved any of the mysteries in this work. I have simply presented the story, and, amazing as it is, it speaks for itself.

CHAPTER ONE

Inheritance

"The ponds supply excellent Fish the Park excellent Venison; there is also great plenty of Pigeons, Rabbits, & all sort of Poultry, a delightful Dairy where is made butter good Warwickshire Cheese and Cream ditto. One Man Servant is called the Baker, He does nothing but Brew and Bake. The quantity of Casks in the Strong Beer Cellar is beyond imagination..."

Cassandra Leigh Austen, 1806[1]

Mrs Austen, Jane Austen's mother, was writing happily to her daughter-in-law Mary about the Stoneleigh estate in Warwickshire. It was August 1806, and Mrs Austen, with Jane, was visiting her cousin the Reverend Thomas Leigh, who had just had the great good fortune to inherit the magnificent estate of Stoneleigh.

This 1806 visit undoubtedly influenced Jane Austen in her writing: Stoneleigh has been plausibly identified as a model for Sotherton, the estate of Mr Rushworth in *Mansfield Park* (1814).[2] More generally, the inheritance of property is one of the central matters in Austen's novels. The plot of *Pride and Prejudice* (1813) is driven by the entail on the Longbourn estate. *Sense and Sensibility* (1811) opens with old Mr Dashwood troubled, on his deathbed, about what is likely to be the inheritance of

---

1. 13 August 1806: from Deirdre Le Faye, *A Chronology of Jane Austen and Her Family 1600-2000* (Cambridge University Press, 2013), p. 331. Quoted in Victoria Huxley, *Jane Austen and Adlestrop: Her Other Family* (Windrush Publishing: Moreton-in-the-Marsh, Gloucestershire, 2013), pp.139–140; p.218 n.4 simply as "J A Papers"; quoted also in Gaye King, "The Jane Austen Connection," in Bearman (ed.), *Stoneleigh Abbey: The House, Its Owners, Its Lands* (Stoneleigh Abbey Limited, 2004), 163–178, p.171 (and referenced on p. 278 n.18, as "Austen Papers, 244–247").
2. Huxley, p. 137; John Wiltshire, "Exploring *Mansfield Park*: in the Footsteps of Fanny Price," *Persuasions* 28 (June 2006), 81–100, p. 88.

his second wife and their daughters. And *Mansfield Park* is, among other things, a protracted meditation on the responsibilities of an estate owner and family head such as Sir Thomas Bertram.

It is understandable that inheritance played such a major role in Austen's works. Women could not go into the church, the armed forces, the law, or business. They could not be respectably employed for money except as governesses, or in a very few cases authors. Inheritance and marriage were the only means whereby they found financial security. Of course, this was also the case for many men. We only have to look at such characters as Wickham and Willoughby to note that their hopes of either inheriting or marrying money were key motives in their lives.

Against this background, it is not surprising that in recent decades, Austen studies have begun to focus on the inheritance scenarios in her own extended family. This trend probably began with Deirdre Le Faye's groundbreaking work *Jane Austen: A Family Record* (first published in 1989, and subsequently appearing in several editions). The Jane Austen Society of Australia also published a landmark in the field with the late Jon Spence's *A Century of Wills from Jane Austen's Family 1705–1806* (2001).

In this book, Spence collected and edited key wills from the Austen family. For the general reader, seventeenth and eighteenth-century wills make tough going. The sentences are quite long, with few commas to help the understanding, and there is a specialist terminology requiring explanation. In addition, complex family and marriage relationships form a key element. The technical aspects of the wills are the key feature at first glance; but, beneath the surface, each will represents a network of human emotions, some laudable, others not so attractive. The wills of Edward Lord Leigh (1786) and of Mary Leigh (1806, Spence's end point) represent to some extent the starting points for this story.

The Reverend Thomas, who was affectionately remembered by Jane Austen, was, prior to his elevation to master of Stoneleigh, the rector of the village of Adlestrop in Gloucestershire. Stoneleigh, about 35 miles north from Adlestrop, and across the county border, was the greatest estate in Warwickshire. An agricultural survey printed for the government in 1813, the year of the Reverend Thomas' death, indicates its pre-eminent position.

"The state of property in Warwickshire, may be considered as very unequal in its division: the most extensive estate is that of Stone-Leigh [sic], possessed by the Rev. Thomas Leigh, supposed to contain upwards of 25,000 acres; a great proportion of which is very excellent land."[3]

Stoneleigh had begun as a Cistercian house in the Middle Ages, before suffering the same fate as many other religious houses in the sixteenth century. By the time of the survey of the wealth of church lands in 1535–6, it was reported that the house itself was ruinous, but that the whole abbey complex was worth £208.3s.0d, somewhat less than its current debt of £212.19s.10½d.[4]

Henry VIII gifted the ruins to his brother-in-law Charles Brandon, the Duke of Suffolk, who left it undeveloped for some years before selling it to Thomas Leigh.[5] This Thomas Leigh (c.1498–1571), the first (identified as number I, to distinguish him from all the subsequent Thomas Leighs), was the ancestor of Jane Austen, of the Reverend Thomas, and of all the Adlestrop and Stoneleigh Leighs.

Thomas Leigh (I) was a business leader who had been Lord Mayor of London. He married Alice Barker, the niece and heiress of his business partner Rowland Hill, and they had several children.[6] Thomas acquired a number of former religious estates, in addition to Stoneleigh.[7] Gradually, during the seventeenth century, the Stoneleigh estate was rebuilt. To this day, there are remnants of the medieval abbey to be seen in the building's fabric, in a manner which recalls Austen's *Northanger Abbey* (1817).

The eighteenth-century Leighs embarked on a series of building phases, developing the abbey into a baroque palace. In the 1760s, a new programme began under the guidance of Edward, the young fifth Baron Leigh (1742–1786), who directed skilled craftsmen to produce

---

3. Adam Murray, *[A] General View of the Agriculture of the County of Warwick: With observations on the means of its improvement, drawn up for the consideration of the Board of Agriculture and Internal Improvement* (London: B. Mcmillan, 1813), p. 25.
4. Andrew Watkins, "The Medieval Abbey: Its lands and Its Tenants," in Bearman (ed.) 2004, 198–213, p. 213.
5. Mairi Macdonald, "'Not Unmarked by Some Eccentricities': the Leigh Family of Stoneleigh Abbey," in Bearman (ed.), 2004, 131–162, p. 133.
6. Macdonald (2004), p. 131.
7. Macdonald (2004), p. 133.

fine decorative work in the classical style, notably a fine series of reliefs depicting events in the Heracles legends.[8]

But after a promising youth at Oxford, and taking part in all the duties and pleasures expected of a young lord (including attendance at the Stratford races), Edward began to exhibit symptoms of mental illness.[9] Family records show sums paid for his care to the leading physicians of the day, including John Monro and Francis Willis, both of whom were to attend on George III.[10] By 1773 it had become clear that Edward would not recover, and he was committed to the care of his relative William Lord Craven and his unmarried sister Mrs (a courtesy title) Mary Leigh (1736–1806). Mary Leigh was assisted in a variety of ways by her agent Joseph Hill and other trusted servants. A touching item in the family papers is a prayer, recorded in 1780, by Mary Leigh that "thy afflicted servant [i.e. Edward] be restored to reason and understanding."[11] Edward appears no more in official accounts of the Leigh family, although he lived for another six years after his sister's prayer.

Two stories about Edward in this twilight period indicate that he may have been conscious of the vexed nature of the Stoneleigh inheritance. One story appears to relate to earlier incidents than the other. Both may arise from sources which seem to have an interest in presenting Edward in this way: that is, from sources linked with estate claimants. However, they also appear to shed light on the personality of Lord Edward: fussy, a little querulous, but conscientious, and—surprisingly, in view of his official status as a lunatic—completely lucid.

The earlier anecdote relates to an episode in which Edward is said to have instituted his own inquiries about his relatives. He employed the Garter King at Arms, Sir Isaac Heard (1730–1822), to undertake research at the College of Heralds. Heard produced only a Leigh family tree which was compiled from the heralds' visitation of 1682. The story goes that Edward tore up this document, stating that it was of no use.[12]

---

8. Andor Gomme, "Abbey into Palace: A Lesser Wilton?" in Bearman (ed., 2004), 82–115, pp. 107–111.
9. Macdonald (2004), p. 150.
10. SBTRO DR 18/17/27/200, 2 November 1769. Letter from Dr Monro to Joseph Hill.
11. SBTRO DR 18/17/28/79, c. 1780.
12. George Leigh, *The Leigh Peerage: Being a full and complete history of the claim of George Leigh, Esq. to the dormant title of Baron Leigh, of Stoneley, in the county of Warwick: comprising a report of*

The second account appeared in the *Gentleman's Magazine* in April 1823. It purported to have been written as a letter to the editor ("Mr Urban"[13]), by a man calling himself *Senex, an. aet. 82* (Latin for "Old Man aged 82").

> "I became acquainted with the late Lord [Edward Lord Leigh], at Sir Roger Newdigate's of Arbury, about the Christmas of 1763 or 1764. I cannot recollect which year, but it was soon after his Lordship came of age—this acquaintance ripened into a friendship, and I was more intimate with him than many of the neighbouring gentlemen. I visited him frequently between that period and the year 1782, in which latter year, accompanied by my eldest son, I spent a few pleasant weeks with my old friend. He was at times a little eccentric, and on that account was attended by a celebrated physician, a Doctor Ash of Birmingham, who brought with him frequently a very pleasant gentleman, Mr Sturges of Northamptonshire. One day after dinner, Dr Ash and Mr Sturges being present, I remember the conversation reverted to his favourite subject; namely, who was his nearest male relation, and who would succeed to his title. I told him I did not apprehend he had any near relation who could succeed to the title; he said that he had reasons to suppose the contrary. I enquired upon what grounds he entertained such an opinion; he replied that from family documents he had no doubt he must have distant relations in Lancashire or Cheshire who would succeed to the title.
>
> I seemed incredulous at this remark, as did Dr Ash. Have you seen, *(said he) with some warmth*, a monument in Stoneleigh church, to the memory of Christopher Leigh, son of my great-great grandfather, the first Lord of the family. I replied I had not. You know then nothing about the matter, said his Lordship. The conversation then dropped. The following morning, accompanied by my son, I rode over to Stoneleigh Church, and found the monument as my friend had described, to the memory of Christopher Leigh

---

the evidence taken before the Lords' committee for Privileges, with notes, analytical and explanatory: and certain additional evidence, forming the ultimatum to this very mysterious case. In two volumes (Henry Kent Causton, jun.: London, 2nd edn, 1834), vol. I, p. x. Hereafter: Leigh (1834).

13. Edward Cave (1691–1754), the magazine's founder, had been the first to use the pseudonym "Silvanus Urban." Subsequent editors were by convention also "Mr Urban."

and his family. The inscription I copied, and when I return into Kent I will send to your valuable Magazine for insertion, if it has not been inserted before. By this inscription it will appear that Christopher, fourth son of the first Lord, was settled near Wigan in Lancashire, and if there are any male descendants from Christopher now living, the title will certainly devolve to them. Last week I again visited Stoneleigh Church, and found two plain marble tablets to the memory of my old friend the late Lord, and his sister the Honourable Mary Leigh, which I transcribed, and will send to you, with the inscription, to the memory of Christopher, &c, &c whose monument, during some late improvements as they are called, has been taken down and not yet replaced. Senex, an. Aet. 82."[14]

This account seems to contradict the earlier one, which had implied that Edward had no useful knowledge of potential heirs.

One writer suggested that the reason for the earlier confusion was that Edward was not in the habit of visiting the village church. In turn the reason for this was that the Leigh family's practice had been for many years to receive divine service in the chapel in Stoneleigh Abbey.[15] The suggestion was, further, that this was because the reforming nature of the standard village service did not accord with the Leigh family's traditional loyalty to the Stuart dynasty.[16] Edward's confident assertions in the second story may reflect a greater acquaintance with the village church in his later life.

The Stoneleigh Abbey chapel may well have inspired Jane Austen's account of the chapel at Sotherton, in *Mansfield Park* (1814). The Leigh situation is, however, the converse from the one Austen portrays, in which Fanny is dismayed that the home chapel has fallen into disuse by the family.[17]

Whether or not Edward was really aware of the reported inscription, it failed to see the light of day in the *Gentleman's Magazine*. If "Senex" actually existed and transcribed the monument, he never supplied this

---

14. 1 January 1823, appearing in *The Gentleman's Magazine and Historical Chronicle,* January to June 1823, volume 93, April 1823, p. 326.
15. Causton in Leigh (1834), vol. I, p. xi.
16. Causton in Leigh (1834), vol. I, p. xi, note.
17. *Mansfield Park* Volume I, Chapter 9.

to the magazine.[18] In 1823, a claim by George Leigh to the Stoneleigh estate was well and truly in train, and it is possible that his agents placed this account in the popular press as a tactic.

On the other hand, the careful references to Dr John Ash (1723–1798), a noted physician and Birmingham celebrity, Mr Sturges,[19] and the writer's son, indicate that whoever wrote the account was aware of the fact that any quoted utterances of Edward needed to be bolstered by other witnesses. The placement of the name of Sir Roger (1719–1806), a well-known member of Parliament and collector of antiquities at his Warwickshire estate of Arbury, also added verisimilitude. The Leigh family noted the *Gentleman's Magazine* account: a copy appears in their family records.[20]

One final anecdote about Edward appeared in the *Gentleman's Magazine* during 1824, in the tenuously related context of an obituary of a vicar of Fillongley (part of the Stoneleigh estate). The writer, having touched upon Edward, goes on:

> "[He] heu meminisse dolet [it is painful to recall] in a very early stage of his life, by an unhappy disease of mind, became insensible of all the innocent and rational pleasures of human life, with the exception of one only, that which related to the powers of music. For at Stoneleigh Abbey, where he constantly resided, under the watchful care of a Fellow of All Souls, whom I well remember, he led the band, and conducted the whole management of his concert with the same zest of pleasure which he felt in the happier moments of his life, as a nobleman at Oriel College."[21]

Edward died without legitimate issue in 1786, aged 44. He left Stoneleigh Abbey and all his associated estates to his sisters and their issue, then to

---

18. Confirmed in *Gentleman's Magazine*, Vol. 99, January-June 1829, p. 638, footnote.
19. Unidentified, but possibly the clergyman Mr Sturges named in the *Gentleman's Magazine* roundup of clerical appointments: to Kempton near Exeter in 1762 (vol. XXXII, p. 505) and to Ealing in 1773 (vol. XLIII, p. 583).
20. SBTRO DR 18/17/49/12, 26 May 1823.
21. Wm. Chas Dyer, obituary of Rev. J. Dyer Hewitt, MA, *Gentleman's Magazine* vol. 94, part 2, July 1824, pp. 84–85.

"the first and nearest of my kindred, being male, and of my name and blood, that shall be living at the time of the determination of the several estates herein before limited and devised, and to the heirs of his body lawfully begotten."[22]

The wording of this will is important. Its ambiguity was to be exploited by a number of claimants over the coming decades. He also made personal bequests, including to friends and fellow-students from Oxford. One major bequest which the Leigh family was later to view with particular resentment was the gift of his mathematical instruments and his entire library to Oriel College. This may well have added to the concern which in general surrounded the terms of Edward's will.[23]

Edward's sister and heir, Mary Leigh, was a very rich woman, in charge, after her brother's confinement, of huge resources. She maintained houses in London and in Bath. Her charitable activities included a payment, in 1794, to a William Penn "for consenting to have his children inoculated."[24] As the practice of inoculation was still subject to a good deal of suspicion in the late eighteenth century, it would appear that Mary was not only generous but progressive in some matters.

She was remembered as somewhat eccentric, but also appears to have been loved by her servants. Thomas Wagstaff had served as her gate porter at her town house at Kensington Gore. He reported that she was "a very nice lady", very proud of her family. Mary would go out in her carriage every day. She once told Thomas Wagstaff, as he was "drying a newspaper by the fire," that her nearest relations lived at Lancashire, but that she had never seen them[25] (the anecdote reveals how precious a newspaper was, even in the wealthy environment of the Leigh family).

Mary herself, as implied in her brother's will, had only a life interest in the estate; Edward's half-sister Anne Hackett had also died without issue. It therefore fell to Mary to determine the next step, in accordance

---

22. Document no. 3, Will of Edward Lord Leigh, dated 1767, proved 1786. Leigh (1834), vol. I, p. 26.
23. Macdonald (2004), p. 153.
24. Macdonald (2004), p. 155.
25. Leigh (1834). vol. I, p. 207.

with Edward's wishes that the ultimate heir be "male, and of his name and blood."

Meanwhile, Mary had given some thought to how she wanted her own funeral to be celebrated. A codicil to her will drafted in 1803 sets out her plan for an impressive exit:

> "I wish my funeral, whenever that may happen, to be as follows: my corpse in a hearse and six horses; immediately following it my own chaise and four, drove by my coachman and postilion in black jackets, and the glasses of my chaise down to shew it empty, my three footmen and groom, two on each side my chaise, in black jackets, made in the same form as their riding jackets; two coaches and six to follow my chaise, in one my house-keeper, my own maid, and the upper house-maid—in the other, my steward and undertaker, and whoever else may be necessary…"[26]

In the event, Mary Leigh died in 1806. "I lost a good mistress," Wagstaff reported.[27] Her funeral was a great event in Stoneleigh, with a large crowd filling the church, pushing and shoving to see the funeral procession.[28]

Mary had had a series of wills and codicils drawn up. According to her will of 1786 and its codicil of 1788, her main executor was to have been her relative William Lord Craven. On Lord Craven's death in 1791, new executors had to be found. She appointed the Reverend Thomas Leigh of Adlestrop and Joseph Hill.[29] The Reverend Thomas was also to be her heir. Mary's will of 1806 gave the freehold and copyhold lands in trust to the use of the eldest representative of the senior line, the Reverend Thomas, for his life, then to James Leigh Perrot of Scarlets for life, a further life tenancy to James Henry Leigh of Adlestrop (Thomas' nephew), and then to his heirs.

The fact that this sat rather oddly with the terms of Edward's bequest did not go unnoticed. The Reverend Thomas was certainly a male relative

---

26. Leigh (1834), vol. I, p. 29.
27. Leigh (1834), vol. I p. 215.
28. Leigh (1834), vol. I p. 217.
29. Leigh (1834), vol. I, p. 38. William 6th Baron Craven (d. 1791) was a member of the extended Craven, Fowle and Lloyd connections of the Austens: Le Faye *Chronology* (2013), family tree on p. 738.

living at the time of the determination of Edward's estates (1786), but he had no heirs of his body. It could be said that neither James Henry Leigh nor James Leigh Perrot had any claim, under a strict interpretation of the terms of Edward's will.

James Leigh Perrot, the brother of Mrs Austen, was a prominent figure in the life of Jane Austen and her siblings. Like Mrs Austen a first cousin of the Reverend Thomas, James had added "Perrot" to his name as a condition of succeeding to the estates of his great-uncle Thomas Perrot.[30] He seems to have been one of those people who are never satisfied with the wealth that they have, but are always on the look-out for more.

He and his wife, Jane's "Aunt Leigh Perrot", had no children of their own. This led to a strong and persistent expectation, at least in the Austen family, that they would leave money to their more fertile relatives.[31] There is a suggestion that the Leigh Perrots valued their childless status as an advantage from a financial point of view, an attitude which would have seemed perverse at the time.

Aunt Leigh Perrot, famously, was charged with and tried for shoplifting in Bath during 1799. On her eventual acquittal, it seemed to be the expense which bothered her the most.

> "The frightful expense I cannot estimate. I am told it will be nearer *two* than one thousand pounds and from the large demands already made only for conveying the witnesses (and the *two* days' expences for the *house* and *eating* at Taunton which alone amounted to £93 odd money), I can easily suppose it will be full that sum. What a comfort that we have no children!"[32]

Spence rightly notes that this has the true sound of Austen's creation Mrs Norris, in *Mansfield Park*.

Bitter negotiations with James Leigh Perrot went on. Two years after Mary Leigh's death, unpleasant letter exchanges continued between James Leigh Perrot and Joseph Hill, acting for the Leigh family. James

---

30. Macdonald (2004), p. 155.
31. Spence *Becoming Jane Austen: A Life* (Hambledon Continuum: London and New York, third edn, 2007), pp. 161–162.
32. Jane Leigh Perrot to Mountague Cholmeley, Bath, 1 April 1800, quoted in Spence (2007), p. 129; p. 262, n. 22.

Henry Leigh, as a further party to the deal, offered the Leigh Perrots a £2,000 annuity for their lives, plus interest on £20,000 and £3,000 lump sums, with a further bond from James Henry for £3,000 payable in 1813. This represented the kind of wealth which most people could not even imagine, and which would have made the Austen women more than comfortable for life. James Leigh Perrot, however, wrote that he would only accept the offer if James Henry also threw in a grant, to Leigh Perrot, of the "presentations" (the power to allocate clergy jobs) of Broadwell and Adlestrop, plus further guarantees should the Reverend Thomas and James Henry predecease the Leigh Perrots.[33] With impressive cheek, he further noted that his increased income would require a higher standard of living, so he also requested a commensurate increase in gifts of game from Stoneleigh.[34]

Eventually, James Leigh Perrot, having extracted everything he could, gave up his claim to Stoneleigh in return for a deal similar to that offered in 1808 by James Henry. Jane Austen saw this arrangement as a sell-out. She was later to refer to it as a "vile compromise."[35] Having visited Stoneleigh and seen its magnificence, she would be unable to understand how a claim to it could simply be exchanged for cash.

James Leigh Perrot himself died in 1817, an event which proved traumatic for Jane Austen, then in her final illness. He had left all his money to his widow, Aunt Leigh Perrot, who lived until 1836, dying at the age of 92.[36]

It was prescient of Jane Austen to have Fanny Dashwood, in Chapter Two of *Sense and Sensibility* (1811), complain that "people always live for ever when there is any annuity to be paid them." She may well have been thinking of her aunt. For their part, the Stoneleigh Leighs for some time nurtured an unrealistic hope that Mrs Leigh Perrot might eventually

---

33. James Leigh Perrot, Paragon Buildings, Bath, to the Reverend Thomas Leigh. SBTRO DR 18/17/34/34, 11 June 1808.
34. Ibid.
35. 3 July 1813. Deidre Le Faye (ed.), *Jane Austen's Letters* (fourth edn, Oxford University Press, 2011), p. 225. *Contra* Spence (pp. 171–172), it is likely that this represents Jane Austen's own view, not that of Mrs Leigh Perrot.
36. Spence (2007), p. 241.

pay back some of the vast amount of Stoneleigh wealth which she had accumulated over the years.[37]

So, returning to 1806, the widowed Reverend Thomas Leigh moved from Adlestrop to Stoneleigh with his unmarried sister Elizabeth (unmarried sisters seem to be a trend in this story). The Reverend Thomas was 72, and Jane's niece Caroline Austen was later to write that the move to Stoneleigh came too late in their lives to be pleasant to them.[38] Caroline, youngest child of Jane Austen's brother James, recalled a poignant scene from a visit to Stoneleigh when she was a young child. Elizabeth Leigh — nominally the lady of the house — was not informed where her guests were to be sleeping:

> "That Miss Elizabeth never felt quite at home at Stoneleigh Abbey was proved the evening of our arrival [in 1809], when she wandered about the house trying in vain to discover *what* room had been prepared for me and my maid. She *knew* she had ordered it to be near my mother's but she could not find either apartment…"[39]

One contemporary writer indicates that the Reverend Thomas (not named, but clearly implied) was a helpless landowner, knowing nothing of farming himself, and controlled in decision-making by his employees. Adam Murray wrote the *Agricultural Report for Warwickshire* which was published in 1813. In collecting information from the Warwickshire farmers about their practices, Murray found many farmers, and even the landholders of highest rank — which at Stoneleigh, at this time, were the Reverend Thomas and his immediate heir James Henry — less than cooperative.

> "It is to be regretted, that sometimes people of large property and liberal education are unhappily the dupes of those about them; and though perhaps

---

37. Chandos Leigh to Julia-Judith Leigh, DR 18/17/55/7, 29 Nov 1830.
38. Huxley, p. 147 and p. 219 n. 2.
39. Caroline Austen (with introduction by Deirdre Le Faye), *Reminiscences of Caroline Austen* (The Jane Austen Society, 1986), p. 21.

willing of themselves to afford information, are biassed [sic] by their bailiffs, and act contrary to their own original good intentions."[40]

It is clear that Murray thought little of the Reverend Thomas as a landholder responsible for effective management of the finest estate in the county. Murray, whose own farming knowledge may have intimidated his interview subjects, was critical of many inefficient practices at Stoneleigh and its environs, and was not shy about reporting his concerns.[41]

The Reverend Thomas died after an illness in 1813. Under the terms of Mary Leigh's will, the next inheritor was to be the Reverend Thomas' nephew James Henry Leigh, also of Adlestrop. James Henry was married to Julia-Judith Twisleton, daughter of Lord and Lady Saye and Sele of Broughton Castle in Oxfordshire. After their marriage in December 1786, Julia-Judith and James Henry Leigh divided their time between Adlestrop and London, where their son Chandos was born in 1791. Four daughters, Julia, Caroline, Mary and Augusta, were born in the following years. James Henry does not seem to have had a profession until his elevation in 1802 as a Member of Parliament, through the interest of relatives.[42] Ever after 1786, the year of the death of Edward Lord Leigh and of James Henry's marriage, the couple lived in expectation of eventually ascending to the property at Stoneleigh.

It was to be a long wait, and there was definitely ill-feeling in the family over the succession. The terms of Edward Lord Leigh's will were widely known, and throughout the period the prospective heirs must have seemed to await the incumbents' deaths with uncomfortable eagerness. It was known, for example, that Mary Leigh, sister of Edward Lord Leigh, did not like her immediate successor, the Reverend Thomas.

---

40. Murray (1813), p. 34.
41. Murray (1813), p. 83, *inter alia*.
42. R. G. Thorne, 'Leigh, James Henry (1765–1823), of Adlestrop, Glos. and Stoneleigh Abbey, Warws,' http://www.historyofparliamentonline.org/volume/1790–1820/member/leigh-james-henry-1765-1823 (Accessed 18 November 2015).

"'I don't like him,' said she, after one of those periodical and by no means frequent visits, which courtesy required he should pay. 'I don't like him—he's a death-hunter—he's a death-hunter.'"[43]

As for the Reverend Thomas, there is no doubt that his own demise was awaited with ill-disguised impatience by Julia-Judith and her husband. On the news of the Reverend Thomas' death, Jane Austen wrote to her brother Frank:

"The respectable, worthy, clever, agreable [sic] Mr Tho. Leigh...has just closed a good life at the age of 79, & must have died the possessor of one of the finest Estates in England & of more worthless Nephews and Neices [sic] than any other private Man in the united Kingdoms."[44]

By "worthless Nephews and Neices," she must have meant not only James Henry Leigh, but Julia-Judith, the Reverend Thomas' niece by marriage.

In the following year, an estate claim was made on the Chawton, Hampshire properties which belonged to Jane Austen's brother Edward Austen Knight. The claim was brought by relatives of Edward's adoptive father Thomas Knight.[45] Proceedings dragged on, and it was April 1818 before an expensive settlement was reached. Edward had to cut down and sell a considerable amount of timber in order to realise the payout required.[46] At the time of her death in July 1817, therefore, on top of the disappointment occasioned by the will of James Leigh Perrot, Jane Austen herself was affected by the worry and uncertainty of a pending estate claim. The question of inheritance was of central concern to her life as well as to her fiction.

---

43. Leigh vol. I (1834), xxxi, source unclear.
44. 3–6 July 1813. Deidre Le Faye (ed.), *Jane Austen's Letters* (fourth edn, Oxford University Press, 2011), p. 225.
45. Spence (2007), p. 221.
46. William Baker, *Critical Companion to Jane Austen: A Literary Reference to Her Life and Work* (Facts on File Inc.: New York, 2008), pp. 19-20.

CHAPTER TWO

Julia-Judith

"Oh, that cursed woman; that cursed woman!"

Sarah Smallbone[1]

Julia-Judith Twisleton (1771–1843), the future Mrs James Henry Leigh, was the second child and first daughter of an ambitious man. Thomas Twisleton (c.1735–1788) was an Army officer, promoted on his merits. But he wanted more: a title. Through his family background, Thomas Twisleton was able, in the latter years of his life, to lay a successful claim to the defunct barony of Saye and Sele.

While the viscounty of Saye and Sele had been continuously inherited, the associated barony had fallen into extinction in the 1670s, on the death without male issue of James Fenys (or, the more usual spelling, Fiennes), the second Baron and Viscount Saye and Sele.[2] Several previous members of Thomas' family, through the seventeenth and eighteenth centuries, had been considered legally the title-holders of the barony, even though they did not exercise the privilege of taking it up. These included female members. Thomas' great-grandmother, Cecil Twisleton (d.1723), had been considered, *de iure*, Baroness Saye and Sele, but (in the

---

1. Quoted by James Leigh as having been spoken by Sarah Smallbone in late 1846; James Leigh evidence at Charles Griffin's libel trial: *Report of the Trial for Libel (The Queen, on the prosecution of the right honourable Lord Leigh, v. Charles Griffin)* in calumniously alleging murders to have been committed at Stoneleigh Abbey, thirty-four years ago. Tried at the Warwickshire Lent assizes, 1849, before Chief Justice Sir Thomas Wilde, Knight. From the type of the Warwick Advertiser of Saturday, April 7th, 1849; with corrections and additions (Henry Sharpe, Warwick, 1849), p. 25, column 2. Hereafter: *Report* (1849).
2. Sir [Samuel] Egerton Brydges (ed.), "Twisleton, Lord Say and Sele," in *Collins's Peerage of England: Genealogical, Biographical, and Historical. Greatly Augmented, and Continued to the Present Time, by Sir Egerton Brydges, K. J.* In nine volumes. Vol. VII (London: F.C. and J. Rivington (etc.), 1812), p. 32.

words of Burke) "did not assume the title." Her son Fiennes Twisleton (1670–1730) was also *de iure* Baron, but never took up the title. His heir, John Twisleton (baptised 1698) was *de iure* the twelfth Baron. He took initial steps towards claiming the title in the 1730s, but the proceedings had not been completed before his death in 1762.[3]

It was left to his son Thomas to make a formal claim to the title of Baron. By the time of his claim, Thomas was Colonel of the 9th Regiment of Foot, promoted to Major-General in 1782.[4]

Thomas was in command of a militia unit during the chaos of the Gordon Riots during June 1780. The riots, which began with a crowd of about 60,000 people, fomented by a disaffected officer on behalf of militant Protestantism, began as a protest against laws relaxing some of the restrictions imposed upon Catholics. As time went on, however, they assumed the general character of a radical revolt against authority, and in particular against wealthy and powerful institutions. In this regard, and in their social impact, the Gordon Riots have been considered a precursor of the French Revolution.[5]

This made for a most difficult position for Twisleton and for other Army leaders. At first, the authorities were reluctant to exert the full force of martial law. In any event, many soldiers had some sympathy for the rioters. This lessened with the growth of the violence against ordinary Catholics, and the destruction of many London institutions. London landmarks such as the Fleet Prison and the Bank of England were under attack. Newgate Prison was opened and prisoners freed.[6] Ten thousand troops were deployed to regain control.

Gradually, after about a week of mayhem, and considerable loss of life (210 were killed outright, with 71 dying later), the troops gained the upper hand. Subsequently, 160 people stood trial for their activities during the riots, of whom 62 were sentenced to death, and 25 eventually hanged.[7]

---

3. Brydges (1812), p. 34.
4. www.cracroftspeerage.co.uk/online/content/saye1603.htm Accessed 18 November 2015.
5. John Rule, *Albion's People: English Society 1714–1815* (London and New York: Longmans, 1992), p. 221.
6. Peter Linebaugh, *The London Hanged: Crime and Civil Society in the Eighteenth Century* (Verso: London, 2006), pp. 333–370.
7. Rule (1992), p. 221.

The involvement of many educated people in the insurrection was a puzzle for the authorities. Colonel Twisleton's observations were recorded. He noted that the mob attacking the Bank of England was led

> "by 'a person in a navy uniform with his sword drawn...many decently dressed people...till they were near the Guard...they then retired and pretended to be spectators...a very well dressed man was killed whose face they took great pains to hide, but after most of them dispersed a curious watchman looked at the body, expressed some surprise, and said he knew the person. Upon which they seized the watchman and dragged him to Moorfields, where they swore him in the most sacred way to secrecy.'"[8]

Twisleton was also quoted as saying that the politician John Wilkes and others, who had been agitating on Protestant issues prior to the riots, were "republican in principle."[9]

Whatever the original motivation for the Gordon Riots, they ultimately represented an occasion for unprecedented soul-searching in England about class relations, religious toleration, and the role of the military in civil disorder.[10] Like the riots in many cities of England during 2011, they gave rise to a sense of bewilderment that they could have occurred in a country which prided itself on the rule of law. The anonymous historian of one version of the *Newgate Calendar*, writing some decades after the events, opened his chapter on the Gordon Riots:

> "We have now arrived at that awful period in the history of England, when a lawless mob excited by party zeal threatened its capital with destruction, and held all the constituted authorities in terror; a commotion of apparently so little importance in its commencement, and so rapid and daring in its progress has seldom occurred in any civilised country."[11]

---

8. Tom Vague, "The Madness of King George and the Great London Riots of 1780," http://www.housmans.com/kingmob.pdf (Accessed 18 November 2015). Useful collection of primary sources.
9. Ibid.
10. Linebaugh (2006), p. 330.
11. *The Newgate Calendar*, introduction by Clive Emsley (Ware: Wordsworth Classics of World Literature, 1997), p. 296. This version has no bibliographic information, but (from stylistic evidence) probably incorporates sections from the 1818, 1822, and 1826 versions. It may borrow, so to speak, even from George Borrow's version, *Celebrated Trials* (1825). Useful bibliographical

They were a formative event for those who were young at the time: Julia-Judith was only nine when her father was involved in the military action. The Gordon Riots may well have impressed upon her a dread of popular uprising against authority.

It is commonly thought that Jane Austen was referring to the Gordon Riots, and later London disturbances, in *Northanger Abbey* (1817), where Catherine speaks of "something very shocking indeed" expected to "come out in" London. She means a new Gothic novel, but Eleanor Tilney — to her brother's amusement — thinks she means a real-world civil crisis.[12] *Northanger Abbey* reflected the preoccupations of Austen's youth, a fact for which she had occasion to apologise when revising the work in the last years of her life.

> "…Some observation is necessary upon those parts of the work which thirteen years have made comparatively obsolete. The public are entreated to bear in mind that thirteen years have passed since it was finished, many more since it was begun, and that during that period, places, manners, books and opinions have undergone considerable changes."[13]

One aspect of that earlier world was the unease occasioned in the last two decades of the eighteenth century by the Gordon Riots.

Although Colonel Thomas Twisleton may have been planning to stake a claim for the Saye and Sele barony previously, a complicating factor was that Richard Fiennes, the Viscount and Baron Saye and Sele, was still living, although he had no male issue. Twisleton apparently did not wish to contest the title while this member of the elder generation was alive.

In the spring of 1780, Twisleton's claim to be the heir in the male line of Fiennes Twisleton was challenged by one Josias Cockshutt. Cockshutt claimed that the will of one John Twisleton (not Thomas' father) had

---

essay (author unknown) at http://www.exclassics.com/newgate/ngbibl.htm (Accessed 18 November 2015).

12. *Northanger Abbey* Volume I, Chapter 14.
13. "Advertisement, by the authoress, to *Northanger Abbey*", 1816: James Kinsley and John Davie (eds.), with an introduction and notes by Claudia L. Johnson, *Northanger Abbey, Lady Susan, The Watsons, Sanditon* (Oxford: Oxford World's Classics, 2003), no p. number, but two leaves after p. l; discussed at note on p. 357.

actually extinguished the male-line entail of the family.¹⁴ The case was heard at the Spring Assizes in York, by a special jury.

While our sources do not actually spell out the terms of this will, the chief question came to be whether Thomas Twisleton was the legitimate heir of his father. Evidence had to be brought of his father's marriage, and Thomas' subsequent birthdate.¹⁵ The evidence was presented and approved by the court, and Thomas was therefore confirmed as the legitimate heir to Fiennes Twisleton.

Having established that he was the heir of the family, Thomas was urged to proceed without delay to stake his claim to the defunct barony. As we have seen, in the summer of 1780 he was occupied in dealing with the riots. But by the following year, a case was made to the Privileges Committee of the House of Lords, and, by the summer of 1781, Thomas Twisleton was summoned to Parliament as Lord Saye and Sele.¹⁶

Twisleton only enjoyed his status as Lord Saye and Sele for seven years. He suffered from violent headaches, according to a family account. In 1788, he took his own life at the second attempt, in Harley Street in London, cutting his throat with a razor and falling on his regimental sword.¹⁷

There may have been an element of survivor guilt contributing to Thomas Twisleton's mental state at the time of his death. A curious death notice in the *Gentleman's Magazine* relates a macabre episode from earlier in Twisleton's military career.

> "At the bloody battle of Bucker [sic: usually Brucker] Muhl, in Germany, fought in 1762, the cannonade was so exceedingly violent, and the British detachment, which was chiefly composed of the foot guards, suffered so severely, that the soldiers piled up the dead bodies of their slain comrades, and sheltered themselves behind them, as behind a parapet. Thomas Twisleton (the late Lord Say [sic] and Sele), in the height of the slaughter, reprimanding a serjeant [sic] whom he heard utter some expressions of horror, was answered by him, 'Oh, Sir, you are now supporting yourself on

---

14. Brydges (1812), p. 35.
15. Ibid. p. 36. Note that we are now no longer sure of the birthdate of Thomas: it is "c. 1735."
16. *Burke's Peerage and Baronetage*, 105th edn., 2nd impression, prob. 1981, p. 2382.
17. Family account by descendant Ranulf Fiennes, "My Family and Other Misfits,' *The Daily Mail* 17 October 2009. Referenced by Huxley, p. 48 and 215, n. 14.

the body of your own brother!' This was his elder brother, John, a lieutenant in the Coldstream regiment, who, unknown to Thomas, had just been slain; and the serjeant had been a servant in the family."[18]

Of course, if his elder brother John had survived, Thomas would never have become Lord Saye and Sele. Similarly, if John had had surviving male children, Thomas would have been very unlikely to succeed. However, John had never married.

The *Gentleman's Magazine* obituary makes clear that a second fortuitous circumstance had enabled Thomas Twisleton to claim the title. It argues that a chance observation during the Gordon Riots encouraged Twisleton to proceed.

> "He owed his peerage to the following inscription, which he met with in [the burial ground of] Bunhill-fields, while on duty there during the late riots, 1780: 'Here lieth the body of Elizabeth Twisleton, the eldest daughter of the Right Honourable the Lord Viscount James Fenys, Say and Sele, wife to John Twisleton, Esq., of Dartford, in Kent. She died on the eighth day of March, Anno Domini 1673;' and proving himself collaterally related to the late Richard Fienes, Viscount and Baron Say and Sele, who died July 29, 1781; substantiated his claim to the barony, and was called up to the House of Lords, June 29, 1781."[19]

The younger Saye and Sele generation, like the Bertram children in *Mansfield Park*, seem to have missed the direction and control which their father, had he lived, might have provided. It is not clear whether the widowed Lady Saye and Sele had ever exerted any moral or social guidance. By 1806, when Jane Austen and her mother visited Stoneleigh, Lady Saye and Sele had become something of an embarrassment. Mrs Austen wrote to her daughter-in-law Mary:

---

18. "Obituary of Considerable Persons, with Biographical Anecdotes," *Gentleman's Magazine: and Historical Chronicle*, volume LVIII (London, 1788), pp. 660–661.
19. Ibid, p. 661.

"Poor Lady Saye & Sele is rather tormenting, tho' sometimes amusing, and affords Jane many a good laugh—but she fatigues me sadly on the whole."[20]

Julia-Judith's elder brother Gregory William, aged 19, succeeded to the barony on the tragic death of their father. The second brother, Thomas James, 18, was obsessed with amateur dramatics. Within months of the suicide, the young Thomas Twisleton was performing in numerous plays at Adlestrop. The productions included the tragedies *Matilda* (by Thomas Francklin, 1775) and Thomas Otway's classic *Venice Preserv'd* (1682), as well as lighter pieces such as David Garrick's comedy *Bon Ton* (1775) and Hannah Cowley's *Who's the Dupe?* (1779).[21]

The inappropriateness of the bereaved family taking part in these performances sheds some light on the attitude of Edmund Bertram, in Jane Austen's *Mansfield Park* (1814), to the amateur theatre. In Austen's novel, Edmund feels that it is insensitive to perform while their father Sir Thomas is absent at sea, possibly at risk of his life.

"It would show great want of feeling on my father's account, absent as he is, and in some degree of constant danger…"[22]

It was surely far more jarring for the second son of a great family, who had recently lost his war hero father to suicide, to indulge in adolescent amusements rather than facing an adult career.

In another prequel of *Mansfield Park*, in 1790, two years after their father's suicide, the youngest sibling, Mary-Cassandra, by then about 16, eloped with Edward Jervis Ricketts. The two married in London and had three children, but in 1799 they were divorced on the basis of Mary-Cassandra's alleged adultery.[23]

On Thomas' accession to the title, Julia-Judith, his second child, was ten years old. Her father, already a respected officer, was now also a lord; her mother was Lady Saye and Sele. Her grandfather and great-grandfather had been noble *de iure* noble, but not *de facto*. Her father had fought

---

20. 13 August 1806. Huxley p. 138.
21. Le Faye, *Chronology*, pp. 119–120.
22. Volume I, Chapter 13.
23. Huxley, p. 49; Le Faye, *Chronology*, p. 128.

for the position and had established the family as indisputably of noble title. These facts were not lost on Julia-Judith. She was nobly born, and she was beautiful. What could lie ahead but a brilliant marriage?

James Henry Leigh saw her when she was 14, he six years older, and fell in love with her. The two were related, a generation apart. Julia-Judith's mother Elizabeth Turner, now Lady Saye and Sele, was James Henry's first cousin. James Henry was at Adlestrop on a visit from Oxford when he met his younger cousins. Mrs Mary Leigh (1731–1797, wife of the Reverend Thomas), described the meeting in a family memoir which she wrote in the 1780s:

> "On entering—he was instantaneously shot!—shot in a vital part by the mischievous wicked eyes of his fair cousin—the Sorceress was not quite fiveteen [sic]."[24]

The two were married at the Saye and Sele seat of Broughton Castle, Oxfordshire, in December 1786, by which time Julia-Judith was fully 15.

It was not, however, the brilliant match to which Julia-Judith might have aspired. Her bridegroom James Henry Leigh was not known as particularly intelligent. The official history of Parliament suggests that he was treated with thinly disguised contempt. Known as "Bunny" Leigh, he was, successively, MP for three different constituencies—essentially warming the seat for his son Chandos Leigh—and was regarded as a reluctant and unpolished politician.[25] The resemblances to Mr Rushworth, in Jane Austen's *Mansfield Park*, are evident.

A kindlier portrait was supplied by the journalist and radical activist Leigh Hunt (1784–1859), in his autobiography. Hunt's father, Isaac Hunt, an American loyal to English power, had virtually been forced to flee to England during the American War of Independence. Isaac Hunt eventually had the good fortune to be employed by the third Duke of Chandos as a tutor to his nephew, James Henry Leigh. It was no doubt

---

24. SBTRO 671/677, cited by Huxley, p. 46 and 215, n. 10. The MS was written in 1788: Le Faye *Chronology*, pp. 112–113.
25. R. G. Thorne, "Leigh, James Henry (1765–1823), of Adlestrop, Glos. and Stoneleigh Abbey, Warws," http://www.historyofparliamentonline.org/volume/1790-1820/member/leigh-james-henry-1765-1823 (Accessed 18 November 2015).

gratitude which led Isaac Hunt to name his youngest son after his pupil: the journalist's full name was James Henry Leigh Hunt.

In turn, many decades later, Leigh Hunt reflected with gratitude on the family which had offered a refuge to his father.

> "I have spoken of the Duke of Chandos, to whose nephew, Mr Leigh, my father became tutor. Mr Leigh, who gave me his name, was son of the Duke's sister, Lady Caroline, and died member of parliament. He was one of the kindest and gentlest of men, addicted to those tastes for poetry and sequestered pleasure, which were conspicuous in his son, [Chandos] Lord Leigh…"

Hunt went on to quote with approval Chandos' likening of James Henry to Squire Allworthy, the ideal country squire from Fielding's novel *Tom Jones* (1749).[26] Even this likeness, however, implies something of the innocent, even the dupe, whose good nature has a tendency to be imposed upon. Having married his clever, attractive and forceful daughter to a fool may also have contributed to Thomas Twisleton's descent into depression.

The next few glimpses we have of the younger Twisletons are courtesy of Jane Austen. Jane met Julia-Judith and Mary-Cassandra in 1801 at an assembly in Bath. Julia-Judith and her sister were distant relatives of Jane through two connections: as great-nieces of the Reverend Thomas, as well as through Julia's marriage with her relative James Henry.

Jane prided herself on recognising Mary-Cassandra from her resemblance to Julia-Judith: "[I have] a very good eye at an Adultress." A few years older than their country cousin Jane, the Twisleton girls may have been in a relation to her similar to that of the Bertram sisters to Fanny Price, in *Mansfield Park*. In the same letter, Jane Austen gave a rather unfriendly pen-portrait of the sisters.

---

26. Leigh Hunt, *The Autobiography of Leigh Hunt* (London: Smith, Elder and Co., 1860), pp. 25–26. This chapter appears to have been drafted during the legal proceedings of 1848–1849. It contains a spirited defence of Chandos Leigh against the charges, in a passage probably unintelligible to the majority of readers.

> "A resemblance to Mrs Leigh [Julia-Judith] was my guide [to Mary-Cassandra]. She is not so pretty as I expected; her face has the same defect of baldness as her sister's, & her features not so handsome;—she was highly rouged, & looked rather quietly & contentedly silly than anything else."[27]

By "baldness", Austen probably meant not hair loss, but blankness of expression, common to both sisters. What is not clear is whether Jane Austen realised that Julia-Judith's blank face concealed an unusually ambitious, controlling and selfish personality. Today it is widely believed that such people often manifest a blank facial expression: Austen may not have known of this belief, but she correctly reported the phenomenon.[28]

Our next glimpse of Julia-Judith is on a visit to Stoneleigh, some time before 1806.

> "[John Perks, engineer to the city of London gas light company in 1829] saith he well recollects a carriage coming to Stoneley Abbey belonging...to Lord Saye and Sele, in which carriage was the lady of the late James Henry Leigh, esquire, and several children, when a conversation arose (the carriage having arrived during the lunch time of the workmen) between several of the artificers who were then at work there...about the heir to the estate after the death of the honourable Mary Leigh, the then possessor, when Smith [a carpenter] remarked,—'that from the account on the monument or stone in Stoneley church (meaning that commonly called the Lancashire stone) would be discovered the heir to the estate.'"[29]

It is possible that it was at this moment, if not before, that Julia-Judith realised that there might be a genuine threat to her long-held dream of becoming mistress of Stoneleigh, and having her son become the first lord of a revived Leigh barony.

---

27. 12–13 May 1801. Le Faye, *Letters*, pp. 88–89.
28. Robert Hare, "This Charming Psychopath: How to Spot Social Predators Before They Attack," 10 December 2012, http://www.psychologytoday.com/articles/199401/charming-psychopath (Accessed 18 November 2015). Includes reference to the fixed stare: "The fixated stare, is more a prelude to self-gratification and the exercise of power rather than simple interest or empathetic caring."
29. Leigh (1834), vol, II, p. 303, note.

Having grown up in the knowledge of her father's successful claim, she knew that evidence for an estate or peerage claim would come from monumental inscriptions, coffin plates, parish records, and wills. One monumental inscription was to prove particularly significant: the "Lancashire stone" to which the carpenter Smith referred. Julia-Judith will have known, from her father's experience, how tenuous and circuitous a claim to an estate and title could be.

There was also an instructive case, a perpetual irritant in her husband James Henry's family: the protracted and eventually unsuccessful claim by Samuel Egerton Brydges (brother of Jane Austen's friend Anne Lefroy) to the Dukedom of Chandos.[30] Aware of the risks involved, Julia-Judith must have become utterly determined to secure the Leigh estate and title at all costs.

From about 1810 onwards, the Reverend Thomas suffered from ill health. The Leigh papers indicate that Julia-Judith, based at Adlestrop but increasingly at Stoneleigh, was the person in charge of the estate. Work was continuing on the waterways on the property, with a major new project being a bridge over the River Avon. Repton had recommended this, but it was given to John Rennie (1761–1821), the great Scottish engineer, to direct it, in consultation with Julia-Judith.[31]

Finally, in June 1813, the Reverend Thomas died, and James Henry inherited the estate. With James Henry seemingly in the background, and young Chandos uninterested in estate management, it was left to Julia-Judith to control the vast empire of which Stoneleigh was the centre. She was the unquestioned ruler, with the power of ruining her tenants and servants at will. Like Jane Austen's Lady Catherine de Bourgh, Julia-Judith even employed sycophantic clergymen, *a là* Mr Collins, to further her projects. She was undoubtedly a gifted, if ruthless, manager of the many properties, tenancies and assets which comprised the Stoneleigh group. If she had lived today, she might have become a particularly successful CEO of a major corporation.

---

30. George Frederick Beltz, *A Review of the Chandos Peerage Case, Adjudicated 1803, and of the pretensions of Sir Samuel Egerton Brydges, baronet, to designate himself* per legem terrae *Baron Chandos of Sudeley* (n.d. but from internal evidence c. 1834).
31. Leigh (1834), vol. II, p. 256.

Above all, Julia-Judith wanted her son, Chandos Leigh (1791–1850), to succeed as master of Stoneleigh. Chandos, however, was a womanising poet, a friend of Byron's from Harrow, with no interest in estate management. His interests lay in literature, expensive living, and women.

He was a serious liability in terms of his reckless spending. One of his early appearances in the Leigh papers is an 1818 letter written by Chandos from Paris to the family lawyer Thomas Hill Mortimer, requesting more money be sent to him at Geneva, as he had bought a carriage and spent most of his allowance.[32]

Julia-Judith's grandson, Sir Edward Chandos Leigh (1832–1915), described her.

> "My grandmother had a striking personality. A very beautiful woman…her strong will and powerful intellect sometimes inclined her to be too managing; but her kindness of heart never failed."[33]

"Managing" was a Victorian euphemism for dictatorial, and we shall see little evidence of Julia-Judith's kindness of heart when it comes to the Leigh estate claim. It would be alleged that she engaged in the destruction of monuments, the obliteration of parish records, and even in murder. What is without question is that tenants were thrown out of their homes, or dismissed from their jobs, if they gave evidence of which Julia-Judith disapproved. The story which follows is largely about the lengths to which she was prepared to go, in order to secure the estates and titles of Stoneleigh against all possible rivals.

---

32. SBTRO DR 18/17/44/16, 19 August 1818.
33. Macdonald (2004), p. 157.

CHAPTER THREE

Rivals

"Lees [are] as plentiful as fleas."

Cheshire proverb[1]

The first clouds on the inheritance horizon had arisen as early as 1808, two years after the death of Mary Leigh. A man who was the son of John Smith, and who claimed to be a relative of Edward Lord Leigh through a female line, changed his surname by "His Majesty's licence" to Leigh in 1802, then filed a bill in Chancery claiming that he was the rightful heir at law of Edward Lord Leigh: "the first and nearest of my name and blood."[2] The Lords sought opinions from the greatest legal minds of the day, including noted legal theorist and the reformer Sir Samuel Romilly. Consideration of the issues required trying to imagine what the testator, in this case Edward Lord Leigh, had really meant with his much-quoted stipulation (see *Chapter 1*).

The experts concluded that he had probably meant his heir to be a male, his relative through a male line of descent, and holding the name Leigh by virtue of this. It was not that he was fixated on the name Leigh itself, because his first concern in his will was for his sisters Mary Leigh and Anne Hackett and their putative issue—and if they had had children (which they did not), the surname of such children would not have been Leigh.[3] Rather, he wanted his heir to be a Leigh by descent, and this would exclude Mr Smith Leigh.

---

1. *Report* (1849), p. 5, column 2.
2. Leigh (1834) vol. I, pp. xiv-xv.
3. Leigh (1834) vol. I, p. xxvii.

Meanwhile, Smith Leigh, like James Leigh Perrot (*Chapter 1*), had been demanding a payout in return for going away. A "friend" had intimated that he would be prepared to settle initially for £5,000 to £10,000. Eventually "friends" suggested that an annual sum of £1,200 might be preferable.[4] The Reverend Thomas was unwilling to compromise, and in the event the legal opinion was that Smith Leigh had no reasonable claim. This case received considerable publicity, and may well have frightened not so much the Reverend Thomas, who was safely incumbent at Stoneleigh, but James Henry and Julia-Judith. If a man who simply adopted the name Leigh could present a claim to Chancery, what about people who had been born Leighs? And there were certainly plenty of Leighs in Warwickshire, Cheshire and Lancashire: "Lees as plentiful as fleas" was a local saying.[5]

The next few years saw several people come forward. In July 1812, a letter was sent by the Reverend Thomas to the attorney acting for a possible claimant. It was rather odd in tone.

> "Mr [the Reverend Thomas] Leigh never advertised for an heir at law of Lord Leigh, nor did he ever hear that any has been advertised for, indeed the heir at law, whoever such person may be, is not at all interested, for the late Lord Leigh, who died in 1786, by a devise in his will left all his estates to his sister the hon. Mary Leigh — his heir at law...
>
> If Christopher, a younger son of Thomas, first lord Leigh, had had any male descendants it must have been known in the family, and any descendant from him in tail male would be lord Leigh, but there is no such descendant from any of the five lords Leigh."[6]

The letter indicates that there was already a widespread sense that members of the Adlestrop family were not the only potential inheritors. The expression that the heir, "whoever such person may be, is not at all

---

4. Fiennes Trotman to Rev. Thomas Leigh, DR 18/17/34/8, 16 February 1808; DR 18/17/34/13, 1 March 1808.
5. *Report* (1849), p. 5, column 2.
6. Leigh (1834) vol. I, pp. xxxiii-xxxiv.

interested," is curious. It suggests that the Reverend Thomas was aware that there might be other potential heirs.

The will of Edward Lord Leigh again came before the Court of Chancery in December 1820. George Leigh, the son of a tanner from Wigan, submitted a bill to Chancery alleging serious misconduct by the Adlestrop heirs, including the suppression of key evidence about other Leigh families.[7] We know nothing about George Leigh except what emerged as part of this and subsequent legal actions. He was a cotton manufacturer who had retired to a home he had built at Highfield House, Blackrod, Lancashire. He was in middle-age by the time of the claim, and had been brought up in the belief of a relationship with Stoneleigh Abbey.[8] It is evident that the claim, worked on over decades, consumed his life and undoubtedly his resources: one of the few facts emerging about him was that at some point in the mid-1820s he spent time in custody, as an insolvent debtor.[9]

The tradition of connection with Stoneleigh, in George Leigh's family, was unfortunately verbal only, and not supported by much documentary evidence. John Leigh of Houghton, the uncle of George Leigh, stated that he recalled a prayer book in the possession of his father (also John Leigh), which recorded the names and descent of the family of Leigh of Stoneleigh. He particularly recalled the names of Christopher Leigh and of his son Roger Leigh, from whom John Leigh claimed descent. This prayer book was said to have been taken by John's half-brother Andrew Taylor, and was never produced in evidence. Andrew Taylor of Rivington, in Lancashire, confirmed the existence of this prayer book, and its entries, but also confirmed that it had been lost.[10] Several witnesses, mostly friends and neighbours, were brought forward who confirmed that the Lancashire Leighs had claimed a family relationship with the Stoneleigh Leighs. William Rylance, a carpenter of Wigan, remembered George Leigh's grandfather Robert Leigh. Robert had told William Rylance that

---

7. Leigh (1834), vol. I, p. xxxv.
8. George Leigh, in his claim, put forward his descent as follows: himself, George (bapt. Blackrod 1759); father James (bapt. Blackrod 1729–30); grandfather Robert (bapt. Blackrod 1707); great-grandfather James (bapt. Blackrod 1680); great-great-grandfather Roger (bapt. ?Stoneleigh, unknown date): Leigh (1834), vol. II, pp. 11–14.
9. Leigh (1834), vol. I, p. 64. Insolvent: vol. I, p. 322.
10. Leigh (1834), vol. I, p. 51 (16 May 1820).

The Missing Monument Murders

he (Robert) had been summoned once to Stoneleigh to attend the funeral of one Lord Leigh (possibly Thomas the fourth Lord, who died in 1749). He was treated with respect as a member of the family. Robert showed the mourning suit he wore at the funeral, and it passed to his grandson, George Leigh the claimant.[11]

The only documentary support, however, provided for a link with Stoneleigh was a tenuous one. This was the will of Roger Leigh of Haigh (Wigan), dated 28 January 1690, the great-great-grandfather of George Leigh the claimant. One of the witnesses was Francis Willoughby. One man of that name was the brother of Hugh Baron Willoughby de Parham (c.1637–1712), who married Honora Leigh of Stoneleigh, one of the sisters of Thomas (V), the second Baron Leigh (1652–1710). Whether the witness Francis Willoughby was the same man as the brother-in-law of Honora (Leigh) Egerton Willoughby is not clear. The identification was questioned at the time.[12] Indeed, it must be questionable, because Honora's first husband, Sir William Egerton of Worsley in Lancashire, was still living in January 1690; his death took place in December 1691.[13] At the time of Roger Leigh's will, then, Honora was probably still married to her first husband, Sir William Egerton, and was not linked by marriage to Francis Willoughby. With so little documentary evidence to support his claim, George Leigh displayed great persistence and tenacity in its pursuit. The fact that he squandered a life's savings from trade, in the quest for a far greater fortune from the Stoneleigh estate, was to provide lawyers for the Leigh family with a readymade argument that all such claims were simply fraudulent gold-seeking. On the other hand, it took away from them the argument that George Leigh bribed his many witnesses — because he was simply unable to.

George Leigh brought his claims before the Court of Chancery. This ancient court had become England's premier court for determining civil disputes, under the supervision of the Lord Chancellor. In the early nineteenth century, it was in a period of transition. Many observers questioned how a court subject to the will of the Lord Chancellor could be

---

11. Deposition of William Rylance: Leigh (1834), vol. II, p. 324.
12. Leigh (1834), vol. I, p. 53; see also p. 12 and notes.
13. Egerton was MP for several Lancashire seats. http://www.historyofparliamentonline.org/volume/1660–1690/member/egerton-sir-william-1649-91 (Accessed 19 November 2015).

seen to operate fairly. It was thought to be a court peculiarly resistant to progress, even as the volume of its workload was increasing dramatically.[14]

In his first claim in 1820, George Leigh's principal accusations were that:

- James Henry Leigh had improperly cut down and used a large amount of timber on the Stoneleigh estates;
- He had pulled down a mansion called Fletchampstead Hall and also that at Watergall, two hamlets close to Stoneleigh;
- He had removed the monument of Christopher Leigh from the Stoneleigh church;
- He had carried away, concealed or destroyed several family records, which would have been evidence of George Leigh's pedigree.[15]

The first accusation, that considerable amounts of timber had been illegally felled and sold, is certainly borne out by the Leigh papers. In 1813, Adam Murray expressed his opinion that the resource had been going to waste under the Reverend Thomas.

> "The estate that is considered to possess the largest quantity of oak timber in the county, is the Leigh estate: I was creditably informed, that the quantity that is ready for cutting on this estate, if sold, would exceed the sum of 150,000. I was sorry to observe a great deal of timber decaying on this estate."[16]

Many letters deal with the felling and sale of timber. In July 1815, estate manager George Jones Snr wrote to Julia-Judith noting that a large quantity of timber had been sold for £7,009, a large sum. He noted with satisfaction:

---

14. Joseph Parkes, *A History of the Court of Chancery; With practical remarks, on the recent Commission, report, and evidence, and on the means of improving the administration of justice in the English courts of equity* (London: Longman, Rees, Orme, Brown, and Green, 1828), p. 353.
15. Leigh (1834), vol. I, p. xxxix.
16. Murray (1813), p. 140.

"I think upon the whole the timber sold remarkably well and will average 4 shillings a foot."[17]

It seems that by 1817, however, the resource had been exhausted, for Jones was writing to Julia-Judith, noting regret at the current felling, and claiming that a halt would be called until she gave further instructions:

"[The current timber] is too coarse for home market and fit only for naval purposes."[18]

In all probability, the tree-felling had begun as soon as Julia-Judith and James Henry took possession in 1813 (possibly before), and, if so, this could have been in Jane Austen's mind as she wrote those passages of *Mansfield Park* (1814) which express Fanny's regret at the mooted sacrifice of trees at Sotherton.[19]

George Leigh's second complaint was that the Leighs had pulled down ancient mansions at Fletchampstead and Watergall. As owners of both hamlets as part of the Stoneleigh estate, technically they were allowed to do this. However, there was later a suggestion that in the case of the Watergall house, important evidence of ownership and entitlement had been destroyed or illegally removed to Stoneleigh.[20]

The critical accusation, for the purposes of George Leigh's claim, was the removal of the monument to Christopher Leigh from Stoneleigh village church. Much of the subsequent consideration of the claims of George and others would focus on this matter. The significance of Christopher Leigh is as follows. The Adlestrop Leighs, of whom James Henry was one, were descended from Rowland, one of the sons of Sir Thomas Leigh (Thomas I, c.1498–1571), the first of the name to inhabit Stoneleigh. This Sir Thomas' great-grandson, also Sir Thomas (Thomas III: 1595–1672), was created the first Baron Leigh in 1643. Thomas III,

---

17. SBTRO DR 18/17/41/9, 2 July 1815.
18. SBTRO DR 18/17/43/10, 1 May 1817.
19. Volume I, Chapter 6.
20. Charles Griffin, Solicitor, *Stoneleigh Abbey, Thirty-four Years Ago, Containing a short history of the claims to the peerage and estates, and a catalogue of the confessed and suspected crimes, &c. &c. &c.* [sic] (Birmingham: R. J. Salter), 1848, p. 64. Hereafter: Griffin (1848).

the first Baron, had sons Thomas IV (1616–1662), who predeceased his father; Charles (1625–1704): Christopher (1626–1672); and Ferdinando (1633–1655), as well as three daughters.[21] The son of Thomas IV, Thomas V (1652–1710), became the second Baron Leigh.

After this, Thomas V's son Edward (1684–1738) became the third Baron; his son Thomas VI (1713–1749) became the fourth Baron; and his son Edward (1742–1786), whom we met in *Chapter 1*, the fifth, dying of unsound mind and without issue.[22] It thus appears that if a male Leigh descendant were to be found who could prove descent through a male line from this family, he would be closer in relationship to Edward Lord Leigh than the Adlestrop Leighs, whose link was further back, two generations prior to the creation of the Barony.

On this basis, it became important to establish whether any of these male Leighs had, or could have had, living descendants. Remarkably, many died either unmarried, or without legitimate issue, or both. Of the sons of Thomas III, first Baron Leigh, Thomas IV, as noted, predeceased his father. He married twice, his first wife dying without issue, but luckily for the family, his second wife produced an heir. Charles Leigh, who inherited the family property at Leighton Buzzard, died in 1704 without male issue. And Ferdinando, also, did not marry prior to his death at the age of twenty-two.

This left Christopher. It was known that he married in 1670 a woman named Constance Clent. They had one son, Thomas, who died unmarried in 1698. George's peerage claim, however, alleged that Christopher Leigh had previously been married, and had legitimate male issue. On the face of it, this has plausibility. Christopher had been born in 1626. It would have been unusual if he had not married before the age of 44, as he would have been in 1670.

George Leigh claimed that there had been, until some recent time, a memorial stone located in Stoneleigh Parish Church, to the memory

---

21. Table 1, "The Leighs of Stoneleigh, to 1806," in Bearman (ed., 2004), p. 130, gives Christopher's death year as 1673, rather than the 1672 which is widely attested. See, e.g., Stoneleigh burials register as provided to the Attorney-General's inquiry, showing Christopher's burial on 16 September 1672: J. S. Copley, *Report of the Attorney General*, 25 April 1826, in Leigh (1834), vol. I, 38–58, p. 43. Ferdinando's dates: baptism in 1633 (Copley 1826, p. 43), death in 1655 (Bearman 2004, p. 130).
22. Details in Table 1, 'The Leighs of Stoneleigh to 1806', Bearman (ed.), 2004, p. 130.

The Missing Monument Murders

of Christopher Leigh. The stone described a first marriage to a woman by the name of Cotton of Combermere in Cheshire, and listed children Mary, Katherine, Roger, and Ferdinand. George Leigh claimed legitimate male descent from Roger.[23]

On the other hand, as the claimant and his agents found during their search for documentation during the period from about 1817 onwards, there were no extant records of such a marriage. The memorial stone was nowhere to be seen. Nor was there a parish register of the marriage. The parish where such a record might be found was that of Wrenbury in Cheshire, where the Cottons of Combermere worshipped. However, the Wrenbury parish register of marriages had a missing section for the 1640s. The writing on the register appeared, according to the claimant, to have been chemically obliterated. Some ink stains remained, indicating that records had previously been legible.[24]

If deliberate mutilation of the Wrenbury register took place, it could only have happened after 6 May 1813. This was the date on which the Reverend Gilbert Vaudrey, minister of Wrenbury, submitted a return to his diocesan court which recorded that

> "...the register of marriages commences in the month of September, 1593, and is continued without any interruption, down to the end of the year 1679."[25]

Nor were there parish records of the births of children. The birth register for Stoneleigh, again, for the relevant period, seemed to have been altered. There were no baptisms recorded for the period 1644 to 1647 or from 1648 to 1665.[26]

Christopher Leigh's presence at Stoneleigh during the 1650s is attested in several documents, including a 1655 assignment of land by Alice, Duchess of Dudley, to Christopher, his brother-in-law Sir Justinian Isham, and a third party.[27] A draft deed from 1657 shows Sir Thomas

---

23. Copley (1826) in Leigh (1834) vol. I, p. 44.
24. Claim of George Leigh in Privileges Committee: Leigh (1834), vol. I, p. 9.
25. Leigh (1834), vol. I, 9–10.
26. Leigh (1834), vol. I, p. 53, note. Also Griffin (1848), p. 41.
27. SBTRO DR 18/2/25, 24 July 1655.

Leigh (III) undertaking to pay to Christopher £1,000, half of a £2,000 commitment made under a settlement in 1641.[28] Why Sir Thomas (III) had made a settlement on behalf of Christopher in 1641, when he would only have been 15-years-old, is unclear. Much, in fact, remains unclear about Christopher Leigh's life, leaving room for a variety of speculations.

Five months elapsed before James Henry Leigh made any formal response to George Leigh's accusations, in May 1821. The substance of the response focused on a formal process whereby the Reverend Thomas and James Henry had sought to pre-empt any claims on the estates. This process involved what were known as *fines* and *recoveries*. In essence, an estate holder could undergo a kind of sham contest with another stakeholder, the outcome being that once an agreement had taken place, this prevented any further claim from being made.[29] Legal opinion varied as to whether these fines and recoveries did, in fact, cut off any chance of further claims.[30]

The claim remained dormant for several years. James Henry disappeared, believed dead, in 1823 (in itself a strange proceeding, discussed in *Chapter 12*). George Leigh continued to seek legal advice. In 1827, he obtained a ruling which required the defendant—this was now James Henry's son Chandos Leigh—to respond to the claims made by George, the plaintiff. Chandos admitted that James Henry had cut down a considerable amount of timber, but claimed that it had been done in order to pay off encumbrances on the estate, in the same manner as Jane Austen's brother, Edward Austen Knight, was obliged to do at Chawton.[31] Interestingly, he added (the statement is in the third person):

> "He denies according to the best of his knowledge, information and belief that Roger Leigh was the first or eldest or any other son of Christopher Leigh, fourth son of the first Lord Leigh, for that defendant [Chandos] believes he had an only son, Thomas, who died without issue in or about December 1698…that he never was in Stoneley church prior to the repair

---

28. SBTRO DR 18/3/47/24, [no day or month] 1657.
29. Leigh (1834), vol. I, xliv, xlv.
30. Leigh (1834), vol. I, l, liii.
31. Leigh (1834), vol. I, lxiv. *Chawton: Caroline Austen* (with an introduction by Deirdre Le Faye), *Reminiscences of Caroline Austen* (The Jane Austen Society, 1986), p. 38.

thereof alluded to in the said bill, and that he denies according to the best of his knowledge, information and belief that there was any monument of the said Christopher Leigh erected and fixed on the south wall or in any part of the body of the parish church of Stoneley..."[32]

Thus Chandos denied knowing about the stone, rather than confidently asserting that it never existed. Chandos further denied that the church repairs were carried out in order to remove the Christopher stone. In any event, they were done on the orders of the Reverend Thomas, prior to James Henry's inheriting the estate. Further, he denied that other family evidence—funeral memorials, ensigns, banners—were removed from the church.[33] Time was running out for George Leigh, as there was a statute of limitations on estate claims. This was a term of 20 years in which an aggrieved claimant was entitled to contest the outcome of a will, and Mary Leigh had died in 1806. In June 1826, George Leigh's lawyers served "declarations in ejectment" on several Leigh tenants and family members, including Chandos Leigh.[34] This was essentially a claim for the particular lands to which George Leigh believed himself entitled. Chandos' response was to call upon the plaintiff to provide details, but a judge over-ruled this prior to an actual case being in progress.

Since the critical piece of information was the Christopher stone, which several witnesses had sworn they remembered in the church, a motion was made in the Court of King's Bench (a common-law court) for a rule calling upon the defendant, Chandos Leigh, to show cause why a search should not be made in Stoneleigh Abbey for the monument. The application was over-ruled by the court.[35] Meanwhile, Chandos Leigh's lawyers maintained that the statute of limitations applied, and that the period of 20 years having passed since Mary Leigh's death, any action of ejectment by George Leigh should be barred. This meant that a claim in the Privileges Committee of the House of Lords remained George Leigh's only option.[36]

---

32. Leigh (1834), vol. I, lxiv.
33. Leigh (1834), vol. I, p. lxvi.
34. Leigh (1834), vol. I, p. lxvii.
35. Leigh (1834), vol. I, p. lxviii-lxx.
36. Leigh (1834), vol. I, p. xcii.

George had actually begun his attempt to have this case heard in the Lords as early as August 1819. His petition was referred to the Attorney-General for primary assessment. James Henry Leigh's lawyer, Thomas Hill Mortimer (heir of Mary Leigh's right-hand man Joseph Hill, and a key player in subsequent events), requested that he be advised of any evidence in support of the claim.[37] This was over-ruled.

Evidence was heard, and in November 1822, the Attorney-General, Sir Robert Gifford, announced that he had reported to the king (George IV) his opinion on the evidence. George Leigh tried unsuccessfully to obtain a copy of this report. In December 1822, the under-secretary of the Home Office Henry Hobhouse, for the Home Secretary Robert Peel, wrote to George to advise him that the Home Secretary could not advise the king to refer George's case to the Lords' Privileges Committee.[38]

Worse was to come. In January 1823, George received another letter from Hobhouse to advise that his petition had been put before His Majesty. But a third letter followed the next day, advising that His Majesty had not signified his pleasure on the claimant's petition. George and his associate, Henry Kent Causton, persisted in writing to the Home Secretary. Finally, "one of these random shots," as Causton put it, resulted in a partial explanation of the difficulties.

"Whitehall, 12th April 1823.

Sir,

Application having been made to Mr Secretary Peel by a person assuming the character of your agent for a copy of the Attorney General's report on your claim to the Leigh peerage, I am directed by Mr Peel to inform you he cannot comply with that request, but he has no difficulty in informing you that the two points upon which you have failed in tendering to the Attorney General any such probable evidence as would justify him in advising a reference to the house of peers, are the marriage of Christopher

---

37. Leigh (1834), vol. I, p. lxxiv-lxxv.
38. Leigh (1834), vol. I, p. lxxvii.

Leigh, son of the first Lord Leigh with a lady named Cotton, and the birth of Roger Leigh the alleged son of that marriage.

Whenever you shall be able to produce evidence on those points, Mr Peel will be ready to refer your claim for the further consideration of the Attorney-General.

I am, &c.,

H. Hobhouse."[39]

In this context, it is important to clarify the role of Henry Kent Causton, a member of a prominent family of London printers.[40] Causton became interested in George Leigh's claim, possibly as early as before 1820. Causton's son attended school in Wigan in 1814, and their connection may date from this period.[41] Causton lent money to George Leigh, and therefore his interest became financial as well as historical and moral. At the time of the Lords hearings in 1828, he was still a creditor of the claimant, who owed him between £1,000 and £1,500.[42] Causton may have printed one of the handbills which called for witnesses concerning the Christopher stone to come forward, although he was evasive about this in his Lords evidence.[43] Chandos' lead lawyer, Sir James Scarlett, pointed out that it was illegal to have printed the handbill with no authorising information about its source.[44]

Following the Lords case in 1828–1829, Causton, no doubt in an attempt to recoup some funds from his expensive and long-running involvement, published the transcripts of evidence. He added considerable editorial comment, mostly in footnotes, but also in appended articles. This was first published in 1832, with a second edition appearing

---

39. Leigh (1834), vol. I, pp. lxxxi-lxxxii.
40. John S. Causton, "The Causton Family in the Printing Trade in London, Including a brief history of Sir Joseph Causton and Sons Ltd., printers, publishers and stationers." http://homepage.ntlworld.com/john.causton/Causton-Printers.htm (Accessed 24 November 2015).
41. Causton cross-examined by Sir James Scarlett, Leigh (1834), vol. I, p. 79.
42. Leigh (1834), vol. I, p. 79. Amount owed: Leigh (1834), vol. I, p. 83.
43. Leigh (1834), vol. I, p. 80.
44. Leigh (1834), vol. I, p. 85.

in 1834. In its modern facsimile form, it appears in two hefty and small-printed volumes. By convention it is referenced under the name of George Leigh, as the claimant responsible, but it should be clear that the writer — qualified by his detailed knowledge of all aspects of the case and its evidence — was Causton. Notes to this and other chapters, however, in regard for the convention, refer to "Leigh (1834)."

Some time afterwards, undoubtedly owing to the perseverance of George Leigh and Henry Kent Causton, the case was referred once more to the Attorney-General. Appointed in 1824, the new Attorney-General was Sir John Singleton Copley (1772–1863), son of the American artist of the same name. Copley, later Lord Lyndhurst, had made his name as the defence counsel for James Watson and others of the Spa Fields Rioters in 1816 and 1817. Watson was acquitted (as was Arthur Thistlewood on this occasion, but was later executed for his part in the Cato Street Conspiracy of 1820).[45] Copley had a reputation as a champion of the oppressed, and his elevation to the position of Attorney-General may well have encouraged George Leigh. Numerous sworn depositions were made for the preliminary investigation before the Attorney-General. As early as 1817, George Leigh's agents had placed advertisements in newspapers and on placards, inviting witnesses who remembered the Christopher stone to come forward, and a large number of witness statements had already been collected.[46]

In April 1826, just as the statute of limitations was running out, Copley signed off on a report which recommended that the king refer the claim to the House of Lords for further consideration.[47] George Leigh had achieved what he had worked towards for a decade or more. But he had run out of money. A year passed without his being able to follow up the claim. Meanwhile, in April 1827, Chandos Leigh placed a request with the Lords that George Leigh should, in effect, put up or shut up.

---

45. Account of both plots in *Newgate Calendar* (introduction by Clive Emsley, 1997), pp. 326–336, noting "ability" of Watson's counsel (Copley) in 1817, p. 331.
46. SBTRO DR 18/17/46/60, 30 Oct 1820, newspaper cutting announcing George Leigh's claim on estates. Warwickshire archives CR2981/6/3/37, handbill (dated 30 August 1817), offering £10 reward for recovery of monument taken from Stoneleigh church http://archivesunlocked.warwickshire.gov.uk/CalmView/Record.aspx?src=CalmView.Catalog&id=00304%2f6%2f3%2f5%2f5&pos=103 (Accessed 24 November 2015).
47. Leigh (1834), vol. I, p. 58.

In particular, Chandos wanted to combat what he called "the foul calumnies affecting the honor [sic] of [his] family."[48]

In all probability, Chandos and his mother Julia-Judith were keen to pursue the revival of the defunct Barony of Leigh, and wanted to get any outstanding obstacles out of the way. Several members of the Lords Privileges Committee were unsure as to whether they had jurisdiction over the estate claim. Their function was to determine conflicts about peerage titles, but if neither George Leigh nor Chandos Leigh was, at this stage, claiming the barony, could they make a judgment? In any event, the committee decided to proceed with the hearing. Henry Kent felt that this was a special favour to Chandos Leigh. It was probably a tacit recognition that he would proceed to claim the Barony.[49] George Leigh, however, without further resources, was not in a position to proceed. It was a costly undertaking. The claimant had to pay for a short-hand writer to record the evidence, as well as meeting the costs of witnesses.[50] And of course, there was the expense of lawyers to develop strategy and cross-examine witnesses.

In February 1828, George Leigh ran out of time. The clerk of the Privileges Committee wrote to him to request that he produce his evidence on or before the 27th March. As that day proved to be one on which King George IV held a levee, it was 1 April 1828 before the committee met for the first time to consider what came to be known as the Leigh peerage claim, although, as noted, the Stoneleigh estate rather than the defunct Leigh peerage was actually the matter at issue.

---

48. Leigh (1834), vol. I, p. lxxxvi-lxxxvii.
49. Leigh (1834), vol. I, p. xci.
50. Leigh (1834), vol. I, p. xcvii.

CHAPTER FOUR

Witness

"'Ned, there stands poor old Christopher.'"

John Ilett, quoted by Edward Baylis, 1827[1]

At least 34 people, in the course of a number of years, swore to remembering the Christopher stone (or Lancashire stone) mounted on the south wall of Stoneleigh village church. A number of others were prepared to give sworn evidence, but were not called to do so. In the main, these people were builders, carpenters, plumbers (several of whom had worked on the church repairs), or members of the parish committee. There was even the woman who cleaned the Christopher stone. Through their evidence, we can hear the authentic voices of classes of people who are often thought to have been overlooked and silent in the novels of Jane Austen. Theirs is the language which she would have heard every day, in the voices of servants and tradespeople. It is a plain, strong and vigorous English, with a few survivals of more archaic usage.

In several cases the witnesses had lived at Stoneleigh in their childhoods, but now lived and worked elsewhere. This is significant: as they no longer lived on the estate, they had less to lose from giving evidence which would make them highly unpopular with the all-powerful Julia-Judith and Chandos Leigh. While no one authentic copy of the stone ever emerged from successive investigations, the consensus was that the inscription was broadly as follows:

---

1. Leigh (1834), vol. II, p. 135.

> "Sacred to the memory of the Honourable Christopher Leigh fourth son of the Right Honourable Thomas Lord Leigh, and Lady Mary his wife. He married Penelope Cotton, daughter of Sir G. Cotton, Bart. of Cumbermere Abbey, Cheshire, by whom he had issue, Mary, Catherine, Roger, and Ferdinand. He married secondly Constance Clent, daughter of John Clent, Esqr. of the Borough of Warwick, by whom he had issue, Thomas.
>
> Roger Leigh of Haigh Hall, eldest son of the above Honourable Christopher Leigh, he married Margaret Higham, eldest daughter of James Higham, Esqr, of Wigan, Lancashire, by whom he had issue, Robert and James.
>
> CHRISTOPHERUS LEIGH, OBIIT SEPTEMBER XVI,
>
> MDCLXXII.
>
> AETAT, XLVI."[2]

The same John Perks who recalled Julia-Judith's visit to Stoneleigh church before 1806, had made a statement in 1824. He had gone to school in Stoneleigh as a boy, then followed his father's business as a plumber and glazier at Kenilworth, and had frequently worked in Stoneleigh church on repairs. While attending the school in Stoneleigh, John Perks used to be given the job of going into the church to ring the bell to summon the children to school. He said that he well remembered having seen on the south wall of the church a monument to the memory of Christopher Leigh, which stood next to another monument to the memory of John Webster. The Leigh monument was commonly known by the name of the Lancashire stone. He clearly recollected it being in place on the wall

---

2. This version given in Griffin (1848), p. 10, with caveats. The purported description of Christopher as the fourth, rather than the third, son of Lord Leigh, is incorrect. A different version was presented by Causton as highly dubious (appearing as it does to be a convenient amalgam of several conjectured variants), in the deposition (date unclear but from internal evidence after 31 January 1829) of Charles Evans Lloyd, watchmaker, of Coventry, who had visited Stoneleigh regularly from the late-eighteenth century onwards: Leigh (1834), vol. II, pp. 244–245, note.

at the time of his marriage to his wife Ann, in January 1806.³ At the time of his statement, Perks was working as an engineer in London with the London Gas Light Company. By the time of the Lords hearing in 1828, John Perks was employed in Berlin, with the Continental Gas Company. The development of gas lighting (using coal gas) had proceeded rapidly since its origins in the late eighteenth century. Birmingham was a local centre of the new industry.

In 1813, the technology had advanced so far that Westminster Bridge in London was lit by gas. Most streets in the district of Westminster were gas-lit in 1814. By 1815, almost 15 miles of gas mains had been laid in London.⁴ John Perks' career reveals that alongside the ancient agricultural Warwickshire economy which Adam Murray chronicled—powered, as for 5,000 years, entirely by humans, horses and oxen—there was a new world unfolding: a world driven by steam and gas. Involved in this new business, John Perks was a successful professional working overseas, and he had little to fear from the Leighs.⁵

John's wife Ann Perks, born Ann Whitmore, who had also grown up in Stoneleigh, also gave a statement. As a child, she had always been brought to church services at Stoneleigh. She remembered the Christopher stone being on the wall, and recalled that it had the names (besides that of Christopher Leigh), Cotton, Catherine, Roger and Ferdinand, as well as Higham, Wigan, and Lancashire. Ann stated that she particularly recalled the names of Wigan and Lancashire, because in 1804 she had taken a tour with her family to the Lake District, and had passed through Wigan.⁶ This evidence reminds us of the tour which Elizabeth Bennet takes with her aunt and uncle the Gardiners in *Pride and Prejudice* (1813). It was the only way in which a young woman could respectably enlarge her experiences through travel. Having the means to take her on such a holiday, Ann's family must have been middle-class.

---

3. Leigh (1834), vol. I, p. 50.
4. M. Dorothy George, *England in Transition: Life and Work in the Eighteenth Century* (Penguin Books, 1953), p. 113.
5. Leigh (1834), vol. II, p. 303.
6. Maiden name Whitmore: record from Familysearch.com (Accessed 11 May 2014), marriage 6 January 1806. Ann's evidence: Leigh (1834), vol. I, p. 50.

John Perks had not only gone to Stoneleigh church as a child and young bridegroom, he may well have worked on it as well. In the period 1810–13, Julia-Judith and James Henry Leigh organized repairs to the church. In October 1810, a John Perks issued an invoice to the Leighs for recasting of the roof lead on the church.[7] This John may be the gas lighting engineer's father, who as we have seen had a local plumbing and glazing business.

John junior's brother Richard Perks also gave evidence confirming the existence of the Christopher stone. Richard was a plumber, who worked, probably with his father, on the church roof. In the Lords hearings of 1828, Richard Perks was subjected to a thorough grilling about his recollections. Like his brother, Richard Perks had gone to school at Stoneleigh. In 1811, he was employed following a public meeting at the *Swan* public house, which had voted that the parish should pay for repairs to the church. The second time he worked on the church roof, it was on the orders of Richard Darley, who was the steward for the Leigh family.[8] Richard Perks maintained that prior to the repairs, there were two monuments on the south wall of the church, one to Christopher Leigh, and the other to John Webster. During the second repair phase, the Christopher stone was taken down. Richard Perks testified that it was placed in the vestry, and that he saw it most evenings when he worked in the church.

> "I used to go into the vestry after I went off the roof of the church, merely to put away our working tools, and I put them behind this monument, several."[9]

Asked what kind of tools he placed behind the stone:

> "Tools that plumbers lay lead with, such as dressers, and such things as we have for our tools; they go into a flat basket; rollers and other things."[10]

---

7. SBTRO DR 18/3/50/6/1, 28 October 1810.
8. Leigh (1834), vol. I, p. 138.
9. Leigh (1834), vol. I, p. 140.
10. Leigh (1834), vol. I, p. 141.

This was confirmed by another witness, John Whitehead, a carpenter, who said that he saw tools placed behind both Leigh and Webster monuments during the renovations.[11] One of the claimant's lawyers was Fitzroy Kelly, who was destined for a prominent career in the law, finishing as Lord Chief Baron of the Court of Exchequer.[12] Kelly asked Richard Perks if he had seen the stone taken away from the church.

> "I did not. At the time we were leading the roof our repairs might detain us about a fortnight; but I put in some windows after that, and other repairs kept us five or six weeks before we had finished, backwards and forwards; but the first repair was about a fortnight, and during this fortnight this [stone] was in the vestry—I saw it every evening."[13]

Richard Perks further testified that the south wall of the church did not, in 1811, really require repair, but he understood that the rationale for the wall changes was to "make a different elevation, and to do away with the tiles of the old roof."[14] Under further questioning, Richard Perks recollected some Leigh family escutcheons (shields and banners) being present in the Stoneleigh church in 1810, but later removed.[15]

The response of Chandos Leigh's lawyers was to impugn Richard Perks' motivation. Thomas Denman was a lawyer of considerable standing (Common Sergeant, an ancient legal office of the city of London), and later Lord Denman and Lord Chief Justice. Denman was already a friend of the Leigh family and noted Whig lawyer, having acted in the protracted proceedings concerning Queen Caroline.[16] At this time, he was one of England's leading lawyers, and was growing in reputation as a rival to Henry Brougham. An anonymous sketch from 1830 gives a vivid impression of Denman's skill.

---

11. Griffin (1848), p. 14.
12. Dalrymple Belgrave, 'Romances of High Life,' *Manchester Times*, 1898.
13. Leigh (1834), vol. I, p. 140.
14. Leigh (1834), vol. I, p. 140.
15. Leigh (1834), vol. I. p. 145.
16. Both the Leighs and the Denmans attended the annual birthday celebrations for Samuel Parr: John Nichols, "Toasts Given at the Celebration of Dr Parr's Birth-days 1820–24," *Gentleman's Magazine*, Volume 144, August 1826, p. 104.

> "There is something peculiarly captivating about [Denman]... It is not that he arrests the attention by the brilliancy of his language, or surprises by the boldness of his conceptions; not that he exceeds other men by the richness of his imagery, or the originality of his eloquence, but that he surpasses most men in singleness of purpose, and honesty of intention... His person is tall, his voice deep-toned, flexible and full, his manner natural and unstudied, his countenance open, prepossessing, and noble; it has something of the finely chiselled, finished appearance of a statue."[17]

Harriette Wilson, the famous Regency courtesan, claimed that she would not mind being sentenced to death by Denman, which sounds like a metaphor for finding him attractive.

> "This I know, that, for my own part, next to not being hanged at all, *plaît à M. Wellington*, I should like Denman to pronounce sentence upon me: so pleasing a voice and so persuasive a manner I never witnessed, and the most placid, benevolent countenance!"[18]

Acting for Chandos Leigh, Denman suggested that Richard Perks had fallen out with the Leigh family over his excessive charging for work. He further pointed out that a relative of Richard Perks, Hannah Gumley, had been deprived of her tenant farm, and implied that Richard Perks was motivated by a spirit of revenge.[19] Richard Perks firmly denied this. Thomas Denman pointed out that Richard Perks had carried out some work in recent years for the claimant's agent Henry Causton, implying that this rendered his evidence suspect.[20]

The next witness to appear was Jasper Palfrey of the local hamlet Finham, an "Agriculturist" by his own description. In his *Agricultural Report for Warwickshire*, Adam Murray mentions Palfrey with approval as a breeder of large polled Warwickshire sheep.[21] In 1810–1811, he was

---

17. "Personal sketches No. VII: Mr Denman," *The Dublin Literary Gazette, Or weekly chronicle of criticism, belles lettres, and fine arts*, Number 23, Saturday June 5 1830, p. 353.
18. *Harriette Wilson's Memoirs* (selected and edited with an introduction by Lesley Blanch) (first published by Joseph Stockdale in 1825; London: Century Publishing, 1985), p. 359.
19. Leigh (1834), vol. I p. 147.
20. Leigh (1834), vol. I p. 148.
21. Murray (1813), p. 161.

a member of the parish committee which met to discuss repairing the Stoneleigh church. He also confirmed that the Christopher stone had stood on the south wall alongside the Webster monument. Jasper Palfrey had attended the first few meetings concerning the repairs, but in 1811 he became frustrated with the fact that whenever the committee had decided on a course of action, Richard Darley intervened to direct that Mrs Leigh — Julia-Judith — preferred a different approach.

> "Mr Darley said Mrs Leigh had been there [in the church] after we had met at our regular meetings, and she would go and order everything different; and I said at one of our meetings that what we ordered was not attended to, and I could spend my time better than in coming here."[22]

In 1811, the Reverend Thomas Leigh was still the estate owner. Until his death in June 1813, Julia-Judith had no official authority at all, let alone the power to override a committee of parish representatives meeting to discuss church matters. Nor did Richard Darley, who was neither a Stoneleigh parishioner, nor, officially, representing the Reverend Thomas. Clearly, Julia-Judith, with her agent Richard Darley, was in control of events at Stoneleigh, despite having no formal standing.

Another parish committee member, John Lee, confirmed Palfrey's account. He was a long-term Stoneleigh resident. He recalled the Christopher stone on the south wall until the changes of 1811. John Lee said that he remembered Richard Darley talking about the Christopher stone, in the context of the parish committee repairs.

> "Mr Darley, the steward at Stoneley Abbey, said the monument should be taken down to the Abbey, and he would have it fresh painted, and it should be replaced... I was by when Mr Darley mentioned in the church that it should go down there and be fresh cleaned and put up again."[23]

Several older people made sworn statements about their memory of the Christopher stone. William Soden was a builder, aged 50 and now

---

22. Leigh (1834), vol. I, p. 152.
23. Leigh (1834), vol. I, p. 188.

living in London. He had lived in Stoneleigh until the age of 14, when he was apprenticed in trade at Kenilworth (the market town three miles west of Stoneleigh). He regularly attended church in Stoneleigh until the age of 21, when he moved to London. His statement indicated clear recall of the Christopher stone.

> "[Witness, William Soden] sat in his father's pew close to the south side wall, recollected a monument on that wall over the back part of that pew, also a smaller monument on that wall with Webster on it: recollected the names 'Christopher Leigh' and 'Cotton' on the larger one: thought when a boy, 'Leigh' ought to be called Leech. Had read this monument many and many a time."[24]

William Soden's evidence is interesting in part because it indicates the difference in pronunciation which might occur to a child. As he left Stoneleigh at 21 — in 1799 — it confirms that the Christopher stone was in place at that time (We have seen that John Perks clearly recalled its presence in 1806). Soden was cross-examined in the Lords hearing on the second day of proceedings, 29 April 1828. Lawyers for both sides questioned him closely on his recollections. They were particularly concerned with his ideas, when a boy, about the pronunciation of "Leigh." William Adam, counsel for the claimant, focused on this point, possibly to demonstrate the credibility of the witness.

> **William Soden:** In my infant life, perhaps at seven years old, I could never sound the name of Leigh as Lee, in my boyish, my simple opinion.
> **Mr Adam:** The spelling attracted your attention?
> **William Soden:** That took my attention particularly, I thought it ought to be called Leech.[25]

Sir James Scarlett (1769–1844), a successful lawyer and Whig politician, later raised to the peerage as Baron Abinger, was another member of Chandos Leigh's star-studded legal team. Both he and the

---
24. Griffin (1848), pp. 12–13. Statement date 24 January 1828: Leigh (1834), vol. I, p. 125, note.
25. Leigh (1834), vol. I, p. 128.

Attorney-General, supposedly acting for the crown, homed in on the pronunciation question. For them, it might serve to indicate the witness' ignorance.

> **Sir James Scarlett:** You were puzzled about Leigh; you thought it ought to be pronounced Leech?
>
> **William Soden:** I used to use the name of Leech; that was my idea as a boy; it was very excuseable [sic].[26]

Then the Attorney-General had a turn.

> **Attorney-General:** You are sure the word Leigh was upon this monument, because you used to pronounce it like Leech?
>
> **William Soden:** Yes.
>
> **Attorney-General:** But your expression was, that you thought so?
>
> **William Soden:** Yes; that was my idea as a boy.
>
> **Attorney-General:** When you were twenty years old?
>
> **William Soden:** No; when I was seven years old.
>
> **Attorney-General:** How might it be when you were twenty?
>
> **William Soden:** I was then satisfied it was the name of Leigh. I had taken more notice, from the circumstance of the honorable Mrs Leigh's waggons being written in the same way...
>
> **Attorney-General:** Did you know, from seeing the honorable Mrs Leigh's name on the waggons, that Leigh on the tombstone should be pronounced like Leigh on the waggon?
>
> **William Soden:** Yes.[27]

From this evidence, we learn that in the time of Mary Leigh, the carts belonging to the abbey were inscribed with the name of Leigh. Adam Murray describes the waggons in common use on Warwickshire farms, noting that their weight was detrimental to the local roads.

---

26. Leigh (1834), vol. I, p. 130.
27. Leigh (1834), vol. I, p. 134. Special taxation arrangements applied to certain kinds of carts, which were required to display the owner's name and place of abode: Deirdre Le Faye, n. 7 to Letter 78 (Jane Austen to Cassandra Austen), 24 January 1813: *Jane Austen's Letters* (Oxford: Oxford University Press, 2011), p. 419.

"The carriages in use throughout the county, are the large four-horse waggons, and two and three-horse turn-up carts, which are made remarkably strong, and are extremely heavy for the horses to draw."[28]

That an intelligent village boy should have to work out for himself, by reading the estate waggons, how the landholder's name was pronounced, surprised the lawyers. The villagers and the estate owners lived parallel but quite separate existences, meeting only in circumstances such as the present situation.

Eventually William Soden, irritated with the patronising emphasis on his childish mistake, took a swipe.

> **Attorney-General:** Have you never asked, as you were a church-goer, how it was to be pronounced, whether it was to be Leigh or Leech: a good sharp boy of eight or nine years old would be enquiring how to pronounce it?
>
> **William Soden:** Yes, probably if I had been at the University, as you were, perhaps I might have asked that question.[29]

The focus on the pronunciation issue also served Chandos' lawyers in distracting from the substance of William Soden's evidence, which was his clear recall of the existence of the stone.

Another witness who recalled the stone from his church attendance as a boy, was Thomas Bryan. He was a carpenter living in London. He recalled the monument to Christopher Leigh, and the names of Cotton and Higham on it. He particularly noticed the name of Cotton.

> **Thomas Bryan:** My reason for remarking it was, that my father had a servant of the name of Cotton, and I supposed it very extraordinary, being a boy, that lord Leigh, or one of his family, should have married a person so mean as a Cotton, my father having a servant of that name.

Thomas Bryan, as a child, was also puzzled by the word "issue."

---

28. Murray (1813), p. 61. Impact on roads: p. 172.
29. Leigh (1834), vol. I, p. 134.

"I recollect it perfectly well; my reason for remembering it was that I did not know the meaning of [the word "issue"] at that time, nor for some time afterwards; but there was the name of Roger, and Mary, and Ferdinand, I recollect particularly well."

The name of "Higham" on the monument also led to a pronunciation problem. Thomas Bryan as a boy thought that it would be pronounced "Hig-ham".

"I always called it Hig-ham, but afterwards understood it was High-am; the same as Leigh, which I always called Leach, with most of the persons in the village; when I was a schoolboy I were surprised that they should take the trouble of spelling it with so many letters."[30]

Bryan thus confirmed the fact—so surprising to the educated classes—that the common pronunciation of the estate owners' name was "Leach/Leech." No doubt Mrs Austen would have been dismayed that her family name was treated with such disrespect.

William Soden and Thomas Bryan had left Stoneleigh as young men, to follow their trades elsewhere. Some witnesses, however, had remained in the local area. The most explosive evidence was given by a man named John Wilcox (sometimes written Wilcooks or Wilcocks). Wilcox was a bricklayer based in Coventry, at the time of the hearings. In his statement, he described his recollections from the period of his employment at Stoneleigh Abbey. From 10 June 1810 until June 1814, he had lived at the abbey. In 1810, he was the post-boy whose job was to bring the mail bag from Coventry.

One day in spring or early summer (the year may have been 1812 or 1813, Wilcox thought more likely 1812), he arrived at the abbey with the mail bag, and went in search of the house steward, John Ilett, who generally unlocked the mail bag. Not finding Ilett, he saw some men carrying a monumental stone covered in part with matting. He was able to see that it was one he had seen in Stoneleigh church as belonging to

---

30. Leigh (1834), vol. I, pp. 382–384.

the Leigh family. Still seeking John Ilett, he followed the men along a passage. Wilcox saw James Henry Leigh standing near the back stairs not far from the first wine cellar, and Mrs Leigh — Julia-Judith — standing near the back stairs with a lighted candle to guide the men, carrying the stone, towards the wine cellar. As the men approached, Julia-Judith entered the cellar, with the men following. James Henry Leigh departed up the back staircase. John Wilcox tried to peer into the cellar, but Julia-Judith shut the door in his face. After the stone was taken into the cellar, the men returned and went away.[31]

John Wilcox was cross-examined. Fitzroy Kelly, for the claimant, got Wilcox essentially to reiterate his evidence. It also emerged that on the same day, Wilcox saw again, in the servants' room, the men who had brought the stone to the cellar.[32]

Sir James Scarlett, for Chandos Leigh, pursued Wilcox's recollection of the lettering on the stone. Some of the Lords also queried why Wilcox had not told anyone about the events at the time. Wilcox responded that he told his father about a month later.

> "I was telling my father about the circumstance of the servants not being in the hall to receive me when I came with the letters; and then I related to him what I had seen."[33]

The demeanour of James Henry Leigh came in for some comment.

Lord Chancellor: What became of Mr Leigh?
John Wilcox: He went up the back stairs near the door.
Lord Chancellor: Did he appear to be very much rejoiced?
John Wilcox: I did not speak to that.[34]

---

31. Summary of Wilcox deposition at Leigh (1834), vol. I, pp. 48–49. Verbatim version at vol. II, pp. 193–194.
32. Leigh (1834), vol. II, p. 197.
33. Leigh (1834), vol. II, p. 206.
34. Leigh (1834), vol. II, p. 207.

Witness

The Lord Chancellor seemed concerned that Wilcox, in his statement, had claimed that James Henry had seemed cheerful about the cellar transaction.

John Wilcox: He seemed brisk; he might be rejoiced.[35]

Edward Baylis was also cross-examined. He had given his first sworn deposition as early as 15th January 1820. Baylis was 64 in 1828. He had gone to the abbey in 1797, lived there in the service of Mary Leigh as usher for nine years, then stayed on as baker. He may, therefore, have been the baker who, Mrs Austen observed in 1806, "did nothing but brew and bake" (*Chapter 1*). He remained in the family's service until 1818, when he got married and went to live at the neighbouring hamlet of Ashow.[36] In 1819 he went into business for himself. Edward Baylis recalled the Christopher stone standing on the south wall of the church. After the repairs, it was never replaced. His deposition confirmed that John Wilcox's bizarre allegations reflected the common belief among the servants.

> "[Deponent, Edward Baylis] saith,[37] that after the monument was taken down it was never replaced in the church, but as deponent has heard and believes it to be true, was clandestinely removed by order of Mr [James Henry] Leigh or the direction of some of his agents, and conveyed by a horse and cart to the Abbey, and there either broken up or deposited in one of the old vaults or cellars, which was thereupon immediately bricked up and closed.
>
> And deponent is more confirmed in his belief of this circumstance, because on the morning of that very day on which he considers the said clandestine transaction took place, the cart arrived at the Abbey containing a package very like in size to the dimensions of the said monument, and which he believes was the said monument so concealed.

---

35. Leigh (1834), vol. II, p. 208.
36. Leigh (1834), vol. II, p. 180.
37. Depositions traditionally used this archaic form to record the testimony being given.

And deponent saith, that according to his usual custom he offered his assistance to unload the cart, but instead of his offer being accepted he was ordered away from his daily and usual avocation in the house which would have led him to the vaults or cellarage to draw beer, etc., and was set to work out of doors to fill in the ruts in the dog kennel lane, which order appeared to him the more strange as he had never before been so employed, and on the following morning was ordered to resume his usual avocation [as baker and brewer] in the family."[38]

This evidence is the more damning because it is clear that Edward Baylis was a loyal servant of the Leighs, remaining in his role for many years after these events. Under cross-examination by Mr Adam, for the claimant, Edward Baylis revealed that, when he was sent out to work in the lane, he met a man who generally worked as a carrier. This man's name was Sprawson. Baylis had seen a horse and cart, presumably Sprawson's, standing at the back gate of the abbey, without any person with them. Baylis also said that stones had been brought into the abbey the day before, but only on this particular day was one covered with matting.

Edward Baylis was asked if he had any conversation with the house steward, John Ilett. Mrs Austen, as it happens, may have given a miniature pen-portrait of John Ilett in her 1806 letter from Stoneleigh.

> "At nine in the morning we meet and say our prayers in a handsome Chapel...then follows Breakfast, consisting of Chocolate Coffee & Tea—Plumb Cake, Pound Cake, Hot Rolls, Cold Rolls, Bread & Butter and *dry toast for me* [emphasis in original]—The House-Steward (a fine large respectable looking Man) orders all these matters..."[39]

John Ilett had been the house steward in the service of Mary Leigh and her successors, from about 1792 until August 1815, first as under-butler, then as house steward and head butler.[40] John Ilett sometimes employed Edward Baylis in cleaning the wine cellars.

---

38. Quoted at length in Leigh (1834), vol. II, pp. 178–179.
39. Maggie Black and Deirdre Le Faye, *The Jane Austen Cookbook* (London: The British Museum Press, 1995), p. 33.
40. Leigh (1834), vol. II, p. 3, note.

> **Edward Baylis:** [John Ilett] said that if Mrs Leigh knew that he employed me in the wine cellar, she would send both him and me to the devil, for we should be both discharged.[41]

Edward Baylis had made another statement on 10 July 1827. In this detailed statement, he reported another remark of John Ilett's.

> "[Edward Baylis saith] that the bricks of the old binns [sic] were used in building up a recess formed by the chimney of the servants' hall in the first wine cellar, and also in building in the second wine cellar a kind of stand about breast high, projecting from the wall which divided it from the former, for the purpose of setting bottles on, which he has often done when working there for Ilett, and he has reason to think that the monument is built up in that erection, as Ilett has said to deponent, pointing to the place, 'Ned, there stands poor old Christopher.'"[42]

For his part, when cross-examined on 11 July 1828, John Ilett, now 74 and by his own account unemployed, denied the allegations made by John Wilcox and Edward Baylis. He did, however, admit that on one occasion Julia-Judith had accompanied him to the cellar.

> **Thomas Denman:** Did you ever see Mrs Leigh carrying a candle to the cellar in the day-time?
> **John Ilett:** No; I carried the candle!!![43]
> **Thomas Denman:** When did you carry the candle?
> **John Ilett:** She had been having a repair in the cellar, shifting the wine cellar, and I had arranged the wine in the new cellar, and put them in the tiers; and I went to let her know it was all done to the best of my judgment.[44]

Further, he confirmed part of Wilcox's story.

---

41. Leigh (1834), vol. II, p. 183.
42. Leigh (1834), vol. II, p. 185.
43. Exclamation marks in Leigh transcript, no doubt Causton's emphasis.
44. Leigh (1834), vol. II, p. 7.

Attorney-General: Wilcocks [sic] was the errand-boy?

John Ilett: He was the errand-boy; and we always kept two keys for the mail-bag, one at the office in Coventry, and one at home; Mrs Leigh and I were at the very time in the cellar, when he came about the key.[45]

Ilett also confirmed that Wilcox was subsequently dismissed from the Leighs' service.[46] Off the record, in 1821 or 1822, John Ilett had told Henry Kent Causton some important information.

"He [Ilett] knew a great deal about the said monument, but that it was his interest not to know or say any thing about it, for that Mrs Leigh behaved very kind to him and he expected more favors [sic] from her."

John Ilett was quite free with his off-the-record remarks. Another witness, Thomas Smith, had said to Ilett that he understood that Edward Baylis knew a good deal about the stone.

Ilett, quoted by Smith: I know more than Baylis does, for I know where the monument was put and which side was put downwards; more than that, Smith, when I was at the Abbey I had a book in my possession containing every name of the Leighs, their births, baptisms, christenings, and burials, and in one of the rooms in the Abbey House there was Christopher Leigh's picture, and two of his children who died in their infancy.[47]

Under cross-examination, Ilett maintained the opposite.

Mr Adam, for the claimant: Do you know the pictures in the Abbey; is there a picture to Christopher Leigh?
John Ilett: No.
Mr Adam: No picture that goes by the name of Christopher Leigh?
John Ilett: No; there never was in my time; I never saw such a thing.[48]

---
45. Leigh (1834), vol. II, p. 11.
46. Leigh (1834), vol. II, p. 11.
47. Leigh (1834), vol. II, p. 5, note.
48. Leigh (1834), vol. II, p. 15.

"Poor old Christopher"'s visage was not, however, completely airbrushed from history. One portrait is extant, which shows him as a young man, possibly still in his teens. It is located at Lamport Hall, Northamptonshire. In 1653, Christopher's sister, Vere Leigh, married the widower Sir Justinian Isham (1610–1675) of Lamport.[49] She probably brought her brother's portrait with her. At Lamport, it escaped the scorched-earth treatment of everything relating to Christopher which apparently took place at Stoneleigh.[50]

One later portrait of Christopher, by the artist Henry Stone (1616–1653), may have survived at Stoneleigh. It was placed in a Christie's sale in 1981, but then withdrawn and returned to the owner, the Stoneleigh Abbey Preservation Trust Limited. This portrait apparently shows Christopher Leigh, three-quarter length, dressed in a brown cloak, leaning on a pedestal. It is described as having been a companion piece to the (surviving) Stone portrait of Thomas Lord Leigh, of 1649. This, then, would be a portrait of Christopher as a man in his twenties.[51]

The consequences of giving evidence that the Christopher stone existed could be serious for someone of lower standing who still lived on the Leigh estate. Benjamin Faulkes, aged about 70-years, of Stoneleigh, made a statement in May 1825. At that time he was in the service of the Leigh family, as keeper of one of the entrance gates, and lived in the lodge house there. He had lived in the village and parish of Stoneleigh all his life. He well remembered seeing two monuments on the south wall of the church, prior to the repairs of 1810–1811, one to Christopher Leigh, and one to Mr Webster of Canley. Between this statement and the Lords' hearing, Faulkes made another statement to the effect that he had been dismissed from his job.[52]

---

49. E. R. Edwards, "Isham, Sir Justinian, 2nd Bt, 1611–1675, of Lamport Hall, Northants," http://www.historyofparliamentonline.org/volume/1660-1690/member/isham-sir-justinian-1611-75 (Accessed 24 November 2015). The letter-writer Dorothy Osborne had rejected Sir Justinian's proposals: no doubt he consoled himself that Vere Leigh was a better match than Dorothy, anyway.
50. Portrait at http://www.bbc.co.uk/arts/yourpaintings/paintings/the-honourable-christopher-leigh-49187 (Accessed 24 November 2015).
51. Christie's sale 20 November 1981, lot 94. Information on the portrait kindly supplied by Ms Harriet Reed, of Christie's Archives, in an email to the author, 24 November 2015.
52. Leigh (1834), vol. II, p. 317.

The Missing Monument Murders

Another witness who suffered adverse consequences was Mary Irons, also variously Iorns or Hiorns, aged 54.[53] She recalled there being two monuments on the south wall of the church, one to John Webster of Canley, the other to Christopher Leigh. Mary's job was to clean the monuments on Michaelmas Sunday, 18 years before (so in 1811).

> "The church had been all over whitewashed, and I was the person as they picked out to clean the church; I was strong, and able to do it; and Mr Handley [one of the churchwardens] chose me to do it."[54]

She recollected the name Leigh and the name Cotton. Much was made by the learned counsel of Mary's simplicity. She had difficulty spelling the name Christopher.

> **Sir James Scarlett:** Did you ever say that you thought the word was Christmas?
>
> **Mary Irons:** Yes, I did; when I was a little girl I thought it was the gift by a gentleman that died, that gave the bread and beef to be given at Christmas, till I got bigger.

Mary, from her experience in cleaning it, was able to recall some details about the stone which no other witness had recalled.

> "There was a flaw from the right corner nearly to the middle of it. A crack right into the stone; for when the cloth went over it, it went over it very rough from the right corner to the middle of it."[55]

Further, Mary recalled using a fork to pick out the splashes of whitewash from within the letters on the two monuments.[56] She had in the past received poor relief at Stoneleigh Abbey, but ceased to receive it after giving evidence of her memory of the monument. This reason was expressly

---

53. Irons in Leigh (1834), vol. II, pp. 116ff. Iorns in Griffin (1848), pp. 18–19. Family name of Hiorns appears in Leigh papers.
54. Leigh (1834), vol. II, p. 118.
55. Leigh (1834), vol. II, p. 124.
56. Leigh (1834), vol. II, p. 126, note.

given to her by Mr Jeacock the parish clerk.⁵⁷ Mary Irons reported in her statement that Mr Jeacock was injudicious enough to add:

> "that old leather breeches [a village name for the claimant George Leigh] would never get the estate; and told [Mary] that she must not say she recalled the monument for it was gone to the Abbey and would not come back: that P****n ******* and he had determined to stick to it that there never was such a monument, and she must do as they did or she would not be countenanced by the ***** ***** any more!!!"⁵⁸

P****n ******* is probably Parson James Roberts, the curate of Stoneleigh, whose evidence is discussed in the next chapter. The second set of asterisks no doubt refers to the Leigh family, although the precise verbal equivalent of the asterisks is debatable (one of the two five-character words may stand for "Leigh.")

Following her examination in the Lords, Mary Irons received notice to leave her house next to the Stoneleigh churchyard.⁵⁹ Mary was not the only parishioner affected. Elizabeth Shirley, who also recalled the Christopher stone, had three children who had predeceased her and were buried in the churchyard. Two of these were removed from their graves to make room for the Leigh mausoleum which was built in the 1820s, adjoining the church.⁶⁰

A total of about 34 witnesses for the claimant, all of whom recalled the Christopher stone, were cross-examined.⁶¹ It was then the turn of the witnesses for Chandos Leigh to be called. There are few modern works dealing with the case. The most prominent of these are two articles in the 2004 collection edited by Robert Bearman, *Stoneleigh Abbey: The House, Its owners, Its Lands*. The first, by Mairi Macdonald ("'Not Unmarked by Some Eccentricities': The Leigh Family of Stoneleigh Abbey") already cited frequently for information on Edward Lord Leigh and Mary Leigh,

---

57. Leigh (1834), vol. II, p. 119.
58. Leigh (1834), vol. II, p. 127, note. Exclamation marks in transcript.
59. Leigh (1834), vol. II, p. 127, note.
60. Leigh (1834), vol. II, p. 320.
61. Listed in Griffin (1848), pp. 11–24, summarising their evidence.

gives a straight summary of the allegations made in the Lords case.[62] The second article, however, by Norma Hampson ("The Poet and the Paternalist") includes the following statement:

> "There were almost as many witnesses who saw the monuments in the church as there were to testify against their existence."[63]

This is a misrepresentation, possibly inadvertent. Hampson's immediate context concerns later court actions, rather than the Lords hearings of 1828–1829. The misapprehension may have arisen because of a reliance on source material from the Leigh family papers, rather than the actual witness statements contained in the transcripts of the Lords case. It is unfortunate, however, in that the vast majority of readers would have no way of checking the facts for themselves.

In reality, the transcripts reveal that there were far more witnesses for the Christopher stone's existence than there were who denied it. Hampson also appears to muddy the waters by referring to monuments in the plural. There may well have been several monuments which were removed from the church (as Edward Baylis' evidence indicates, and which Richard Barnett would later confirm), but the main legal battle was always over the Christopher stone. The evidence of those who asserted the stone's existence was far more rooted in actual experience than that of the deniers. These, as will be shown in the following chapter, relied largely on a lack of recall. Hampson also fails to note that, with some exceptions such as Lionel Place, it was the less well off in Stoneleigh who were prepared to put their futures on the line to maintain the stone's previous existence. There was certainly a class aspect to this contest.

---

62. Macdonald (2004), p. 158.
63. Norma Hampson, "The Poet and the Paternalist," in Bearman (ed. 2004), 179–196, p. 185.

CHAPTER FIVE

Denial

"I should certainly say, speaking without reference to what I now know and have since observed, with respect to my recollection within the period mentioned, 1804 and 1810, I should not say that I have a distinct recollection of any monument on that side."

The Reverend Vaughan Thomas, 1828[1]

The first witness called to give evidence against the claim was Richard Darley, land steward on the Stoneleigh estate from the period 1806 to 1822. He did not live in Stoneleigh, but in the Dial House in the neighbouring parish of Ashow, two miles from Stoneleigh village church. Darley testified that, in 1810, this church was in a "most deplorable state of repair." This required the renovation programme agreed by the parish committee.[2] He admitted, however, that he was not in the habit of visiting Stoneleigh church every week. His visits might be once in two or three months.[3] The Lord Chancellor asked:

"Are you perfectly positive there was no monument to the memory of Christopher Leigh?"

Darley responded:

"I am positive there was none during this time; I saw the church from the beginning of 1807; there was nothing of that kind."[4]

---
1. Leigh (1834), vol. II, p. 42.
2. Leigh (1834), vol. I, p. 441–442. Two miles away: p. 444.
3. Leigh (1834), vol. I, p. 444.
4. Leigh (1834), vol. I, p. 444.

When he was not collecting rents from Chandos Leigh's tenants, Richard Darley seems to have been an amateur architect or designer. He had been brought up in Wiltshire.[5] Prior to working at Stoneleigh, he had been a clerk with the firm of Blacks, land surveyors and valuers, near Epping.[6]

Over several years, between 1808 and 1812, Richard Darley prepared a series of plans and drawings of the church to assist in planning the repair project. He even designed the new section of the roof.[7]

> "I made a plan of the church in such a way as to shew all the different stones containing inscriptions, that when we narrowed the different passages they should be replaced in the same situation as nearly as possible; in consequence of that, if there had been a monument I must have seen it."[8]

We shall meet Darley's argument, such as it is — "If X had existed I must have seen it; I do not remember seeing it, therefore X did not exist" — many times and in a number of forms, in the course of this case, as put forward by the Leigh team. For readers from (the present author's) New South Wales, Australia, it bears an uncanny resemblance to one used in April 2014 by the then Premier of the state, Barry O'Farrell, in appearing before the Independent Commission Against Corruption (ICAC). He claimed not to have received an expensive bottle of wine from a business lobbyist.

> "What I do know is if I received a bottle of 1959 Penfolds Grange [Hermitage red wine] I would have known about it, and I did not receive a bottle of Penfolds Grange."[9]

Mr O'Farrell resigned as Premier the following day, as his thankyou note for the wine was about to be tabled at ICAC. For convenience,

---

5. Leigh (1834), vol. I, p. 445.
6. Leigh (1834), vol. I, p. 459.
7. Leigh (1834), vol. I, p. 453, 463.
8. Leigh (1834), vol. I, p. 444.
9. Mark Coultan, "The $3000 drop O'Farrell couldn't recall", *The Australian* 16 April 2014, p. 6.

then, this argument and its variants will in future be referred to as "the O'Farrell defence," or "O'Farrell" for short.

On the witness stand, Darley was unable to produce his drawings or plans. One copy, he thought, might have been kept in the parish chest with other important documents. He destroyed many documents after ceasing to work for the Leigh family.

> "I kept but two plans. When I left Stoneley the Leigh family and myself were rather unfriendly, and I might burn, perhaps, nearly a cart load of papers which were of no use to me."[10]

At one point in giving evidence, Darley appeared distressed and confused. He was being asked about another stone inscription, the one dedicated to Humphrey Howe, which was also removed during the repairs, and later replaced.

> "In the first instance I had it placed in a little pew—which—according to the then situation of the church—was a little square place that belonged or was occupied—if it ever was occupied—by a tenant at four miles distance,—his name was Hands,—his father was the warrener [gamekeeper];—it was afterwards removed from that place and placed in the belfry; I saw it moved, I think, five or six different times, but I never lost sight of it."[11]

For his part, Richard Hands (presumably the man to whom Darley was referring) had given a deposition saying that he had no recollection of any monument other than those of Webster and Howe, and—curiously—that his father, "the warrener", had had no recollection of any such monument, either.[12] Causton commented on Darley's testimony here:

---

10. Leigh (1834), vol. I, p. 445.
11. Leigh (1834), vol. I, p. 451.
12. Leigh (1834), vol. II, pp. 300–301.

"Whether it was owing to the heat, which was excessive, we are not aware, but the witness at this time appeared much distressed and confused, as his reply plainly indicates. He however soon recovered his self-possession, and continued throughout his long examination the deliberate manner of delivery for which he had hitherto been distinguishable."[13]

Causton was implying that Darley's loss of self-possession in speaking about the Howe monument was caused by the fact that he really did feel guilty about the fate of the Christopher stone. Jasper Palfrey, in his affidavit, had testified that James Roberts was present when Richard Darley, pointing to the Christopher stone, had said:

"That monument the parish have nothing to do with; it belongs to the Leigh family; let it be taken down carefully; I will send it to the Abbey; they may have it cleaned or put up again, or do what they please with it."[14]

Repeatedly, Darley denied that he had directed the Christopher stone to be sent to the abbey.[15] He denied ever hearing of the monument until the villagers began to talk about it, in September 1817.[16]

Of the eleven members of the parish committee for the repairs in 1810–1811, seven were living in 1828. Of these, four—Jasper Palfrey, John Lee, William Harris, and John Dry—all made statements which confirmed their recollection of the Christopher stone, and several, in particular, recalled Darley giving directions about it.[17] Another churchwarden, George Handley, often referred to in evidence, was not called as a witness, but anecdotally would have confirmed the stone's removal also. Only Richard Darley and the Reverend James Roberts would deny that it had existed.[18]

The repairs seemed to have been undertaken with the sole object of removing the very section of the wall which supported the putative

---

13. Leigh (1834), vol. I, p. 451, note.
14. Leigh (1834), vol. II, p. 47, note.
15. Leigh (1834), vol. I, p. 451.
16. Leigh (1834), vol, I, p. 452.
17. Depositions in Leigh vol. I: Palfrey: p. 149, note; Lee: p. 49; Harris: p. 48; and in vol. II: Dry, p. 308.
18. Leigh (1834), vol. I, p. 473, note.

Christopher stone. William Adam (the distinguished lawyer mentioned in the previous chapter, here acting here for the claimant), in questioning, got Darley to admit that the only part of the church which was thought to be in need of repair was the south wall. In fact, it was only one section of that wall which was taken down and replaced.

The Lords committee was shown drawings of the south wall (not Darley's), including some prepared for the claimant. Darley maintained—as he had to, for consistency—that the plan purporting to show the wall prior to the repairs was not accurate. He objected not only to the depiction of the Christopher stone, but the positioning of one of the windows. Following the repairs to the wall and roof, a large new window (possibly one of those put in by Richard Perks) replaced the small windows which had previously stood on the left side, to the viewer, of the Webster and putative Christopher monuments. The workmanship of the repairs was not considered entirely satisfactory. Adam questioned Darley about whether he himself had said that the new wall was not perpendicular.[19] Darley was vague.

> "I should say that a great part of it is perpendicular...It is not straight, that I know."[20]

It is not clear why Darley eventually parted on bad terms from the Leigh family in 1822. Causton's view was that this allegation of bad blood was a ruse, set up in order to lend credibility to Darley's evidence. This may be so; however Darley's language was stronger than such a tactic might have required.

> "I thought myself exceedingly ill-treated by the family, and I think so still."[21]

He added that he was in poor health when he left Stoneleigh.[22] Under cross-examination, incredibly, Darley claimed to have had no dealings

---

19. Leigh (1834), vol. I, p. 462.
20. Leigh (1834), vol. I, p. 462.
21. Leigh (1834), vol. I, p. 471. Causton's view of ruse: pp. 473–474, note.
22. Leigh (1834), vol. I, p. 471.

with Julia-Judith Leigh until 1814. It was as if he was pretending that she had barely existed.

> "I never saw nor heard of Mrs Leigh till long after [the church repairs in 1810–1811]; I believe in the year 1814."[23]

This is directly contradicted, not only by the evidence of Richard Perks and Jasper Palfrey, but by the Leigh papers. It would appear that Darley was already working at Stoneleigh in the Reverend Thomas Leigh's lifetime (that is, prior to June 1813), which would mean that he would have met Julia-Judith there. In addition, records include a letter from Darley to Julia-Judith concerning bridge repairs in October 1813.[24]

Several episodes in the period 1821–1822 may have contributed to Darley wanting to leave his position. The first was the dismissal of William Walker, the publican of the *Swan Inn* in Stoneleigh. The *Swan* was a prominent building, occupying a corner of the village green (it no longer exists in any form). In the latter years of the eighteenth century it was in a poor state of repair. John Soden (probably the father of William and Jonathan Soden) had his stabling there.[25]

In 1783 the residents met at the *Swan* to petition Edward Lord Leigh (or by now his minders and agents) to agree that the villagers should build a workhouse for the poor.[26] The *Swan* was where significant village decisions were made. It was also to become intimately concerned with the issue of the monument and George Leigh's claim on the estate.

From 1812 to 1815, Joseph Hallam was the publican of the *Swan*. Hallam was also a member of the church committee. In his evidence, Darley referred several times to Hallam having taken a keen interest in the Webster monument being replaced after the repairs.[27] However, referral

---

23. Leigh (1834), vol. I, p. 450.
24. Letter from Darley to Rev Thomas: SBTRO DR 18/3/3/16/4, 6 January 1812; from Darley to Julia-Judith: SBTRO DR 18/17/39/28, 25 October 1813.
25. Stoneleigh Historical Society, "The Swan Inn," revised 2015, http://issuu.com/stoneleighhistorysociety/docs/swan_revised_2015_for_website/3?e=9414998/13481082 accessed 24 November 2015, p. 3. Hereafter: SHS (2015).
26. SHS (2015), p. 4.
27. Leigh (1834), vol. I, p. 447.

to Joseph Hallam's recollections was impossible, as Hallam was one of those no longer living. In 1816. He had "cut his throat being a lunatic."[28]

"Poor Hallam!" Causton commented: "It is a truism as antiquated as it is approvable with modern practice, that 'dead men tell no tales.'" A writer in 1849 made reference to the "awful deaths" of several witnesses "both clerical and lay," and Hallam's death may have been one of those to which he referred.[29]

Hallam's widow, Mary, who took over the *Swan* licence in 1815, married Joseph Whitehead, a master shoemaker of Coventry (and brother of John Whitehead the carpenter, who recalled seeing the tradesmen's tools stored near the Leigh and Webster monuments). Mary Whitehead made a deposition but was never cross-examined. She stated that she recalled two monuments on the south wall, with the larger having Christopher Leigh's name upon it, and that it stood nearly above John Soden's pew. Her new husband, Joseph Whitehead, also stated that, having attended church at Stoneleigh every Sunday, he recalled a monument to Christopher Leigh; it seemed old and dirty.[30]

From March 1817, a Mrs Walker was leasing the *Swan*. The Walkers had been operating the Stoneleigh workhouse, but applied to take on the licence there.[31] Correspondence with Julia-Judith—who was, as usual, micro-managing the situation—reveals that the Walkers wished to purchase some household goods from the workhouse to use at the inn. Julia-Judith refused permission for most of the items to be purchased.[32]

In August 1817, agents for George Leigh advertised for anyone knowing about the removal of the Christopher stone to meet them at the *Swan* in Stoneleigh, or the *Craven Arms Inn* in Coventry.[33] According to a statement he made in January 1821, William Walker claimed that by the terms of his licence he had to give lodging to all travellers. This included George Leigh and his agents, who stayed for some days at the *Swan* about two years previously (so in 1819).

---

28. SHS (2015), p. 6.
29. No tales: Leigh (1834), vol. I, p. 447, note. Deaths: Griffin in *Report* (1849), p. 10, column 1.
30. Leigh (1834), vol. II, pp. 320–321.
31. SHS (2015), p. 7.
32. SHS (2015), p. 7.
33. Handbill dated 30 August 1817: SHS (2015), p. 5.

As a consequence of this, Walker was told that James Henry Leigh would refuse to renew his licence to operate the *Swan* when it next came up for renewal. Walker and his wife went to Stoneleigh Abbey to object to this treatment. They reported that, "having been admitted to the presence of the honorable Julia-Judith Leigh, she said to [Mrs Walker] that 'as they (the Walkers) had taken in *strollers* and *vagrants*, and had chosen their friends, she would choose her's [sic].'"[34]

William Walker found himself without any supporters among the powerful in the village. He applied to the then curate Mr Morrison, to endorse his application for renewal of the licence. Morrison stated that he could not sign this until the churchwardens had signed it. Walker then applied to Richard Darley, who was one of the churchwardens at that time. Darley also refused to sign it, "giving as a reason, that [name blank in text] had desired him not to do it, and had sent him to Mr Morrison to *direct* him likewise to refuse doing so."[35]

On 15th September 1820, Walker attended the bench of magistrates meeting for the announcement of the licencing outcome. Walker's licence was refused, without any reason given. Walker went again to the abbey to protest. This time it was James Henry Leigh who told Walker that "he should suffer for it."[36]

Behind the scenes, Darley was attempting to get the best possible outcome for the Walkers. He wrote to Julia-Judith, noting that although they could not give a full reference for Walker to obtain another licence elsewhere:

> "But if it met with your approbation and Mr Leigh's, we would and could truly and honestly certify 'that [Walker] was a man of sober life and conversation and had kept The Swan that time'—which I believe would be sufficient. The fact is, the man's conduct would justify the certificate and be the means possibly of removing him quietly from this place and give him an opportunity of procuring a livelihood for his family."[37]

---

34. Leigh (1834), vol. I, p. 395–396, note (deposition of William Walker, January 1821).
35. Leigh (1834), vol. I, p. 396, note.
36. Leigh (1834), vol. I, p. 396, note.
37. SBTRO DR 18/17/47/37, 2 October 1821; SHS (2015), p. 10.

With or without assent from Julia-Judith, Darley, Morrison and the other churchwardens signed this certificate on the same day (2 October 1821), deeming William Walker fit to keep a public house — though not at Stoneleigh. He subsequently operated a licence at the *Red Lion* in Coventry.[38]

In June 1822, Richard Darley wrote to Julia-Judith to intercede for a tenant, Thomas Parkes, who was behind in paying his rent. Darley hoped that Parkes would be given additional time to pay, as he was still on crutches (presumably following an injury) and was not neglecting his farm.[39]

Thomas Parkes and his wife Martha were the parents of seven children, the youngest of whom was Henry Parkes (1815–1896), much later the father of Australian federation. Darley's appeal to Julia-Judith's clemency went unheeded, and the Parkes were evicted from the Stoneleigh estate. They moved to Glamorganshire and then settled in Birmingham. Thomas Parkes got work as a gardener and odd-job man, which meant extreme poverty for his family.[40] It is quite possible that the history of Australia might have been different, had there been a more humane landlord at Stoneleigh than Julia-Judith. It is also tempting to think that this was the last straw for Richard Darley.

Two tradesmen were brought forward as witnesses by the lawyers for Chandos Leigh. These were John Baddams, a weaver who had lived in Stoneleigh all his life. He claimed not to have heard of the Christopher stone until claims began to be mooted in 1810–1811.[41] John Alcott, a stonemason of Coventry, was cross-examined. He worked on the church in 1811. He was vague when pressed about how closely he had inspected the church before the work began. This was surprising, in a master mason.

"I was not in [the church], never, till I received the orders; not to take any particular notice."

---

38. SHS (2015), p. 11, speculating that Walker was the lessee of the Red Lion in Coventry: confirmed in Leigh (1834), vol. II, p. 306, note.
39. SBTRO DR 18/17/48/17, 13 June 1822.
40. A. W. Martin, "Parkes, Sir Henry (1815–1896)," *Australian Dictionary of Biography* vol. 5 (Melbourne: Melbourne University Press, 1974), online version http://adb.anu.edu.au/biography/parkes-sir-henry-4366 (Accessed 24 November 2015).
41. Leigh (1834), vol. II, p. 17.

The Missing Monument Murders

> **Attorney-General:** Before you received the orders, had you had occasion to go into the church, to look exactly at the state of the wall?
> **John Alcott:** It was concluded to be taken down, so it did not signify...
> **Attorney-General:** When you went there, had you occasion to look at the South wall, to see what monuments and stones were there?
> **John Alcott:** No; I do not know that I did.[42]

There remained some confusion, no doubt intentional on the part of the Leigh side, as to which monument or monuments John Alcott took down and replaced, or did not replace. In May 1825 Alcott had made an admission to a Mr Vale, an alderman of Coventry, that his men did remove the (sc. Christopher) monument and that he saw it lying in one of the pews of the church, but what became of it afterwards he could not say.[43]

Alcott also stated to Vale that there was Latin on the monument which he took down, which alone would identify it as the Christopher stone rather than the monument to John Webster, which was entirely in English. In addition, Alcott said that he could read the name of Leigh on the stone, which would confirm the identification. Alcott was reported to have added, "For God's sake don't let Mrs Leigh know what I've said."[44] His remark expresses the fear with which even a master tradesman, based in Coventry rather than Stoneleigh, regarded Julia-Judith.

Jonathan Soden was cross-examined. His brother, William Soden, had given evidence that he remembered the Christopher stone (*Chapter 4*). Now Jonathan appeared to claim that he had no knowledge of a monument on the south wall, other than Webster's.

> **Mr Denman:** Was there any other monument besides that of Mr Webster's?
> **Jonathan Soden:** Not to my knowledge.

---

42. Leigh (1834), vol. II, pp. 24–25.
43. Leigh (1834), vol. II, p. 27, note.
44. Leigh (1834), vol. II, p. 27, note. At Charles Griffin's libel trial in 1849, a witness, Thomas Smith, ribbon maker and parish clerk, testified under oath that Alcott had shown him the Christopher stone, hidden at his Coventry workshop, after its removal from Stoneleigh village church: *Report* (1849), p. 23, column 2. If true, this might account for the lapse of time between its removal from the church (no later than October 1811) and its being brought to the abbey (probably in 1812, according to Wilcox).

Mr Denman: Did you ever see any other?
Jonathan Soden: No, I never did.⁴⁵

The lords were struck by the fact that two brothers, who had grown up attending church and sitting in the same pew, could maintain two different opinions about the monuments on the wall just above that pew. Lord Hood, who as it happened was a Warwickshire estate owner and associate of the Leighs, persisted:

Lord Hood: Are you quite sure there was no other monument on that wall?
Jonathan Soden: I have no recollection of any monument there, except Webster's; and I think, if there had been any other there, I must have seen it.⁴⁶

Causton's editorial footnotes to the transcripts are often characterised by mordant moralising, and his notes on Jonathan Soden are lurid even by this standard. Describing that Jonathan Soden became ill after giving his evidence, he added:

"During [Jonathan Soden's] long and painful illness the subject of the monument to the memory of Christopher Leigh was of continual recurrence in his conversation, and although throughout, he always said he had no recollection of it whatever, *admitted his conviction that it must have existed,* as it was fresh in the memory of so many persons, amongst whom were numbered the nearest and dearest of his own relatives. It is well known, and before stated, that his father, Mr John Soden, was well informed of the inscription upon it. Eight of his family connections, including his aunt, Mrs Baylis, his brother and others who had occupied for a series of years the same pew, had been examined and given testimony the reverse of his own."⁴⁷

---

45. Leigh (1834), vol. II, p. 36.
46. Leigh (1834), vol. II, p. 38.
47. Leigh (1834), vol. II, p. 39, note.

The leading witness against the existence of the Christopher stone, cross-examined on 16 July 1828, was the Reverend Vaughan Thomas (1775–1858). In 1803 Vaughan Thomas became vicar of Yarnton in Oxfordshire. In June 1804 he was appointed vicar of Stoneleigh, and in March 1811 he received the rectory of Duntisborne Rouse in Gloucestershire. He held these three livings for the rest of his life.[48]

Plurality—the holding of more than one clergy job, in parishes separated by a greater or lesser distance—was not uncommon at the time. As some parishes only generated a small income from tithes, plurality was sometimes the way that clergy were able to make enough money for themselves and their families to live on. A Parliamentary discussion in 1838 suggested that plurality was not needed unless the value of a living was less than about £300 a year.[49] (Naturally, it was considered perfectly acceptable for a working man and his family to survive on a fraction of this amount: a skilled working man such as a ploughman, working six days per week, might earn a total of £20 if he were in work for the whole year.[50])

The eighteenth century had been somewhat more relaxed about the practice. Jane Austen's father, the Reverend George Austen, was lucky enough to hold the rectory of Steventon in Hampshire from 1761 until he bequeathed it to his eldest son James on his retirement in 1800–1801. Steventon was better off than many parishes, but even so, George's benefactor, his uncle Francis Austen, still bought the "presentations" to neighbouring Ashe and Deane as well. This meant that both were available to the Austen family, if and when they should wish to take them up. It was considered a mild example of plurality.[51]

James Austen, following his father to Oxford and the church, had been appointed as curate of the parish of Overton in Hampshire in 1790. In

---

48. G. Martin Murphy, "Thomas, Vaughan (1775–1858)," Oxford DNB online, http://www.oxforddnb.com.wwwproxy0.library.unsw.edu.au/view/article/27241?docPos=2 (Accessed 25 November 2015).
49. Irene Collins, *Jane Austen: The Parson's Daughter* (London: The Hambledon Press, 1998), p. xx. 1838: John Henry Barrow (ed.), *The Mirror of Parliament, Sessions 1837–1838*, 2nd series, vol. VI (London: Longman etc.), p. 4643.
50. Estimates of income need to be treated with caution, but are sufficiently clear on the broad outline. Murray, *Agricultural Survey* (1813), p. 169.
51. Collins (1998), p. 4. Claire Tomalin, *Jane Austen: A Life* (London: Penguin, 1998) pp. 168–169.

the following year, family friend and patron William Chute appointed him vicar of Sherborne St John, also in Hampshire. Sherborne had no parsonage house, so James Austen was not expected to live there.

Finally, Mary Leigh of Stoneleigh appointed James to the living of Cubbington in Warwickshire. The three appointments together raised James Austen's income to about £200, which he considered a sufficient basis for beginning married life with Ann Mathew in 1792.[52] His marriage resulted in yet more plurality, as in 1794 his father-in-law General Mathew bought for him the chaplaincy of the 86th Regiment, his duties to be performed by another clergyman paid to do so.[53]

By the early nineteenth century, however, the holding of more than one living was beginning to be considered inappropriate. New standards saw the eighteenth-century practice as worldly, even corrupt, and neglectful of the spiritual needs of the parishioners in each area. Finally, in 1838, Parliament passed the Pluralities Act, which actually forbade any clergyman from holding more than one benefice "with cure of souls", except where the travelling distance between churches was less than ten miles, and the joint annual income under £1,000. As we have seen, this would permit such pluralities as James Austen's, but it is clear that the practice was now thought to be improper. As one politician remarked during the debate,

> "No colonel is allowed to hold two regiments at one time, and to devolve the command of the one upon another officer; and it is highly improper that a clergyman should be allowed to hold two benefices."[54]

In the spare time afforded through employing deputies in his various livings, Vaughan Thomas conducted antiquarian research. He began collecting materials in 1806 for his most important work, *The Italian Biography of Sir Robert Dudley, Knight* (Oxford, 1861). Sir Robert Dudley (1574–1649), illegitimate son of his namesake the Earl of Leicester, married Alice, one of the daughters of Sir Thomas Leigh (II, d. 1626) and

---

52. Collins (1998), pp. 99–100.
53. Le Faye (2013), p. 163.
54. F. L. Cross (ed.), *The Oxford Dictionary of the Christian Church* (London: Oxford University Press, 1961), s.v. 'Pluralities Act, 1838,' p. 1085. Debate: Barrow (ed., 1838), p. 4648.

the great-aunt of Christopher Leigh. Dudley was thus a close connection of the Stoneleigh Leighs, and the tomb of his widow, the Duchess Alice, is the best known monument in Stoneleigh church.

It was all the more surprising, therefore, that Vaughan Thomas proved to be so vague about monuments on the south wall of the church. In his initial deposition (dated 3 January 1828), he stated that if there had been a monument to Christopher Leigh on the south wall, "he must have noticed it and well remembered it."[55] (This, of course, is an instance of the O'Farrell approach.)

Admittedly, Vaughan Thomas was effectively an absentee incumbent. He conceded under questioning that he never resided at Stoneleigh, and seldom performed divine service there.[56] His curate undertook the day-to-day parish work and the Sunday sermon.

> "Between the periods of my institution [11 June 1804] and the period to which my attention is to be directed [1810–1813], I performed divine service there very seldom indeed."[57]

Subsequently he said that he may not have visited Stoneleigh more than once in a year.[58]

Denman examined Vaughan Thomas, and asked him point blank.

> **Denman:** Between your institution and the time of the repairs being in contemplation in Stoneley church, did you ever see any monument on the South wall of that church?
> **Vaughan Thomas:** Most certainly not.
> **Mr Denman:** Any monument?
> **Vaughan Thomas:** On that wall you are speaking of,—as to my recollection within those periods,—as you call upon me to say—whether I saw any monument—within those periods,—I cannot change [sc. charge]

---

55. Leigh (1834), vol. II, p. 40, note.
56. Leigh (1834), vol. II, p. 41.
57. Leigh (1834), vol. II, p. 41.
58. Leigh (1834), vol. II, p. 45.

my memory;—as to that time,—I should certainly say—I recollect no monuments.[59]

Thus Vaughan Thomas denied recalling even the Webster monument, whose existence had never been in question by anyone else. This was a false step in the view of the family's lawyers. Denman attempted to get him to confirm a memory of Webster's memorial, but in vain.[60]

Even Vaughan Thomas, later on, seems to have had doubts about whether had taken the right approach in his evidence. In the July following the hearings, he wrote to the Leigh family lawyer, Thomas Hill Mortimer, expressing unhappiness about certain aspects of his testimony.[61] Causton, in his footnotes, had a field day.

> "'Alas! What a falling off was there!'—after rearing so beautiful and important a fabric: vicar of Yarnton, in the county of Oxford, and of Stoneley, in the county of Warwick,—a gentleman of literary observation and enquiry—a monumental modelist, and addicted to 'matters of that sort', forsooth; and after all, to fall irrecoverably deep into the abyss of error. Heavens! What a lapse…"[62]

Vaughan Thomas' evidence may have been influenced by the fact that for many years, he had been campaigning to receive an increase in his parish tithes from Stoneleigh.[63] During 1819, he wanted to enlist the Leigh family's support in increasing his tithes, and found them less than responsive. At one point, in writing to Richard Darley, he threatened legal action.[64] The image of an absentee vicar expending his energies in seeking more money is not an attractive picture.

Relations may have thawed over the issue of the Leigh family wish to expand their family vault, the development of which resulted in disruption of parishioners' graves and homes. On the "grant" of five guineas

---

59. Leigh (1834), vol. II, p. 42.
60. Leigh (1834), vol. II, p. 44.
61. SBTRO DR 18/17/53/10, 18 July 1828.
62. Leigh (1834), vol. II, p. 42, note.
63. Vaughan Thomas to Julia-Judith, SBTRO DR 18/3/65/4/27, 22 May 1819; Vaughan Thomas to James Henry Leigh, SBTRO DR 18/3/65/4/30, 24 May 1819.
64. Vaughan Thomas to Richard Darley, SBTRO DR 18/3/65/4/48, 22 September 1819.

from the Leighs to the church, Vaughan Thomas was happy to give permission for the expansion.[65]

In the wider world, as opposed to little Stoneleigh, Vaughan Thomas' legacy was on the whole a positive one. One of his interests was in the development of medical training in Birmingham. He was in general a promoter of philanthropic causes, with a strongly religious flavour.[66] It was in 1828, the year in which Vaughan Thomas gave his unsatisfactory evidence to the Lords hearing, that a decision was made to set up a medical school in Birmingham General Hospital.[67] Vaughan Thomas' collection of papers relating to the history of medical training in Birmingham is now part of the National Archives.[68]

He, then, seems to have been a bundle of contradictions. He was an antiquarian who failed to notice a monument to a relative of the subject of his life's work. He was a philanthropist who wanted to enrich himself at the expense of poor parishioners. He was an absentee minister of the church, who wanted every privilege accorded to clerical status without the bother of delivering sermons or visiting the poor. Vaughan Thomas was not the first or last witness to sacrifice the appearance of competence on the altar of apparent consistency: he was only the most distinguished in this case.

Next to give evidence was the Reverend James Roberts, the curate of Stoneleigh from the early 1790s until 1819. Unlike Vaughan Thomas, who would not have known his parishioners by sight, James Roberts—"Parson Roberts"—was well-known to everyone in Stoneleigh. His father had been the vicar of Stoneleigh until his death in 1791, then the position was held by Robert Sumner until the accession of Vaughan Thomas in 1804. James Roberts served all three as curate, performing divine service each Sunday.

---

65. Vaughan Thomas to James Henry Leigh, SBTRO DR 18/3/65/4/58, 8 September 1820; and DR 18/3/65/4/59, 14 September 1820.
66. Notes to the Vaughan Thomas Collection, 1834–1858, http://www.nationalarchives.gov.uk/a2a/records.aspx?cat=150-vt&cid=0#0 (Accessed 24 November 2015).
67. G. Martin Murphy, "Thomas, Vaughan (1775–1858)," *Oxford Dictionary of National Biography*, Oxford University Press, 2004; online edn, Jan 2015, http://www.oxforddnb.com/view/article/27241 (Accessed 17 Feb 2016).
68. Notes to the Vaughan Thomas Collection, 1834–1858, http://www.nationalarchives.gov.uk/a2a/records.aspx?cat=150-vt&cid=0#0 (Accessed 24 November 2015).

An absentee vicar paid his curate to undertake his duties, at a lower rate than the vicar's own income from the position. It was, therefore, unlikely that Parson Roberts would contradict his vicar Vaughan Thomas in essentials, that is to say, on the question of the existence of the Christopher stone. In his deposition, dated 11 January 1828, James Roberts claimed that he had no recollection of a monument to Christopher Leigh having been on the south wall of the church.[69] Correcting the error of his vicar, Roberts confidently asserted that he remembered Webster's monument.

> **Thomas Denman:** Was there any other monument upon that wall?
> **James Roberts:** I believe — certainly not.[70]

Under questioning, Roberts maintained that he was the instigator of the repairs to the church undertaken in 1810 and 1811. This meant that he was involved with the parish committee discussions. As we have seen, the majority of the committee members at the time asserted that the Christopher stone had been taken down, under Richard Darley's supervision, and never replaced. Roberts' deposition declared this to be false and unfounded, but inevitably he was questioned about it.

> **Denman:** Were you present when Darley said, "that monument", pointing to a monument of Christopher Leigh, "the parish have nothing to do with; it belongs to the Leigh family; let it be taken down carefully; I will send it to the Abbey"?

Adam momentarily objected to the question, before then supporting it, and in the event Roberts did not have to give an answer. Moments later, the Lord Chancellor sought a direct commitment.

> **Lord Chancellor:** Will you say positively, upon your oath, that there was no other monument there?
> **James Roberts:** I say, as strongly as I suppose I can be called upon to do upon my oath — I have the firmest and strongest conviction of my

---

69. Leigh (1834), vol. II, p. 46, note.
70. Leigh (1834), vol. II, p. 48.

mind, speaking under the awe of an oath—that there never was any such monument there.[71]

All Roberts had to have said was "Yes." His long-winded actual response is somewhat along the lines of Vaughan Thomas' statement quoted at the start of this chapter.

Again, however, Roberts found his testimony under question. His wife was also brought into evidence. It had been reported that in the presence of others, including his wife and a Mr and Mrs Thomas Hall Vaughton, the Reverend Roberts had spoken of the removal of the Christopher stone.

> **Adam:** Do you ever remember Mrs Roberts in your presence conversing about Christopher Leigh's monument, or supposed monument?
> **James Roberts:** Very often.
> **Adam:** Do you remember her conversing with Mr Vaughton?
> **James Roberts:** I do not recollect that; but I think it may have occurred…
> **Adam:** Do you remember Mrs Roberts to have said to Mr Vaughton, in your presence, that if she were called upon to say whether there had existed a monument to the Leigh family in the church, she must and would do so, or any thing to that effect?
> **James Roberts:** I certainly never heard anything like that said by her; not only not so, but not any thing like it.[72]

This contradicted a letter which Thomas Hall Vaughton of Fillongley (a parish within the Stoneleigh estate) had written to the Attorney-General, in which he wrote that Mrs Roberts had said that she must, if required, testify to the monument's existence.[73] Mr Vaughton also quoted Mrs Roberts as saying that she had asked workmen in the church about the

---

71. Leigh (1834), vol. II, p. 49.
72. Leigh (1834), vol. II, pp. 54–55.
73. Thomas Hall Vaughton of Fillongley Lodge: letter to Attorney-General (10 April 1826), Leigh (1834), vol. II, p. 55, note; notice of death, 18 February 1841, in *Gentleman's Magazine* vol. XV (=vol. 169) (new series), January-June 1841, p. 670.

monument, and was told that it had been placed in the belfry.[74] As it turned out, Mrs Roberts was not called to give evidence.

The claimant George Leigh was another who had heard Mr and Mrs Roberts speak on the subject. In the early days of his claim, he had approached Mr Roberts in order to view the relevant Stoneleigh parish registers. Mr Roberts charged George Leigh two guineas for extracts from the parish registers. They had shared a bottle of wine, and Mrs Roberts had said, "You may get the title, but I would not give you much for your chance of the property."[75]

In addition to being contradicted by several witnesses, ultimately James Roberts contradicted himself. In giving evidence before the Attorney-General, Roberts had admitted that the Stoneleigh marriage registers, for the relevant period for Christopher Leigh, had been deliberately damaged, appearing to have been cut. In his affidavit prior to the Lords hearings, however, Roberts said that he had never claimed that the registers had been mutilated.

Under detailed questioning, Roberts' attempt to reconcile these statements was less than convincing.

> **James Roberts:** I reconcile them by stating that there were omissions of marriages, in what way cut out I cannot say.[76]

Roberts tried to deflect this unfortunate step. Led by Denman, he tried to suggest that any damage to the registers might have been caused during the political turmoil of the period 1640 to 1660, for which period he had never seen an undamaged register.

> **James Roberts:** Never during the commonwealth; I never saw one that was perfect.[77]

---

74. Leigh (1834), vol. II, p. 56, note.
75. Leigh (1834), vol. II, p. 60, note.
76. Leigh (1834), vol. II, p. 65.
77. Leigh (1834), vol. II, pp. 65–66.

The Missing Monument Murders

Yet another witness, however, had written to the Attorney-General in April 1826. This was Lionel Place, a Warwickshire landowner and former magistrate. Place had written:

> "In the early part of my acquaintance with Mr Roberts I have, more than once, heard him speak of a monument which had existed to the memory of Christopher Leigh in Stoneley church, and which had been removed."[78]

James Roberts denied this under questioning, even claiming that Lionel Place had not asserted this, but Lionel Place himself was about to give evidence.[79]

---

78. Leigh (1834), vol. II, p. 59, note.
79. Leigh (1834), vol. II, p. 58.

CHAPTER SIX

Not Far From Here

"Good God! How can Mr Roberts deny this? How can he deny the existence of this monument, when I heard him speak of it himself?"

Lionel Place, c.1826[1]

In 1826, Lionel Place (1766–1838) had held the position of High Sheriff of Warwickshire. This post, traditional in each ancient county (now ceremonial in nature), is of very long standing, having first been occupied over 1,000 years ago. The High Sheriff was for centuries the principal law enforcement officer in the county. Place took over the Warwickshire role from Chandos Leigh, who had held it in 1825. This background may have had some bearing on Lionel Place's decision to give evidence which directly contradicted that of one of Chandos' key witnesses, James Roberts. It is possible that there was personal as well as political antagonism between the two Warwickshire grandees.

Since about 1810, Place had occupied Weddington Castle in the north of Warwickshire. (The castle was demolished in the 1920s to make way for a housing estate.[2]) He had the grounds landscaped during the early period of his tenure there, earning praise from Robert Lugar, who wrote about Weddington in 1811.[3] Despite holding high positions in the Warwick magistracy, Place had several run-ins with the law himself, and in 1818 badly injured a labourer.[4]

---

1. Leigh (1834), vol. II, p. 75.
2. Weddington Castle website, http://www.weddingtoncastle.co.uk/ (Accessed 25 November 2015): Introduction to the castle. Time at Weddington "about eighteen or nineteen years" (in 1828): Leigh (1834), vol. II, p. 69.
3. Weddington Castle website, http://www.weddingtoncastle.co.uk/ (Accessed 25 November 2015): Key people 10: Lionel Place.
4. Weddington Castle website, http://www.weddingtoncastle.co.uk/ (Accessed 25 November 2015):

In the Lords hearing of 1828, Place was subjected to a lengthy cross-examination. He had first become acquainted with James Roberts in about 1813, when Place wished to consult with him about changes to roadways.

> **Lionel Place:** Our conversation turned upon the accession of fortune and property which had come to the late Mr James [Henry] Leigh, who had only a few years back come to reside at Stoneley. He [Roberts] mentioned how fortunate they were, and how accidental it was that they should have come into it; that they were not the rightful heirs, but that the rightful heir must have descended from the Christopher Leigh to whom that monument had been erected; that the descendants of that family were supposed, all trace of them, to have been lost, and in consequence I suppose that Mr James Henry Leigh had come into possession.[5]

At that time, Place said, he had no particular interest in the issue, and did not pursue it with Roberts. In Place's part of Warwickshire, he thought, nobody took any interest in the Stoneleigh matter.[6] Many years later — in about 1826, when Attorney-General Copley undertook some inquiries — he met again with Roberts.

> "When he [Roberts] told me he had denied the existence of a monument, I immediately turned round to Mrs Place, after he was gone, and said, 'Good God! How can Mr Roberts deny this? How can he deny the existence of this monument, when I heard him speak of it himself?'"[7]

Place did more than exclaim to his wife. By now — and probably especially after succeeding Chandos Leigh in the High Sheriff's office — he had become interested in the rivalry about the Leigh inheritance. Place first made acquaintance with Henry Kent Causton. Through Causton, he met the second of the claimant George Leigh's sons, and then George

---

Key people 10: Lionel Place.
5. Leigh (1834), vol. II, pp. 70–71.
6. Leigh (1834), vol. II, p. 81.
7. Leigh (1834), vol. II, p. 75.

Leigh himself.[8] It was probably in this context that Place wrote to the Attorney-General to attest that James Roberts had previously spoken of the Christopher stone as having existed.[9] It was not long before he experienced some blow-back.

James Roberts, together with a Captain Mason of the Royal Navy, paid a visit to Place later in 1826. The Captain Mason, who went as Roberts' friend and supporter, was Francis Mason (b.1779). Mason's career well illustrates the stop-start nature of a naval officer's employment during the Napoleonic Wars, one of the themes of Jane Austen's *Persuasion* (1817). A peace treaty would see the officer return to England on half-pay; then he would eagerly search for another appointment at the first opportunity. Mason took every opportunity going. Both during and between hostilities, Mason had a distinguished naval career, involved in operations in the Mediterranean, and, after the short lived Peace of Amiens, in action against the French off Dieppe. Mason's second-last ship appointment, the *Fisgard*, was found to be beyond repair in 1812, and was paid off. Mason transferred to the *President*, in which he was present at the siege and capture of San Sebastian in Spain in 1813. This was a decisive action in the Peninsular War: Arthur Wellesley, afterwards Duke of Wellington, was pressing on east to the Pyrenees after his victory at the battle of Vitoria. San Sebastian was situated on the Bay of Biscay, and it was no doubt here that Mason's ship was stationed.

In 1814 Mason was posted to Cork Harbour, which must have seemed dull by comparison. "Peace being certain, and his lady being in a precarious state of health," Mason resigned his commission.[10] Mason's wife was Selina, daughter of the second Viscount Hood, Henry Hood (1753–1836). The Hood family seat was at Whitley, in Warwickshire. Selina's grandfather was a famous naval commander, Samuel Hood, who had been created Baron and Viscount Hood in 1778. It was no doubt through his connection with the Hoods that Mason had become known to the

---

8. Leigh (1834), vol. II, p. 91.
9. Leigh (1834), vol. Ii, p. 59, note.
10. John Marshall, *Royal Naval Biography; Or, memoirs of the services of all the flag-officers, superannuated rear-admirals, retired-captains, post-captains, and commanders, whose names appeared on the Admiralty List of Sea-Officers at the commencement of the year 1823, or who have been since promoted; etc.* Supplement: Part I. (London: printed for Longman, Rees, Orme, Brown, and Green, Paternoster Row, 1827), pp. 55–64. "Peace being certain": pp. 63–64.

and add, "I think it probable you may have equally mistaken what Mr Roberts said"?[19]

Place agreed to none of it. Meanwhile, one of the Lords (his name given as only a dash in the transcript) picked up on the issue of the inscription copy, which Denman had done his best to bury in the preceding exchanges.

It seems that, apart from the disagreement about the Leigh evidence, the Roberts, Place and Mason families were, or had been, friends for several years. Mason was so much in the habit of visiting Place that Place's servant knew him and was able to pass on a message about when Place would be available.[20] Place attested that one of Roberts' sons was dining with Place, a short time after Place had written to the Attorney-General in April 1826. "He told me his brother [Henry Roberts] had got a copy of the inscription, and that the first words were, '*Haud procul ex hoc loco.*'"[21] This opening is Latin for: "Not far from this place." The phrase *haud procul* ("not far") was common in Latin literature of classical Roman times, as a poetic indicator of location: instead of simply "nearby", it was a poetic locution to expand the idea to "not far from." The phrase appears in several places in the poetry of Ovid (43 BCE-17/18 CE), and as such would have been familiar to men such as Roberts and Place.[22] During the seventeenth and eighteenth centuries, the phrase *haud procul* was used in a range of non-literary contexts. Its formal and evocative nature, as well as its vagueness about specific distances and locations, had value. A plant catalogue published in 1730 had the title: "*Catalogus plantarum: tam exoticarum tum domesticarum: quae in hortis haud procul a Londino sitis a venditionem propagantur*: a Catalogue of trees, shrubs, plants and flowers, both exotic and domestic, which are propagated for sale, in the gardens near London."[23] Here, probably for

---

19. Leigh (1834), vol. II, pp. 84–85.
20. Leigh (1834), vol. II, p. 101: Place at Mason's house in October 1825; p. 105, Place's servant knew Mason; p. 107, Place and his wife dining and staying with Roberts in 1817.
21. Leigh (1834), vol. II, p. 88.
22. E.g. Ovid *Metamorphoses* 5.385: *Haud procul Hennaeis lacus est a moenibus altae*; 8.624: *Haud procul hinc stagnum est, tellus habitabilis olim;* etc.
23. Philip Miller, *Catalogus Plantarum* (London: Society of Gardeners, 1730). Biodiversity Heritage Library, www.biodiversitylibrary.org/bibliography/819#/summary (Accessed 25 November 2015).

commercial reasons, the expression "near/not far from London" removes the specifics of particular growers. The phrase also served as an opening for memorial inscriptions: "Not far from here, Person X lies buried." As well as bringing its poetic associations, it was usefully vague about the exact location of the said burial in relation to the inscription, and thus could be set up at whatever distance was convenient. A 1710 inscription from Trinity church in Kingston-upon-Hull, in Yorkshire, reads:

Haud procul hinc jacet Georgius Barker, Miles.[24]

"Not far from here lies George Barker, Knight..." The inscription goes on to record George Barker's achievements and virtues, and to explain that although he died in 1667, the stone was erected by his nephew in 1710. This shows that such inscriptions could be put up after a considerable lapse of time. Another example, at Great Stoughton church in Huntingdonshire, dates from 1719. It records Sir John Conyers, who, it states, lies "not far from this marble [*marmore*], next to the ashes of his dearest wife:"

Ab hoc haud procul marmore, juxta charissimae suae conjugis cineres...[25]

A final example dates from 1694, in the church of Saint Nicholas in Newcastle-upon-Tyne.

Memoria Patricii Crowe olim de Ashlington Armigeri. Cujus corpus haud procul marmaro isto sepultum jacet...

"To the memory of the honourable Patrick Crowe, sometime of Ashlington, whose body lies buried not far from this marble."[26]

---

24. John Tickell, *History of the Town and County of Kingston-upon-Hull, From its foundation in the reign of Edward the First, to the present time; etc.* (For Thomas Lee, Thomas Browne, Richard Millson, booksellers, and G. W. Browne, stationer, 1798), pp. 791–792.
25. Thomas Wotton, *The English Baronetage: Containing a genealogical and historical account of all the English Baronets now existing: their descents, marriages, and issues; etc.* Vol II. (London: printed for Tho. Wotton, 1741), p. 102.
26. Henry Bourne, *The History of Newcastle-upon-Tyne; Or the ancient and present state of that town* (Newcastle-upon-Tyne: printed and sold by John White, 1736), p. 81.

The Missing Monument Murders

For Henry Roberts (or Henry Mason), therefore, to allege that the Christopher stone copy started with the words *Haud procul ex hoc loco*, was on the surface plausible. It is to be noted, however, that none of the examples quoted share this exact wording, and in fact the only example of this precise phrase known to Google is this very example from the Lords transcript. It may not even be particularly correct Latin. None of the other examples use the preposition *ex* to indicate "from", most using instead *ab* or *a*. This error was probably in Place's recollection of what Henry Roberts had told him.

Henry Roberts himself was then called as a witness. He maintained that the inscription was "reported" only, not genuine. He claimed that the wording was *Haud procul ab hoc loco*. (The veteran Lord Eldon approvingly noted this correction of *ex* to *ab*.[27]) The inscription, he said, had been given to him by a Mr Warde, who had taken copies of a number of inscriptions in Stoneleigh church.[28] Henry Roberts no longer had his copy, but thought that the inscription had been in Latin.[29] Mr Warde was said to be a clergyman at the village of Weston, near Leamington, about four or five miles from Stoneleigh. Under questioning, Henry Roberts agreed that Mr Warde had claimed that the copy represented the monument inscription, but that Mr Warde himself had not claimed to have seen the monument in question.[30] Henry Roberts thought that the copy mentioned a marriage, but did not think it included the names of children.[31]

Mr Warde is not otherwise known to the record, but a "Mr J.W. Warwick, of Coventry", appears in the Leigh family papers. In February 1828 he had written to Chandos Leigh concerning a list of inscriptions from the Stoneleigh church, made 20 years previously by his brother. He would not act in the matter until he heard from Chandos.[32] The abstracts of the Leigh papers are not without some errors, and it is possible that "Mr J. W. Warwick, of Coventry" is, in fact, Mr J. Warde, of Warwick,

---

27. Leigh (1834), vol. II, p. 114.
28. Leigh (1834), vol. II, pp. 112–113.
29. Leigh (1834), vol. II, p. 112.
30. Leigh (1834), vol. II, pp. 114–115.
31. Leigh (1834), vol. II, p. 114.
32. SBTRO DR 18/17/53/4, 7 February 1828.

or Coventry. It seems unlikely that two men with similar initials would have made copies of the inscriptions. It appears that a version of Mr Warde's copy may have been preserved in the Leigh papers. A detailed description of coffins and inscriptions present in the old vault survives, although it is not entirely clear when this record was made.[33] It records the burial there of Christopher Leigh, along with evidence about many other burials in the vault, and is discussed in more detail in *Chapter 14*. This transcript does not, as it survives, record any inscription from the church relating to Christopher Leigh.

Without the actual copy of the putative inscription, speculation could go no further. Probably Chandos, in response to Mr Warde/Warwick, had arranged for the inscription trail to go silent. Mr Warde was not called as a witness. He had written to Causton in May 1828, claiming to have had no recollection of the Christopher stone, but that he had heard, at second or third hand, that it read:

Haud procul ab hoc loco jacet Christopheri Leigh, armiger, filius quartus Thomae Leigh, Baro de Stonely, qui quidem Christopherus obiit mensis Septembris, 1672, Aetat. 75.[34]

"Not far from this place lies the honourable Christopher Leigh, fourth son of Thomas Leigh, Baron of Stoneleigh, who (Christopher) died in the month of September, 1672, aged 75." Warde emphasised that he did not know the person who told him this:

"I know nothing of the person who said it; he was an entire stranger to me."[35]

Warde also wrote to the lawyers Goren & Price, at one time acting in the case, to deny all knowledge of the inscriptions. Warde's protests that he did not know the person ("some person at the rooms") who, out of the blue, spouted a Latin inscription at him, seems bizarre. In

---

33. SBTRO DR 18/3/50/1, undated but watermark 1813; suggests not original version from c. 1808 (see later chapter). Photocopy kindly provided to me by SBTRO, 2015.
34. Leigh (1834), vol. II, p. 115, note.
35. Leigh (1834), vol. II, p. 115, note.

addition, the recollection of Christopher's age at death as 75 is entirely inaccurate; having been born in 1626, his age at death was 46. These matters strongly suggest that Warde was disguising any actual information about the inscription. The status of this supposed Latin version of the Christopher stone, ultimately, was a red herring. Any inscription which made no mention of marriage or children was of no use whatever to the claimant George Leigh. This was why James Roberts, Henry Roberts, and Francis Mason had had no hesitation in testifying about this putative *Haud procul* version. The investigation took up time, generated no results which benefited George Leigh, and diverted attention from the potentially damaging testimony of Lionel Place, which had emphasised both James Roberts' inconsistency, and his and Mason's attempts to intimidate a witness.

But there was additional evidence that the "supposed inscription" had been the subject of conversation inside and outside the Roberts family. A Mrs Hannah Gumley (or Gumbley) provided a deposition in which she maintained that she remembered the Christopher stone, and that as a friend of the Roberts family she regularly left her pony, on which she rode to church, in James Roberts' stable. She was also a frequent visitor for dinner or tea at the curate's. Mrs Gumley asked James Roberts what had become of the Christopher stone after its removal from the church. She reported Roberts' reply that "Mrs Leigh (meaning the honorable Mrs [Julia-Judith] Leigh) had advised Mr Leigh (meaning the reverend Thomas Leigh) to have it taken down to the abbey to be cleaned and recut." Mrs Gumley added that she had heard both Roberts and his wife express surprise that the monument had not been replaced. That the Reverend Thomas was still living dates this exchange to before June 1813.

Roberts had said more. Hannah Gumley maintained that she had heard him say that the possessors of Stoneleigh were not the rightful owners, "but that he thought no one else would claim it, as he understood the right heir was somewhere abroad." This belief was apparently widespread, with some people of the view that George Leigh himself had come from America. This idea may have been a distorted reflection of the fact that at least one branch of Leighs, related to the Stoneleigh family, had emigrated to America during the previous century.[36] James Roberts had even lent some weight on his own behalf to George Leigh's claim. Hannah Gumley recalled him having said that he was sure that George Leigh was the rightful heir, because his physical resemblance to Mary Leigh (d.1806) was so striking. According to Causton (who took care to warn that this widespread belief did not constitute evidence), this view was shared by a large number of people in Stoneleigh and Coventry.[37]

Hannah Gumley's final piece of evidence, aimed at destroying the credibility of James Roberts, was that the Christopher stone was frequently the subject of conversation in the Roberts household, until such time as James Roberts' daughter, named only as Miss Roberts, became friends with "the ……… ……… at ……… ………" The dots appear in Causton's text, presumably as they stood in Hannah Gumley's deposition. We may infer that the final two words are *Stoneley* and *Abbey*. The only question is over the first and second words. The phrase may stand for *Leigh family*. Miss Roberts may have become friends with the Leigh girls, or possibly—a more fraught scenario—with Chandos himself. After this friendship began, according to Hannah Gumley, "the subject was disagreeable and it was dropped accordingly, as it would have given offence to have named it."[38]

Hannah Gumley was the widow of a farmer whose family had lived in Stoneleigh for several generations.[39] She was respected, and of sufficient means to keep a riding pony. Her decision to give evidence which was so at odds with the official Stoneleigh line may have been driven by her treatment at the hands of the Leigh family. At about the time James Henry and Julia-Judith Leigh took over the estate, and possibly around the time of her husband's death, Mrs Gumley had been unable to keep up the rental payments, and in November 1813 had appealed for assistance to Viscount Hood. He had undertaken to pay her rental on

---

36. Hannah Gumley deposition: Leigh (1834), vol. II, pp. 110–111, note. Spelling "Gumbley" in Leigh papers: see n. 11 above. American family: belief about George Leigh: Leigh (1834), vol. II, p. 111, note; also descendants allegedly of Christopher Leigh: email from Nancy Law to author, 2014.
37. Leigh (1834), vol. II, p. 111, note.
38. Leigh (1834), vol. II, p. 111, note. Hannah Gumley deposition dated 24 January 1828.
39. SBTRO DR 18/3/47/41/6, 1 May 1769, "Survey of Late Jenkins's Farm in Stoneley Let to Lant, Rawlins & Gumley."

Tossill Farm, and asked the Leighs to let her and her daughter stay on. By 1821, the Leighs were endeavouring to remove Hannah Gumley from her home, although it is not clear that this is because of unpaid rent or other reasons. By this time Viscount Hood wanted no more to do with the matter, and Mrs Gumley was evicted in that year.[40]

By 1824, the unfortunate Hannah Gumley was in prison. She was making complaints about and probably to the Leigh family, as we find Julia-Judith writing to the family solicitor, Thomas Hill Mortimer, regarding the "impudent claims and shameful conduct" of Mrs Gumley. Permission was being sought to release her from prison.[41] It was nearly a month before Hill Mortimer replied in detail, and his considered view was that Hannah Gumley should remain in prison "till she amends her Schedule."[42] This may mean that she had made public or private claims along the lines of her later deposition, regarding the Christopher stone. In the Leigh papers, the term "impudent" is routinely reserved for matters with the potential for wider embarrassment, such as the claims of Jane Rhodes against her former lover Chandos Leigh.[43] In the event, Hannah Gumley was not called to give evidence before the Lords, possibly because she had been a prisoner at some time in recent years. However, it is more surprising that one further witness was not called. This was the Reverend William Robinson of Wishaw in Warwickshire. He made a deposition which stated that he had been dining with James Roberts in about 1821 or 1822. The subject of the Leigh inheritance had come up, and Robinson had remarked that he understood that a monument which had been removed would shed some light on the matter. He stated that Roberts replied words to the effect: "I know all about the monument; I know what became of it."[44]

---

40. SBTRO DR 18/17/39/30 8 November 1813, Lord Hood undertaking rent; DR 18/17/39/31 15 November 1813, Lord Hood requesting Mrs Gumley's tenancy continue; DR 18/17/47/13 22 April 1821, unsigned but presumably from James Henry Leigh to Lord Hood, requesting he use his persuasion to assist in removing Mrs Gumley; DR 18/17/47/14 23 April 1821, Lord Hood to James Henry, refusing to act in the matter. Hannah Gumley left Stoneleigh in 1821: her deposition, 24 January 1828, Leigh (1834), vol. II, p. 110, note.
41. SBTRO DR 18/17/50/4, 29 March 1824.
42. SBTRO DR 18/17/50/6, 26 April 1824.
43. SBTRO DR 18/17/50/19, 9 Sept 1824; DR 18/17/50/20, 10 Sept 1824, both regarding Jane Rhodes.
44. Robinson deposition, dated 16 December 1828: Leigh (1834), vol. II, p. 110, note.

Robinson came to London in the expectation of being called for cross-examination, but was not called. This appeared to have been because the Lords Committee adhered to the practice that as Roberts had not been advised that new witnesses would contradict his evidence in particular details, it was not proper for these witnesses to be called.[45]

In the event, a hiatus of many months intervened after the evidence of Lionel Place and another group of witnesses. The tenth day of hearings was Wednesday 23 July 1828; the eleventh was not until Monday 18 May 1829.[46] On this eleventh day, a surprising witness took the stand. This was none other than Gregory Roberts, brother of the Reverend James. He had emerged late in the proceedings, and there was some question in the committee whether his evidence could be admitted. Gregory Roberts was questioned aggressively by Denman, who was attempting to show both that Gregory was an unreliable person, and that his evidence was prompted by some quarrel with his brother. Denman questioned Gregory about his livelihood and many previous places of residence.

> **Denman:** Did you ever carry on any business?…What business?…When did you first carry on that business?… Did you ever carry on business there [at Liverpool] before that time?…How long did you live in Birmingham?…Had you only three residences in Birmingham?…You went from Kinver to Birmingham; where is that?…[47]

Denman extracted from Gregory that he had previously worked as a farmer, a button manufacturer, and a factor and merchant. He had not been in contact with his brother the Reverend James since about 1817. Despite Denman's grilling, Gregory Roberts did not become confused. He maintained that he recalled the Christopher stone near the Webster monument on the south wall, and claimed that the inscription began *Haud procul*. Gregory stated that he had often been present when his brother, the Reverend James, read aloud the inscription in the church.

---

45. Leigh (1834), vol. II, p. 112, note.
46. Tenth day: Leigh (1834), vol. II, p. 101; eleventh day: Leigh (1834), vol. II, p. 116.
47. Leigh (1834), vol. II, pp. 225–229.

Denman's next approach was to try to establish that Gregory Roberts had been in contact with the claimant's agents, with the implication that he was motivated by greed for the reward they offered for evidence. Gregory denied this, claiming that he first found out about George Leigh's claim and the search for the stone after a conversation with a Dr Burgess at Liverpool.[48]

The evidence, taken as a whole, indicates that the Reverend James Roberts was a gossip, who had been unable to conceal his knowledge of, and keen interest in, the Christopher stone. Lionel Place, Hannah Gumley, the Reverend William Robinson, and Gregory Roberts, all testified that James Roberts had spoken of the stone and its disappearance. The Reverend James Roberts, however, was a curate with a wife and several children to support into adulthood; and his allegiance to both his vicar, Vaughan Thomas, and the Leigh family, was too important to their very livelihood for him to admit publicly the existence of the Christopher stone, and the doubt it threw upon the Leigh inheritance. Causton summed up:

> "Upon the whole evidence of Mr Roberts we will not blot his character with an observation. The test of truth is upon him. Let the county of Warwick, *where he is best known* [suggestive italics in original], decide upon his testimony."[49]

Of witnesses for the Leigh team, responsibility for the various aspects of the case was distributed around. Richard Darley had taken responsibility for designing the church alterations. James Roberts had claimed to have proposed them in the first place. Thomas Hill Mortimer was supposed to have been in charge of improvements to the abbey cellars. One Leigh family member who might have been thought to have played a key role in these events was apparently missing in action. This was the incumbent of the Stoneleigh estate, Chandos Leigh.

---

48. Leigh (1834), vol. II, p. 236.
49. Leigh (1834), vol. II, p. 112, note.

CHAPTER SEVEN

Chandos: The Severest Satire on Lord Byron

"[The Whigs] all had the same intense conviction that every thing but Whiggism was *bête* [stupid]; that they could teach 'the people' every thing that it was good for them to know; and that the way to do it was by addressing them in a coaxing and admonitory way."

Harriet Martineau, 1855[1]

At the time of Chandos' birth and for many years after, James Henry Leigh, Julia-Judith and their family were living in Harley Street in London, at the expense of the Reverend Thomas and the Adlestrop estate. Chandos Leigh was born in London on 27 June 1791, five years after the marriage of his parents. The lengthy hiatus prior to their first child's birth may perhaps be explained by Julia-Judith's youth, as she was only 15 at her marriage. Four daughters followed: Julia (1793–1871), Caroline Eliza (1794–1870), Mary (b.1797), and Augusta Elizabeth (birth date unknown).[2] In the 1802 census, James Henry's household comprised 20 persons, seven males and 13 females.[3] In the same year, James Henry first became a Member of Parliament, through the interest of relatives.

---

1. Harriet Martineau, with a new introduction by Gaby Weiner, *Harriet Martineau's Autobiography* (London: Virago, 1983), vol. I, p. 340.
2. Chandos birth date: David Hill Radcliffe, "Leigh, Chandos, first Baron Leigh (1791–1850)," *Oxford Dictionary of National Biography*, Oxford University Press, 2004; online edn, Sept 2010 http://www.oxforddnb.com/view/article/16375 (Accessed 1 December 2015). Birthdates of sisters: not given in *Burke's Peerage*, but according to various internet sites; Julia dates from Julia Leigh Colvile gravestone (added Julia Tansell 13/11/11, #80376961, www.findagrave.com (Accessed 25 November 2015); Caroline Eliza dates from *DNB* article on her husband, G. C. Boase, "East, Sir James Buller, Second Baronet (1789–1878)," rev. Beth F. Wood, *Oxford Dictionary of National Biography*, Oxford University Press, 2004 http://www.oxforddnb.com/view/article/8409 (Accessed 1 December 2015).
3. Huxley (2013), p. 64.

The need to live a gentleman's lifestyle at Adlestrop and in London, without a job to support it, must have placed great stress on the family, and underlines the tension which surrounded the relationship with Mary Leigh at Stoneleigh. As we have seen, Mary regarded the Reverend Thomas as eager for her death, and no doubt James Henry, Julia-Judith and their growing family were no less keen. Interestingly, the official history of Parliament records, erroneously, that in 1806 it was James Henry himself, not the Reverend Thomas, who succeeded to the Stoneleigh estate.[4] The misapprehension was no doubt fostered by James Henry and his family. That the James Henrys felt a sense of entitlement to Stoneleigh so early helps to account for the fact that, well before the death of the Reverend Thomas in 1813, Julia-Judith was directing improvements on the estate.

Chandos was sent to Harrow School in north-west London in 1799, aged only eight.[5] In a few years, Harrow's most famous student arrived: George Gordon, Lord Byron. Byron was three years older than Chandos, and became an influence on the younger boy. Byron's time at Harrow was characterised by a state of almost permanent insurrection, in which the charismatic young lord was a perpetual ringleader. Student unrest was almost a tradition at Harrow, having been sparked as early as 1771, when the Reverend Samuel Parr (1747–1825), who had worked as head assistant at Harrow, was not, despite his own expectations and those of his friends, appointed to the headmaster's job. Students petitioned and protested in favour of Parr, even destroying a carriage belonging to one school governor.[6] The new governor, Benjamin Heath, restored order and improved morale.

---

4. Huxley (2013), p. 51, that James Henry was first elected in 1802; R.G. Thorne, 'Leigh, James Henry (1765–1823), of Adlestrop, Glos. and Stoneleigh Abbey, Warws,' (1986), http://www.historyofparliamentonline.org/volume/1790-1820/member/leigh-james-henry-1765-1823#footnote1_1fpboxu accessed 1 December 2015.
5. David Hill Radcliffe, 'Leigh, Chandos, first Baron Leigh (1791–1850)', *Oxford Dictionary of National Biography*, Oxford University Press, 2004; online edn, Sept 2010 http://www.oxforddnb.com/view/article/16375, accessed 1 December 2015.
6. 'Schools: Harrow School', *A History of the County of Middlesex: Volume 1: Physique, Archaeology, Domesday, Ecclesiastical Organization, The Jews, Religious Houses, Education of Working Classes to 1870, Private Education from Sixteenth Century*(1969), pp. 299–302. URL: http://www.british-history.ac.uk/report.aspx?compid=22134 Date accessed: 03 September 2015.

Chandos: The Severest Satire on Lord Byron

His successor Joseph Drury (1785–1805) oversaw a prosperous period in which student numbers briefly exceeded those of Eton. Next came George Butler (1805–1829), against whom Byron directed a new blast of dissent, prior to his own departure from the school in the summer of 1805. The Harrow poems in Byron's first published volume of verse, *Hours of Idleness* (1807, when the poet was only 19) reveal that while Byron greatly valued school friendships, he strongly resented many features of the official modes of education.

The poem "On a Change of Masters at a Great Public School" (July 1805) was aimed at Butler.

> Where are those honours, Ida! Once your own,
> When Probus fill'd your magisterial throne?
> As ancient Rome, fast falling to disgrace,
> Hail'd a barbarian in her Caesar's place,
> So you, degenerate, share as hard a fate,
> And seat Pomposus where your Probus sate.
> Of narrow brain, yet of a narrower soul,
> Pomposus holds you in his harsh control:
> Pomposus, by no social virtue sway'd,
> With florid jargon, and with vain parade;
> With noisy nonsense, and new-fangled rules,
> Such as were ne'er before enforced in schools.
> Mistaking pedantry for learning's laws,
> He governs, sanction'd but by self-applause...[7]

The official education imparted at Harrow seems to have been an unwelcome interruption to Byron's rambles with friends through the neighbouring countryside, and his performances in school theatricals.

> Again I revisit the hills where we sported,
> The streams where we swam, and the fields where we fought;
> The school where, loud warn'd by the bell, we resorted,

---

7. *The poetical works of Lord Byron* (Geoffrey Cumberlege, Oxford University Press, edition of July 1904 reset in 1945, reprinted 1950), p. 9.

> To pore o'er the precepts by pedagogues taught...
> I once more view the room, with spectators surrounded,
> Where, as Zanga, I trod on Alonzo o'erthrown;
> While, to swell my young pride, such applauses resounded,
> I fancied that Mossop himself was outshone:
> Or, as Lear, I pour'd forth the deep imprecation,
> By my daughters of kingdom and reason deprived;
> Till, fired by loud plaudits and self-adulation,
> I regarded myself as a Garrick revived...[8]

Byron did, however, imbibe a life-long passion for ancient literature at Harrow. *Hours of Idleness* includes several poems which are translations from Anacreon, as well as a piece from Aeschylus' *Prometheus Bound*. They exhibit his typical strength, agility, and command of the constraints of both the Greek and the English. It is not surprising that Byron also translated poems by the Roman love poets Catullus and Tibullus. These writers developed a persona of the hapless lover at the mercy of his mistress, a type with eternal appeal to the young in love.

It is clear that Byron was a natural leader at Harrow, and one tradition is that Chandos was his "fag" there: a junior boy who did the older boy's bidding.[9] Byron was not without a cruel streak, and part of the student unrest in the years following his departure was in protest at restrictions on the power of older students to beat others as they saw fit. This suggests that Byron, in his time, had enjoyed and approved of wielding the power of corporal punishment.[10]

---

8. From "On a Distant View of the Village and School of Harrow on the Hill" (1806), *Poetical Works* (195), pp. 11–12. Henry Mossop (1729–1773) was an Irish actor who featured in the role of Zanga in the tragedy *The Revenge* (1721, by Edward Young). David Garrick (1717–1779) was the actor and theatre manager most associated with the eighteenth-century English stage.
9. Macdonald (2004), p. 157, giving no reference. Information possibly from article by Hélène Leigh (Lady Frances Hélène Leigh, d.s.p. 1909, wife of Francis Dudley Leigh, third Lord, 1855–1938), "Stoneleigh Abbey," in Alice Dryden, *Memorials of Old Warwickshire* (London, 1908), p. 29.
10. "Schools: Harrow School," *A History of the County of Middlesex: Volume 1: Physique, Archaeology, Domesday, Ecclesiastical Organization, The Jews, Religious Houses, Education of Working Classes to 1870, Private Education from Sixteenth Century* (1969), pp. 299–302. URL: http://www.british-history.ac.uk/report.aspx?compid=22134 (Accessed: 25 November 2015).

Even at the time, some liberal commentators expressed concern about the institutionalised violence of the public (that is, private) school system. The Reverend Sydney Smith (1771–1845), reviewing a new book in 1809, protested about the cruelty involved.

> "At a public school (for such is the system established by immemorial custom), every boy is alternately tyrant and slave. The power which the elder part of these communities exercises over the younger, is exceedingly great—very difficult to be controlled—and accompanied, not infrequently, with cruelty and caprice."[11]

Indeed, Smith argued that the fact that it was almost exclusively the older boys who had responsibility for moulding the younger ones, which caused the great evil here.[12] Smith concluded that in many cases, such influence had a profoundly bad effect on later character:

> "Submission to tyranny lays the foundation of hatred, suspicion, cunning, and a variety of odious passions."[13]

Smith dismissed the claim that public schools afforded students a wider knowledge of the world. He argued that men who had not experienced this supposed benefit

> "…have probably escaped the arrogant character so often attendant upon this trifling superiority; nor is there much chance that they have ever fallen into the common and youthful error of mistaking a premature initiation into vice for a knowledge of the ways of mankind."[14]

In concluding his broadside against the public schools, Smith touched upon the reason why many parents sent their sons to them. It was "the

---

11. Rev. Sydney Smith, "English Public Schools," review of *Remarks on the System of Education in Public Schools* (apparently published anonymously; London: Hatchard, 1809), in *Essays Social and Political* (first and second series in one volume) (London: Ward, Lock and Co., n.d. but from internal evidence early twentieth century), 67–74, p. 68.
12. Smith (1809), p. 73.
13. Smith (1809), p. 68.
14. Smith (1809), p. 69.

opportunity, of which so many parents are desirous, of forming great connections for their children."[15] This was no doubt the object of James Henry and Julia-Judith Leigh in sending Chandos to Harrow. The one connection we know he made—with Byron—is unlikely to have been exactly what they had in mind.

After leaving Harrow, Chandos matriculated at Christ Church, Oxford, in 1810.[16] This meant that he satisfied the conditions for entry into the university. Apparently he only attended for some terms before leaving Oxford for good. It is not clear why Chandos never completed his degree. It may have had something to do with events at Stoneleigh.

Throughout his career from about 1814 onwards, Chandos cultivated a persona of a retiring, literary, family man, dedicated to the promotion of progressive, if not radical, reform. Apart from holding the largely symbolic position of High Sheriff of Warwickshire in 1825, he is not known to have taken part in public life. Even after his elevation to the peerage in 1839—the ultimate aim of all Julia-Judith's manoeuvring—Chandos made no contribution to Parliament. *Hansard's* official account of his activity in the House of Lords, from his elevation until his death in 1850, registers zero.[17]

Wherever Chandos was based in the period 1810–1814, he must have been accumulating life experiences which he was to exploit in his first volume of poetry, *The Island of Love*, published in 1812.[18] Chandos' early verse imitates Byron's *Hours of Idleness*. Both volumes emphasised the youth of their authors. Typically, Byron was self-conscious about being classed among the "mob of gentlemen who write:" It is not clear that Chandos had any sense that this could be embarrassing.[19]

---

15. Smith (1809), p. 73.
16. David Hill Radcliffe, "Leigh, Chandos, First Baron Leigh (1791–1850)," *Oxford Dictionary of National Biography*, Oxford University Press, 2004; online edn, Sept 2010 http://www.oxforddnb.com/view/article/16375 (Accessed 1 December 2015).
17. High Sheriff: *The London Gazette*, 5 February 1828, issue 18105, p. 203. Zero contributions to Parliament: *Hansard, 1803–2005, People*: "Mr Chandos Leigh, June 27, 1791—27 September, 1850: Contributions by year: 0 in total." http://hansard.millbanksystems.com/people/mr-chandos-leigh (Accessed 29 November 2015).
18. Anonymous obituary of Chandos in *Gentleman's Magazine* (NS 34, December 1850), 656–658: http://spenserians.cath.vt.edu/BiographyRecord.php?action=GET&bioid=35175 (Accessed 29 November 2015).
19. Byron (1950), p. 1. Byron's phrase recalled Alexander Pope, "The mob of gentlemen who wrote with ease," satirising the Caroline wits (among the targets of his *Imitations of Horace*, Ep. I, *to*

As well as the overall enterprise, several individual poems of Chandos' seem to be in direct recollection of Byron's. There is a reference to Aeschylus' *Prometheus Bound,* which we have seen Byron took as the basis for one poem. Versions of Catullus' Lesbia poems appear in both: both Byron and Chandos undertook a version of the most famous of these, to Lesbia's sparrow (Byron: "Translation from Catullus," Chandos: "To Miss — on the Death of Her Canary Bird"[20]). There are also some references to Harrow.

As clear, however, as Byron's influence is upon Chandos' work, just as glaring is the major difference: that Byron, even at his most pedestrian, displays a skill, a power, an ease which entirely escapes his imitator. The scientist and lawyer Henry Brougham (1778–1868, eventually revealed to have been the "Scotch reviewer" of the *Edinburgh Review)* complained, not unjustly, of the uniformity of tone exhibited in *Hours of Idleness.*

> "[Byron's] effusions are spread over a dead flat, and can no more get above or below the level, than if they were so much stagnant water."[21]

If it was a failing in Byron, it was considerably worse in the case of Chandos. Time and again, Chandos' verse plods just below the threshold of memorability. It is disfigured by the kind of awkward rhymes on which Byron loved to play, but which are no joke in Chandos (e.g. rhyming "Erin" with "endearing".[22]) Chandos is laboured where Byron is easy. In tone, also, Byron frequently shows a sense of humour, often at his own expense (as in his self-mocking account of his acting ability): Chandos is without a sense of the ridiculous.

Early reviewers naturally spotted Chandos' model. An anonymous reviewer in the *Champion* saw the world-weariness of the *Poems* as cynical in the style of Byron. Interestingly, this reviewer noted that Chandos,

---

Bolingbroke (*The Works of Alexander Pope Esq.,* vol. IV (Satires), London: C. Bathurst, 1770), p. 157.
20. Byron (1950), p. 5; Chandos Leigh, *Poems of Chandos Leigh* (second edn., with additions), London: for W. Lindsell, 1818, p. 107.
21. Henry Brougham but at the time anonymous, "Art. II, *Hours of Idleness: A Series of Poems, Original and Translated.* By George Gordon, Lord Byron, a Minor," *The Edinburgh Review, Or Critical Journal,* Vol. XI, October 1807-January 1808, pp. 285–289, 285.
22. Chandos Leigh, *Poems* (1818), p. 173.

in quasi-confessional mode, appeared to have more to be confessional about than many a noble poetaster.

> "Assuredly some of these [gentlemen poets] owned to more crimes than they were entitled to, and talked of a self-abasement which was only verse-born. We fear, however, from many passages in the book before us, that Mr. Leigh has seen quite enough of dissipation to justify a good deal of honest regret, and a little of gentlemanly moroseness."[23]

Chandos seemed to be out-Catullus-ing Byron in hinting at past affairs and disgraces. He used the word "crime" repeatedly:

> My fair confessor many were my crimes…
> ("Dedicatory Stanzas: to Mary"[24])

> No conscious guilt disturb'd my rest at night.
> May no sad contrast to these happy times
> Add weight to woe, or aggravate my crimes.
> ("Verses Written Upon Leaving Harrow School"[25])

> My crime was *then*—the same as *now*. ("The Deserted Friend"[26])

> Fame, fortune, genius sacrificed to crime… ("The Lament, Written After Seeing *Timon of Athens* Performed at Drury-Lane Theatre, 1816"[27])

It is possible that this is merely poetic, recalling the Latin term *crimen*, which meant any kind of wrongdoing, not necessarily something against the law. A *crimen*, in a Roman literary context, could be any kind of accusation, charge, reproach. In erotic authors, such as Propertius and

---

23. Anonymous review of Leigh, *Poems. The Champion* 28 September 1817, p. 309. http://spenserians.cath.vt.edu/CommentRecord.php?action=GET&cmmtid=7456 (Accessed 29 November 2015).
24. Chandos Leigh (1818), 9–19, p. 19.
25. Chandos Leigh (1818), 41–44, p. 44.
26. Chandos Leigh (1818), 57–60, p. 58.
27. Chandos Leigh (1818), 160–164, p. 152.

Ovid, it is strongly associated with unlawful sex.[28] Chandos, like Byron, had certainly had relationships with girls and women from a young age. Byron's sexual career was well advanced by the time *Hours of Idleness* appeared. For Chandos, a key experience was a long affair with a girl called Jane Rhodes, 14-years-old at the start, whom he knew in London from 1814 onwards. As "courtesan" is so archaic, we lack a suitable word for such women. Jane Rhodes was a sex worker, based at the Berkeley Street, Piccadilly, premises of one Mrs Porter. This lady at one time also employed the famous Harriette Wilson, mistress of many distinguished men including the Duke of Wellington. From the point of view of Mrs Porter and Jane Rhodes, Chandos represented a source of income. Jane's madam drew up a contract under which Chandos was committed to paying her certain sums, contingent on his inheritance and other events.[29]

This form of financial arrangement was an accepted part of the relationships which aristocratic, or would-be aristocratic men formed with available women. It provided a living for the woman who was likely to be rejected by large sections of society, including potential husbands, but it also tied her to the man under whose "protection" she was said to be. Harriette Wilson's memoirs make it clear that sometimes the impetus came from the woman or girl, and sometimes, as a form of inducement, from the man.

Wilson describes Lord Deerhurst (later the Earl of Coventry) as offering a settlement of 300 pounds a year to her young sister Sophia, on the condition that if proof of Sophia's "inconstancy" was established, the payout would be reduced to 100 a year. Sophia was at this time only 13.[30] She claims that one of her own lovers, John Ponsonby (Viscount Ponsonby, the cousin of Byron's lover Lady Caroline Lamb), offered her a provision of 200 pounds per year, for the remainder of her life. Really in love with Ponsonby, who was married, she rejected the offer, tearing up the document and throwing it out of his coach window:

---

28. See, e.g., *Crimen Amoris* (Propertius 2 (3), 30, 24; Ovid *Met.* 9, 24).
29. Hampson (2004), p. 180.
30. *Harriette Wilson's Memoirs* (selected and edited with an introduction by Lesley Blanch) (first published by Joseph Stockdale in 1825; London: Century Publishing, 1985). Sophia's settlement: p. 108. Her age: p. 92.

"'I am no liar, Ponsonby,' said I; 'and when I most solemnly declare to you that I will never accept of any annuity from you, unless you were to become so rich as to make one without the slightest inconvenience to yourself or your family—I hope you will believe me.'"[31]

Some time later, Wilson's sister Sophia took the initiative in proposing an arrangement to Colonel William Berkeley. He reacted angrily:

"Do you fancy me then so humble and so void of taste, as to buy with my money the reluctant embraces of any woman breathing? Do you think I cannot find friends who have proved their affection, by the sacrifices they have made for me, that I should give my money to buy the cold-blooded being who calculates, at fifteen years of age, what the prostitution of her person ought to sell for?"[32]

Chandos, whose own income was not of ducal proportions, entered into an arrangement which paid Jane an annuity of 60 pounds during the joint lives of Chandos, Jane and James Henry Leigh, payable twice a year, on 8 January and 8 July. On the death of James Henry and the consequent succession of Chandos to the estate of Stoneleigh, the annuity would rise to 300 pounds.[33]

From the point of view of a Harriette Wilson or a Jane Rhodes, these payments, and often the provision of a home, represented a living wage earned through the provision of companionship and sex. There was also a pretence of quasi-married status. Chandos appears to have followed custom in allowing, or possibly obliging, Jane Rhodes to call herself Mrs Chandos Leigh. Harriette Wilson's sister Amy was called, at times, Mrs Sydenham after her lover's name. Another sister, Fanny, took the name of Mrs Parker, at the insistence of her new lover Colonel Parker. As "Mrs Chandos Leigh", Jane was removed from Chandos' box at the *Theatre Royal*, in May 1814[34] (Harriette Wilson indicates that boxes at the

---

31. Wilson (1985), p. 117.
32. Wilson (1985), p. 144.
33. Hampson (2004), p. 180.
34. Hampson (2004), p. 181.

theatre and opera were a key location in which the demi-monde women met potential lovers: "At the opera I learned to be a complete flirt."[35])

Protection arrangements also performed the secondary function of dissuading the woman from making trouble for the man. Chandos agreed to the arrangement not out of any generosity to Jane, but because he did not want his parents—and, later, his wife—finding out about her.

Hampson speculates that Chandos may have become involved with the demi-monde after a rejection by a local young woman in the Adlestrop district. A surviving letter, possibly from 1813, suggests that he had offered relationship status to an unknown recipient:

> "As for marriage with any being under the sun I can never think of it at present but our union will perchance be as lasting as that of marriage…all the enjoyments of the town are insipid unless I have a kind friend to participate in them with me…Be not angry at my proposal."[36]

Many middle-class young women would have been angry at such a proposal, because what Chandos had in mind was sex without the encumbrance of marriage: exactly what he eventually got with Jane Rhodes. It was a plan far more feasible in the crowds of London than at quiet Adlestrop. Here, as elsewhere, Chandos was indulging in the pursuits of the wealthy young noblemen of the Regency.

According to Jane Rhodes' version of events, she repelled Chandos' advances, and he responded by spreading damaging gossip.

> "He then spread a report that I was not formed properly and could not either be the wife or the mistress of any man in the general sense of the term."[37]

Such a report would amount to damaging Jane Rhodes' future currency in the sexual market: a loss of future earnings, as well as being offensive at the time. It added to her demands for compensation through

---

35. Wilson (1985): Amy 'Mrs Sydenham': p. 70. Fanny 'Mrs Parker': p. 181. Theatre and opera boxes: pp. 40–41.
36. Hampson (2004), p. 181.
37. Hampson (2004), p. 181.

blackmail, which persisted for many years. This emotional, legal and financial entanglement may well have influenced several of the *Poems*, in which women are depicted as deceitful. Seduction is often referred to, at times in a manner recalling the temptresses sketched by the great Elizabethan poet Edmund Spenser, in his epic *The Faerie Queene* (1590). Chandos' clear references to Spenser, and his intermittent use of the Spenserian stanza form, mean that he is considered to fall in the Spenserian tradition of English verse. This is perhaps the only channel through which his poetry has been, to some extent, preserved.[38]

Chandos was also writing for the London theatre in 1813. His prologue to *Lose No Time*, a new comedy at Drury Lane by the nobleman and fop Lumley Skeffington, was spoken by "Mr de Camp," no doubt a member of the noted theatrical family of that name.[39] Two poems are addressed to Maria Foote, "Miss Foote of Covent Garden Theatre." The second poem, "On her performance of Statira in the tragedy of Alexander the Great," is thus dated to June 1815, as it was in that month when Maria Foote, who was only 17, appeared in the role.[40] (In the same year, Maria became the mistress of that Colonel Berkeley whom we last met rebuffing Harriette Wilson's sister Sophia.)

The only other thing which we know for certain that Chandos was doing in the early months of 1814, was making moves towards the purchase of Byron's home, Newstead Abbey. Ever short of ready money, Byron planned for several years to sell his property. He wrote to his agent John Hanson:

> "My dear Sir/ — by all I hear — & some of it very tolerable authority — *Leigh* & not Claughton is the *real* purchaser — if so — he is well able to adhere to the contract and the only question is have we made good our title? Leigh has certainly *been here* with Mr C[laughton] — & his *own* people talk openly of it being for him the purchase was made — & from Mr C[laughton]'s asking

---

38. Useful collection of Spenserian writers compiled by David Hill Radcliffe at http://spenserians.cath.vt.edu/ (Accessed 1 December 2015).
39. Review in *The Universal Magazine*, vol. XIX, January-June 1813, p. 495.
40. Joseph Knight, "Foote, Maria [married name Maria Stanhope, countess of Harrington] (1797–1867)," rev. K. D. Reynolds, *Oxford Dictionary of National Biography*, Oxford University Press, 2004; online edn, May 2013 http://www.oxforddnb.com/view/article/9807 (Accessed 1 Dec 2015).

him frequently 'would he like this—that or the other done' I think there can be little doubt of it…"[41]

Peter Cochran has speculated as to whether Byron was correct in identifying Chandos Leigh as the purported purchaser, suggesting instead that since Claughton was connected by marriage with another man named Legh [sic], this may have been the source of error.[42] This, however, is unlikely, if only because Byron will have remembered Chandos from Harrow, even if they were not as close in succeeding years as Chandos would have liked.

Claughton (whether or not in concert with Chandos) did not proceed with this transaction, forfeiting his deposit, which may have been as high as £25,000.[43] Chandos is described in the notes to this letter as "a landed gentleman of considerable wealth," but in early 1814 Chandos himself had no wealth to speak of. Having to forfeit such a vast sum could well have been financially disastrous for the Leigh family.

Undoubtedly, in nurturing an ambition to purchase Newstead, Chandos was indulging his fantasy of not only imitating, but *being* Byron, as nearly as possible. Byron's editor remarks:

> "It is an interesting coincidence that Leigh, who was raised to the peerage in 1839, was not only rich but was also a poet, and an apparent admirer of Byron, for he owned a Phillips portrait of the author of *Childe Harold.*"[44]

It was no coincidence, but the sincerest form of flattery. There is little evidence that this feeling was reciprocated; Byron made no further mention of Chandos in his surviving letters.

---

41. Byron to Hanson, January-February 1st 1814. *Byron's Letters and Journals: "Wedlock's the Devil"* (ed. Leslie A. Marchand) (Harvard University Press, 1975), vol. 4 1814–1815, pp. 43–44.
42. Peter Cochran, review *Byron and Newstead* (John Beckett with Sheila Adey), Newark: University of Delaware Press, 2002. No page numbers; note 19. http://petercochran.files.wordpress.com/2010/03/john-beckett2.pdf (Accessed 29 November 2015).
43. J. V. Beckett with Sheila Adey, *Byron and Newstead: the Aristocrat and the Abbey* (University of Delaware Press, 2001), pp. 170, 174, 180.
44. Marchand, footnote 1 to letter Byron to Hanson, January-February 1st 1814. *Byron's Letters and Journals: "Wedlock's the Devil"* (ed. Leslie A. Marchand) (Harvard University Press, 1975), vol. 4, 1814–1815, p. 43.

Byron seems, however, to have conferred one great favour on his disciple. In 1815, embarking on his ill-fated marriage to Annabella Milbanke, he moved to Piccadilly. Chandos took over Byron's bachelor quarters at Albany, the prestigious apartment complex set back from Piccadilly.[45] There is a mythology around Albany, cultivated by Byron himself, and no doubt relished by Chandos. Lady Caroline Lamb wrote that she visited Byron at "the Albany," but Byron himself insisted that the name had no definite article. It was, therefore, like a private and luxurious town, not simply an hotel.[46] It was also, to the surprise of another of Byron's female visitors, infested with rats. Eliza Francis, who had more than one romantic encounter with Byron in 1814, as he prepared with mixed feelings for his marriage, reported: "It seemed to me wonderful that rats should invade the [sic] Albany, but I remarked, 'Well, at any rate you have no children here.'"[47]

The tenants at Albany were often the sons of nobles who left upon inheriting their titles. The politician George Canning lived at A5. Ironically, Henry Brougham, by now in Parliamentary rather than *Edinburgh Review* mode, occupied another "set" as the apartments were called.[48] A further benefit, from the point of view of James Henry and Julia-Judith, was that the Leigh family lawyer, Thomas Hill Mortimer, was also based at Albany. He was therefore on hand to exercise some control, or least surveillance, over Chandos.[49]

The authorised nineteenth-century version of Chandos' life, which is to be found in his entry in the 1909 *Dictionary of National Biography*, states that "while a young man"—and therefore, probably, in this London period—Chandos was part of the liberal and well-off circle which centred on Holland House. The Holland House group included Byron, his friend John Cam Hobhouse, and Sydney Smith. The most recent history of the group, however, makes no mention of Chandos, and it is

---

45. Hampson (2004), p. 180.
46. Bernard Beatty, "A2 at Albany: Byron in 1814," *The Byron Journal*, volume 39, issue 1, 2011, 1–10, p. 6.
47. Leslie A. Marchand, *Byron: A Portrait* (London: Futura Publications, 1976), p. 186.
48. Beatty (2011), pp. 5–6.
49. See, e.g., Thomas Hill Mortimer, "Albany," to Julia-Judith, 25 March 1814: SBTRO DR 18/17/40/13.

likely that the story of his involvement is yet more cover for Chandos' far less respectable preoccupations, with the theatre and Jane Rhodes.[50]

Albany may have afforded Chandos the setting in which he wrote the bulk of his *Fragments of Essays*, which appeared in 1816. The misogynist tendencies visible in the *Poems* are more pathological here. The opening essay, "On Women," begins:

> "We all know that there are women who pretend to great correctness of conduct, but who in reality have not much virtue.—They may be in outward appearance good; but their minds are perverted."[51]

Another essay, "On Intrigue", is similar in tone. This essay was dated 12 October 1814, so dates from the Jane Rhodes period.

> "If a woman (I do not speak here of the miserable race of prostitutes, under which appellation I include all who are not *ostensibly* virtuous) *intrigues* from selfish motives, take care to raise a disinterested affection in her mind for you, which can easily be done, otherwise she will lead you on to a precipice."[52]

In prose, as well as poetry, Chandos regularly lapses into cliché. His essay "On Extreme Delicacy of Feeling" turns into a diatribe against novel-reading for women, as leading to loose and undesirable conduct.[53] For 100 years, novel-reading had been a key point of judgment concerning women's behaviour from a male perspective. Byron is reported to have attributed Caroline Lamb's unusual and socially awkward behaviour to the same origin:

> "[Her] imagination was heated by novel reading which made her fancy herself the heroine of romance and led her into all sorts of eccentricities."[54]

---

50. Linda Kelly, *Holland House: A History of London's Most Celebrated Salon* (London: I.B. Tauris, 2013).
51. Chandos Leigh, *Fragments of Essays* (London: G. Sidney, 1816), p. 1. Hereafter Chandos Leigh (1816).
52. Chandos Leigh (1816), pp. 12–13.
53. Chandos Leigh (1816), pp. 16–18.
54. Thomas Medwin alleged that Byron made this comment, but Medwin did not meet Byron until

Jane Austen attacked this view as dated (and anti-feminist) by the time she came to revise *Northanger Abbey*, at about the same time as Chandos' essays appeared. Her defence of women's novel-reading is probably one of those passages which reflected the preoccupations of her youth, and for which she apologised—as for an old-fashioned preoccupation—in the "Advertisement" to the novel as it eventually appeared.[55]

The other notable feature of Chandos' *Fragments* is the attempt to appear well-read and scholarly, probably as compensation for not having completed studies at Oxford. Chandos wears his learning heavily, as he discusses such historical figures as Machiavelli, Henri IV of France, and Philip of Macedon. Many of the fragments seem entirely without point, except to demonstrate Chandos' recent reading. As it happened, the essay in English was at this period enjoying one of its golden ages: William Hazlitt, Charles Lamb, and the author with a deep family loyalty to Chandos, Leigh Hunt, were re-creating the vibrant art form which Addison had pioneered a century previously. In such company, Chandos' essays have justly been forgotten.

Occasionally, as in the *Poems*, Chandos strikes what appears to be a confessional note. The essay "On Hunting" is particularly interesting for its autobiographical hints.

> "I have gained no little celebrity in my time, in the athletic amusement of fox-hunting, so justly termed by the poet the 'mimicry of noble war.' But extreme weakness, arising, perhaps, from early dissoluteness, or a natural delicacy of constitution, now prevents me from delighting myself with the second great happiness of life [love]..."

Chandos rejects the prospect of taking up field sports again, as his health would not bear it.

1821, long after the Lamb affair. The quote suggests post-hoc rationalisation rather than Byron's own sentiments. Quoted in Deborah Lutz, introduction to Caroline Lamb, *Glenarvon* (1816; Valancourt Books, 2007), p. xiii.

55. "Advertisement, by the authoress, to *Northanger Abbey*", 1816: James Kinsley and John Davie (eds.), with an introduction and notes by Claudia L. Johnson, *Northanger Abbey, Lady Susan, The Watsons, Sanditon* (Oxford: Oxford World's Classics, 2003), before p. 5; note on p. 357.

> "Life has very *few pleasures*, but there is a mysterious horror that environs death. It is this horror which makes us rather 'bear the ills we have, than fly to others that we know not of.' It is this horror which darkens my brightest prospects, and gives an increased gloom to my hours of sickness."[56]

That Chandos recalled the hunting of his younger days is interesting from another viewpoint. In the evidence which would be brought forward in 1848–49, one of the Stoneleigh employees who had been closely associated with the alleged killings, was the gamekeeper Hay (Hayward/Haywood). Hay had been at the bridge on the fateful night (*Chapter 12*), and according to Richard Barnett, it was Hay who later shot and killed William Blissett, who had worked on the bridge foundations.[57]

Hay was a man of some celebrity in hunting circles. Charles James Apperley, author of cheery and florid works which detailed many of the hunts and hunting characters of the period, wrote that Hay had revived the sport in Warwickshire. "Nimrod", as Apperley called himself, met the Warwickshire hunt at Stoneleigh, then (19 December 1825) the seat of Chandos.

> "In society, the manners of Mr Hay are particularly mild and agreeable, but his conduct with his hounds is firm ... He addressed his brother sportsmen in a short but pithy speech, when on the point of finding his fox, and begged to explain to them the literal acceptation of those two little monosyllables, 'HOLD HARD!' *One* word to the wise has ever been esteemed sufficient; and *two* in this instance had a most happy effect; for no field has been better kept than Warwickshire since that hour, and much to its credit be it told."[58]

Clearly, Hay had maintained his position as keeper at Stoneleigh, and only increased his importance in the period after the bridge construction

---

56. Chandos Leigh (1816), pp. 35–36.
57. Griffin (1848), p. 51. Mary Draper's version alleged that Blissett was shot by "John Haywood and James Farden" (*Report* 1849, p. 18, column 1). Various sources refer to Haywood rather than Hay. There was also confusion because another stonemason was Alexander Hay, cross-examined as a witness on behalf of Chandos in 1849, doubtless to distract attention from the gamekeeper Hay: *Report* (1849), p. 28, column 2.
58. *Nimrod's Hunting Tours, Interspersed with characteristic anecdotes, sayings, and doings of sporting men, including notices of the principal crack riders of England* (London: M. A. Pittman, 1835), p. 281.

described in later chapters. The anecdote indicates that he was a forceful, indeed possibly menacing, man. Nimrod's implication is that Chandos was patronising the hunt at this period, even though in 1816 he had declared that his hunting days were over.

But what was wrong with Chandos' health? In 1816 he was only 25. Jane Rhodes would much later allege that his final illness was caused by his youthful "excesses."[59] This was Victorian code for sexually transmitted disease, and certainly Jane Rhodes would be likely to know.

Another writer in the period expressed concern about Chandos. This was none other than the Dr Samuel Parr, former teacher, who had been championed by the students at Harrow, as long ago as 1771. Parr was a political friend as well as a Harrow connection. After numerous career disappointments, Parr was given the living of Hatton in Warwickshire, less than ten miles from Stoneleigh.

By the early years of the nineteenth century, Parr, now retired, had become a Warwickshire institution. His literary and social contacts were extensive, particularly among Whig figures. Charles James Fox, until his untimely death in 1806, was a personal friend, and Parr's supporters believed that—yet another "what if?" in Parr's life—if Fox had become Prime Minister, he might have appointed Parr to a bishopric. Fox, however, never achieved the Prime Ministership, and Parr remained the curate of Hatton.[60] Regarding this fact as a shame was a kind of touchstone of political allegiance. The reliably liberal Sydney Smith concluded a review of an 1801 work of Parr's with a ritual statement of regret about it:

> "How painful to reflect, that a truly devout and attentive minister, a strenuous defender of the church establishment, and by far the most learned man of his day, should be permitted to languish on a little paltry curacy in Warwickshire!"[61]

---

59. Hampson (2004), p. 185.
60. Leonard W. Cowie, "Parr, Samuel (1747–1825)", *Oxford Dictionary of National Biography*, Oxford University Press, 2004 http://www.oxforddnb.com/view/article/21402 (Accessed 2 Dec 2015).
61. Smith, "Dr Parr's Spital Sermon," 1801, in Smith, *Essays Social and Political* (n.d.), 251–256, p. 256.

Yet it did not escape Smith, nor did he omit to point it out at length in a review in 1809, that Parr's written work was characterised by pomposity and small-town self-importance, which disfigured even his better pieces.[62] This might have afforded sufficient reason, leaving aside the political animus which he provoked, why Parr's career had fallen short of his ambition.

It was no doubt in his capacity as friend of all the Whig great and good, that Samuel Parr was patronised by James Henry Leigh. In 1813, on succeeding to Stoneleigh, James Henry sought out Parr's friendship.

> "[Parr] had also, in 1813, the happiness of acquiring an excellent neighbour and friend, in the late J. H. Leigh, Esq.; who, about that time, came into possession of the noble mansion and vast estates of Stoneleigh Abbey; and after his death another, in his son and successor, Chandos Leigh Esq.; of whom Dr Parr expressed his opinion in the following terms—'a lively companion, an elegant scholar, a zealous patriot, and an amiable and honourable man.' He often congratulated the friends of liberty in Warwickshire, on the support which their cause must derive from the residence among them of one, so ardently devoted to it, and possessing the influence, which rank and fortune always command; and most of all, when adorned and dignified by cultivated talent, and by pure and elevated character."[63]

Smith had found this kind of flattery of the great, in Parr's works, highly irritating, probably the more so in a writer who was on the same political side. It strikes the modern reader as grotesque. As always with Parr, it was partly political: "zealous patriot" and "friend of liberty" were Whig self-descriptors. Parr's gushing endorsement, therefore, probably means little more than that he and the Leighs flattered each other: Parr enjoyed all contact with the Whig rich, and the Leighs sought the authority which Parr lent in intellectual circles.

---

62. Smith, review of *Characters of the Late Charles James Fox*, by Philopatris Varvicensis [Samuel Parr], n.d. but Parr's work 1809. Smith, *Essays* (n.d.), 170–176, p. 174.
63. William Field, *Memoirs of the Life, Writings, and Opinions of the Rev. Samuel Parr, LLD* (London: Henry Colburn, 1828), Vol. II, Chapter X, AD 1816–1820, pp. 138–139. Reproduced at http://lordbyron.cath.lib.vt.edu/monograph.php?doc=SaParr.1828&select=II8 (Accessed 1 December 2015).

It is useful to examine what these Whig principles were, on which the Leighs and their associates so prided themselves. Conveniently, these were summarised in the toasts given at a dinner, held every year in the period 1820–1824, to celebrate Parr's birthday (Parr died in 1825). Those attending the feast included the Earl and Countess of Blessington (the Countess being the friend of Byron), James Henry (until his death in 1823) and Julia-Judith, Thomas Denman and his wife (Denman, yet to act for Chandos in the 1828 case, was on the rise as a celebrity Whig lawyer second only in prominence to Henry Brougham), and Mr West of Alscott (a connection by marriage of the Leighs). They drank to the following, among other goals:

"A patriot King and an uncorrupt Parliament;

The memory of Queen Caroline and her daughter [Caroline had died in 1821, and her daughter Charlotte, in childbirth, in 1817];

The memory of Charles Fox;

Liberty to subjects, and independence to nations;

The cause of Greece, South America, and the Peninsular;

May the Lion of Old England never crouch to Russian Bears or French Baboons;

Destruction, defeat and disgrace to all the members of the Holy Alliance…"[64]

The Holy Alliance was the grouping of Russia, Austria and Prussia, which served to restrain secular and republican movements in Europe in the period after the final defeat of Napoleon. This list indicates the global concerns of the Warwickshire Whigs.

---

64. John Nichols, "Toasts Given at the Celebration of Dr Parr's Birth-days 1820–24," *Gentleman's Magazine,* vol. 144, August 1828, p. 104.

For his own part, Chandos was keen to secure Parr's support for his literary work. He presented Parr with copies of his books, which Parr, with pathetic diligence, inscribed:

> "The gifts of the author, an ingenious poet, an elegant scholar, and my much esteemed friend. S. P."[65]

It was probably in 1817 that Parr wrote to James Henry with some concern about Chandos. During this year, Chandos had embarked on travels in Europe, accompanied by Philip Shuttleworth, later Bishop of Chichester, and of impeccably Whig opinions (toned down in later life[66]). In all probability, Shuttleworth was employed by James Henry and Julia-Judith to try to keep Chandos out of trouble on the continent.

> "I write to you with some haste; but you know very well my unfeigned solicitude for the intellectual improvement of Chandos. His travels, and the conversation of his enlightened comrade Mr Shuttleworth, have fortunately turned his mind towards the curious and valuable learning which is contained in Latin inscriptions…"

This was ironic, considering the history—of which presumably Parr knew absolutely nothing—of the Christopher stone. Parr goes on to recommend that Chandos study the inscriptions collected by Muratorius and Burman.[67] There is no suggestion that he ever took this up. Chandos wrote from Stoneleigh to Parr.

> "Will you do for me what you can in relation to my poems. I am anxious, very anxious, to bring out a second edition of my poems immediately, and therefore wish for an extensive sale; your recommendation would perform

---

65. No date, Parr to J. H. Leigh, in John Johnstone (ed.), *The Works of Samuel Parr, With memoirs of his life and writings, and a selection from his correspondence* (1828), vol. VII, Appendix, p. 314.
66. C. W. Sutton, "Shuttleworth, Philip Nicholas (1782–1842)," rev. M. C. Curthoys, *Oxford Dictionary of National Biography*, Oxford University Press, 2004 http://www.oxforddnb.com/view/article/25492 (Accessed 2 Dec 2015).
67. Parr to J. H. Leigh, p. 315.

wonders, perhaps you might recommend them at *Birmingham* [italics in original]..."

Chandos was keen to enhance his reputation within Warwickshire itself.

"I am endeavouring to sustain an elevated flight without approaching to bombast...Is it not too daring to study Aeschylus as a model? I bitterly regret, now, that I did not read when at Oxford. My politics must be offensive to [William] Gifford..."[68]

Eighteen months later, Chandos again sought Parr's support with an introduction to the leading philosopher (widely believed to be a political radical), Dugald Stewart.

"As I intended to leave Stoneleigh on Wednesday, I came over to Hatton for the purpose of requesting you to give me a letter of introduction to the celebrated Dugald Stewart, in case I set off for Edinburgh in June...The truth is, I want to get out of the mire in which the malevolent critic who attacked me in the B.C. last year has plunged me..."

Chandos proposes publishing a "satire" in response to the hostile reviewer, in an attempt to emulate Byron's broadside "English Bards and Scotch Reviewers" (1809). The offending criticism was probably an anonymous review of Chandos' poems which had appeared in the Tory journal, the *British Critic*, in April 1818. The reviewer was equally dismissive of Chandos' talents and his character, as displayed in the persona of the poems.

"Now we certainly have something better to do than to lecture Mr Chandos Leigh upon his 'crimes and vanities,' we should as soon think of lecturing him upon the marvellous doggrel [sic] which he has written, under the name of poetry."

---

68. 14 September 1817, Chandos to Parr. Correspondence at Parr *Works* (1828), vol. VII, Appendix, pp. 315–316.

Curiously, and in an echo of the earlier review which perceived something out of the ordinary in Chandos' profession of past misdeeds, this reviewer went on to use language which suggested mental tribulation in the poet.

> "The tone of this unhappy man's mind, seems to us so utterly depraved, that we have no doubt, that the wickedness he ascribes to his heart, are [sic] as natural to him as the weakness we find in his understanding…"

The reviewer claimed not to admire Byron's work, but admitted that a proof of Byron's talent was the fact that his works had "blinded so many to the total want of good feelings" they betrayed. Chandos, however, in the reviewer's opinion, had not the talent which led readers to overlook Byron's moral failings.

> "That [Chandos' works] resemble the original [Byron's] is, perhaps, the severest satire that can be passed upon his lordship."[69]

That this devastating review had caused Chandos consternation is not surprising. It is unlikely that Parr was able to offer any compensating support, other than to point out that the *British Critic*'s attack was partly political, with Byron the ultimate target, and Chandos only collateral damage in the liberal cause.

Finally, Chandos sought information from Parr on a surprisingly theological topic. Here, perhaps for the only time, he anticipated rather than imitated Byron, whose theological discussions with Dr James Kennedy, in Greece during 1823, afterwards formed a curious side-light in Byroniana.[70]

> "Will you be kind enough to inform me what are the *most* powerful and strongly argumentative discourses on the '*atonement*', as I should like very much to study them with attention."[71]

---

69. Review, "Art. IX, *Leigh's Poems*, Lindsell, 1818," *The British Critic*, vols 9–10, 1818, pp. 415–417.
70. William Maginn, review, "Dr Kennedy and Lord Byron," *Fraser's Magazine*, new series, vol. 2, No. VII, August 1830, pp. 1–9.
71. 12 March 1819, Chandos to Parr. Correspondence at Parr *Works* (1828), Vol. VII, Appendix, 316–317.

Parr's response is not recorded. The atonement, as understood in Christian theology, was a difficult concept. It means "at-one-ness," or reconciliation. It refers to the reconciliation of mankind, after the Fall, with God, through Jesus Christ. Beyond this basic point, various theories have differed; but the atonement was certainly a prominent feature of popular religion at this time.

Partly in reaction against the comfortable "natural religion" so prevalent in the eighteenth century, the early decades of the nineteenth saw a renewed preoccupation with the pressing call for redemption of fallen man, accompanied by more or less Calvinist overtones. One strand of this belief was eventually identified with the Evangelical movement. At its fringes, Evangelical thought touched, to a degree, even such unlikely subjects as Byron, who could never wholly cast off the Calvinist pessimism of his upbringing.[72] It may have been having an effect, also, on Chandos.

One possible reason why Chandos sought assistance with the topic may have been that he was troubled by guilt, and wanted to know whether, in orthodox theory, Christ's sacrifice on the cross served to redeem sinners even of the worst kind. Chandos' emphasis on his "crimes" could, really, refer to actual crimes which he had committed in the period.

One poem in particular seems to express grief for past actions: "The vision," which is worth quoting in full. The epigraph by Petrarch means "I mourn the wreck of years untimely spent," as it was rendered in an anonymous 1823 translation.[73] Britain was enjoying a Petrarch revival in the later eighteenth and early nineteenth centuries; his themes of regret and desire were readily appropriated to a broadly Romantic context.[74]

---

72. Boyd Hilton, *The Age of Atonement: The Influence of Evangelicalism on Social and Economic Thought 1795–1865* (Oxford: Clarendon Press, 1988), pp. 4, 9–10, 29.
73. Published as "Sonnet from Petrarch," *The New Monthly Magazine and Literary Journal*, vol. VII (original papers) (London: Henry Colburn and Co., 1823), p. 451.
74. Edoardo Zuccato, *Petrarch in Romantic England* (Basingstoke and New York: Palgrave Macmillan, 2008), p. ix. http://www.palgraveconnect.com/pc/doifinder/view/10.1057/9780230584433 (Accessed 28 June 2016 accessed 28 June 2016.

I'vo piangendo I miei passati tempi. Pet[rarch] Son[net]. LXXXVI.[75]

When comfortless sorrow diseases the soul,
As the death-watch is heard in the noon of the night;
When no longer inflam'd by the mirth of the bowl;
I slumber in sadness, or wake in affright.
Shame, anguish, despair, storm my bosom within;
What spectre still haunts me? The daemon is sin.
How haggard his visage, how fearful his brow,
How wither'd his aspect of gaiety now.
Lo! The moon sheds her tremulous beams through the room,
Till visible darkness attempers the gloom.
Now I see that the spectre a mirror displays,
Where pass in succession my earlier days.
O those of my boyhood, I ne'er can forget,
Unclouded by sorrows, untainted as yet,
They rapidly fly; too beauteous to last—
Compar'd with the present, how happy the past.
Next others succeed, of ambiguous hue,
False pleasures I follow,—I fancy them true;
Th'illusion continues deceitfully vain,
Till reflection converts even pleasure to pain.
The languor of sickness, the pangs of remorse,
O'erspread my wan cheeks, weaken reason's full force.
Decay'd is my memory, *conscience* alone
Revives the remembrance of days that are gone.
The charms that illude [sic] me, at length disappear,
Still, still must I follow the same mad career?
No! convinc'd of my sins, I regard them with dread,
There *is* hope to the sinner, the spectre has fled.

---

75. Numbering of Petrarch's poems is, it turns out, no straightforward business. This sonnet has also been numbered as XX; in some manuscripts it is numbered as poem 361, in others 365: Teodolinda Barolini and H. Wayne Storey (eds.), *Petrarch and the Textual Origins of Interpretation* (Columbia University Press, 2007), p. 112.

The references in this poem, as in the essay on hunting, suggest severe depression, even suicidal thoughts. Chandos' health problems — dating from this period — may have been mental, and his relatives may well have been conscious of the mental illness which troubled the final decades of Edward, the previous Lord Leigh. His family will also have recalled the depression and suicide of Chandos' maternal grandfather, Thomas Twisleton.

Byron, too, in the period 1815–1816, was believed by some — including his wife — to be suffering from what was termed "insanity."[76] It is ironic that while Byron, Chandos' idol and life model, was vilified for his perceived moral depravity, he was never formally charged with murder. If Chandos was experiencing symptoms of mental illness, it seems that a sense of guilt about his past actions is likely to have contributed to his mental oppression.

---

76. Marchand (1976), p. 211.

CHAPTER EIGHT

A Death's Head

"It was resolved, that it is the opinion of this committee, that George Leigh, esquire, the claimant, hath not made out his claim to the title and dignity of baron Leigh of Stoneley, as claimed by his petition."

The House of Lords Privileges Committee, 1829[1]

Having examined the history and persona of the incumbent of Stoneleigh, it is time to return to the hearings of 1829, from which Chandos was so conspicuously absent. The strength of the evidence in favour of the previous existence of the Christopher stone was covertly admitted even by Chandos Leigh's legal team. In cross-examining Gregory Roberts, whose evidence so thoroughly contradicted that of his brother the Reverend James, Thomas Denman asked whether Gregory Roberts remembered a "death's head or an armorial bearing" on the Christopher stone. Roberts thought there was some kind of ornament, but would not specifically identify it. Causton comments:

> "Throughout the whole of the examinations the Common Sergeant [Denman] appeared extremely desirous to decorate the monument with a *death's head*, which would have been heraldically significant of a *total extinction of that branch of the family* in the party whom it commemorated."[2]

Evidence supporting this heraldic significance of the death's head, as understood in the early nineteenth century, is to be found in the cheerfully named "Our Monthly Crypt" column of *The Monthly Magazine*,

---

1. Leigh (1834), vol. II, p. 288.
2. Leigh (1834), vol. II, p. 231, note.

or British Register, from 1840. The writer, describing an ancient embroidered napkin, depicting heraldic symbols of many families associated with Henry the Seventh, notes:

> "The death's head is an appropriate emblem of the Lancastrians being in the direct line utterly extinct…"[3]

If Gregory Roberts, or anyone else, had testified to recalling a death's head on the monument, it is clear that Denman would have been satisfied. That is, he would have been happy to concede the monument's existence, if he could have been sure that its inscription certified the extinction of any other claim.

For his part, Sir James Scarlett, in summing up, appeared indulgent, even generous, rather than triumphant. He was prepared to allow that people might have been in error, mistaking other monuments in the church for the putative Christopher stone. Scarlett himself, no doubt intentionally, went on to create more of the same kind of confusion:

> "[Scarlett] thought that when the church was rebuilt, *it was very probable that some tablet containing an account of donations might [have been] removed from the South wall* [italics in Causton's text for emphasis]."

This was disingenuous, as there were monuments in the church which recorded donations from past village benefactors, but these were agreed to have been on the north wall. The only element which Scarlett clearly stated to have been a deliberate fabrication was the allegation that Julia-Judith Leigh had supervised the monument concealment:

> "The whole story [of the cellar transactions] was a perfect fabrication."

Again, this cautious approach implies that Scarlett was, at the very least, prepared to admit the possibility of the monument's former

---

3. Camilla Toulmin (1812–1895, miscellaneous writer), "Our Monthly Crypt: Description of a piece of ancient damask, in the possession of W. G. Colchester, Esq.", *The Monthly Magazine, or British Register*, vol. IV, July-December 1840, pp. 316–319, p. 318.

existence, although not of its criminal suppression by the Leighs.⁴ Following his summing-up, Scarlett called only two witnesses against the claim by George Leigh. The first was Julia-Judith herself. Julia-Judith, in her deposition, had outlined her close relationship with "her late uncle, the Reverend Thomas Leigh."⁵ Under examination, her focus was on the visits to the church with the Reverend Thomas.

> **Denman:** Was there any monument in the church to the memory of Christopher Leigh?
> **Julia-Judith:** Certainly not.
> **Adam:** Did Mr [Thomas] Leigh call your attention to Mr Webster's monument at all?
> **Julia-Judith:** Not at all.⁶

This was surprising, since Julia-Judith had, in her deposition, described at some length the other church monuments, such as Humphrey Howe's. She went on:

> **Julia-Judith:** I saw many inscriptions lettered in the church; *charities and gifts of different kinds were lettered in black upon a dirty white ground* [italics in Causton's text]; the church was in a most shameful condition.⁷

Here, Julia-Judith's description of the "black letters upon a dirty white ground" coincided with the recollections of many witnesses about the Christopher stone. Mary Iorns/Irons/Hiorns had described it as of "a lightish stone, with black letters."⁸ William Dee had called it "a dingy white ... as if time or dust had damaged it."⁹ Thomas Hancock had called it "of a light color [sic], not white."¹⁰ Richard Eaton had described it as

---

4. Scarlett summing-up, Leigh (1834), vol. II, pp. 248–250.
5. Julia-Judith Leigh deposition: Leigh (1834), vol. II, pp. 250–253, note.
6. Questioned by Denman: p. 253. By Adam: p. 255.
7. Julia-Judith Leigh deposition: Leigh (1834), vol. II, pp. 252–3, note; cross-examination: pp. 250–257, p. 255.
8. Leigh (1834), vol. II, p. 121.
9. Leigh (1834), vol. II, p. 129.
10. Leigh (1834), vol. II, p. 139.

"a kind of dirty white."[11] Causton did not think it was inadvertent that Julia-Judith echoed the colour description of so many witnesses for the monument's existence. He viewed it as a tactic to give the witnesses the benefit of the doubt, in a pseudo-generous move parallel to Scarlett's in summing up.

> "It was Mrs Leigh who thrust into her evidence the 'black letters upon a dirty white ground:'…This was a judicious adaptation of a probable fiction to suit the particular description of the claimant's witnesses: to give them credit for a general truth, and thus to conquer by the stratagem of a suppositious inscription…"[12]

Only one other witness for the Leigh family, Thomas Hill Mortimer, was called to give evidence, but a small number had provided depositions. That Julia-Judith's deposition resembled other Leigh team statements was no accident. In the protracted lead-up to the Lords hearings, Thomas Hill Mortimer had carefully orchestrated the Leigh witnesses' depositions. This is clear from a letter he wrote from his Albany offices to Chandos, then at Stoneleigh, in December 1827, when George Leigh was seeking a Chancery ruling to support a thorough search of the abbey for the monument.

> "I have prepared sketches of all the affidavits that I think will be necessary for I think even your own affidavits denying there being any such Monument (as is pretended) in your House ought to be sufficient to discharge [with] no deed obtained—but I shall take care that all their Allegations are denied in which there is no difficulty…"[13]

That Mortimer essentially drafted the depositions accounts for the fact that they bear a strong family resemblance to one another. Chandos himself, in his noticeably short and circumspect statement, wrote that he did not believe there had ever been a Christopher stone.[14] Charles

---

11. Leigh (1834), vol. II, p 162.
12. Leigh (1834), vol. II, p. 400.
13. Mortimer to Chandos, 14 December 1827, SBTRO DR 18/17/52/9.
14. Leigh (1834), vol. II, p. 289.

Woodcock of Coventry, "gentleman", who said he had looked in the Stoneleigh cellars in company with Chandos and his butler, stated that he did not believe there had been a monument.[15] George Jones Snr, who would later be alleged to have had a direct role in the monument's criminal suppression, did not mention much about the bridge project discussed in later chapters, for which he had been employed in the first place. No doubt prompted by Mortimer, Jones focused instead on the cellar redevelopment.

> "[Witness deposed that] in the month of November 1813, he received orders to fit up for port wine and claret two cellars at the North end of Stoneley Abbey, and some masons were immediately employed to prepare stones for making the necessary divisions or catacombs, and as soon as the newly fitted cellars were completed the port and claret were removed...and the second cellar from the servants' hall was fitted up with stone catacombs instead of binns, and is still continued to this day as a white wine cellar...He is quite positive that no monument or monumental stone whatever was in any of the cellars at that time."[16]

Jones' deposition makes clear that a number of masons were employed on the cellar works.

The Reverend Theophilus Leigh Cooke (1776–1846) made a deposition on behalf of the Leigh family. He was the vicar of Beckley in Oxfordshire, and son of Jane Austen's godfather, the Reverend Samuel Cooke of Great Bookham in Surrey. It is difficult to avoid the impression that he made his deposition in a spirit of flattery to his great Leigh relatives: he was a nephew of the Reverend Thomas Leigh's late wife Mary.[17] Cooke had visited Stoneleigh in the autumn of 1806 (no doubt part of the procession of relatives which had, in the summer, included the Austen women). He had visited again, frequently he said, in the period up to 1813, and

---

15. Leigh (1834), vol. II, p. 290.
16. Leigh (1834), vol. II, pp. 293–294.
17. Cooke dates from Le Faye, *Chronology* (2013), Tree 7 on p. 734; Samuel Cooke Jane Austen's godfather: p. 66.

"He never saw in any part of the said church, except in the chancel thereof, any monument or tablet to the memory of any member of the Leigh family."[18]

Several other people provided depositions which stated only their non-recollection of the Christopher stone. Some deployed the O'Farrell approach (*Chapter 5*): that if the monument had existed, they must have seen and remembered it.[19] This category included the Reverend Thomas Cox, of Atherton Stower in Warwickshire, Edward Thornton Twycross, of Canley, and William Judd of The Hurst in Stoneleigh parish.[20] As indicated in *Chapter 5*, this category had also, of those Leigh witnesses actually cross-examined, included Richard Darley and Jonathan Soden.

Thomas Howlett, the Stoneleigh blacksmith, made a statement that he had no recollection of any monument other than that of Webster. He quoted his father, also in his time the village blacksmith, who had died in 1818, as saying that there had never been a monument as alleged. Causton, in his notes, commented that Howlett was known as "silly Tommy, the butt and jest of all the neighboring [sic] boys." Causton also pointed out that Howlett's father was unlikely to have supported his son's version of events. He gave as evidence the fact that John Perks, the gas engineer, recalled the elder Howlett being present in the Stoneleigh church in 1806, on the occasion when Julia-Judith and her children appeared in the carriage of her brother, the Lord Saye and Sele. It was on this occasion that various tradesmen were talking about the monument, "meaning that commonly called the Lancashire stone," as the source of information about the heir to the estate.[21]

The most substantial deposition made on behalf of the Leigh family was that of Thomas Hill Mortimer himself. Mortimer outlined his background: from 1798 onwards he had been the clerk of Mary Leigh's solicitor, Joseph Hill, and worked as his assistant until taking over the role as Leigh family solicitor. In October 1811 he spent some weeks at Stoneleigh to organize the estate accounts. He visited the church, and

---

18. Leigh (1834), vol. II, pp. 294–295.
19. See Chapter 5 Denial, note 8.
20. Leigh (1834), vol. II, pp. 295–297, 300.
21. Leigh (1834), vol. II, pp. 302–303. John Perks deposition at p. 303, note.

"saw a splendid monument to the memory of Duchess Dudley," as well as other Leigh monuments in the chancel. Thomas Hill Mortimer, rather strangely, stated that Richard Darley pointed out to him the interesting monument to Humphrey Howe. With some daring, he exploited Darley, as the acknowledged expert on the church, in a variant of the O'Farrell defence.

> "[Mortimer] saw no other monuments either in the chancel, vestry, or body of the said church to the memory of the Leigh family, and if there had been any such the said Richard Darley would no doubt have pointed out the same to deponent's notice."[22]

This was no doubt because he wanted to use the classical O'Farrell approach on his own behalf, in regard to the abbey cellars.

> "[Mortimer stated] that he had the full range of the said house and offices, and must have seen any monument if there had been one."

Mortimer, rather amusingly, spent much of his deposition outlining the background to the cellar alterations.

> "At the time he was taking an account of the contents of the said cellars he was struck with the unfitness for port wine of one of such cellars, in which a considerable quantity of port wine was deposited, deponent considering it too warm … the heat of the sun was very perceptible, and [the] cellar was in the day-time quite light without a candle."[23]

This was a little too obviously directed at the evidence of John Wilcox. Mortimer had been able to read some of the depositions provided by witnesses for George Leigh.[24] Wilcox had alleged that Julia-Judith had carried a candle to the cellar to supervise the interment of the Christopher stone: Mortimer was concerned to indicate that a candle would

---
22. Leigh (1834), vol. II, pp. 272–273, notes.
23. Leigh (1834), vol. II, p. 273, note.
24. Mortimer to Chandos, 14 December 1827. SBTRO DR 18/17/52/9.

The Missing Monument Murders

not have been necessary, with the implied corollary that Wilcox's whole allegation must be false.[25] Mortimer also attempted, at some length, to discredit Edward Baylis' evidence about the cellar changes.

By the fourteenth day of hearings (Thursday 11 June, 1829), the tone of the transcript seems tired.[26] The Lords had clearly had enough of this protracted case. Several final witnesses were called to provide documentary evidence of events such as the 1698 burial of Thomas, the son of Christopher Leigh and Constance Clent. Thomas Denman then announced what he considered to be the clinching argument against the claim of George Leigh. Roger Leigh of Haigh, in Wigan, the claimant's great-great-grandfather, had a child born in 1658. The parish records of Wigan showed the entry:

"12th March 1658, Elin. Daughr. of Roger Lee of Haighe."[27]

If Roger was the son of Christopher Leigh, who had been born in 1626, he is unlikely to have been born earlier than 1646. On this basis, Roger must have become the father of Elin[or] at the age of about 12. This was not entirely out of the question (as Denman seemed to imply), but it was most unlikely. Roger Leigh of Haigh continued to have children well into the 1670s. Parish records were produced which showed that a daughter Ester was born to Roger Leigh of Haigh in April 1677.[28]

These facts were a setback to the credibility of George Leigh's claim. His lawyer, William Adam, stated that it appeared that there were no fewer than three Roger Leighs in or about the parishes of Wigan, in the mid-seventeenth century. He suggested that further investigation should take place on the identity of these men.[29] The Lords were not inclined to give any more time for this. Nor were they receptive to Adam's suggestion

---

25. Summary of Wilcox deposition at Leigh (1834), vol. I, pp. 48–49. Verbatim version at vol. II, pp. 193–194, notes.
26. Leigh (1834), vol. II, p. 278.
27. William Ward, deputy registrar of the diocese of Chester, producing parish returns for Wigan: Leigh (1834), vol. II, pp. 281–283. 1696 burial of Constance (Clent) Leigh, and 1698 of Thomas Leigh: p. 279.
28. William Marsden, producing parish registers of Blackrod (in the parish of Bolton, four miles from Wigan): Leigh (1834), vol. II, p. 283.
29. Leigh (1834), vol. II, p. 284.

that he needed more opportunity to obtain and examine the bishop's transcripts for the relevant parishes, in order to cross-check the parish records.

The Lord Chancellor took this opportunity to mention that a Mr Banks had written to the committee to say that he could produce a document which would prove fatal to George Leigh's claim. This, the Lord Chancellor thought, might have been the parish evidence about Roger Leigh. Adam said "they [the claimant's team] were not afraid of Mr Banks."[30] Clearly in a rush to terminate proceedings, the Earl of Shaftesbury put the final question, and

> "It was resolved, that it is the opinion of this committee, that George Leigh, esquire, the claimant, hath not made out his claim to the title and dignity of baron Leigh of Stoneley, as claimed by his petition."[31]

It was with a certain amount of smugness that the *Gentleman's Magazine* of June 1829 reported the end of George Leigh's claim to Stoneleigh.

> "June 11 [1829]. The *Leigh peerage* case was this day decided in the House of Lords, by the rejection of the claim of Mr George Leigh…To prove the existence of [the Christopher stone], a vast number of witnesses were brought forward; but from the absurd and extremely contradictory testimony of those witnesses, and the examination of documentary evidence, it was clearly proved that no such monument could ever have existed, and that the alleged [first] marriage of Christopher Leigh was a mere fabrication."[32]

This was history as written by the victors. It forms a good example of the rhetorical practice of "poisoning the wells", or pre-emptively mischaracterising evidence in advance of any casual or unbiased observer having the chance to examine the facts for themselves. This view of the matter has persisted successfully to this day, as demonstrated by Norma

---

30. Leigh (1834), vol. II, p. 287. Lords resolution: p. 288.
31. Leigh (1834), vol. II, p. 288.
32. "Domestic Occurrences," in *Gentleman's Magazine* vol. 99, January-June 1829, p. 638. Accompanied by a footnote which recalls the letter from "Senex," in 1823, pointing out that the transcription of the Christopher stone was never, in the event, supplied to the magazine.

Hampson's 2004 dismissal of the claim, without apparent examination of the evidence I have described in this book.

In reality, the testimony of witnesses who recollected the Christopher stone had varied in details, understandably after the lapse of 20 years. But in essentials, which is to say its very existence, the number of witnesses alone was strong evidence of its having stood, until about 1811, on the south wall of the church. So far from it having been proven that no such monument could have existed, the weight of evidence was strongly in favour of its past existence.

This, then, was the end of 20 years of intriguing and consulting, of accumulating witnesses and researching parish records. We know nothing more of the claimant, George Leigh, apart from the date of his death, only a few years later. On 21 January 1834, it was reported in several outlets.

> "Mr George Leigh, claimant to the title and estates of the late Edward, lord Leigh of Stoneleigh."[33]

Being the failed claimant to Stoneleigh had consumed George Leigh's financial resources, and become his identity. It had also, in another manner, consumed the intellectual and emotional resources of Henry Kent Causton. To his annotated transcript of the proceedings, Causton appended a detailed analysis of the evidence. He was a printer, bookseller and stationer, not a lawyer or genealogist, but his reasoning and research are thorough and convincing.

Causton's particular condemnation was for Sir John Copley, Lord Lyndhurst. As Attorney-General in the mid-1820s, Copley had recommended further investigation of George Leigh's case. As Lord Lyndhurst, and Lord Chancellor, in 1829, Copley said that he never believed that the Christopher Leigh monument had existed.[34] In Causton's view, this turnaround was not only reprehensible in itself, but the final view was grossly unfair on the many witnesses who had given evidence of the monument's previous existence. It also failed to acknowledge that considerable doubt

---

33. *The Annual Register...for 1834*, vol. 76 (London, 1835), p. 207; same notice in *Gentleman's Magazine*, vol. I, new series/155 (London, January to June 1834), p. 341.
34. Leigh (1834), vol. II, p. 285.

remained about the issues. Doubt certainly persisted about the key matter: whether Christopher Leigh had, in fact, been married with children, prior to his marriage to Constance Clent in 1670. An agent called A. Manning had written in 1814 to George Leigh to report that he had found, at Combermere Abbey, evidence of a marriage of Christopher Leigh to a daughter of Sir George Cotton. He had found no evidence of children at the time of writing.[35] Manning later named the daughter as Penelope Cotton (as recorded in notes from the Attorney-General's first investigation in 1825).[36] This naming of the putative first wife as Penelope went to discredit Manning's initial claim. This is because the only Penelope Cotton known to history died in 1712, aged 77, unmarried. She was one of the eleven daughters of Sir Robert Cotton of Combermere (c.1635–1712).[37] There may have been a confusion with another daughter, Sydney, who married Nathaniel Lee (baptised 1655).[38]

Causton throws out, as a suggestion heard from someone with knowledge of the fact, that Christopher Leigh's first wife, born a Cotton, was previously married, and widowed, so bearing another name at her marriage.[39] This scenario would have created a whole new set of mysteries, and has not, to my knowledge, been pursued.

In addition to the matter of there having been several Roger Leighs, some further pieces of evidence were, at the time of the claim, cited against a first marriage. There was the pedigree of Leigh prepared by the heralds' visitations in 1682–83, and the notes by the antiquarian Peter Le Neve. These were cited in an article in the magazine *Retrospective Review*, possibly by the journalist and editor Henry Southern, which appeared in 1827, shortly before the Lords hearings.[40] The article summarised the claim and some of the key witness statements taken from the Attorney-General's investigation.

---

35. Leigh (1834), vol. I, p. 318, note.
36. Leigh (1834), vol. I, p. 320, note.
37. Leigh (1834), vol. I, p. 54, note. Eveline Cruickshanks/Richard Harrison, "Cotton, Sir Robert, 1st Bt (c. 1635–1712), of Combermere, Cheshire," in http://www.historyofparliamentonline.org/volume/1690-1715/member/cotton-sir-robert-1635-1712 (Accessed 2 December 2015).
38. John Burke, *A Genealogical and Heraldic History of the Commoners of Great Britain and Ireland*, vol. III (London, 1836), p. 316.
39. Leigh (1834), vol. II, p. 343.
40. *The Retrospective Review, and Historical and Antiquarian Magazine*, ed. Henry Southern and Nicholas Harris Nicolas, second series, vol. I, 1827, 505–511.

The Missing Monument Murders

Throughout the sixteenth and seventeenth centuries, professional heralds would undertake "visitations" to regional areas. Their task was to compile family trees of notable families, and confirm or reject claims of armorial bearings made by individuals or families. Their subsequent notes and reports formed an official record acceptable to formal investigations such as Privileges Committee inquiries. The relevant Warwickshire visitation of 1682–83 was undertaken by a team of heralds, and a number of "pedigrees", or confirmed family trees, were prepared and lodged in London.[41] The heralds cited the nephew of Christopher Leigh, Thomas the second Baron Leigh, as certifying that Christopher was married to Constance Clent, and had "Thomas Leigh, onely child, aet. circa 12, annor. 1683."[42] It should be noted, however, that this just implies that Thomas was the "onely" child of this marriage: it does not entirely rule out a previous marriage.

The other evidence produced in the article is that of the herald Peter Le Neve, afterwards Norroy King of Arms, one of the ancient herald titles of England.[43] In a 1694 manuscript, he noted the same marriage of Christopher to Constance, with the son Thomas "about 18 yrs old 1694."[44] In fact, Christopher's son Thomas, having been born in about 1672, the year of his father's death, was closer to 22 in 1694. Again, this evidence does not go to eliminate the possibility of an earlier marriage of Christopher Leigh. Both the visitation from 1682–83 and Le Neve's notes from 1694 are limited, and the latter in particular show errors. Le Neve described Christopher as the fourth, rather than the third, son of the first Lord Leigh (the four sons were Thomas IV, Charles, Christopher and Ferdinando). The sources for both the 1683 and 1694 information, to be sure, appear to be unaware of a first marriage of Christopher, but they do not rule it out. The heralds made every effort to collect correct

---

41. W. Harry Rylands (ed.), *The Visitation of the County of Warwick, Begun by Thomas May, Chester, and Gregory King, Rouge Dragon, in Hilary vacacon [sic] 1682. Reviewed by them in the Trinity vacacon following, and finished by Henry Dethick Richmond, and said rouge dragon pursuiv in Trinity vacation, 1683, by virtue of several deputations from Sir Henry St George, Clarence King of Arms* (ed. and published by The Harleian Society, 1911), pp. 10–12.
42. Pedigree recorded in Rylands (1911), pp. 10–12. Quoted in *The Retrospective Review, and Historical and Antiquarian Magazine*, ed. Henry Southern and Nicholas Harris Nicolas, second series, vol. I, 1827, p. 510.
43. http://www.british-history.ac.uk/report.aspx?compid=118256 (Accessed 19 November 2014).
44. Cited in article as Harleian MSS 5808 f. 102 (*Retrospective Review* (1827), p. 510.

information in their visitations, but even the family members interviewed did not always provide correct or complete accounts of the marriages and children of their relatives.

Causton dismissed as a polemic the anonymous *Retrospective Review* article, which canvassed these pieces of evidence.[45] The article's conclusion was certainly against the substance of George Leigh's claims, and its tone in producing the Le Neve evidence was triumphant, but it was hardly one which the Leigh family will have enjoyed reading. It quoted at considerable length from the evidence of John Wilcox about the cellar incidents. Clearly, Henry Southern, or whoever wrote the article, found himself fascinated with the bizarre nature of the allegations.

In the absence of positive evidence for a first marriage, it remained for Causton to examine the actual family history of George Leigh. There was no doubt that George Leigh's great-great grandfather was Roger Leigh of Haigh, one of the villages on the outskirts of Wigan.[46] His family was closely involved with that of Sir Roger Bradshaigh, of Haigh Hall near Haigh, particularly in coal mining ventures. Roger Leigh's grandson Robert Leigh became bankrupt in 1747. His possessions had included some property held under lease from the Bradshaigh family.[47] One property was particularly associated with Roger Leigh. This was a farm styled "fine Roger's or Captaine Legh's tenement" in the township of Haigh, which bore an L and R carved in stone over the door. This property was believed by some to have descended to Robert, the claimant's grandfather.[48] Causton was sceptical about this link. His own research found a 1727 document by an Alexander Leigh, aged over 80, describing a Haigh property, "widow Lee's tenement", in which he said that he had been born in or before 1639. Alexander said that his older brother Roger Leigh, the claimant's great-great-grandfather, had also been born there,

---

45. Leigh (1834), vol. II, p. 420–421.
46. George Leigh put forward his descent as follows: himself, George (bapt. Blackrod 1759); father James (bapt. Blackrod 1729–30); grandfather Robert (bapt. Blackrod 1707); great-grandfather James (bapt. Blackrod 1680); great-great-grandfather Roger (bapt. ?Stoneleigh, unknown date): Leigh (1834), vol. II, pp. 11–14.
47. Leigh (1834), vol. II, p. 434 (coal interests); 442 (bankrupt).
48. Leigh (1834), vol. II, pp. 448–449.

previous to 1639.⁴⁹ If this is the case, this Roger, definitely the claimant's ancestor, cannot have been a son of Christopher, who was born in 1626.

Where did this leave the Christopher stone? Causton concluded that it was set up in the mid-eighteenth century, probably at the instigation of Robert Leigh, by then in financial difficulties, and anxious to claim a link with Stoneleigh. He cited the evidence of the elder Job Jeacock, the Stoneleigh parish clerk (who died in 1822), that he remembered the monument to Christopher Leigh being brought to Stoneleigh. Jeacock was on record as recalling that there were objections to the setting up of the stone in the chancel, and a subsequent agreement to its being mounted on the south wall.⁵⁰ Causton argued, boldly, that the Leigh family's agreement to the setting up of the monument was evidence for their acceptance of the substance of its inscription, principally of the fact of Christopher's first marriage.⁵¹

One further piece of documentary evidence was produced, as late as 1849, to destroy, once and for all, belief in a first marriage of Christopher. This may, or may not, have been the potent document held by the equally mysterious Mr Banks, which the Lords committee had not the patience to examine in June 1829. If it was available in 1828 or 1829, however, it seems surprising that Thomas Hill Mortimer, or another agent of Chandos Leigh, did not produce it, as it would probably have extinguished the claim. Causton makes no mention of the document, so he seems to have been unaware of it, or possibly chose to ignore it.

This document was the summary of marriage licences issued by the Dean and Chapter of Canterbury, for August 1670.

"Aug 31 Christopher Leigh of Stoneley, co. Warwick Bach[elor] above 30, Constance Clent of Eudford [sic: sc. Radford] Sp[inster] about 23, with

---

49. Leigh (1834), vol. II, p. 452.
50. Leigh (1834), vol. II, p. 432. Source, curiously, the same Mr Warde of Leamington who was said by James Roberts to have made copies of all the church inscriptions: vol. II, p. 63.
51. Leigh (1834), vol. II, p. 433.

consent of her mother, a Widow: at Stoneley afs [=aforesaid] or [blank], co. Warwick."[52]

So Christopher Leigh was, officially, a bachelor at the time of his marriage to Constance Clent. He certainly was over the age of 30; in fact, he was 44, an elderly time to be entering the marriage state in the seventeenth century.

The Christopher stone, then, probably existed, but was probably a forgery. There seem to have been other strange pieces of evidence concocted at some point. These may have included a deed, dated 1 August 1670, supposedly between Christopher Leigh ('sometime of Stonleigh'), Henry Byrom, and Roger Leigh, assigning a repayment of money to Roger as the son of Christopher.

Even more curiously, a fragment of a marble tablet was said to be in the possession of a Mr Wood, of Manchester. This was said to have had the following inscription:

> "Ursula Legh
> ......and daughter of Christopher
> ......sister unto Christ. Guillam and
> ...lexd [sc. Alexander] Legh.   Buried...
> [Hebrew characters interspersed with some Greek]
> [A cross]
> Christopher Leigh, who Roger Leigh, brother of......
> Sir John Leigh, and son of Sir Thomas......
> Leigh, ... Lord Leigh."[53]

Why a forger would have gone to the trouble of inserting Hebrew and Greek characters in a memorial to Ursula Legh is unclear. A Mr Mozley, who acted as Consul at Liverpool for the Ottoman Empire, was

---

52. Scanned version of Canterbury marriage licences, http://www.ebooksread.com/authors-eng/canterbury-england-province-faculty-office/allegations-for-marriage-licences-issued-from-the-faculty-office-of-the-archbish-tna/page-17-allegations-for-marriage-licences-issued-from-the-faculty-office-of-the-archbish-tna.shtml (Accessed 28 June 2016). Slightly more complete version (possibly embellished), quoted in *Report* (1849), p. 30, column 2.
53. Both apparent forgeries quoted at length in Leigh (1834), vol. II, pp. 328–330.

shown the tablet, and told that it had been unearthed among the ruins of a Catholic chapel at Wildershaw (near St Helens).⁵⁴ On the unlikely view that this was a genuine article, it may have related to other, earlier, Leigh or Legh families, of which there were several, some related to the Stoneleigh branch. The absence of archaeological dating techniques in the early nineteenth century meant that such an artefact could, at least to some, seem plausible.

The Christopher stone was certainly a more convincing forgery than some. The naming of Christopher Leigh's children as Mary, Katherine, Roger and Ferdinand projected considerable plausibility. Roger was the name of the brother and of the father of Sir Thomas Leigh (I) (c.1498–1571), Lord Mayor of London, who first acquired Stoneleigh. Even more evocatively, the choice of the name Ferdinand was inspired.

Sir Thomas Leigh (II) (who died in the year of Christopher's birth, 1626) had a son called Ferdinando (d.1591). And Christopher's own younger brother, who also died unmarried, was named Ferdinando (d.1655).⁵⁵ One reason for the exotic name, although not for the first occurrence of it, may have been the Stoneleigh family's links with the Holy Roman Empire. Sir Robert Dudley, a family connection, was recognsed as Duke of Northumberland by Holy Roman Emperor Ferdinand II, in 1620.⁵⁶ (The first Ferdinando Leigh may have been named after Ferdinand I, 1503–1564). If Robert Leigh concocted a son called Ferdinand for Christopher Leigh, he could not have done better.

There remains, to this day, a large group of people who, without knowing anything about George Leigh's 1828 claim, are convinced of their own descent from Christopher Leigh. A prominent family-history website, www.thepeerage.com (privately created and maintained), names Edmund Leigh, born in 1665, as the son of Christopher Leigh. This information was posted on the website in 2011.⁵⁷ On my contacting the person who

---

54. Leigh (1834), vol. II, p. 330, note.
55. Dates from Table 1 in Bearman (ed. 2004), p. 130.
56. Simon Adams, "Dudley, Sir Robert (1574–1649), Marine and Landowner," rev. K. D. Reynolds, *Oxford Dictionary of National Biography,* Oxford University Press, 2004; online edn, Jan 2008. http://www.oxforddnb.com/view/article/8161 (Accessed 2 Dec 2015).
57. http://www.thepeerage.com/p46598.htm#i465975 (Accessed 2 December 2015), giving as authority: "[S5197] Nancy Law, 're: Leigh family', e-mail message to Darryl Roger LUNDY (101053), 18 February 2011."

had provided this information to the site manager, I learned that she and numerous other people are in possession of a similar pedigree, which gives a line of descent from Christopher and Edmund through to a William Leigh, born in 1814. It does not state the place of Edmund's birth, or his mother's name.[58]

The readiest explanation of this pedigree, if it could be substantiated with other documentation such as a parish record of Edmund's birth, would be that Edmund was born outside wedlock. The putative birth date of 1665 is, of itself, plausible; in that year Christopher would have been 39-years-old. No supporting record of Edmund's birth or baptism, however, is known to me. If Christopher did have illegitimate children, this would have been of no relevance whatsoever to the claim of George Leigh or anyone else. Only legitimate children could inherit, unless special arrangements were made for illegitimate children to be heirs. George Leigh's claim relied crucially on the existence of a first marriage of Christopher Leigh. If there were illegitimate children of Christopher extant at the time of his marriage, this might go towards accounting for the cryptic hints in Constance (Clent) Leigh's will (dated 1692, proved 1696). Constance strongly suggested that Christopher had made separate arrangements for their son Thomas, which she deliberately over-rode with her disposition of matters.

> "And in case my said son [Thomas] shall sue or prosecute my said trustees or executors ... to avoid or question this will ... upon pretence of any settlement made by his father ... then all and every the bequests hereinbefore to him made shall cease ..."[59]

In other words, whatever arrangements Christopher had sought to make, she was over-turning them. Christopher's own settlements are not extant. The likeliest reason for their thorough-going suppression by Constance would be that they made some provision for children born to another woman, before (and possibly after) their marriage in 1670. George Leigh's team, principally of course Henry Kent Causton, chose

---

58. Personal communication from Nancy Law, 8 April 2014.
59. Will reproduced in Leigh (1834), vol. I, pp. 20–25, p. 23.

to infer that the dispossession of legitimate children from a first marriage was Constance's object, but equally, the exclusion of illegitimate children, whom Christopher had attempted to support with a settlement, may have been the aim.

One final matter concerns the relationship of the claimant George Leigh to the Stoneleigh family. The claimant's goal was to establish that George Leigh was legitimately descended from Christopher Leigh. This appears not to have been the case, but that does not mean that he was not at all connected with the Stoneleigh branch. George Leigh and Causton had no interest in attempting to establish this, as such a connection would not have been direct, but there is some evidence of a more distant family relationship. Curiously, this matter comes to light through a family account of one of Jane Austen's admirers. Mrs Austen, in the same August 1806 letter already quoted, vividly described a visitor at Stoneleigh, a Mr Robert Holt Leigh:

> "A great friend of young Mr Leigh's [James Henry Leigh was 45], a very distant Relation, a single man, the wrong side of forty; chatty and well bred, and has a large estate."

Caroline Austen, Jane's niece, later wrote to her own niece, Emma Austen-Leigh, that according to Cassandra Austen, Robert Holt Leigh

> "was a great admirer...of her sister [Jane]. They were all passing guests at Stoneleigh Abbey—& all passed away, & never met again...& I...mention this...only as showing that her pretty face did not pass through the world without receiving some tributes of admiration."[60]

Robert Holt Leigh (1762–1843), as MP for Wigan, was involved in all the complicated political manoeuvring of the day, and was considered an enthusiastic follower of George Canning. He was a cultured man, versed in Greek literature. Holt Leigh was also notorious for having a long-term affair with Sarah Yates, the wife of one of his tenant farmers; he

---

60. Gaye King, "The Jane Austen Connection," in Bearman (ed., 2004), 163–177, p. 173. Caroline letter: in possession of Joan Austen-Leigh: King (2004), p. 173 and p. 278, note 25.

left his estate to her son (possibly his son as well), Roger Leigh.⁶¹ Robert Holt Leigh was descended from a family of Leighs of Adlington, some few miles north of Haigh. We have seen that George Leigh's ancestor was Roger Leigh, born some time before 1639 (who was not, therefore, the son of Christopher Leigh), and was brother of Alexander Leigh of Adlington.⁶² Robert Holt Leigh was described in Debrett as

> "…being in direct descent from the ancient family of Leigh, of Adlington, co. Chester."⁶³

Robert Holt Leigh's grandfather was an Alexander Leigh of Bretherton, Lancashire. The official Parliamentary history relates that this Alexander was attorney and financial adviser to Sir Roger Bradshaigh of Haigh, member for Wigan (1695–1747).⁶⁴ Adlington and Bretherton are two Lancashire villages some 12 miles apart. This Alexander Leigh would not appear to be the same as the Alexander featured in Causton's research, in which Alexander is described as "yeoman" and "husbandman", respectively. Nor does the will published by Causton as that of Alexander Leigh make any mention of wife or children, which the ancestor of Robert Holt Leigh certainly had. Yet both these Alexander Leighs, from the same area, had a longstanding and close connection with the family of Bradshaigh of Haighe. It is likely that they were related to each other.

It was part of the Stoneleigh case in defending against the peerage claim, that these lines of Leighs were not related to the Stoneleigh (or Adlestrop) branches. Yet Robert Holt Leigh was believed by the Stoneleigh Leighs to be a "distant Relation": Mrs Austen had no reason to

---

61. Robert Holt Leigh: M. H. Port/David R. Fisher, "Leigh, Robert Holt (1762–1843), of Whitley, Wigan, and Hindley Hall, Aspull, Lancs." http://www.historyofparliamentonline.org/volume/1790-1820/member/leigh-robert-holt-1762-1843 (Accessed 2 December 2015).
62. Deposition of Alexander Leigh of Adlington, 1727, noting that deponent was then aged "87 years and upwards," (Leigh (1834), vol. II, p. 501; was uncle of James Leigh, son of claimant's ancestor Roger Leigh of Haigh (Leigh (1834), vol. II, p. 452. Items No. 13 and 14 appended to Leigh (1834), vol. II (13: Will of Alexander Leigh of Adlington, 4 September 1728; 14: Deposition of Alexander Leigh of Adlington, 1727), pp. 499–503.
63. John Debrett, *The Baronetage of England*, fourth edn, vol. II (London, 1819), p. 1291.
64. M. H. Port/David R. Fisher, "Leigh, Robert Holt (1762–1843), of Whitley, Wigan, and Hindley Hall, Aspull, Lancs." http://www.historyofparliamentonline.org/volume/1790-1820/member/leigh-robert-holt-1762-1843 (Accessed 2 December 2015).

make this up, or to be mistaken about it. Indeed, it was confirmed in an 1833 volume by the genealogist John Burke, by whom the connection was deliberately made. Robert Holt Leigh's ancestors are given:

> "Alexander Leigh, esq. of Bretherton, in the county of Lancaster, of the ancient family of Leigh, of Adlington, in the county of Chester, whence descended the Barons Leigh (see *Burke's Extinct Peerage*)..."[65]

The link is shown in greater detail in Burke's volume on the extinct peerages. Robert Leigh of Adlington had sons, Robert "progenitor of the Leighs of that place," and Sir Peter Leigh, who died at the battle of Agincourt in 1415. This Peter's descendant was Thomas Leigh (d.1571) (described in *Chapter 1* of this book as Sir Thomas Leigh (I)), former Lord Mayor of London and generally considered first of the Stoneleigh and Adlestrop Leighs.[66]

The Adlington Leighs therefore pre-dated the Stoneleigh and Adlestrop Leighs by some centuries. It would have been ironic if George Leigh of Blackrod, through his ancestor's relationship with the Adlington Leighs, was of a more ancient stock than the actual possessors of Stoneleigh. James Henry's branch, the Adlestrop family, was the most recent, but eventually the final inheritor of Stoneleigh. In 1833, as appearing in Burke's nostalgic volume of extinct nobility, the Leigh peerage was still defunct. George Leigh's claim to the estate had recently been crushed, but the Leigh peerage remained to be revived.

---

65. John Burke, *A General and Heraldic Dictionary of the Peerage and Baronetage of the British Empire*, fourth edn, vol. II (London, 1833), p. 71. The official obituary of Robert Holt Leigh took issue with the connection made by Burke, but offered no more substantial objection than that the Adlington branch had "always been spelt Legh, whereas the branch from which the deceased Baronet was descended, has uniformly been spelt Leigh" (*Gentleman's Magazine*, vol. XIX new series, January-June 1843, 314–315, p. 314). The anonymous writer assumed a constancy of spelling traditions through the fifteenth to the nineteenth centuries which was unlikely to have existed in fact.

66. John Burke, *A General and Heraldic Dictionary of the Peerages of England, Ireland and Scotland, Extinct, Dormant, and In Abeyance* (London: Henry Colburn and Richard Bentley, 1831), p. 310. Burke's account makes clear that, in addition to sharing a common ancestry, the various Leigh branches also intermarried. Thomas I's great-uncle, Roger Leigh, married his relative Ellen Leigh, daughter of Robert Leigh of Adlington.

CHAPTER NINE

"Let go!"

"You keep your mouth shut, or else you'll be one of them."
George Shaw to Richard Barnett, c.1814[1]

Throughout the hearings of 1828, one person who might have been expected to give evidence was not called. This was Chandos Leigh, who on his father's disappearance in 1823 had inherited Stoneleigh. By 1828 he was 37-years-old, married, with several young children. Chandos (as, it appears, everyone, even his social inferiors at times, was in the habit of referring to him[2]) had given a deposition which stated his conviction that there had never been a monument, as described, in Stoneleigh church. He had added that, acting on advice, he "searched all the cellars of Stoneley [sic] Abbey," but had not found the stone.[3] Surprisingly, he was not called to enlarge upon this brief and circumspect evidence, which related to his own conviction, rather than to any particular reasons for it. It was not as if Chandos was someone who had no opinions, or who was reluctant to voice them. As noted in *Chapter 7*, he had been publishing poetry and essays for many years. Indeed, literature was his primary interest in adult life. The reason for Chandos' succinct evidence may, rather, lie in the fact that he knew all too much about the fate of the Christopher stone, and indeed it would be formally alleged that he had played a criminal role in its suppression.

Ostensibly, in the account emerging from the 1828–29 hearings, Chandos was not involved in the management of Stoneleigh during the period

---

1. *Report* (1849), p. 12, column 1.
2. Evidence in *Report* (1849), pp. 22, 24, in which social inferiors refer in the third person to "Chandos."
3. Chandos Leigh deposition dated 9 January 1828: Leigh (1834), vol. II, p. 289.

after he left Harrow School and attended, however briefly, Oxford. His mother, however, as we have seen, was a key player, sometimes through her agents, at Stoneleigh the bailiff George Jones Snr and the steward Richard Darley, and from London the lawyer Thomas Hill Mortimer. Their directions were sometimes at odds with the plans of the parish committee. Regular committee members included the Reverend James Roberts, Jasper Palfrey (until his walk-out in protest at Julia-Judith's interventions), Joseph Hallam, John Dry, George Handley, and Richard Darley. Discussions focused on the repairs to the roof, and the scraping and whitewashing of the walls. From June 1810 onwards, meetings focused on plans for major repairs to the village church.[4]

By 1811, however, the demolition of the south wall began to be discussed. The minutes of the 1 April 1811 meeting record:

> "The committee having met, agreed that the mason work to the south side shall be begun to be taken down, except of the best window, and to be rebuilt as soon as possible after Easter Monday; and that the timber for the roof be hauled and sawn out with expedition."[5]

Easter Monday in 1811 was 15 April, so this meant that quick action was being planned.[6] The wall was taken down that spring. The monument to Christopher Leigh, according to those who said it had existed, remained for some time propped up in the church: Richard Perks the plumber said he often stored his tools behind it. One witness claimed that the monument was taken down as late as September 1811.[7] The Leighs' lawyer, Thomas Hill Mortimer, was careful about the date when he described visiting the Reverend Thomas in October 1811 in order to make assessments on the estate; at that time, he saw no monument to the Leigh family in the body of the church.[8] The stone, therefore, was

---

4. Leigh (1834), vol. II, pp. 467–470, minutes for monthly parish meetings during 1810.
5. Leigh (1834), vol. II, p. 470.
6. "List of Easter Sunday Dates 1800–1899," http://tlarsen2.tripod.com/anthonypolumbo/apeasterdates.html#List18 (Accessed 8 December 2015).
7. Deposition of Charles Evans Lloyd, watchmaker, of Coventry: Leigh (1834), vol. II, pp. 244–245, note.
8. Deposition of Thomas Hill Mortimer, solicitor, of London: Leigh (1834), vol. II, pp. 272–273, note.

certainly gone by October. When the wall was rebuilt, the monument did not reappear. John Wilcox had thought that the removal of the monument into the abbey took place in 1812 or 1813, and he thought that 1812 was more likely. What was Chandos doing in 1812? Many years later, he claimed that he had not been at Stoneleigh at this time, although another account alleged that he had been at Stoneleigh in the autumn of 1812.[9] It certainly appeared that Chandos was deliberately kept away from Stoneleigh from about 1813 onwards. He was in London until 1817, when he travelled in Europe. A letter he wrote from Paris in August 1818 to Thomas Hill Mortimer indicates the extent of his spending.

> "Will you be so good as to get send [sic] more money sent to Sir ─────────? at Geneva for me ; for the purchase of a carriage & c. has made a great hole in my 2 hundred pounds ; & I fear will but carry me to Geneva. If Sir Howe of Great Queen St., Long Acre will sell my carriage, or buy it, so much the better as I have bought a handsome one which I intend to bring to England with me. You had better give me a letter of audit for a certain sum on ─────? and he will [give] me a letter of audit for Milan. We shall stay at Geneva for some few days to make excursions into Switzerland and then proceed to Milan, Florence and home. Pray take care that I have a sufficient supply as otherwise I shall indeed be in status quo. We are off on Saturday for Geneva. I keep a regular account and spend no more than I can help but the Reservations spectacles, and other things have run away a good deal."[10]

This kind of extravagance was not such as Julia-Judith and James Henry wanted to encourage. The best thing would be for Chandos to come home, get married, and stay out of trouble. This duly happened in the following year. In June 1819 Chandos married Margarette Willes, the daughter of the Reverend William Shippen Willes of Astrop House, Northamptonshire. The couple then moved to Adlestrop House. The Reverend Willes was not just a village minister; he had been Prebendary

---
9. Griffin in *Report* (1849), p. 13, column 1.
10. SBTRO DR 18/17/44/16: Letter from Chandos to Mortimer, 19 August 1818.

of York, and for many years was rector of Preston Bissett, Buckinghamshire.[11] A portrait of him by Thomas Lawrence exists.

The Reverend F E Witts, of Upper Slaughter in Gloucestershire, wrote in his diary of meeting Chandos during this Adlestrop period.

> "Chandos Leigh is an eccentric mortal, possessed of talent and studious in an odd way. He has been an admirer of theatrical performances and performers, male and female, a poet in a small way…He resides much at Adlestrop but without taking a share in the public business of the county and neighbourhood."[12]

In this same period, the late Edward Lord Leigh, certified insane, was described as having been "eccentric."[13] This means that the term was a euphemism, with the connotation of a manner and/or behaviour suggesting a state of mental health not quite the norm. This is supported by Witts' additional use of the phrase "in an odd way." Chandos represented something of a puzzle for his Adlestrop neighbours. He did, however, with Margarette, conform to the expectation of his class that they were, if at all possible, to bring a healthy male child into existence.

Two girls were born (Julia in 1820, Emma in 1822). James Henry Leigh's disappearance took place in October 1823, and after this, Chandos, Margarette and their children moved from Adlestrop to Stoneleigh. A male heir, William Henry, was born in January 1824.[14] In this period, Chandos seems to have been writing non-fiction: "tracts," as he called them. While he may not have taken much of a role in the county, he seems to have had a theoretical interest in the key ideological battlegrounds of the day: Parliamentary reform, free trade, and Catholic emancipation. The tone of the essays is much as would be expected from our knowledge of

---

11. Portrait: http://www.artnet.com/artists/thomas-lawrence/portrait-of-rev-william-shippen-willes-of-astrop-mFFsX2IwfDUgVXXmyNemQA2 (Accessed 3 December 2015). Death notice in *The Gentleman's Magazine*, vol. XCII, June-December 1822, p. 476.
12. *Diary of a Cotswold Parson*, quoted in Hampson (2004), p. 184.
13. 1 January 1823, appearing in Sylvanus Urban, *The Gentleman's Magazine and Historical Chronicle, from January to June 1823*, volume 133, being the sixteenth of a new series. (London: John Nichols and son), April 1823, p. 326.
14. Birth dates of first three children: http://www.thepeerage.com/p1569.htm#i15687 (Accessed 8 December 2015).

Chandos as a consistent Whig. He promoted voting reform, and the end of the East India Company's monopoly on the silk trade.

In the period 1821–1823, Chandos' essays include the following titles: "A Few Hints to any Administration," "A Few Remarks on Parliamentary Reform," "A Few Thoughts on the Invasion of Spain," and "Natural and Revealed Religion." Essays written in the first year of the Chancery hearings, 1828, include: "On Free Trade, Pensions and Salaries, and Currency," "On East India Trade," and "Causes of Present Distress."[15] The collected essays were privately printed by John Merridew of Warwick, in 1832. Many of the points made by Chandos would later seem ironic, in view of subsequent events, but they were, indeed, already suffused with irony, if not hypocrisy. Chandos inveighed against the corrupt system of allocating electorates via the influence of borough patrons.

> "If Patrons of Boroughs could not succeed in bringing their dependants into the House of Commons, ministers would be compelled to introduce economy into every branch of the public expenditure, and to confide in a disinterested House of Commons, freely chosen by an intelligent People."[16]

Chandos, who had never been able to control his own ruinous extravagance, was calling for the reform of public spending. Not only this, but at the very time of writing, Chandos' father, James Henry, held the electorate of Winchester entirely through family connections.

> "'Bunny' Leigh...had been returned for Winchester in 1818 on the old Chandos interest revived by his cousin's husband, the second marquess of Buckingham."[17]

This cousin's husband was Richard Temple Grenville, who had married James Henry's cousin Lady Anne Eliza Brydges, daughter of the Duke of Chandos, in 1799. James Henry Leigh had been brought up in

---

15. Chandos Leigh, *Tracts, Written in the Years 1823 & 1828* (Warwick: John Merridew), 1832.
16. "A Few Remarks on Parliamentary Reform," in *Tracts* (1832), p. 24.
17. Philip Salmon/David R. Fisher, "Leigh, James Henry (1761–1823), of Adlestrop, Glos. and Stoneleigh Abbey, Warws." http://www.historyofparliamentonline.org/volume/1820–1832/member/leigh-james-1765–1823 (Accessed 4 December 2015).

the household of his uncle the Duke (brother of his mother Lady Caroline), and had probably expected to inherit his wealth and possibly his title. This did not occur, and on the Duke's death in 1789, the title had become extinct. This disappointment may well have contributed to the resentment, and determination, of James Henry and Julia-Judith to obtain an estate and title at all costs.

Richard Temple Grenville, through having married Lady Anne Eliza, was eventually created (among other titles) Marquess of Chandos. It may well have been that he felt that he owed something to James Henry, the protégé of his late father-in-law; and thus, in 1818, Temple Grenville procured for his cousin-by-marriage the seat of Winchester. The official Parliamentary history goes on to record that James Henry was granted the seat as a stop-gap for Chandos himself, but that it was James Henry who was again returned in the election of 1820, probably because Chandos did not wish, or was not thought suitable, to stand.[18]

James Henry is recorded as being a "lax attender" in Parliament. His voting history was mixed, voting on several occasions in 1821 and 1822 against Catholic relief bills (bills with the intention of removing some of the traditional restrictions on Catholics in public life), and also in 1822 to preserve some of the protection duties on imported corn.[19] These voting trends seem to be in contradiction to the more consistently held liberal beliefs of his son Chandos, who wrote in favour of greater freedoms for Catholics, and for an end to trade protection, but did not himself stand for Parliament in order to argue for his views.

Being a beneficiary, through his father's position, of corrupt Parliamentary selection, while calling for reform of that very system, was not the only way in which Chandos appears liable to a charge of hypocrisy. In the year in which his agents were pressing in Chancery to dismiss the claims of George Leigh, Chandos was writing on the "Causes of Present

---

18. R. G. Thorne, "Leigh, James Henry (1761–1823), of Adlestrop, Glos. and Stoneleigh Abbey, Warws." http://www.historyofparliamentonline.org/volume/1790–1820/member/leigh-james-henry-1765–1823 (Accessed 8 December 2015).
19. Philip Salmon/David R. Fisher, "Leigh, James Henry (1761–1823), of Adlestrop, Glos. and Stoneleigh Abbey, Warws." http://www.historyofparliamentonline.org/volume/1820–1832/member/leigh-james-1765–1823 (Accessed 8 December 2015).

Distress." He called forcefully for greater equality and a more just distribution of wealth:

> "The number of the idle classes bear too large a proportion to that of the laborious: hence there is general distress, though individuals have amassed large fortunes... The productive classes have less than their just share in the annual distribution of wealth."[20]

This was at the very time in which his lawyers, Sir James Scarlett and Thomas Denman, were quietly ridiculing the working people ("productive classes") who testified to the existence of the Christopher stone. Clearly, no redistribution of wealth was going to take place within the Stoneleigh Abbey estate.

In 1836, by which time Chandos and Margarette had eight children, the family visited Europe, with great ceremony and expense. Their granddaughter recalled hearing about this legendary trip.

> "As to my grandfather [Chandos] Leigh, I believe he travelled with his family for about two years, to Switzerland, France, and the north of Italy. They had three carriages, one for the parents, one for the schoolroom, and one for the nursery. A courier escorted them, and an avant-courier rode on in front with bags of five-franc pieces to secure lodgings when they migrated from one place to another. On one occasion on the Riviera they met the then Grand Duke Constantine, who thrust his head out of the window and exclaimed: 'Toute Angleterre est en route!'"[21]

Chandos wrote to his nephew from Nice that he had

> "...rented a palace for the season, engaged two governesses and a dancing master for the children and obtained the services of a capital cook."[22]

---

20. "Causes of Present Distress," *Tracts* (1832), p. 194.
21. Margaret Elizabeth Leigh Child-Villiers, Countess of Jersey, *Fifty-one Years of Victorian Life* (London: John Murray), 1922, p. 6.
22. SBTRO PR 231/12, 16, quoted in Hampson (2004), p. 185.

The Missing Monument Murders

In 1838, on the return journey, in Paris, Margarette (quaintly called in the family papers "Mrs Chandos," probably to distinguish her from her mother-in-law, Mrs [Julia-Judith] Leigh) gave birth to twins.[23] The responsibilities of a large family, and possibly of other matters, were beginning to weigh upon Chandos. He wrote to Julia-Judith:

> "I must become much less busy than I have been and do what I think I ought very quietly, otherwise I fear I must quit these shores again and perhaps never return. The great point is not to be anxious about anything but to do what one thinks best and discipline one's mind so as not to be put out by anything, but this, for a nervous person is not an easy matter but ought to be trained by quiet habits, it is hard work for a single man to regulate a large property but much harder for one with a large family with large encumbrances. After all who should be fussed about a few fleeting things of this brief existence?"[24]

The tone of this passage indicates considerable uneasiness of mind, and the suggestion of having to leave England permanently is surprising. In view of such a frame of mind in Chandos, it was probably through the agitation of Julia-Judith, rather than Chandos himself, that in 1839 the defunct peerage of Leigh was revived. An expired peerage could only be revived by the monarch, after application by the heir apparent (or, probably in this case, his representative).[25] Letters patent were granted by the monarch on 11 May 1839 which summoned Chandos to the House of Lords as Lord Leigh of the second creation. Queen Victoria had become the monarch in 1837, but records from the time suggest that the decision had been made by her predecessor, King William IV.[26]

Having seen this process to its conclusion, Julia-Judith died in 1843. Meanwhile, Chandos was still writing verse as well as non-fiction. In 1844, he published a volume called *Walks in the Country*. Its poems included wishes for peace and increased commercial activity, but less greed:

---

23. Hampson (2004), p. 185.
24. SBTRO DR 18/17/55/114, quoted in Hampson (2004), p. 186.
25. http://www.debretts.com/people/essential-guide-peerage/creation-and-inheritance-peerage (Accessed 4 December 2015).
26. *Report* (1849), p. 4, column 1.

which were eventually published in the group's journal.³¹ Was this Charles Griffin the solicitor?

In the 1841 census, there are several men called Charles Griffin listed in Warwickshire: a collector (of what it does not say), a paper-tray maker, a publican, a farmer, a dressmaker, and a solicitor. Of these, it is the solicitor who is most likely to have called himself "esquire," and had the leisure to pursue electrical experiments. The author of the papers is careful to state that he has no expert knowledge of mathematics, emphasising his amateur status.³²

The London Electrical Society was made up of such amateurs: described as "cultivators of electricity," or "electricians," they included military men such as Lieutenant Morrison of the Royal Navy, scientific clergymen such as the Reverend Mr Shillibeer, and "natural philosophers" such as Sir Richard Phillips.³³ Such men believed, rightly, that electricity had "a general tendency to improve the condition of mankind."³⁴ While it might seem to us improbable for a lawyer to devote considerable time to scientific pursuits, a precedent from the previous generation was afforded by none other than Henry Brougham, who has already appeared in our story in more than one persona. In his teens and twenties, the precocious Brougham published scientific papers on light, prisms, and wave motion, before giving his time fully to journalism and the law.³⁵ One of the scientific controversies in which he took part in the early years of the nineteenth century was one with contemporary relevance: the extent of

---

31. See, e.g. abstract of a paper read on 2 June 1838, "A Paper on the Homogeneous Attraction of Electricity, by C. Griffin, Esq., Leamington," in *Transactions and Proceedings of the London Electrical Society from 1837 to 1840* (London: Smith, Elder and Co., 1841), p. 148.
32. Charles Griffin, Esq., M.L.E.S., "Why do Electrised Bodies Recede From Each Other?" in *The Annals of Electricity, Magnetism, and Chemistry; And guardian of experimental science*, vol. VIII, January 1842, pp. 1–17.
33. First annual report of the London Electrical Society, 28 May 1838, first item in *Transactions and Proceedings of the London Electrical Society from 1837 to 1840* (London: Smith, Elder and Co.), 1841, no page numbers.
34. Address by W. Sturgeon, 7 August 1837, *Transactions of LES* (1841), p. 6.
35. Michael Lobban, "Brougham, Henry Peter, first Baron Brougham and Vaux (1778–1868)," *Oxford Dictionary of National Biography*, Oxford University Press, 2004; online edn, Jan 2008. http://www.oxforddnb.com/view/article/3581 (Aaccessed 8 Dec 2015).

influence of solar activity on terrestrial climate, and hence on economic markers such as the price of wheat.[36]

Certain similarities of style between the electricity papers, and the polemical booklet *Stoneleigh Abbey Thirty-four Years Ago*, would seem to lend support to the view that the same Charles Griffin wrote both. Both are, for example, written in a personal, almost conversational style, as these two extracts show. Both works make liberal use of the first person.

> "I have thought it best, considering my own ignorance of mathematics and the abstruseness of my subject, to err on the side of prolixity rather than on that of brevity; to risk saying something unnecessary, rather than leave anything necessary to my being understood, unsaid" (Charles Griffin, "'Why Do Electrised Bodies Recede From Each Other?", 1841, p. 1).

> "I am the more anxious my meaning should be here understood, as I shall have to observe on the past and present conduct of the Abbey parties in this matter, as an indication of a consciousness there is something to conceal...I shall not pretend to state or argue fully both sides of the question..." (Charles Griffin, *Stoneleigh Abbey Thirty-four Years Ago*, 1848, p. 68).

If, as seems likely, Charles Griffin the "electrician" is our man, this has implications for his subsequent forensic work. As a scientist, Griffin was conscious of the importance of the slow accumulation of observed facts. As a lawyer, he was described by a legal adversary in 1849 as "shrewd," which suggests an appreciation of his intelligence and judgment.[37] He may even have been a local polymath, a small-town Brougham.

At about the time he represented the men who had broken into the abbey, Charles Griffin received a statement from a man named Richard Barnett. Barnett, a stonemason who had worked on the project for a new bridge at Stoneleigh Abbey over the River Avon (mentioned later

---

36. Lev A. Pustilnik, Gregory Yom Din, "Influence of Solar Activity on [the] State of [the] Wheat Market in Medieval England," 2003 and widely cited; http://arxiv.org/ftp/astro-ph/papers/0312/0312244.pdf (Accessed 8 December 2015), p. 4, note 1, unfortunately giving no reference for source of Brougham's contemptuous dismissal of Herschel's correlation between solar activity and prices.
37. Whitehurst in *Report* (1849), p. 6, column 2.

in this chapter) in the period, claimed to know about the removal and disposal of the Christopher stone, nine coffin plates from the church vault, another monument and plate, and a child's coffin.[38]

Two years later, Griffin was asked to take a statement from Sarah Smallbone, née Silk. She had worked as a cook at Stoneleigh Abbey during the earlier period, reporting directly to Julia-Judith. She was in a disturbed state of mind, and refused to make a sworn statement, as she feared punishment for her involvement in several criminal activities. She did, however, make confessions to several people about crimes in which, she said, Julia-Judith forced her to take part. These included several murders.[39] A third person, George Shaw, made confessions regarding events at the bridge. The evidence of the three persons was referred to Warwickshire magistrates, and the result was that at a hearing on 6 May 1848, Chandos Leigh, by now Lord Leigh "of the second creation," and one William Wood, a former Stoneleigh employee, were charged with murder.[40]

It is worthwhile, at this point, to prepare the reader for the fact that the ensuing chapters cover events and evidence from both this May 1848 hearing and the trial of Griffin for libel in March 1849. As the whole of this complicated matter covers events as far back as 1811 or even 1806, it will be important to focus on the evidence concerning the actual events, rather than retailing in chronological order the evidence as it gradually emerged. In some instances, the evidence presented in 1849 filled in the bare outlines sketched in the previous year. Ultimately, both court cases formed the latter two parts of the same process, which had begun with the Lords hearings of 1828 and 1829: the exposure of Stoneleigh's scandals from the first 25 years of the nineteenth century.

At the May 1848 trial, the key witness was Barnett, as by this time both Smallbone and Shaw had died. Barnett, under oath, stated that he was a stonemason, aged 52. In 1814, in his teens, he had been part of a large group working on the foundations of the new bridge. "Lady Leigh, meaning the late Honourable Mrs Leigh, directed the alterations; Lord

---

38. Griffin (1848), p. 46.
39. Griffin (1848). p. 47.
40. Griffin (1848), pp. 47–48.

The Missing Monument Murders

Leigh [Chandos] superintended also, and Mr Jones, his steward, who was [by 1848] dead."[41] Barnett remembered the names of fellow workmen Thomas Proud, Joseph Smith, John Wilcox, George Shaw, Matthew Billinge (or Billinges), William Forbes, Alexander Munro, William Wood, and William Blissett.[42]

One night during work on the bridge, Barnett alleged, he was holding the rope which was to guide into place one of the massive stones forming the abutment. The abutment of a stone arch bridge is the structure at either end, embedded within the earth and supported by substantial foundations, which absorbs the considerable forces exerted by the tension of the arch. William Mason, who was the foreman that night, should have given the direction to lower the stone carefully into place. Instead, Barnett stated, Julia-Judith, Chandos, and George Jones Snr all said "Let go" together. Billinges should have steadied the rope, but instead, he and Forbes, who were standing in the hole, were crushed by the stone's sudden fall.[43]

Barnett himself, at a distance of about 50 yards away, could not see what was happening. A few minutes later, Barnett came to the abutment to see blood working up around the stone. He asked Shaw "how that blood came there, Shaw replied 'hold your noise, Billings [sic] and Forbes are there'." Barnett did not know what to say, and said nothing.[44]

The chairman of the hearing must have queried why Barnett did not speak out.

> "[I] was not surprised, expected how it was; did not ask any one to get the bodies out; was but a youth amongst them, if [I] had said anything, [I] might have been served the same."[45]

In fact, as was revealed in 1849, George Shaw had personally threatened Barnett: "You keep your mouth shut, or else you'll be one of them."[46]

---

41. Griffin (1848), p. 52–53.
42. Griffin (1848), p. 50.
43. Griffin (1848), pp. 51–52.
44. Griffin (1848), p. 53.
45. Barnett's evidence: Griffin (1848), pp. 51–53.
46. *Report* (1849), p. 12, column 1.

"Let go!"

Barnett did not speak to anyone about the events other than Shaw. Shaw later told him, "If you had gone up [to the abbey] with the rest you would have had £10." Barnett replied that he did not want blood money.[47] He also claimed to know of the killing of two other men, Proud and Smith, whose bodies, he said, had been shown to him by John Wilcox, the former Stoneleigh post-boy. He believed that they, too, had been buried in the abutments of the bridge. He had worked with Proud and Smith, and was sure that he recognised their bodies.[48]

The next witness to be questioned was none other than John Wilcox himself. By now he was 51-years-old. He reprised his evidence from the 1828 hearings about the removal to Stoneleigh Abbey of the Christopher stone, recalling that both Julia-Judith and James Henry supervised the operation. He stated that a number of portraits, previously hung in the family gallery (called the print gallery) were burnt on the kitchen fire: Sarah Silk, later Smallbone, helped to burn them.[49] Wilcox also testified that a black man called John Thomas was brought to Stoneleigh by the Leigh family's London lawyer, "Mr Mortimer Hill" (sic: actually Thomas Hill Mortimer). His function was to pay money to the servants "for keeping the abbey secrets." Wilcox himself claimed to have been paid eight pounds by John Ilett, as early as 1812.[50]

Concerning events at the bridge, Wilcox was surprisingly circumspect.

> "[He] had seen hand carts going to the bridge once, with something covered with a mat; found a glove near the river, *kept it many years* [italics in original], it was nearly black, but stained much with something."

Griffin's text goes on: "Wilcox here began to falter and [appeared] afraid to speak."

Mr Pollock, the lawyer engaged to prosecute the murder charge, produced a statement made previously by Wilcox. Wilcox admitted that he had signed this document, but claimed not to have been sober at the time. Griffin explained: "This was a statutory declaration, containing

---

47. Griffin (1848), p. 53.
48. Griffin (1848), pp. 50, 53.
49. Griffin (1848), p. 54.
50. Wilcox's evidence: Griffin (1848), p. 54.

extraordinary disclosures, which [Wilcox] chose to deny."[51] Some further debate took place about the admissibility of evidence from Smallbone and Shaw. Jones claimed that for Chandos to be examined would "degrade his noble client." Very little more discussions took place, and the magistrates determined that they would not grant a warrant for an examination of the bridge or the abbey. This was apparently equivalent to an abrupt discharge of Chandos Leigh (the charges against Wood had been withdrawn).[52] After this May 1848 hearing failed to result in any investigation of Barnett's, Shaw's and Smallbone's allegations, Griffin took matters into his own hands. Within two months he had put together a short but explosive book, entitled *Stoneleigh Abbey Thirty-four Years Ago, Containing a Short History of the Claims to the Peerage and Estates, and a Catalogue of the Confessed and Suspected Crimes, &c. &c, &c* (printed by R J Salter in Birmingham, "for Charles Griffin, the Proprietor and Publisher, Leamington Spa").[53] In his introduction, addressed "To the Public," Griffin writes that it was not so much the high level of public curiosity about the Stoneleigh case which justified his publishing the book. Rather, he considered that publication was the only likely means of seeing justice served:

> "The press is perhaps the only true safeguard of right and justice against so wealthy an individual as Lord Leigh has become by the possession of property so strongly, and probably suspected to belong to another…"[54]

Griffin summarised the evidence presented in the 1828 and 1829 Lords hearings; he had read and absorbed the analysis and judgments of Henry Kent Causton. In treating the allegations of criminal activity, and for the first time placing these in the context of the failed claims of the early years of the century, Griffin was careful not to accuse Chandos of any wrongdoing. Instead, he presented what Barnett had sworn under oath, and Smallbone had told several listeners. Griffin then included a somewhat truncated transcript of the May 1848 hearing.

---

51. Griffin (1848), p. 54.
52. Griffin (1848), pp. 57–58.
53. Dated Leamington Spa, May 1848, p. vi.
54. Griffin (1848), p. iv.

"Let go!"

Griffin appended a summary of the allegations, together with hints he had gathered from witnesses not yet publicly examined.⁵⁵ He pointed out that the evidence probably existed, in the possession of the Leigh family, to shed light on the bridge events:

"I shall not pretend to state or argue fully both sides of the question, Lord Leigh having ample means of meeting my facts and arguments, if unfounded, in every nook which they chance to reach. I do not allude to pecuniary means only, but the accounts of Mr George Jones deceased, and others of those employed in building the bridge, and similar sources whence [Chandos] may obtain almost every information he is likely to require as to dates, names, and other circumstances. The expense of advertisements, too, if necessary, to find out parties he cannot otherwise trace, would be but a bagatelle to him."⁵⁶

In short, Griffin called upon Chandos to refute the allegations by a thorough investigation. In relation to suggestions that the claims by Barnett, Shaw and Smallbone were incredible, Griffin riposted:

"I do not think it so absurd so to believe [in the allegations], for history is full of such things. 'I do *not* believe' in death-bed confessions of crimes *never committed*. 'I do *not* believe' in three ignorant persons, at a hundred miles distance from each other, forging the *same* tale of horrid crimes in which they were engaged thirty-four years ago, and two of them going to their final account with a lie on their lips, 'damning themselves to everlasting fame.' I do *not* believe history ever recorded *such* confessions, [were: the actual text says 'we<r>e': see footnote 36 in *Chapter 16*] there never such to record. With the facts before me, it would be absurd, indeed, if my belief were other than it is."⁵⁷

Griffin noted that he himself, on first hearing of the allegations, had thought that victims who suddenly disappeared must surely have been

---

55. Griffin (1848), pp. 63–66.
56. Griffin (1848), p. 68.
57. Griffin (1848), p. 68.

missed. He later concluded that this might not have happened, as they were poor, from Scotland or the north of England, or itinerant. Griffin claims he learned later that rumours were, in fact, current at the time, but that Julia-Judith prevented contact between work gangs on the estate. In addition, a person who had any communication with George Leigh's supporters was summarily dismissed.[58] Griffin pointed out that the Leigh team's strategy in 1848 consisted not of providing evidence to combat the charges, but to "ridicule, falsehood, and evasion." He queried why George Jones junior, having claimed to be open to any evidence, in fact would not admit George Shaw's statement, or any information which had emanated from Sarah Smallbone.[59] In concluding his book, Griffin said he hoped that Chandos was not guilty of the charges.

> "I am still unwilling to believe he is. The literary tastes, the domestic virtues, the general mildness and benignity of character that he has credit for, (and I ardently hope justly so) forbid me to conclude him guilty of the crime recently laid to his charge, without the most cogent and indubitable evidence."[60]

Perhaps Chandos had been misled by others into failing to allow an investigation:

> "I should be ashamed to think the worse of Lord Leigh, or William Wood (in a criminal matter especially) through the indiscretion of others, I trust the delay hitherto in *meeting* the recent charges, and *grappling* with them instead of *evading* them by legal astuteness or otherwise, has arisen from Lord Leigh's too great confidence in others, and a too retiring, a too timid natural disposition."[61]

In an ironic nod both to Chandos' famous penchant for poetry, and to Warwickshire's greatest poet, Griffin quoted from *Hamlet* Claudius' confessional soliloquy about guilt and atonement:

---

58. Griffin (1848), p. 68–69.
59. Griffin (1848), p. 70.
60. Griffin (1848), p. 77.
61. Griffin (1848), p. 80.

> "May one be pardon'd, and retain the offence?
> In the corrupted currents of the world,
> Offence's gilded hand may shove by justice;
> And oft 'tis seen the wicked prize itself
> Buys out the law…"[62]

"But," Griffin continued, "how [to] reconcile the honesty of Barnett's testimony with his lordship's innocence?"[63] In order to clear the air, once and for all:

> "I ask [Chandos] to offer up to the vindication of public justice, and of his own innocence, the whole of his personal exertions, the whole of his personal influence for a short time, and a fraction, a contemptible one indeed, of that private property which at present hangs on a mere thread, on a title thrice questioned, and on a refutation of the sworn evidence of scores of disinterested witnesses."[64]

Griffin's book was incendiary enough. It was followed by meetings held in Leamington, Coventry, Birmingham and Manchester, at which Griffin addressed large crowds on the Stoneleigh Abbey "mysteries." At a meeting in Leamington, attended by some 200 people, Griffin gave an address on the Stoneleigh affair, and was said to have asked for a show of hands on whether the audience thought Chandos was a murderer.[65] Noting Griffin's caution in his book to avoid this kind of direct accusation, it is more likely that he had actually called for a show of hands on whether proper investigation should take place. This, after all, had been the thrust of his book.

In late-1848, Griffin gave a three-hour lecture on the Stoneleigh affair, attended by nearly 1,000 people, in the Manchester Corn Exchange. He charged entry to these lectures, he claimed, in order to raise money both towards funding his own defence (shortly to be required), and to

---

62. Act III, Scene III, lines 56–60.
63. Griffin (1848), p. 83.
64. Griffin (1848), p. 87.
65. *Report*, p. 7, column 2.

form a fund to rebuild the Stoneleigh bridge after a proper excavation.[66] Chandos had had enough. According to his counsel, Mr Whitehurst, reluctantly, Chandos prosecuted Griffin for libel. Griffin was arrested and, in his words, "dragged in custody through the principal streets of Warwick, for no kind of purpose."[67] The record of his status as an accused prisoner is to be found in the Warwickshire Archives. Under the heading "Literacy," the clerk has recorded, ironically enough in the case of a lawyer and scientist, that Griffin "reads and writes well."[68] The case was heard at the Warwickshire Lent Assizes, commencing on 31 March 1849.[69]

This time, the gloves were off. Griffin, who by now had nothing to lose, threw everything at his own defence. He must have had an opportunity to arrange the attendance of numerous witnesses, including Mary Draper and William Faxon, who had been overlooked in 1828 and 1848. This was an expensive undertaking: Griffin claimed to have spent between £2,000 and £3,000 in assembling witnesses.[70] Among other vital evidence, the explosive, and in 1848 redacted, statements of John Wilcox were finally aired, although Wilcox himself did not appear. Wilcox had told several people about what he knew of the bridge events. One of these people was Mary Draper, also a friend of Sarah Smallbone. Mary Draper had made a statement in 1828, but was not called to answer questions at that time.[71] She knew all the protagonists, having lived in Stoneleigh for many years (she was now very elderly).

According to Mary Draper, John Wilcox had come to her house, bringing a bloodstained glove with him.

> "He told me there had been two men killed in the abutment of the bridge, by a heavy stone falling on them, but it did not kill them dead, and Chandos Leigh rushed upon one and with the assistance of [George the elder] Jones cut his throat. At the same time he said Mrs Leigh rushed upon the other

---

66. *Report*, p. 9, column 2; p. 10, column 1.
67. *Report*, p. 9, column 2.
68. Calendars of Prisoners, 1801–1900. Reference QS 26/1/034. County Record Office, Heritage and Culture Warwickshire, http://apps.warwickshire.gov.uk/prisonersdb/prisoners/6799 (Accessed 8 December 2015).
69. *Report* (1849), p. 3.
70. *Report* (1849), p. 8, column 2.
71. Mary Draper deposition dated 23 January 1828: Leigh (1834), vol. II, p. 311.

and with the help of Jones they strangled him; and [Wilcox] never was so frightened in his life, and [Chandos] fainted and dropped his glove, and it was as much as they could do to get him out of the abutment of the bridge."[72]

Another witness at the libel trial, William Faxon, claimed that Wilcox had told him a further story. Sarah Smallbone and Wilcox both claimed that several workmen on the estate were poisoned by Julia-Judith and her staff. Faxon added that, according to Wilcox, one of these poisoning victims escaped into the Stoneleigh Abbey privy. Wilcox said that Chandos "went to Wilcox and said 'Jack, which way is he gone?' Wilcox pointed after him, and his Lordship followed, telling Wilcox to make haste after him. Chandos followed [the workman] into the privy and cut his throat."[73]

Faxon had also heard a version of the bridge murders from George Shaw, who had been closer to the action than Barnett had. "[Shaw] said the stone fell on one of them above the waistband, and the other about the middle of the thigh. He said Chandos Leigh cut Joe Billinge's throat, and Jones was strangled They wound the stone off them and then buried them in the hole."[74]

Could these events actually have happened? Could Chandos Leigh, the mild-mannered, eccentric, literary lord of Stoneleigh, have slaughtered several men with his bare hands? And could Julia-Judith Twisleton Leigh — Jane Austen's cousin — have ordered the deaths of up to nine or even ten other people on the estate, becoming England's first serial killer? In addition to Billinges, Forbes, Proud and Smith, the victims were said to be: four unnamed masons who worked on the wine bins (plus the possible fifth victim, the man slain in the privy); Daniel Dingley; William Blissett; John Sprawson, the carrier; John Thomas, the black man employed in securing the allegiance of Shaw and other parties to the bridge murders; and finally, in 1823, John Leigh (I), would-be claimant to the estate.

---

72. *Report* (1849), p. 18, column 1.
73. *Report* (1849), p. 22, column 2.
74. *Report* (1849), p. 22, column 1.

The Missing Monument Murders

CHAPTER TEN

Drink to the Dead Men

"I build a magnificent bridge to gratify my vanity; yet, in after-times I shall hear nothing of it; perchance nothing of this, of any world!"
    Chandos Leigh, "On a Future State", *Fragments of Essays* (1816), pp.10–11.

The Stoneleigh Abbey bridge at the centre of these bizarre allegations had its genesis in the time of the Reverend Thomas Leigh. As early as 1808–1809, he engaged Humphry Repton (1752–1818) to advise him on "improvements" to Stoneleigh Abbey. Famously, Humphry Repton was one of the few living people to whom Jane Austen directly referred in her works (in *Mansfield Park*, 1814). Part of the reason why Austen mentioned so few real people by name may have been that, because her novels were a long time in gestation, she was conscious that they might easily become dated by references which were specific in time. This is confirmed by her apology in the "Advertisement" to *Northanger Abbey* (1817) for topics which by then must, she thought, have appeared out of date.[1] By the time Austen was writing *Mansfield Park*, Repton had been a celebrity landscape designer long enough to stand as an institution, and therefore did not attract this risk of tying the text too closely to one person's lifetime. This is confirmed in that one of the other few actual people mentioned by Austen was James King, Master of Ceremonies at the Assembly Rooms in Bath from 1785 to 1805.[2] He too held his role long enough to be able to act as a marker for the period as a whole.

---

1. "Advertisement, by the authoress, to *Northanger Abbey*", 1816: James Kinsley and John Davie (eds.), with an introduction and notes by Claudia L. Johnson, *Northanger Abbey, Lady Susan, The Watsons, Sanditon* (Oxford: Oxford World's Classics, 2003), no p. number, but two leaves after p. l; discussed at note on p. 357.
2. *Northanger Abbey* vol. I, chapter 3 (Oxford World's Classics, 2003), p. 15.

When Austen referred in *Mansfield Park* to Repton, and in *Northanger Abbey* to King, she was referring in each case to a cultural phenomenon, a "brand" as much as a person.

Repton's domination of the celebrity designer market had only been achieved after he had failed at several other professions. He had begun in business in 1773 in the textile industry. This failed to prosper, and Repton tried journalism, art, and the role of political staffer (he worked as private secretary to William Windham, Whig politician and then briefly secretary to the Lord Lieutenant of Ireland). He joined with John Palmer in a project to reform the mail-coach system, but lost money in the venture.[3] In 1788, aged 36 and with children to support (he and his wife had 16, seven of whom survived to adulthood),[4] Repton hit upon the idea of using his drawing skills, in combination with his experience of laying out gardens at his home in Norfolk, to become a "landscape gardener" (a term he coined). Since the death of Lancelot 'Capability' Brown in 1783, no one had filled the void in high-end garden design. Repton offered his services to noble clients, achieving his first commission in his first year. Commissions quickly followed during the 1790s.

It is significant that Repton represented a trend about which Austen herself was equivocal, if not actually hostile. The employment of Repton is mooted by three characters in *Mansfield Park* who have no taste, no judgment, and are addicted to empty display. Rushworth visits his friend Smith's estate, Compton, and sees the transformation effected by Repton. His fiancée Maria Bertram, always sensitive to promoting their status as a couple, suggests that Rushworth employ Repton also. Mrs Norris, with her passion for spending the money of others, suggests that Repton's fee of five guineas per day should be no object.

"Well, and if they were *ten*," cried Mrs Norris, "I am sure *you* need not regard it…" (Chapter 6 of *Mansfield Park*)

---

3. Stephen Daniels, "Repton, Humphry (1752–1818)," *Oxford Dictionary of National Biography*, Oxford University Press, 2004; online edn, Jan 2012 http://www.oxforddnb.com/view/article/23387 (Accessed 9 Dec 2015).
4. W. P. Courtney, "Repton, Humphry (1752–1818)," *DNB* (ed. S. Lee), vol. XVI, 1909, 914–916, p. 915.

Mr Rushworth is a fool, and as we have seen he may have been to some degree inspired by James Henry Leigh. Maria Bertram shares some similarities with Julia-Judith Twisleton Leigh, notably a desire for social advancement through her marriage. And Mrs Norris is, along with Sir Walter Elliot, Austen's nearest approach to a truly evil character. To have Repton and his "improvements" recommended by these three is about as close as Austen comes to outright condemnation.[5]

As it happens, James Henry and the Reverend Thomas Leigh had already employed Repton at Adlestrop in 1800, to "improve" the Rectory gardens and unite them with those of Adlestrop Park.[6] One of his innovations at Adlestrop was a plunge pool and bath house. Repton also created a running stream in view of both the Park and the rectory, falling into a lake. Repton was an accomplished marketer, and included his own account of this feature at Adlestrop in his 1803 work, *Observations on the Theory and Practice of Landscape Gardening*.

> "A lively stream of water has been led through a flower-garden, where its progress down the hill is occasionally obstructed by ledges of rocks, and after a variety of interesting circumstances it falls into a lake at a considerable distance, but in full view of both the mansion and the parsonage, to each of which it makes a delightful, because a natural feature in the landscape."[7]

The irony that Repton's interesting, delightful and above all, "natural" features were only achieved at colossal effort and expense was one which must have appealed to Jane Austen. A skilled Warwickshire farm worker such as a ploughman might normally earn 20 guineas over the course of a year.[8] This allows us to place in perspective Repton's charge of five guineas per day, amounting to at least 1,500 guineas per year (based upon a rough calculation five guineas per day times six days per week, times 50 weeks—assuming two weeks' holiday in the year). To employ

---
5. Alistair M. Duckworth, 'Mansfield Park and Estate Improvements: Jane Austen's Grounds of Being,' *Nineteenth-Century Fiction*, vol. 26, no. 1 (June 1971), 25–48, pp. 28–29.
6. Huxley (2013), p. 107.
7. Quoted in Huxley (2013), p. 109.
8. Murray (1813), p. 169.

Repton was to announce, in the most ostentatious way, one's wealth, taste and desire to keep up with the times.

By 1816, when Shelley's friend, the satirist Thomas Love Peacock, published *Headlong Hall*, every reader would know that Repton was the original of his landscape gardening consultant, Mr Milestone. Mr Milestone is genial and ever-ready to explain the scenery, which is invariably accompanied by a rich and stupid client spoiling the view.

> "Here sweeps a plantation, in that beautiful regular curve: there winds a gravel walk: here are parts of the old wood, left in these majestic circular clumps, disposed at equal distances with wonderful symmetry...The stream, you see, is become a canal: the banks are perfectly smooth and green, sloping to the water's edge: and there is Lord Littlebrain, rowing in an elegant boat."

Mr Milestone explains an overhanging rock:

> "In the other [hand] is a ponderous stone, so exactly balanced as to be apparently ready to fall on the head of any person who may happen to be beneath: and there is Lord Littlebrain walking under it."

Lord Littlebrain is again perceived driving four-in-hand along a belt of lime-trees, and finally:

> "Here is the new house, without a tree near it, standing in the midst of an undulating lawn: a white, polished, angular building, reflected to a nicety in this waveless lake: and there you see Lord Littlebrain looking out of the window."[9]

Peacock's satire confirms Jane Austen's depiction of the employment of Repton as a resort of the landed with more money than sense. Naturally, this meant that his services were sought once the Leighs were settled at Stoneleigh.

---

9. Thomas Love Peacock, *Headlong Hall* (London: Dent, Everyman's Library, 1969), pp. 56–58.

Repton was engaged to make an assessment. He first visited in 1808.[10] He considered that Stoneleigh Abbey, as it stood, was "a curious specimen of the architecture of every date" from the tenth century to the eighteenth.[11] It was unique: "I look upon Stoneleigh Abbey as a place *Sui generis* and not to be compared to any other place."[12] Regarding the interior, he found the rooms old-fashioned, with

> "...all the dignity together with the gloom of those Cedar Parlours occasionally mentioned in the works of Richardson, when society existed without the Music, the Pamphlet, or News Papers, of the present day."[13]

For the outdoor setting, Repton prepared a Red Book for Stoneleigh. This was a book of sketches which allowed the viewer a "before and after" perspective, using a transparent page overlay. The Stoneleigh book is a large volume, similar in scale to Repton's books for Brighton Pavilion and Woburn Abbey.[14] Conscious of the place's rich history, Repton emphasised the importance of retaining ancient features such as the abbey gatehouse. One of his chief concerns was to improve the access into the abbey and park.

> "The Approach to a place is one of the first considerations in all modern Improvement, and it is impossible for any place to require it more than Stoneleigh Abbey, because from its situation, on a large peninsula, formed by the Winding of the [Avon] river and the badness of the Cross Roads to Dunchurch, it is at present difficult of access from all directions."[15]

A pair of bridges formed part of Repton's plan for improving access. The need for one on the western, or main, approach to the abbey seemed clearer than for one on the southern side. In the end, the southern bridge

---

10. Hazel Fryer, "The Park and Gardens at Stoneleigh Abbey," in Bearman (ed.2004), 243–261, p. 248.
11. Geoffrey Tyack, "Stoneleigh Abbey in the Nineteenth Century," in Bearman (ed. 2004), 116–130, p. 117.
12. Fryer (2004), p. 243.
13. Tyack (2004), p. 117.
14. http://www.plants.info/gardens/stoneleigh-abbey-repton.htm (Accessed 8 December 2015).
15. Fryer (2004), p. 249.

remains "a temporary structure," while the western bridge was a key feature of Repton's vision.[16]

For the bridge, the merits of a cast-iron construction were debated, but Repton recommended stone. He suggested a three-arched form, "rather picturesque in outline (with) a hint from the simple, rude but celebrated bridge of Llanwrst built by Inigo Jones."[17] This was rather a daring suggestion: the 1636 Jones bridge, which survives today, looks surprisingly modern, and not at all classical, in its use of local dark stone. Repton's designs for Stoneleigh were not completely carried out. This may have been in part because in January 1811, on returning home with his daughters from a ball, Repton met with an accident which put an end to his professional work.[18] In the event, it was John Rennie who designed the bridge, while a number of other professionals such as Charles Smith undertook improvements to the abbey proper. It is unfortunate, but perhaps in the event understandable, that while Repton will forever be associated with Stoneleigh and its Austen links, John Rennie (1761–1821) is forgotten in Stoneleigh lore: in the 2004 Bearman volume, Rennie receives only two mentions as the bridge engineer. Of these, only one is listed in the index to the volume.[19]

Where Humphry Repton was very much part of the world we know from Austen's works, standing as he did for the earlier era in which wealthy landowners promoted their own status with estate improvements, his younger contemporary John Rennie represented the new world of industrial development. Repton had stumbled into his brilliant career after many false starts: Rennie began in business for himself as a teenage scientific prodigy. He went on to design and build canals, docks, harbours and bridges which promoted industry, transport and defence, on behalf of local and national corporations. As we saw in the evidence of the gas lighting engineer John Perks, this industrial world existed in parallel with the agricultural one Austen described. The two worlds came

---

16. Fryer (2004), p. 252.
17. Fryer (2004), p. 254.
18. Stephen Daniels, "Repton, Humphry (1752–1818)," *Oxford Dictionary of National Biography*, Oxford University Press, 2004; online edn, Jan 2012 http://www.oxforddnb.com/view/article/23387 (Accessed 9 Dec 2015).
19. Bearman (2004), index on p. 289 lists a brief mention of Rennie on p. 119; the other (unlisted in the index) is on p. 254.

together when Rennie was chosen in 1811 to build the Stoneleigh bridge. He was a man of extraordinary skill and energy, which is reflected in his achievements. Growing up in lowland Scotland, he impressed visitors to Dunbar High School with his mathematical knowledge: "a second Newton," wrote one.[20] He funded his university studies at Edinburgh in science through working as a millwright. In 1784, in his early twenties, he decided to visit the nerve centre of the new industrial age: Birmingham, where Matthew Boulton and James Watt were producing their steam engines which powered new developments in both England and throughout Europe.[21]

Rennie spent two months in Birmingham, presumably becoming familiar with Warwickshire. In the following years he set up in business for himself in London, building the milling equipment for the famous Albion Mills, designed and built by Samuel Wyatt, near Blackfriars. The Albion was a massive milling complex, the equipment and systems designed and built by Rennie and other engine makers, including major innovations in the use of steam power.[22] Rennie showcased the mill to many visitors, and it became a tourist attraction in state-of-the-art technology.[23] It burned down in suspicious circumstances in 1791, but by then Rennie's career was well and truly made. In fact, Rennie — then only 30-years-old — was already complaining of being chronically overcommitted. By 1790 he was preparing four major projects for Parliament; in 1791 he was involved, among other works, with the Rochdale Canal, the Lancaster Canal and the Stowmarket Navigation.[24] The design and construction of canals, which brought water transport to areas previously inaccessible, was at its height in the last two decades of the eighteenth

---

20. David Loch, HM Inspector of Fisheries, visiting the school in 1776. Quoted in Cyril T. G. Boucher, *John Rennie 1761–1821: The Life and Work of a Great Engineer* (Manchester University Press: Manchester, 1963), p. 5.
21. Andrew Saint, "Rennie, John (1761–1821)," *Oxford Dictionary of National Biography*, Oxford University Press, 2004; online edn, Sept 2013 http://www.oxforddnb.com/view/article/23376 (Accessed 9 Dec 2015).
22. Boucher (1963), p. 10.
23. Boucher (1963), p. 11.
24. P. S. M. Cross-Rudkin, "Rennie, John, FRS, FRSE (1761–1821)," in A. W. Skempton *et al.* (eds.), *A Biographical Dictionary of Civil Engineers in Great Britain and Ireland, Volume 1: 1500–1830* (London: Thomas Telford Publishing on behalf of the Institution of Civil Engineers, 2002), 554–569, p. 557.

century. As various industries increased their production, the problems of transport in large areas of Great Britain became more obvious, and water transport became a priority.²⁵ The technical and logistical challenges involved were huge. Rennie designed and built the channels themselves, the dams required to control water flow (and allow compensation for aggrieved mill owners who complained of losing water supply), and the aqueducts which took the flow over roads and rivers. Many of his canal bridges still stand.²⁶

One influential friend was John Jervis, later Lord St Vincent, First Lord of the Admiralty, who in 1793 was a shareholder in the Chelmer and Blackwater Navigation, one of Rennie's major projects (completed as the Chelmer and Blackwater Canal in 1797).²⁷ Jervis' nephew and eventual heir was Edward Jervis Ricketts (later Jervis Jervis), who had briefly been the (wronged) husband of Julia-Judith's sister Mary-Cassandra. It is possible that this connection eventually led to his undertaking the work on the Stoneleigh bridge, following Repton's injury. Without some personal connection to Warwickshire or the Leighs, it is a little difficult to understand why Rennie would have taken on such an insignificant private contract.

To give an idea of his workload at this period, Rennie, by 1811, was working on a range of ongoing projects, of both national and local significance. These included the Bell Rock Lighthouse off the coast of Angus in Scotland, the Grand Trunk Canal (Uttoxeter branch), Ramsgate and Margate harbours, the Plymouth Breakwater, the long-running mega-projects of the London Docks and Waterloo Bridge, and other lower-profile works.²⁸ Several of these projects survive. The Bell Rock Lighthouse, for which Rennie, as engineer, and Robert Stevenson, assistant engineer, were both responsible, is of such durable construction that it has stood, without alteration or replacement, under the harshest of conditions, for two centuries. For its part, another Rennie project in the Plymouth Breakwater has also stood the test of time, from its initial

---

25. A. W. Skempton, *Civil Engineers and Engineering in Britain, 1600–1830* (Aldershot: Variorum Ashgate, 1996), p. 28.
26. Boucher (1963), p. 97.
27. Cross-Rudkin (2002), p. 562; completion: p. 566.
28. Plans: Cross-Rudkin (2002), p. 568; projects: p. 566.

Drink to the Dead Men

purpose in protecting British ships of the Channel Fleet against possible French attack.

Waterloo Bridge (opened in 1817), is no longer extant, but is often regarded as Rennie's masterpiece: built of granite, it was then the most expensive bridge ever built in Britain. Technologically it broke new ground, with foundations laid within coffer dams (box-like structures in which workers could labour under water), and the piles driven by steam engines.[29] Engravings from 1817 show a remarkably beautiful and modern-looking bridge with nine arches, nearly 750 metres long in total. The bridge became a symbol of London throughout the nineteenth century, being replaced only in the twentieth.

In addition to the management of his projects, Rennie in 1811 was preparing plans or reports for the Kennet and Avon Canal extension, the Liverpool Docks, the road from Dumfries to Port Patrick, the Queensferry Piers in the Firth of Forth, and the proposed London and Cambridge Junction Canal. The preparation of these reports was a key element of Rennie's work as a consulting engineer. A typical printed report ran to 20 pages, often with folding plans enclosed. It would be sent to the authority responsible for the project, and often printed in quantities sufficient for circulation among commissioners, management board members, or interested members of the public.[30] Without any automated copying, Rennie's fine hand-drawn plans had to be reproduced by professional copyists for publication. Nobody, not even John Rennie, could be personally responsible for every element of this programme of works. The only way in which he could manage his schedule was to delegate day-to-day project control, after creating the initial plans, designs and cost estimates himself. He developed a network of men he could nominate as resident engineers, although it could be difficult to find the person with the right mix of skills for the job. The resident engineer was responsible for the supervision of construction and for certifying work carried out by contractors.[31] The resident engineer was employed by the client, and Rennie made it clear that he was not responsible for

---

29. Waterloo Bridge: Cross-Rudkin (2002), p. 556.
30. Reports: Skempton (1996), p. xiv; Cross-Rudkin (2002), p. 568.
31. Skempton (1996), p. xvi.

the nominee's actions. On some rare occasions, Rennie was forced to dismiss a resident engineer who had departed from his brief.³²

The resident engineer engaged for the Stoneleigh Abbey bridge was George Jones. Jones' father, Charles Jones, was a civil engineering contractor who worked on the Bridgewater Canal and other canals in the 1780s. Jones senior tendered for the Sapperton Tunnel, a challenging excavation project on the Thames and Severn Canal, but was unable to complete the work, partly because of his alcohol problem and spells in prison for debt.³³ His sons Charles junior and George worked with him on the Sapperton Tunnel, and one son was agent on the Norwood Tunnel on the Chesterfield Canal, with indifferent results. The family repeatedly tendered for tunneling work, but rarely completed a job.³⁴ It is probably this George Jones who had worked with Rennie on the Royal Military Canal near Romney Marsh in 1804–1805.³⁵ This project was taken out of the hands of Rennie and his contractors in 1805, after slow progress on what was seen as an important initiative for national defence. Rennie blamed the contractors and poor project management.³⁶

It is perhaps indicative of the low priority Rennie placed on the Stoneleigh contract that he again appointed Jones to undertake it. Jones made a deposition to the 1828 Lords hearing in which he stated:

> "That in the year 1811 he was appointed by the late John Rennie, esquire, to superintend the erection of a bridge over the Avon in the grounds belonging to Stoneley Abbey, which was to be built by contract for the reverend Thomas Leigh; and after the death of the reverend Thomas Leigh he was appointed by the late James Henry Leigh, esquire, to superintend all the trades-people, workmen, and labourers, employed on the estate, and he now holds the same official situation under Chandos Leigh, esquire."³⁷

---

32. Cross-Rudkin (2002), p. 563.
33. Chrimes, Mike, "Jones Family (fl. 1770–1835)," in Skempton *et al.* (eds., 2002), pp. 378–379, p. 378.
34. Chrimes (2002), p. 379.
35. Cross-Rudkin (2002), p 566.
36. http://www.royalmilitarycanal.com/pages/history.asp (Accessed 8 December 2015).
37. George Jones deposition (4 January 1828), Leigh (1834), vol. II, p. 293.

Thus, Jones arrived at Stoneleigh as the resident engineer on Rennie's behalf, and only later took on his expanded role in charge of all estate labour. Like Hay the gamekeeper, Jones found himself with increasing influence in the Stoneleigh world as time went on.

We have seen in *Chapter 9* that Richard Barnett, in 1848, accused Chandos Leigh, the late Julia-Judith, and the late George Jones of having caused the deaths of Billinges and Forbes at the bridge. One of the many questions raised by this accusation is why John Rennie, who embodied the profession of engineering in his time, would have permitted one of his building projects to become a murder scene. Part of the answer, as we have seen, is that Rennie himself was far too busy to be personally involved at Stoneleigh. He will have made a site visit, drawn the plans, designed the bridge, given a cost estimate, and appointed the resident engineer, but the actual build was left to Jones. If Rennie was too busy and too distant to be culpable for misdeeds at the bridge, the same cannot be said for his resident engineer. Jones' record, as we have seen, was mixed at best. He may well have felt that this was his last chance to work on a Rennie project. Perhaps he had nothing to lose from being party to murder: he may have had a great deal to gain, in terms of a new career. If the Leighs required Jones to commit murder, they were bound, on the "hang together or hang separately" principle, to keep him employed and within their sight.

In surviving evidence, it appears to have been part of the Leigh family's strategy to be vague about the timeline of the bridge construction. Julia-Judith, in her 1828 evidence, was asked about the bridge. This in itself was striking, because nowhere else in the case material is the bridge mentioned. Clearly, George Leigh's legal team had heard that the bridge may have been the site of the disposal of the Christopher stone: they may even have heard that it was the site of a killing. Julia-Judith, in her evidence at the 1829 hearings, was asked by William Adam, for the claimant:

> **Adam:** Did you take the charge of the building and the ornamenting of that bridge?
> **Julia-Judith:** No; Mr Rennie had the management.
> **Adam:** But he consulted you as a person of taste?

> **Julia-Judith:** He consulted me, and so did Mr Thomas Leigh...[38]

Julia-Judith did not seem to be aware that Adam was making fun of her: her self-importance was such that she did not see anything absurd in the idea that she might have been a consultant on the build to John Rennie, the genius of the age (Richard Barnett, for his part, seems to have believed that Julia-Judith was in charge at the bridge: "Lady Leigh [sic] directed those alterations."[39]) She did not make any mention of Jones' role, possibly to shield him from scrutiny. Nor did Jones, in his deposition, make any further reference to the bridge, focusing only on the wine cellar alterations, and his non-recollection of the Christopher stone.[40]

Julia-Judith was deliberately vague about the commencement date of the bridge works.

> "I do not recollect when it was begun, but I can tell that a foundation stone waited for me; they said they had waited for me a day or two to see the foundation stone laid; and that happened to be on the birth-day of the present king, and I gave the men five guineas to drink His Majesty's health."[41]

This must have been in 1812, as Julia-Judith implied that the Reverend Thomas was still alive (he died in June 1813). The birthday of the then Prince Regent (from 1820 King George IV) was 12 August, so this dates the episode to the height of summer: probably the time when night works, as described by Barnett, could have taken place. Causton, in a footnote, pointed out that Julia-Judith had seemed "considerably distressed" up to this point, but on mentioning the King's health, "gave the latter part of her answer in an elevated tone accompanied with action becoming to the toast."[42]

The reason for Julia-Judith's apparent distress may well have been that the early days of the bridge construction were characterised by crime and concealment. There seems little doubt that Julia-Judith, with this

---

38. Leigh (1834), vol. II, p. 256.
39. *Report* (1849), p. 10, column 2.
40. Leigh (1834), vol. II, pp. 293–294.
41. Leigh (1834), vol. II, p. 256, with footnote.
42. Causton in Leigh (1834), vol. II, p. 256, footnote.

tale of the toast to the Prince Regent, was pre-emptively accounting for moneys later paid to the workmen in connection with keeping them quiet. Barnett, in 1848, claimed that after the night of the killings, "the men [about ten men were on site] were offered money to be silent." [43]

During the trial of Charles Griffin in 1849, Barnett's evidence was presented in a more lengthy form than by Griffin himself in his 1848 work. Here Barnett is quoted:

> "I was between 14 and 15 when I first worked at Stoneleigh Abbey. I am now [in 1848] 52; I am positive I was more than 14 but not more than 15, and when this occurrence took place I should think I was 16 or 17."[44]

That is, if Barnett was born in 1796, the bridge killings could have taken place at the earlier end of the construction spectrum, which is to say in 1812, or one or two years later.

The Leigh papers record the first payments made for work on the bridge in 1812.[45] Trees were being felled for the site in early August.[46] Numerous bills came from blacksmiths, iron founders, and wheelwrights. John Rennie had greatly promoted the use of cast iron in all kinds of industrial contexts, including developing the first known iron gears (previously gearing had been made from wood), so it should not surprise that in the construction of his bridges, considerable amounts of iron machinery were required.[47] Rennie himself hired out "portable crab cranes" to the site. These were probably brought from London, where Rennie's Stamford Street workshop supplied machinery of all kinds for plants great and small across Britain, Europe, and even Japan.[48]

The other striking feature of these early days of the build was the amount of money paid to George Jones. In 1812, initial estimates for the

---

43. Griffin (1848), p. 53.
44. *Report* (1849), p. 11, column 2.
45. SBTRO DR 18/3/48/3–41.
46. SBTRO DR 18/3/48/5.
47. Ironworkers: SBTRO DR 18/3/48/13, 29 January 1813; blacksmith (Thomas Howlett, Causton's "Silly Tommy") DR 18/3/48/16, 20 February 1813. Rennie's developments in use of iron, including gearing: Boucher (1963), p. 83.
48. Crab cranes at Stoneleigh: SBTRO DR 18/3/48/18, 19 April 1813. Rennie's equipment supply: Boucher (1963), p. 86.

bridge cost, after consultation with both Repton and Rennie, had been £3,725.[49] Rennie was known for quoting construction costs which were on the high side, preferring to lose work rather than make an unrealistically low estimate.[50] In March 1813, Jones was paid £1,697.4s.0d. In June 1813, Jones received another £1,250.7s.11d.[51] In February 1814, Jones was paid a further £2,695.10s.0d.[52] Not counting shillings and pence, these payments to Jones total over £5,642, a blow-out against the estimate of £1,917, or 51 per cent, by March 1814, with the project still having some time to run. Under the system current at the time, Jones will probably have had to pay the subcontractors and labourers out of these sums.[53] Nevertheless, it looks as though Jones himself was probably receiving a generous portion, particularly in comparison with Rennie himself.

In 1797, as principal engineer on the Lancaster Canal, John Rennie had been paid a total of £262.10s: more than ten times what a skilled rural workman could earn, but not a particularly high salary. We recall that clergy were considered entitled to seek a second living if their first amounted to less than 200 or 300 pounds.[54] By 1809, as the leading engineer of his day, Rennie's yearly income from all his consulting work was £975 plus salaries.[55] While we cannot be sure how much of the Stoneleigh payments, totaling over five and a half thousand pounds in a two-year period, were going to Jones himself, it is difficult to avoid the conclusion that he was doing well out of the project. The Stoneleigh bridge cost more, in fact, than the £4,000 which Byron paid to the Greek revolutionaries at Missolonghi in 1823: you could buy a fleet in Greece for less than a smallish Rennie bridge in Warwickshire project-managed by

---

49. SBTRO DR 18/17/38/54, 29 December 1812.
50. Boucher (1963), p. 75.
51. SBTRO DR 18/3/48/16, 20 February 1813 (£1,697.4s.0d); DR 18/3/48/22, 26 June 1813 (£1,250.7s.11d).
52. SBTRO DR 18/3/48/36, 19 February 1814 (£2,695.10s.0d).
53. Rennie's system of relying on resident engineers to evaluate and properly pay contract work: Cross-Rudkin (2002), p. 564.
54. Irene Collins, *Jane Austen: The Parson's Daughter* (London: The Hambledon Press, 1998), p. xx. 1838: John Henry Barrow (ed.), *The Mirror of Parliament, Sessions 1837–1838*, 2nd series, vol. VI (London: Longman etc.), p. 4643.
55. Rennie's fee in 1797: Boucher (1963), p. 73. Income in 1809: Cross-Rudkin (2002), p. 565.

George Jones.[56] It may be that the Leighs were paying Jones for more than simply his above-board services.

While in the context of Rennie's other works, the Stoneleigh bridge must have seemed relatively straightforward, it was not without challenges. While his stone bridges, such as Stoneleigh bridge and Ellel Grange bridge on the Lancaster Canal, look simple and classical, this is partly because Rennie himself had solved an architectural problem which had occupied theorists for centuries. Rennie and his professor at Edinburgh, John Robison, had both worked on the principles governing the size and forces involved in the creation of stone arched bridges. Rennie introduced a feature called an inverted arch, which supports the main arch. Rennie also established the ratio in which the arch stones should increase from the keystone in the middle, out to the piers or abutments. He was the first to correctly calculate the required size of the abutment, which is the portion of the bridge embedded in the banks of the river or canal, in order to support the bridge under the forces generated by the arch system.[57] The Stoneleigh bridge consists of one main span across the river Avon, and at each bank one smaller "dry arch". Between the arches are niches, "set in rusticated stonework."[58]

Barnett gives some information in passing about the construction: as a stonemason himself, he can be considered as an informed witness. Preparation for the abutments included the creation of space for the giant blocks required to sustain the bridge. "A cavity was made and a stone [was cut] to fit it."[59] Barnett and the other masons would have used hand tools to cut and shape the blocks of stone: as for thousands of years, their tools were the square, the level, the plumb-line, the hammer, the chisel, the mallet, and the saw.[60] The hole was made purposely large so that the stone could fit comfortably: "it is made to fit in easy on purpose."[61]

---

56. Marchand (1970), p. 423.
57. Boucher (1963) 42–45.
58. Description at https://historicengland.org.uk/listing/the-list/list-entry/1000377 (Accessed 9 December 2015).
59. Griffin (1848), p. 52.
60. *The Book of English Trades, and Library of the Useful Arts* (London: J. Souter for Richard Phillips, 1818), p. 374.
61. *Report* (1849), p. 11, column 2.

The Missing Monument Murders

Barnett saw Billinges and Forbes get into the hole to receive the block. "I should say the hole would be two feet by three feet, to receive a stone a ton and a half." Billinges and Forbes were ostensibly sent into the hole to spread mortar for the stone, but Barnett queried why two men were needed: "there was only room for one."[62] Another man who had worked on the bridge was William Faxon, who gave evidence at Griffin's trial for libel in 1849. By this time he was a rag-and-bone collector, scraping a living from the waste left by others. He stated that in 1812 or 1813 he had helped to dig the foundations of the new bridge, driving piles and pumping out water on Sundays and at night, between the normal work shifts. He then worked on the abutment, digging out earth and carrying it away in barrows. One day Faxon saw George Jones, Julia-Judith and Chandos Leigh come to the site, while two sawyers (men who cut wood for structures on site) carried "something on a truck" (a cart for holding heavy loads). The object was wrapped in matting. The sawyers left, and the object was taken out of the cart. Faxon claimed that two masons, Jones, Julia-Judith and Chandos stood in the foundation hole at the same time.

> "One of the masons gave Lord Leigh a mallet, and he struck the matting three times; the man then put some mortar down, gave the trowel to Lord Leigh, and he spread it about…The matting was in the hole. When his Lordship had spread the mortar, Lord Leigh, Mrs Leigh, and Jones got out of the hole: the hole was on the foundation. The first blow sounded sharp like as if platters or something of that sort were in the matting; the other blows I did not hear."[63]

Faxon's account may help to explain Barnett's. Understandably, Barnett was concerned with the killings themselves rather than any possible explanation or motive for them. If Billinges and Forbes were these two masons who had helped Chandos bury the monument in the foundations, this would give a motive for the attack on them, which appears to

---

62. *Report* (1849), p. 11, column 2.
63. *Report* (1849), p. 22, column 1.

have taken place that very night. Faxon confirms that it was the day after the object was buried in the foundations, that he saw blood on the site.

> "The next day I was at work in the same place, and I saw Shaw and another man in the hole; they asked me to come down there, and to take the tool I was working with. I did so, and when I got there he pointed to the hole, and I saw something like crimson froth. When I moved it with my tool it changed colour and was just like blood. I put dirt over it, or most of it, and then returned to my work. When I was in the hole, I disturbed what was in it, and then my spade had marks of blood on it, when I was told to leave the hole directly. I saw that the ground was not in the same state around the hole as on the previous day."[64]

For his part, Barnett reported that while the men's bodies caused the stone to sit six or eight inches higher than the others, it was pared off to make it level. On the same night as the murder, the men placed a course of stones over the bodies. He stated confidently that "The bodies are under the middle of the dry arch" (on the Stoneleigh side of the river).

One bridge expert, called at the trial of Chandos Leigh in 1848, gave as his opinion that the invert used to support the dry arch (Rennie's signature inverted arch), would make it relatively easy to search the location indicated by Barnett.[65] "I'll lay my life down, sir, if they are not found," was Barnett's comment on signing his deposition. As we have seen, however, permission to search under the bridge was not granted by the Warwickshire magistrates.[66]

The Stoneleigh bridge was not formally signed off as complete until 1818, the year it appears in the voluminous list of Rennie's works.[67] Once completed, it featured in the increasing range of guidebooks to Warwickshire which appeared for the use of the tourist. Francis Smith, in his 1827 account of Leamington Spa and environs, realised that the name of Rennie was a selling point.

---

64. *Report* (1849), p. 22, column 1.
65. Barnett's account of body location: *Report* (1849), p. 11, column 1. Expert opinion: by one James Leigh (no relation, and not named in text to minimise confusion), Griffin (1848), p. 57.
66. Griffin (1848), p. 58.
67. Boucher (1963), p. 135.

"Stoneleigh Abbey is most delightfully situated in the midst of a luxuriant and fertile country, adorned by extensive and venerable woods, and watered by the Avon, which being here of ample breadth, flows through the grounds with a noble effect. Over one part of this river is a fine Bridge, of one arch, erected from a plan of Mr Rennie, and is the principal approach to the Abbey."[68]

Another Smith, this time William, took the opportunity to praise Chandos in connection with the bridge.

"The present possessor has recently made considerable alterations and improvements in this grand mansion; and under his direction a handsome new bridge has been constructed over the Avon, which adds much to its beauty and magnificence."[69]

Finally, the Stoneleigh bridge appeared in a technical manual published in 1839. This work showcased a number of recent bridges, including London Bridge (by Rennie's son, also John, later Sir John Rennie), and the elder Rennie's bridges over the Avon at Stoneleigh and over the Earn in Scotland.

"We have [in the volume under review] next the drawings of Stoneleigh Bridge in Warwickshire, constructed by the late John Rennie, and consisting of one arch, with two land arches in the abutments. The design of this work is beautifully balanced..."[70]

As Richard Barnett would try to explain in 1848, in response to a sceptical question as to how the corpses could have been placed without ruining the build, the entombment had not spoiled the architectural effect:

---

68. Francis Smith, *An Historical and Descriptive Guide to Leamington Spa, With a brief account of Warwick, Kenilworth, Guy's Cliff, Grove Park, Stoneleigh, Baginton, Offchurch, etc.* (Leamington, London: Southam, 7th edn, 1827), no page numbers.
69. William Smith, *A New and Compendious History of the County of Warwick, From the earliest period to the present time, etc.* (Birmingham: W. Emans, 1830), p. 116.
70. Anonymous review of E. Cresy, *A Practical Treatise on Bridge Building* (London: John Williams), in *The Civil Engineer and Architect's Journal*, vol. II, May 1839, pp. 189–190.

> "Two human bodies in a cavity to which a stone had been exactly fitted, do not make the stone too large."[71]

This chapter's epigraph shows that Chandos himself, understandably if Barnett, Faxon, Wilcox and other witnesses were to be believed, had mixed feelings about the "magnificent" Rennie bridge. There must also have been local rumours. In the 1849 proceedings against Charles Griffin, one witness was Ann Burford. She had been still-room maid at Stoneleigh, living at the abbey from 1819 to the end of 1821 or start of 1822. She remembered a group of the servants having a trip in a boat down the river.

> "When we were under the bridge, the men, as a joke, I suppose, said, 'Come, now, we must drink to the dead men.'"[72]

---

71. *Report* (1849), p. 11, column 2.
72. *Report* (1849), p. 21, column 1.

The Missing Monument Murders

CHAPTER ELEVEN

The Billinges Problem

"[William Billinge(s)] said if I valued my life I should go away. I asked after Joseph, and he said he was killed by a stone falling on him. [I] expressed surprise, and Billinge hung down his head, and said no more."

William Faxon, 1849[1]

Charles Griffin first took Barnett's statement at around the time he represented the Stoneleigh Abbey rioters. He also heard about the witness William Faxon. After Sarah Smallbone's death in December 1846, former abbey worker George Shaw came to Warwickshire. Like Barnett, Shaw made a formal statement about the tragedy at the bridge.[2] Charles Griffin felt that this information was too serious to be left to the vagaries of local authorities. He wrote to the Home Secretary, Sir George Grey (1799–1882), and was granted an interview in November 1846.[3] The Home Secretary, Griffin reports, began to read Shaw's (or possibly Barnett's) deposition, then—upon reaching "a particular name," closed the documents and referred Griffin back to the Warwickshire magistrates.[4]

The name was doubtless that of Chandos Leigh. Grey will have been sensitive to the political implications. Chandos Leigh was a well-known Whig member of the House of Lords, if not as vocal as in his younger years; Grey, some years Chandos' junior, was also a born-in-the-purple

---

1. *Report* (1849), p. 22, column 1.
2. Griffin (1848), pp. 46–47. Smallbone's death: according to Mary Draper (March 1849), "she died two years ago, on the 15th of December." *Report* (1849), p. 18, column 2; death record confirms year and last quarter, if not precise month: "England and Wales Death Registration Index 1837–2007," database, *FamilySearch* (https://familysearch.org/ark:/61903/1:1:2JM5-B9V (Accessed 18 February 2016)), Sarah Smallbones, 1846.
3. *Report* (1849), p. 9, column 1.
4. *Report* (1849), p. 9, column 1.

Whig. His uncle, Lord Grey, had been a key Whig politician in the first quarter of the century, succeeding to the *de facto* leadership of the group on the death of Charles James Fox, and retaining that position until the Whigs eventually returned to government in 1830.[5]

Griffin may have been optimistic, but he had been within his rights to approach Grey, since the Home Secretary was the ultimate authority for the recently created police forces in England. Robert Peel, as Home Secretary in 1829, had introduced the Metropolitan Police Act, which established an organized police force in London. Griffin's wish to take advantage of the new policing resources was consistent with his preference, as a man of science, for the most up-to-date approach.

On the other hand, the younger Grey's reluctance to deal with the matter reflected both the realities of contemporary politics and the limits of policing as it stood. The emphasis of the metropolitan force at the time was on crime prevention, with detection a secondary focus.[6] In any event, detectives in our understanding of the term barely existed: a detective department of the Metropolitan Police had been created as recently as 1842, consisting only of eight men.[7] A proposal for the new London force to send inexperienced investigators out to rural Warwickshire, to pursue claims of murder made by two tradesmen against a member of the House of Lords, would represent a precedent which only the most adventurous, or radical, of Home Secretaries could be expected to entertain.

Grey will have been conscious of the national scandal which had resulted the first, and last, time the Metropolitan Police had intervened in Warwickshire, on the direction of one of his predecessors as Home Secretary and fellow Whig, Lord John Russell. Fearing Chartist rioting in 1839, the local authorities in Birmingham, which had no police force

---

5. David Frederick Smith, "Grey, Sir George, Second Baronet (1799–1882)," *Oxford Dictionary of National Biography*, Oxford University Press, 2004; online edn, Jan 2008 http://www.oxforddnb.com/view/article/11533 (Accessed 9 Dec 2015).
6. Sir Richard Mayne (1796–1868), first and longest-serving Commissioner of the Metropolitan Police, 1829: "The primary object of an efficient police is the prevention of crime: the next that of detection and punishment of offenders if crime is committed." http://content.met.police.uk/Site/historypolicing (Accessed 5 January 2015).
7. https://englishlegalhistory.wordpress.com/2013/07/23/detection-in-england-from-bow-street-to-the-met/ (Accessed 5 January 2015). Team of eight: Elaine A. Reynolds, *Before the Bobbies: The Night Watch and Police Reform in Metropolitan London, 1720–1830* (Stanford: Stanford University Press), 1998, p. 152.

of its own, had requested support from London. One hundred officers were sent; having no jurisdiction outside London, they were sworn in as "special constables" in Birmingham. Clashing with demonstrators and coming off worse, the London police had to be rescued by a local military unit. Upon the third confrontation with protesters, the police responded with open cutlasses. The rioting was quelled, but an outcry followed.[8]

It was absurd that a major industrial centre such as Birmingham lacked its own police protection. The situation represented, in microcosm, much of the difficulty in effecting any reform of law enforcement anywhere in Britain. Local magistrates, resenting a challenge to their traditional power base, had opposed the grant of incorporation to the Birmingham city authorities. That charter had been granted in 1838, but the opponents of incorporation claimed that the new body had no power to raise funds for a police force. The town corporation was obliged to make an urgent appeal to the Home Secretary for ten thousand pounds to set one up. This was agreed, on the basis that, for the interim, the Birmingham police force remained under central (the Home Secretary's) control. Predictably, this resulted in local complaints about centralised despotism.[9]

It was partly this resentment of London interference which caused the delays in the development of organized policing in rural areas by local authorities. The events in Birmingham confirmed the need for such development, which had been in train since the 1836 Royal Commission into the best way to establish a rural system. In the event, the County Police Act 1839, passed shortly after the Birmingham riots, allowed, but did not require, local authorities to set up forces. Such a requirement was not eventually made until the County and Borough Police Act of 1856.[10]

Meanwhile, in the 1840s, law enforcement in Warwickshire persisted largely as it had for several hundred years, administered by incompetent and self-important constables in the style of Shakespeare's Dogberry (notionally of Sicily, but quite possibly, in origin, a Warwickshire figure). Most towns now supplemented these archaic institutions with a few paid night-watchmen, but across England most rural forces comprised only

---

8. T. A Critchley, *A History of Police in England and Wales* (London: Constable), 1978, p. 81
9. Critchley (1978), pp. 82–84.
10. https://www.cityoflondon.police.uk/about-us/history/Pages/British-Police-history.aspx (Accessed 9 December 2015).

five men or fewer.[11] Policing was thus rudimentary, even after the establishment of the first local force in 1840. The service was unpopular, and it was found difficult to recruit men to serve as constables.[12]

Detection, as ever, was a secondary concern. There was also the problem that if one private citizen wished to bring an action against another, he or she had to fund investigations and witnesses himself or herself.[13] Astonishingly, England lacked a universal, independent system of public prosecution until 1986. Until this recent date, every prosecution in England and Wales was, in law, a private prosecution.[14]

In the early nineteenth century, if a prosecutor succeeded in having the case heard by the court, this meant by the local magistrates, who were all landowners. In Warwickshire, none of these was the equal of Lord Leigh. He was the *de facto* social leader of the county, in virtue of both his title and the fact that his landholding was the largest and grandest. It was unlikely that such a bench would find against him. Knowing that a referral to the Warwickshire magistrates was unlikely to secure an adequate investigation into the claims of Barnett and Shaw, Griffin bitterly resented Grey's inaction.

Grey's attitude has been characterised as representative of "a certain nonchalant opportunism" towards police affairs during the 1840s. "The Home Office was content to see nothing, hear nothing, and do nothing—unless correspondence came its way, and then it did as little as possible."[15] Grey did at least, as the decade went on, focus on Chartist agitation, which seemed increasingly likely to threaten order in the metropolis and elsewhere.

---

11. Supplementing the ancient system with paid watchmen: Critchley (1978), p. 58. Small size of most rural forces: David Taylor, *Policing the Victorian Town: The Development of the Police in Middlesbrough c. 1840–1914* (Basingstoke: Palgrave Macmillan, 2002), p. 29.
12. Inspector A. J. Hinksman, *The First Hundred Years of the Warwickshire Constabulary* (1957), 'Knightlow Force.' http://warksconstabularyhs.co.uk/the-first-hundred-years-1857-1957/knightlow-force/ (Accessed 28 June 2016).
13. Reynolds (1998), pp. 70–71, referring to the eighteenth century, but the situation persisted well into the nineteenth.
14. Bob Morris, "History of Criminal Investigation," in Tim Newburn, Tom Williamson and Alan Wright (eds.), *Handbook of Criminal Investigation* (Cullompton, Devon/Portland, Oregon: Willan Publishing, 2007), 15–40, p. 15.
15. Critchley (1978), p. 98.

The Billinges Problem

From 1839 to its culmination in April 1848, the Chartists sought what they considered to be the traditional rights of Englishmen: these included fair pay, and electoral reforms such as the vote for every male over 21, secret ballot, and the payment of MPs to allow men from less wealthy backgrounds to stand.[16] Government nervousness about possible rioting rose to a peak in April 1848, as the Chartists planned a mass rally and march on Parliament in London, with an estimated 150,000 people taking part. The rally passed without violence, but as Europe continued to be convulsed by revolutionary activity, English authorities remained on high alert lest a Chartist mob should rise against the aristocracy.[17]

Charles Griffin was not a revolutionary, or even a radical. After being rebuffed by Grey in 1846, he did not rush into action. It had, after all, been two years since he had first heard of the strange allegations. But nor was he deterred by the prospect of his allegations being dismissed as inspired by political radicalism. Griffin applied to one of the Warwick magistrates (not named), who "read all the papers, but could not believe"[18] them. The allegations were so extraordinary that they were, indeed, difficult to believe. The only proper course, Griffin maintained, was to investigate them.

No doubt to the growing dismay of the Leigh family and its agents, Griffin consulted widely among lawyers in the midlands. He approached William Prowting Roberts (1806-1871) of Manchester, who had for some years acted as paid advocate for trade unions. Roberts acted to resist individual acts of oppression, even in cases which he had no expectation of winning.[19] He was known as an active, able and persistent advocate for working people.

The mid-1840s were a critical juncture in which radical lawyers were beginning to have considerable impact on the administration of justice

---

16. Thomas Attwood, MP for Birmingham, introduced the Charter to Parliament on 14 June 1839: G. M. Young and W. D. Handcock (eds.), *English Historical Documents*, vol. XII (1) 1833–1874 (London: Eyre and Spottiswoode, 1956), pp. 415–417.
17. *Illustrated London News*, 15 April 1848, reporting the rally. Official apprehension: Mr Whitehurst, lawyer for Chandos Leigh: *Report* (1849), p. 6, column 1.
18. Griffin (1848), p. 47.
19. Raymond Challinor, "Roberts, William Prowting (1806–1871)," *Oxford Dictionary of National Biography*, Oxford University Press, 2004; online edn, Jan 2008 http://www.oxforddnb.com/view/article/23781 (Accessed 9 Dec 2015).

in regional England. For his part, Roberts challenged a number of decisions made by rural and regional magistrates, taking them to the Queen's Bench in London. The Queen's Bench (or King's Bench, as appropriate) was, until its abolition in 1875, a senior court with a particular responsibility for amending unlawful actions by public authorities. In this period, Roberts placed unprecedented scrutiny on the decisions of local magistrates, which were often characterised by slack procedure and summary hearings.[20] The Queen's Bench (which featured, by this time, such judges as Chandos' friend Thomas, now Lord, Denman) overturned a number of magistrate decisions in which working people had been denied the full protection of the law.[21]

Richard Barnett made a statement to William Prowting Roberts at his Manchester chambers, apparently in the early months of 1848.[22] The involvement of Roberts, as a lawyer identified with organized labour, apparently generated a good deal of concern among the Warwickshire authorities; Barnett seems to have been questioned closely about Roberts' role at the May 1848 hearing. Griffin states that Roberts went on to instruct the prosecution barrister, Mr Pollock, in the prosecution before the Warwickshire magistrates.[23]

Griffin also took advice from other lawyers. He sought counsel from W H Bodkin, a London barrister who was associated with Roberts in some cases at the Queen's Bench.[24] He also approached a Mr Clarkson (not the abolitionist, who had died in 1846), and a Mr Whitehurst, who had acted as a prosecutor in cases at the Derbyshire Assizes.[25] Griffin strongly suggests, without actually quoting them, that it was on the advice of all of these men that a criminal case was made.[26] Roberts, who was present at the hearings but did not speak during the prosecution,

---

20. Christopher Frank, *Master and Servant Law: Chartists, Trade Unions, Radical Lawyers and the Magistracy in England, 1840–1865* (Farnham: Ashgate, 2010), p. 3.
21. Frank (2010), p. 11; Denman: Frank (2010), p. 115.
22. 1847: Griffin (1848), p. 52. 1848: *Report* (1849), p. 12.
23. *Report* (1849), p. 12. Griffin (1848), p. 48.
24. Frank (2010), p. 10.
25. *Sheffield and Rotherham Independent*, 14 August 1841; Whitehurst also appears in several law journals, e.g. *The Justice of the Peace and Poor Law Recorder* (vol. VIII, 1844), p. 631. It would be curious if this were the same Mr Whitehurst who, in March 1849, was to appear as the prosecuting counsel on behalf of Chandos Leigh.
26. Griffin (1848), p. 47.

said that he had submitted a case to Whitehurst, Bodkin, and Clarkson, before proceeding, and on their advice had sent Chandos Leigh notice of the pending charges.[27]

It is not clear how Pollock was chosen to act as the prosecution lawyer on the day. He may possibly have been William Frederick Pollock (1815–1888), who had recently (1846) been appointed a master of the Court of Exchequer, and who was part of a distinguished family of lawyers.[28] He outlined the case for the prosecution, suggesting that Chandos should consent to the removal of part of the bridge in order to ascertain whether human remains and church monuments were interred there.[29]

Chandos' lawyer was George Jones junior, the son of the bridge supervisor. Jones' response to Pollock's opening remarks was that Chandos would not follow the suggestion.

> "If he did, it would prove nothing: he was certain nothing would be found, but that would not stop the calumnies, for the assertion would then be made that the bodies were under the Abbey; and if the Abbey were levelled, and the greenhouses and every building on the estate, they would be no nearer their object: [adding] that [Chandos Leigh] came there totally ignorant of the charges to be made."[30]

Jones added, in a surprising and (it would turn out) delusory show of openness:

> "If the learned gentleman [Pollock] had evidence, let him produce it, they feared it not, whatever might be said."[31]

Richard Barnett offered once more the evidence given in his earlier statement. In addition to the killing of Billinges and Forbes, he spoke of having seen the bodies of Proud and Smith, shown him by John Wilcox.

---

27. Griffin (1848), p. 55.
28. J. M. Rigg, "Pollock, Sir William Frederick, Second Baronet (1815–1888)," rev. Eric Metcalfe, *Oxford Dictionary of National Biography*, Oxford University Press, 2004 http://www.oxforddnb.com/view/article/22480 (Accessed 9 Dec 2015).
29. Griffin (1848), p. 49.
30. Griffin (1848), p. 49.
31. Griffin (1848), p. 49.

"About twelve or one at night they were brought to the bridge in a cart by [John] Sprawson: they were sewn up in a sack a piece, they were put in the abutment."[32]

After the hearing of Barnett's and Wilcox's evidence (though not its details, as Wilcox denied them under oath at this time), a discussion ensued as to whether Shaw's statement should be admitted. Griffin, now sworn as a witness, stated that Shaw's statement had incriminated himself; Griffin believed that Shaw was now dead. Pollock asked what the substance of Shaw's statement had been, but Jones objected to this:

"Mr Pollock having called a witness, who proved Shaw's death, Mr Jones then objected, the statement was not made in the fear of death."[33]

Pollock cited, against this, a ruling by Lord Mansfield, that a confession of crimes was admissible even if not made on a death bed. The issue of the admissibility, or otherwise, of confessions, deathbed or otherwise, was a live issue in the courts of the early nineteenth century. In this period, courts were becoming increasingly reluctant to admit even deathbed confessions.[34]

Against this background, the Warwick magistrates did not admit Shaw's statement in evidence. As it never made it into the court proceedings, this statement, then, was effectively suppressed. It is present neither in the National Archives dossier entitled "Stoneleigh Murders", nor is it available from the Warwickshire Archives.[35]

The content of Shaw's statement, however, was presented by other witnesses at Griffin's libel trial in 1849. Mary Draper stated under oath that Shaw had told her that he was hired to let the stone down upon Billinges and Forbes.

---

32. Griffin (1848), p. 50.
33. Griffin (1848), p. 55.
34. David Bentley, *English Criminal Justice in the Nineteenth Century* (London: Hambledon Press, 1998), pp. 214ff.
35. National Archives dossier: HO 45/2316, consisting entirely of Griffin's 1848 book and his letters to the Home Secretary and other authorities (unanswered). Warwick Archives: email to author from Janette Radcliffe, Warwickshire County Record Office, 8 May 2015.

The Billinges Problem

"Shaw gave the account that he let the stone upon them; he said he was hired to do it,—to let the stone on two men; they had been talking of what had been done, and they must be put away; he was hired to do it, and he received money to do it; there were four men hired to do it, and he was the man that let the stone upon them."[36]

Shaw apparently went on to confirm, in essence, the redacted and explosive evidence of John Wilcox.

"[Shaw] said the men, 'were killed in the abutment by Chandos Leigh and Mrs Leigh: old Jones held one, and Billy Wood held the other.'"

The reason why Shaw was chosen to take part in the killings may have been that he had already committed theft and destruction of monuments from the church. Mary Draper continued:

"After that [Shaw] said he was engaged to go and take the monument out of the church, and he received 17 spade-ace guineas to do it. He said he then took it out; he said he got it through a window; in pulling it out it broke in three pieces; they carried it to a place in the Park and there they dug a hole and buried it."

Whether this was actually the Christopher stone is unclear. Shaw was clear about another monument:

"He took down the first Lord Thomas' monument: when it broke, a piece of brass fell out; he doubled it up and said it would do to buy drink with, but he dare not sell it for fear it should be owned, and Mr Jones should find it out that he had not done as he was ordered. He named the place where it was buried, under the withy tree."[37]

William Faxon, the bone-collector of Ashow, had also heard the substance of Shaw's confessions.

---

36. *Report* (1849), p. 18, columns 1–2.
37. *Report* (1849), p. 18, column 2.

"I saw George Shaw in Kenilworth about 3 years ago [1846], and he said he did not know where Billinge [sic: William Billinges, said to be the father of the man killed] was. At night he told me Joseph Billinge[s] and Forbes were killed underneath a stone. He said the stone fell on one of them above the waistband, and the other about the middle of the thigh. He said Chandos Leigh cut Joe Billinge's throat, and Jones strangled the other. They wound the stone off them and then buried them in the hole."[38]

Faxon's evidence was rambling, and the report in several places includes the note, in parentheses, "Loud laughter." The friends and relatives of Chandos Leigh in the courtroom were determined to treat Mary Draper's and Faxon's evidence as a joke.

There was less laughter when Faxon's allegations went on to implicate other Leigh employees such as Thomas Hill Mortimer, and—once again—Chandos Leigh himself.

"George Shaw said a black man had been brought down to Stoneleigh to swear the murderers to do the deeds: he was brought down by Mortimer or Hill [sic]. Wilcox said they had killed the black man and buried him in the Fountain Court [of the abbey]. Shaw said they were sworn two at a time, and he was one of the last two that were thus sworn. When they left the Abbey Shaw told his other butties [mates] he was not willing to kill Billinge[s], for they would have his family to keep; and while they were going down [to the site] they all agreed not to kill [Billinges].

When they got down they did not go about the work as they had promised, and Chandos came out of the hole, and, with an oath, asked why they did not go to work as they had agreed to do. Shaw told him that they were unwilling because they would have [Billinges'] family to keep, and Lord Leigh replied 'What have you to do with the family? I'll take care of them!' They then let the stone down on the top of these men."[39]

---

38. *Report* (1849), p. 22, column 1.
39. *Report* (1849), p. 22, columns 1–2.

The Billinges Problem

Faxon also said that he had witnessed George Jones senior and Shaw break up a monument with a sledge-hammer, and bury it in a ditch. Faxon had made a statement to William Prowting Roberts.[40]

Because Billinges was the only one of the four murdered masons to have been married with a family, his was the only one whose identity was the subject of any further inquiry. In the absence of missing persons' registers, and without family in the neighbourhood to make inquiries, it appears that working men could simply disappear with barely any questions asked.

It was known that Billinges had a wife and at least one child; Barnett had given evidence to this effect at the 6 May 1848 hearing, naming Billinges as Matthew. He had added that he had seen Mrs Billinges the previous Christmas (1847) in Liverpool.[41] George Naylor, a stonemason from Liverpool, who had known George Shaw, testified in 1849 that Mrs Billinges was still, 35 years on, receiving a payment of 16 or 17 shillings per week.[42]

Within a few weeks after Chandos' abortive magistrates' court hearing, a response came from George Jones junior, of which an account appeared in the *Warwick Advertiser*, 27 May 1848, under the headline "The Stoneleigh Abbey Affair: most important discovery!"

A man had come forward who had provided a deposition to a magistrate at Liverpool, claiming to be named Billinge, and a son of the mason said by Barnett to have been killed. The statement was quoted, in part:

> "I was at the Abbey with my father and brother Joseph when the bridge was going on. They were both stonemasons; my father died in 1825 or 1826; I produce a letter from him to me, dated Stockport, February the 12ᵗʰ, 1822…My father is one of the persons stated to have been buried in the abutments of the bridge; the bridge was building when I was there, and my father lived many years after; he was buried in the ground of the new Methodist chapel at Edgley, near Stockport, I was at the burial, and I afterwards put a stone over his grave… The whole story is a lie and a

---

40. *Report* (1849), p. 22, column 2.
41. Matthew: Griffin (1848), p. 50; wife: p. 52.
42. *Report* (1849), p. 25, column 1.

hoax; my father's name was Matthew Billinge: no other man of that name worked at the bridge; I never heard of any one named Matthew Billinge but my father, and my own son, who is a lad 16 years old, I shall be 51 years old next time."[43]

The newspaper account concludes:

"Mr Jones expressed his gratitude to the magistrate…and then withdrew, proceeding to the office of the electric telegraph company, in order to forward to the home office, &c., an announcement of the important evidence he had procured for the defence of Lord Leigh from a charge so foul as that adduced against him."[44]

Griffin, in quoting this evidence, queried the names used. In the *Manchester Guardian* of 20 May, Griffin argued, the deposition was said to have been by a William Billinge(s), whereas no Christian name was used in the *Advertiser* piece.[45] There certainly remained considerable confusion about the Christian names of the men in the Billinges family. The absence of anything which we would recognise as definitive identification of persons is striking.

By the time of the libel trial in March 1849, the Leigh legal team had apparently decided that more detail was necessary in order to defuse the Billinges matter. A William Billinge (again, not identified by anything other than his own declaration) was examined.

"I am a stone-mason, living at Liverpool. When I was young I worked at Stoneleigh Bridge. My father's name was Matthew. He worked there also. I had a brother Joseph there as well. This was in 1812; and there was no other person of the same name at work there. When I joined them the foundation was not quite got out, I think, and before the first abutment opposite the Abbey was done. My father and I left before my brother left and went

---

43. Griffin (1848), pp. 61–62.
44. Griffin (1848), p. 62.
45. Griffin (1848), p. 62.

The Billinges Problem

to Vauxhall, in London. We worked at the abutment on the Ashow side, farthest from the Abbey."[46]

Perhaps aware that so far, so consistent with the evidence of Faxon, William Billinge went on to contradict it:

"My brother remained at Stoneleigh a fortnight after we left, and he then followed us up to town, and was working at the Strand Bridge. After that I worked for him at Sheerness, where he was drowned in the diving bell. I saw the body taken out of the bell; there was an inquest held on it, but I don't know the coroner."

The coroner's son was duly brought forward, who produced a report on the death of Joseph Billinge [sic], 20 July 1817, verdict "accidental death" in the diving bell at Sheerness.[47]

This 1849 evidence actually contradicts, in one important particular, the statement so triumphantly brought forward in May 1848. In the earlier statement supposedly from (William) Billinge, he stated categorically that the only Matthew Billinges that he knew of were his father and his own son. The man who gave evidence in March 1849, again as William Billinge, said, just as categorically:

"I have known three Matthew Billinges — my father's brother and two sons; one of whom I buried. My brother Matthew lives at Stockport…"[48]

In the first statement, Matthew is described as the speaker's father; in the second, as his uncle. "1848 William" (i.e. the man saying he was William Billinges, making a statement to the newspaper in that year) claimed to have known only two Matthews, his father Matthew and his son Matthew. This contradicted "1849 William" (i.e. the man who who appeared at Charles Griffin's trial in 1849) who claimed to have three relatives with that name: an uncle Matthew, and "two sons" called Matthew — and it is

---

46. *Report* (1849), p. 28, column 1.
47. *Report* (1849), p. 28, columns 1–2.
48. No other Matthew: Griffin (1848), p. 62; three Matthews: *Report* (1849), p. 28, column 1.

The Missing Monument Murders

unclear whether these were sons of his father (and therefore, the speaker's brothers, one surviving), or of his uncle, or of himself.

It is not to be thought that someone 51-years-old (as "1848 William" claimed to be) could be mistaken about whether or not he had a brother, uncle, or son named Matthew. Therefore, either one, or both, of the statements must be wrong. Possibly the witness purporting to be William Billinge was not, either in May 1848 or in March 1849, or neither; or he was, and was lying in either May 1848 or March 1849. As "1848 William" was never publicly examined, but only featured in a meeting with a magistrate and a statement in a newspaper, it was most unlikely that anyone would know if it was he, or a different man, who appeared at the 1849 trial.

The key may lie in the casual statement by "1849 William", in passing while under questioning by Griffin:

> "I saw Mr Jones in the course of last summer… I don't exactly recollect what I said at Liverpool."[49]

By the summer of 1848, Jones junior no doubt thought that it was more productive to expand the number of Matthews, and had briefed "(William) Billinges" (or whoever the witness actually was) to this effect. The whole of the 1849 evidence from "William" is characterised by confusion, probably intentional.

At the 1849 trial, in his own defence, Griffin called as witness Sarah Phillips. She was married and had several children by Matthew Billinge, and knew the Billinge examined the day before ("William", above) to be [Matthew's] son.

> "She gave her evidence in a very strange manner, and stated that her husband lived in London at the time of the erection of the bridge; that he had never left her at any time, except on two occasions—once to work at Bristol, and once at Lord Camden's. The effect of this testimony was to show that Joseph Billinge, who was said to have been murdered, was not

---

49. *Report* (1849), p. 28, column 1.

the brother of the William Billinge who was examined yesterday, but of a different family."⁵⁰

William Faxon said that a week after the bridge events he met William [sic] Billinge, who asked him (Faxon) to go with him to London.

> "He said if I valued my life I should go away. I asked after Joseph, and he said he was killed by a stone falling on him. Witness [= Faxon] expressed surprise, and Billinge hung down his head, and said no more."⁵¹

It is important to realise that this evidence from Faxon, which was overlooked in 1848 and only brought to light in 1849, is significant. It is a quote from the period directly after the bridge events, and Faxon seems clear that it was William to whom he spoke. It suggests that it may well have been Joseph Billinges who died at the bridge in 1812–1814.

With father Matthew also working on the bridge, it was understandable that Barnett may have been in error in 1848 in naming the victim as Matthew. This error allowed the Leigh team to focus on Matthew as a complete red herring, creating useful confusion which sufficed for the time. By 1849, however, in a direct confrontation with Griffin, a little more substantiation was apparently needed.

The inquest report attesting Joseph Billinge's death in 1817 would be evidence, obviously, against his death in 1812–1814. Presumably, if genuine, it had been available in 1848: this raises the question as to why it was not then produced to support the purported Liverpool statement by "1848 William."

In any case, the problem of identity remains. There was almost certainly more than one Joseph Billinge extant at the time. Several appear in the birth, death and marriage records on the *FamilySearch* website, for Warwickshire alone, leaving aside counties such as Lancashire where the name was a common one.⁵² There are numerous Billinges, including a young Joseph, attested in Methodist records from Longnor in

---

50. *Report* (1849), p. 30, column 2.
51. *Report* (1849), p. 22, column 1.
52. Billinge is the name of a village near Wigan, and is probably a location surname for many families.

Staffordshire in the last decades of the eighteenth century.[53] Again, in the absence of other identification, it remains unclear whether the Leigh evidence actually ruled out the death of a man called Billinge or Billinges, whether Joseph or not, at Stoneleigh bridge.

---

53. Extract from the *Leek Wesleyan Methodist Centenary Book,* Longnor Chapel, http://www.rewlach.org.uk/chapellist/lngr2.html (Accessed 9 December 2015).

CHAPTER TWELVE

A Mock Funeral

"I remember the reported funeral of James Henry Leigh. It was said to be a mock funeral; that he was not there. I thought that could not be, then; but I changed my opinion since."

John Toone, 1849[1]

Mary Draper, widow of William Draper, sadler, of Kenilworth, had a sound background knowledge of the history of the Stoneleigh claims. She had given a statement in 1828, but was never called to be cross-examined at the Lords hearings. In the 1848 hearing, she was called to give evidence. She was sworn in, then stated that she had known Sarah Smallbone, and that Sarah had stated that she had committed crimes connected with the Leigh family. Sarah Smallbone said that she had poisoned a man. At this, George Jones junior objected, and no more of Mary Draper's evidence was heard.[2]

Mary Draper had her opportunity, however, at full length, in March 1849, at Griffin's trial for libel. By this time, she was elderly, infirm, and in a chair. Her memory, however, seemed uncompromised. If confirmation were needed, she confirmed having heard from Wilcox about the bridge murders. She had also known Richard Barnett, and described him as being "in as sound a state of health as a man could possibly be; he was perfectly reconciled to tell what he knew about [the bridge events]."[3] Mary Draper had also heard accounts from Sarah Smallbone and George Shaw.

---
1. *Report* (1849), p. 17, column 1.
2. Griffin (1848), pp. 56–57.
3. *Report*, p. 18, column 1.

The Missing Monument Murders

Sarah Smallbone, née Silk, had been second cook at Stoneleigh Abbey. A Sarah Silk, who may be the same person, was born in 1792 to William Silk and his wife Letitia in Birmingham.[4] Sarah Silk married Richard Smallbone at Kenilworth on 23 May 1826.[5] Richard Smallbone/s (both variants are recorded) had owned the *Green Dragon Inn* in the Market Place at Warwick in 1806, as well as holding a property on New Street, so was at that time at least, a man of some substance.[6] (The *Green Dragon*, which survives to this day, apparently dates back to the early decades of the seventeenth century.[7]) It is likely that on her marriage in 1826, Sarah Smallbone left her position at Stoneleigh Abbey. By 1830 the Smallbones were operating a lodging house in Gloucester Street, Leamington.[8] By 1846, she was widowed (Richard may have died in 1836), and living in Kenilworth.[9] According to Mary Draper, in her final months Sarah Smallbone made a number of confessions. John Wilcox had also told Draper that Sarah Smallbone had been involved in criminal activities. One of these was the poisoning of several men. Draper said:

> "Wilcox told me four men had died eating beef and mutton, which had been poisoned, and they all died at the table…I asked [Wilcox] who the beef had been poisoned by, and he said Mrs Smallbone."[10]

---

4. "England Births and Christenings, 1538–1975," index, *FamilySearch* (https://familysearch.org/ark:/61903/1:1:NY9K-CVF (Accessed 5 January 2016)), Sarah Silk, 26 Nov 1792; citing Birmingham, Warwick, England, reference yrs 1792–1809; FHL microfilm 813,717.
5. "England Marriages, 1538–1973 ," database, *FamilySearch* (https://familysearch.org/ark:/61903/1:1:NVWJ-GXF (Accessed 5 January 2016)), Richard Smallbone and Sarah Silk, 23 May 1826; citing Kenilworth, Warwick, England, reference; FHL microfilm 0555348–350.
6. William James, *Survey of Warwick Town (1806)*, at http://freepages.genealogy.rootsweb.ancestry.com/~shakespeare/warks/warwick/warwick_survey_1806.htm (Accessed 5 January 2016), item 292.
7. John Crossling, "History of Warwick Pubs," http://www.hunimex.com/warwick/pubs/g_inns.html (Accessed 15 December 2015).
8. William West, *The History, Topography and Directory of Warwickshire (etc.)* (Birmingham: R. Wrightson, 1830), p. 720.
9. Burial of Richard Smallbones, aged 76, 29 January 1836: "England Deaths and Burials, 1538–1991," database, *FamilySearch* (https://familysearch.org/ark:/61903/1:1:JC84-Y6R (Accessed 18 February 2016)), Richard Smallbone, 29 Jan 1836; citing Parish St. Mary, Warwick Co., England, reference FPG3850 P 27 R 210; FHL microfilm 350,545.
10. *Report* (1849), p. 18, column 2.

Wilcox told Draper that these men had been working on the Stoneleigh Abbey cellar, "making up some bins."[11] In all probability, these bins were those in which the Christopher stone was alleged to have been concealed. Smallbone herself told Draper about several other episodes: the death of John Sprawson, the carrier; the death of Daniel Dingley; the death of William Blissett; the death of John Leigh (I); and the faked funeral of James Henry Leigh.

Back in 1828, Edward Baylis had told the Lords hearing that John Sprawson, the Stoneleigh carrier, was alleged to have assisted in the removal of the Christopher stone to the abbey. It was his cart and horse, minus Sprawson himself, which were seen by Edward Baylis near the abbey back entrance, on the day of the removal: Baylis then saw Sprawson levelling the ruts in the lane, along with another labourer.[12] Now, in 1849, a carpenter called John Thompson told Griffin's trial that Sprawson, whom he met one day at the church with his cart and horse, was quite clear about what he was doing.

> "[Sprawson] said he was going to take the monuments to Stoneleigh Abbey, and [Thompson] saw two men bring one out of the Church to put in Sprawson's cart."[13]

Smallbone told Draper that the four men who were poisoned with the beef were taken in Sprawson's cart to Adlestrop, for burial.

> "There were four of them put into hampers and sent away in their luggage cart; and one broke the basket and discovered what was in, and that caused poor Sprawson to be drowned. Willcox [sic], who went with him, when he came back told what had happened, and then Mrs Leigh said [Sprawson] must be put away."

Draper went on:

---

11. *Report* (1849), p. 18, column 2.
12. Leigh (1834), vol. II, p. 182.
13. *Report* (1849), p. 16, column 1.

The Missing Monument Murders

"The same night he was made drunk, and taken over the green bridge the nearest road to Ashow, and [Smallbone] and Mrs Leigh went into the grove to hear the splashing when he was thrown in; he was thrown in by Billy Wood and others."

Sprawson's death had clearly affected Smallbone.

"She told [Draper], 'Poor Sprawson, poor Sprawson, I was very sorry for him to be drowned, for he was such a good man.'"[14]

Another witness at Griffin's libel trial spoke about Sprawson's death. John Billington went looking for Sprawson and found his body in the river, reclining against the bank.

"It was evident the poor fellow had crossed over the gravel road, and slipped into the water, as there were marks of his feet down the bank. His head was under the surface; his hat was on, and a basket was over his arm. There was no suspicion that he had been murdered."

An inquest was said to have been held. A woman who had been present at the inquest, a Mrs Lapworth, "an old woman of 83," testified at Griffin's trial that Sprawson's body

"…was very clear and [had] not a blemish on it. There was no bruise on the head, and he had a 'colour as fresh as a rose.'"[15]

The findings of inquests from this period are not in general available from the Warwick County Record Office: the office website reports that while coroners' reports were deposited, those dating from earlier than 1900 do not in general survive. Initial searches show no evidence of an inquest for Sprawson.[16] The claim of an inquest having been held was easily made, offered apparent legitimacy, and was unlikely to be refuted.

---

14. *Report* (1849), p. 19, column 1.
15. Billington and Lapworth evidence: *Report*, p. 30, column 1.
16. http://heritage.warwickshire.gov.uk/warwickshire-county-record-office/county-record-office-collections/county-record-office-main-categories-of-records/ (Accessed 15 December 2015).

The evidence, however, of neither Billington nor Lapworth, nor the occurrence of an inquest, are sufficient to discount the evidence of Sarah Smallbone that Sprawson's death was caused by foul play. The fact that Sprawson was carrying his basket when he died is strongly suggestive that he met with an untoward event, and the marks of his feet may well have been caused by his having been dragged down the bank.

The Leigh legal team had little incentive to encourage witnesses to be precise about dates, and Mary Draper's evidence ranged across years and possibly decades. There is, however, an external fix on this particular event. The burial of John Sprawson, aged 74, is recorded as having taken place at the Church of the Assumption of Our Lady, Ashow, on 22 January 1815.[17] The cellar alterations at the abbey, on which the unfortunate masons had been working, had probably taken place during 1814. The Leigh papers include plans for port and white wine cellars (presumably those which Thomas Hill Mortimer was so proud of having drafted), dated April-May 1814. This is later than the impression given in Thomas Hill Mortimer's own evidence to the House of Lords hearings in 1829, in which he implied that the cellar works began late in 1813, shortly after the succession of James Henry Leigh to the estate.[18]

The burial record from January 1815 dates Sprawson's death to the period of the abbey alterations and bridge construction. The bridge, after all, was not formally completed until 1818. The death of Sprawson may not have taken place on the night directly after he transported the masons' bodies, as Draper claimed, but it certainly happened in the months after the completion of the abbey cellar works, which is to say in the latter part of 1814 or early days of 1815. If Sprawson's death had taken place well outside this period, Draper's evidence would be so much less convincing: the fact that it was within the timeframe adds confirmation of the overall tendency of her evidence, if not the precise timing.

Email from Janet Radcliffe, Warwick County Record Office to author, 7 May 2015.
17. Data by Nigel Draper, "Ashow—Church of the Assumption of Our Lady, Burials from 1813 to 1839," http://www.hunimex.net/warwick/bmd/Ashow_burials_1813–1839.html (Accessed 15 December 2015).
18. Plans: SBTRO DR 18/17/17/6 April/May 1814 (list of port); DR 18/17/17/7 April/May 1814 (port); DR 18/17/17/8, 1814 (white wine); Mortimer evidence: Leigh (1834), vol. II, pp. 272–278.

The Missing Monument Murders

The death of Daniel Dingley is more mysterious. It is not clear who he was, or how he came to be at Stoneleigh. Sarah Smallbone told Mary Draper about his death.

> "The second time I went to Mrs Smallbone's, as I was going into the room, she said (referring to Daniel Dingley) 'they cut the string and let him down.' I asked who cut him down? She replied, I did, and I tried to carry him, but I could not, he was so heavy."[19]

Smallbone went on to say that John Hayward (sic) and Billy (William) Wood helped her carry Dingley's body to a hole which she and Julia-Judith had dug. She added that Hayward (or Haywood, see below) and Wood had hung Dingley.[20]

Elizabeth James, another widowed friend, had also heard about Dingley: "There was another man of the name of Dingley cut down that was hanged."[21] She added:

> "Mrs Julia Leigh marked the ground for the grave, and Mrs Smallbone dug it. They buried him there. I think she said before the green-house. They buried him with his clothes on, and the lady threw his hat at his feet. I don't know whether it was true or not."[22]

Sarah Smallbone told a similar story to James Leigh, one of the men tried for the 1844 Stoneleigh Abbey break-in.[23]

The Leigh papers do not shed any light on Daniel Dingley. In response to the allegations, at Griffin's trial the Leigh team brought forward a witness named John Dingley. His evidence was, like that of several of the Leigh witnesses, delivered humorously, as if in contempt of the claims, and received as a joke by the Leigh supporters in court.

---

19. *Report*, p. 19, column 1.
20. *Report*, p. 19, column 1.
21. *Report*, p. 21, column 1.
22. *Report*, p. 21, column 1–2.
23. *Report*, p. 25, column 2.

"'I had a brother, of the name of Joseph, there [at Stoneleigh] also; but there was no other of that name in the neighbourhood. He died of a decline, and was buried in Lillington some years afterwards. He had never been hung himself in an apple tree, nor had his brother, and was never buried by Mrs Smallbone and Mrs Leigh.' (Laughter.)"[24]

Griffin, speaking in his own defence, noted that whereas he had asked for information about Daniel Dingley, or a certificate of his burial, all the Leighs had produced was a John Dingley.[25]

The shooting of William Blissett was another mysterious death on the estate. A William Blisset was born in 1791 at Stratford-upon-Avon; this may have been the man referred to.[26] Barnett had stated that Blisset was among the men who worked on the bridge.[27] This would fit with a birthdate of 1791, as being a young and fit worker in 1812–1814.

Barnett stated that Blisset had worked on the foundations of the bridge.

"[Blisset] was shot by [Stoneleigh gamekeeper] Hay about six at night, [Barnett] heard the gun go off as he went down the road … [Blisset] was the next night taken from the greenhouse and buried, Mr Jones and Lady [sic] Leigh were there when the body was removed."

Mary Draper had heard a slightly different version from Barnett:

"[Barnett] appeared very unhappy, and said he knew one who was shot in the garden; his name was Blissett. I asked who shot him, and [Barnett] said John Haywood and James Farden."[28]

The existence of James Farden, as James Fardon, is testified to in an unrelated source. A family history account of the Fardon family describes

---

24. *Report*, p. 29, column 1.
25. *Report*, p. 31, column 1.
26. "England Births and Christenings, 1538–1975," index, *FamilySearch* (https://familysearch.org/ark:/61903/1:1:NLM4-GYL (Accessed 15 December 2015)), William Blisset, 24 Feb 1791; citing HOLY TRINITY, STRATFORD ON AVON, WARWICK, ENGLAND, reference; FHL microfilm 1,067,508.
27. Griffin, p. 50.
28. *Report*, p. 18, column 1.

James as having been born in Temple Guiting, Gloucestershire, in 1793, but having moved to Stoneleigh to work in 1814. James, 'labourer,' was named as the father of an illegitimate son born to Ann Kinman in 1818, and in 1819 married Sarah Green; the couple settled in Stareton, and James continued to work on the Stoneleigh estate.[29]

John Turner, a joiner who, following his father and grandfather, had worked on the Stoneleigh estate, testified at Griffin's trial.

> "I did not know Blisset. I heard the report that he was shot by a keeper. I knew the keeper well; his name was John Haywood. I heard Blisset was poaching, setting wires or gins, and Haywood aware of him, and wanted to take him into custody, and he would not be took, but ran away, when Haywood shot him.—He was shot in the side, it was reported."[30]

Turner's evidence indicates that, understandably after the lapse of 34 years, there was confusion about the gamekeeper's name: Hay or Haywood/Hayward. As described in *Chapter 7*, the Stoneleigh gamekeeper Hay was a formidable character. As one of the senior employees on the estate, it is not surprising if he was enlisted in the campaign to eliminate witnesses of the bridge events. While it is unclear whether or not the gamekeeper Hay was still alive in 1849 (he was very much alive when profiled by hunting writer "Nimrod" in 1825), the Leigh team, at Griffin's trial, in a now familiar move to sow confusion, brought forward a man named Hay who was not the gamekeeper at all. Alec was a stonemason, by 1849 working at Elgin in Scotland. In 1812 he began work at the Stoneleigh bridge site. Alec Hay's evidence is characterised by what he didn't know.

> "I can't say I ever saw Mr [sic] Chandos Leigh at the bridge when I was there. Mrs Leigh sometimes came to the bridge…I never heard of any such person as Alexander Munro, or William Wood, or William Blissett,

---

29. Brian Harringman, Alan Harmer, and Julie Harmer (née Fardon), *The Fardons of Gloucestershire, England* (online book, dated 6 September 2007, material copyright 2015 Alan Harmer), James Fardon—Chapter 4 http://www.aharmer.co.uk/glosfardons/narrative/c_james_kenilworthnr_m.htm accessed 22 December 2015.
30. *Report*, p. 17, column 2.

or George Shaw, or Thomas Proud, or Joseph Smith working there at the time...I never heard of a William Forbes working there... I assisted in building the catacombs for the vaults in the wine cellar. There was not, and could not have been, without my knowledge, any monument built up in the wall of the wine cellar."[31]

It goes without saying that this evidence entirely fails to address the question of what might have happened to William Blisset in 1812–1814. Turner's story of Blisset's poaching seems like a cover. The laws governing poaching were well-known and stringently applied, and gamekeepers could not summarily execute poachers on sight. The gamekeeper's role was to guard and protect the landlord's game, not to administer vigilante justice; offenders suspected of poaching were to be tried, not slain on the spot.

Sydney Smith, reviewing a book on the game laws in 1818, wrote that poaching was

"[punished] by pecuniary penalties, and summary conviction before magistrates."[32]

The most severe punishment for poaching was transportation, and even this was generally felt to be unfairly severe.[33] Smith does record that some landowners set traps for poachers, but points out that this was illegal.[34]

A parallel case to this putative confrontation between Blisset and the gamekeeper can be found in the experience of the Leighs' Adlestrop neighbour, the Reverend F E Witts. In 1817, an "unqualified man" (the technical term for a person without an official licence to kill game) called John Turner was brought before Witts, as local magistrate, and charged by the gamekeeper of Sherborne manor with having set a snare to catch game. Turner was detained in gaol for further examination, but was released when he incriminated another man called John Day. Both

---
31. *Report*, p. 28, column 2.
32. Review of *Three Letters on the Game Laws*, in Smith, *Essays Social and Political* (n.d.), 368–380, p. 373.
33. Smith, p, 374.
34. Smith, p. 379.

The Missing Monument Murders

Turner and Day were ultimately released.[35] It does not, on the whole, seem likely that Blisset could have been shot simply for poaching, without consultation with a magistrate, in an era when the game laws were the subject of considerable public debate.

A little more information is available about the fate of John Leigh. A man named John Leigh (John Leigh (I)) had been making inquiries about the Stoneleigh succession as early as the immediate aftermath of Mary Leigh's death in 1806.[36] While there were no doubt many John Leighs extant in the first 20 years of the nineteenth century, this man may have been the John Leigh (b. 1775) named in the pedigree of Nancy Law, which claims descent from Christopher Leigh through a putative son Edmund (b. 1665).[37] At Griffin's trial, William Faxon testified that at some point (it is unclear exactly when) he had seen John Leigh at the abbey. He later asked Sarah Smallbone what had become of him.

> "[Sarah Smallbone] said that Mrs Leigh had allowed [John Leigh] to come in and go out when he liked, and said if he could prove his claim they would be very willing to give up the estates to him. [Smallbone] said two men killed [John Leigh] in the cellar, and she stood by and held the candle.
>
> I said, 'Sally, you had some ale over that?'
>
> She replied 'Yes, they had some, and I had one glass'. She said when they had killed him they went into the house and had a good supper, and plenty of liquors and wine after it.'"[38]

Two further pieces of information bear on the death of John Leigh. Mary Draper said that Sarah Smallbone had told her that John Leigh was murdered in the abbey vault.

---

35. P. B. Munsche, *Gentlemen and Poachers: The English Game Laws 1671–1831* (Cambridge University Press, 1981), p. 97.
36. Mary Draper statement (23 January 1828), at Leigh (1834), vol. II, p. 311.
37. John Leighs: e.g. one, of Houghton, Lancashire, extant in 1828, made a statement in the Lords case (Leigh 1834, vol, I, p. 51; vol. II, p, 325). Email from Nancy Law, 8 April 2014; although 1828 statement names deponent's father also as John Leigh, whereas the John (b. 1775) in the Law pedigree was named as the son of William (b. 1731).
38. *Report*, p. 22, column 2.

"[Smallbone] told me that there was a John Leigh murdered there, and he was buried in the wine vault with his clothes and boots on. I said 'Oh dear!' and asked who killed him? She said Mr Kirkland and Mr Webb. She added that it was that which caused James Henry Leigh to leave them, and that he would not stop at the Abbey after he had heard of it."[39]

James Henry Leigh was said to have been found dead in his bed on the morning of 28 October 1823.[40] In fact, he was not seen alive after the evening of the 27 October. If John Leigh's death took place in the period preceding this, some support would be offered for Smallbone's account of James Henry's disappearance from Stoneleigh.

As it happens, the Leigh papers record an event which was certainly the mysterious death of someone called John, and may have been the death of the claimant John Leigh. On 2 May 1823, George Jones senior wrote to Julia-Judith, then at Portman Square in London. After discussing the perennial irritant of Stoneleigh neighbour Colonel Gregory, who persisted in cutting down timber to which he insisted on his hereditary right, Jones added a strangely worded postscript, which the transcriber notes has been crossed out.

"John was perfectly sober and in his business and not the least blame can be attached to any Individual. A Coroner's Inquest will sit upon the body this day and tomorrow. I shall send over a hearse and inter him in Stoneleigh Church Yard, where he expressed a strong wish to be buried. He was perfectly sensible to the last moment and was considering his approaching Disolut[ion: 'page torn'] every thing here is going on well."[41]

Jones' statement that no blame could be attached to any individual is strongly suggestive of something blameworthy having occurred. It is to be noted that Jones omits a surname for "John," and assumes that

---

39. *Report*, p. 19, column 1.
40. Philip Salmon/David R. Fisher, "Leigh, James Henry (1765–1823), of Adlestrop, Glos, and Stoneleigh Abbey, Warws," in D. R. Fisher (ed.), *The History of Parliament: The House of Commons 1820–1832* (Cambridge University Press, 2009), digitised as http://www.historyofparliamentonline.org/volume/1790–1820/member/leigh-james-henry-1765–1823 (Accessed 5 January 2016).
41. SBTRO DR 18/17/49/8, George Jones to Julia-Judith, 2 May 1823. Transcription by Garry Strachan, email to author, 28 October 2014.

The Missing Monument Murders

Julia-Judith will know whom and what he is writing about. It is also curious that the page has been torn just where John's point of death is described. If Draper's/Smallbone's account was correct, it was not the case that an inquest was held, but rather a summary burial. No record of an inquest has been found in the Warwick County Record Office, though inquests prior to 1900 are generally not available even if they definitely took place.[42] Jones is particular about an appropriate burial, which perhaps indicates that no such burial took place. The fact that Julia-Judith was absent from Stoneleigh Abbey for the event itself is consistent with Smallbone's version, that only she and two men (identified as Kirkland and Webb) were present. Finally, the fact that the paragraph was crossed out suggests that Jones had second thoughts about committing to paper even this carefully guarded information.

If John Leigh was, indeed, murdered in the spring of 1823, this may well have formed part of the background to the bizarre circumstances surrounding the disappearance, and purported death, of James Henry Leigh later that year. Sarah Smallbone had told Mary Draper that she had taken part in preparing a fake funeral for James Henry Leigh.

> "She said Mrs Leigh took her, Mrs Colt, and Mr Kirkland, into her (Mrs Leigh's) room, and asked them to assist her in the mock funeral. They had 50 guineas each, and went into the yard to get a piece of timber to represent James H. Leigh. They took the timber into Mr Leigh's room, put it in a shell, all ready prepared for it, and [Smallbone] wrapped a sheet off Mr Kirkland's table round it. She said they sealed the sheet up, and showed how it was done by holding up her apron. She said they had a plaster of Paris face put on this wood, wrapped a napkin round the throat, and then left the room, locking the door."[43]

James Henry Leigh either died or went missing on the evening or night of 27 October 1823. According to Smallbone, in conversation with Draper:

---

42. http://heritage.warwickshire.gov.uk/warwickshire-county-record-office/county-record-office-collections/county-record-office-main-categories-of-records/ (Accessed 7 May 2015). Email from Janet Radcliffe, Warwick County Record Office to author, 7 May 2015.
43. *Report* (1849), p. 19, column 1.

"Mr [James Henry] Leigh had gone away that day after dinner; a man named Mark Bicknell went with him. [Smallbone] said she never saw James Henry Leigh after. There were reports abroad about this mock funeral, but people dare not speak out about it. I [Draper] was told of it in my own house by Barnett. He was afraid to speak of it, and told me in a whisper. I heard others talk of it at different times, and the men who worked at the Abbey said James Henry Leigh did not die when it was reported."[44]

That this event was the subject of speculation was confirmed by other witnesses at Griffin's trial. John Toone, a Leamington builder who recalled the Christopher stone, stated

"I remember the reported funeral of James Henry Leigh. It was said to be a mock funeral; that he was not there. I thought that could not be, then; but I changed my opinion since."

Toone recalled meeting in Leamington a former local resident who had lived in France for some years.[45]

"He said he knew the Stoneleigh family. I said I suppose you know [James Henry Leigh] is dead then? He replied no, he was sure he was not, for he waited on him at dinner only a few days back. I added, report said [James Henry] was dead; and he replied he was sure he was not; he knew him as well as he did his own father."[46]

Phoebe Russell, who owned a boarding house in Coventry, had gone to school when a girl in Stoneleigh. She had been on friendly terms with Sarah Smallbone, and some time in the late-1830s asked her about the late James Henry Leigh.

"I asked her if she had seen the late James Henry Leigh after he was dead, and she said she did not; and she did not know if any one else did except

---

44. *Report* (1849), p. 19, column 1.
45. *Report* (1849), p. 17, column 1.
46. *Report* (1849), p. 17, column 1.

Dr Wake. I enquired, as he died so suddenly, how was it there was not an inquest held, for I considered if he had been a poor man there would have been an inquest? [Smallbone] said no, she believed not. She then put her hand on my arm, and said, don't you ask me any more questions, for she was not exactly at liberty to speak. She seemed a little confused."[47]

The official, Leigh family account can be found in the obituary of James Henry Leigh which appeared in the *Gentleman's Magazine*.

"Oct. 28 [1823]. At his seat, Stoneleigh-abbey, Warwickshire, James Henry Leigh esq. Mr Leigh had retired to rest on the evening of the 27th, apparently in perfectly good health, and on the following morning was found dead in his bed."[48]

At Griffin's trial, a number of witnesses were called to give evidence on the death of James Henry Leigh. Chandos Leigh was the first. With a now customary attempt at humour, his lawyer Mr Whitehurst began:

"Did you ever murder any one at Stoneleigh?
[Chandos] Certainly not.
Did you ever see any one murdered there?"
Never."[49]
Whitehurst went on:
"Did you see your father after he was dead?
You accompanied the funeral?
I accompanied it to Adlestrop."

This funeral procession to Adlestrop had been described, in part, by Smallbone:

---

47. *Report* (1849), p. 23, column 1.
48. *Gentleman's Magazine*, vol. XCIV, December-June 1824, January 1824, p. 87. Strangely, for a version which must have originated with the Leigh family, James Henry's father is wrongly given as John, rather than James, Leigh. This carelessness about family details, while surprising in itself, is of a piece with the Leigh legal team's approach throughout Griffin's trial: as if the facts barely mattered.
49. *Report* (1849), p. 26, column 1.

> "The [Stoneleigh] tenants followed him [sc. James Henry Leigh, presumed deceased] as far as Halford Bridge, where the other [presumably Adlestrop] tenants were to meet him."[50]

Halford Bridge is about 18 miles south of Stoneleigh, and it is a further 14 miles to Adlestrop. In total, such a procession will have been on the road for many hours, representing a considerable demand on the tenants required to follow it. Even Lord Saye and Sele, Julia-Judith's nephew, admitted that there seemed to be no particular reason for James Henry to have been buried at Adlestrop, rather than at Stoneleigh.[51] It may indeed have been purely an elaborate and imposing piece of theatre.

The purported death was the subject of cross-examination of Samuel Kirkland, James Henry Leigh's valet.

> "I recollect Mr Leigh's retiring to rest at his usual time; he had then recently returned from a journey. He complained of being unwell on the road between Doncaster and Rotherham, on the 21st of October. I travelled with him. The next morning [28 October] I went up as usual to put out his things to dress, and in consequence of what the housemaid told me, I went into his room. I opened the shutters, and listened at the foot of the bed, but heard no breathing. I went to the head of the bed, and he was dead."[52]

Kirkland informed Julia-Judith's nephew, Frederick Twisleton-Wykeham-Fiennes (1799–1887), later Lord Saye and Sele, who was staying at Stoneleigh, and the family physician Dr Wake. Wake examined the body, and stated that the cause of death was apoplexy. Kirkland added some details:

> "I never left the apartment, attended the room night and day, saw him put in the coffin, and followed him to Adlestrop, where the coffin was deposited. After his death, I cut some locks of hair off his head, on account of his sudden decease. I also kept one myself. I helped to put the body in the

---

50. *Report* (1849), p. 21, column 2.
51. *Report* (1849), p. 27, column 1.
52. *Report* (1849), p. 26, column 1.

coffin myself. The coffin was open for the body to be seen up to the 5th of November, and I saw it sealed up."[53]

Kirkland denied ("seem[ing] surprised by the question") that he had murdered John Leigh, and that a log of wood had been placed in the coffin. Griffin questioned Kirkland about the events prior to James Henry Leigh's disappearance:

"[James Henry Leigh] arrived home on Saturday night. On the Monday, the 27th of October, he rode out, accompanied by his groom, Mark Bicknell. I don't know where he went. Bicknell kept a public house since he left the service of the family."

Kirkland produced a memorandum in which, helpfully, he had recorded the event.

"Found Mr Leigh dead in his bed at 5 minutes before 8 o'clock on Tuesday morning, 28th of October, 1823. Was buried on Thursday, 5th of November, at Adlestrop."[54]

It is noteworthy that Kirkland does not indicate, other than a vague statement "I recollect Mr Leigh's retiring to rest at his usual time," that he saw James Henry Leigh return after departing with Mark Bicknell, which, according to Smallbone, took place after dinner.[55]

This meal, at least among the very wealthy, was taken during the early evening: ten years prior, Jane Austen had the Bingley family at Netherfield dine at half-past six.[56] If James Henry Leigh had set off after dinner, this must have been no earlier than seven o'clock. It was a late hour, particularly in late-autumn, to set out if he intended to return that night. It is surprising that Kirkland, as a senior servant, did not know where James Henry was planning to go late on the 27th, or when he might have

---

53. *Report* (1849), p. 26, column 1.
54. *Report* (1849), p. 26, column 2.
55. *Report* (1849), p. 19, column 1.
56. *Pride and Prejudice* (1813), Chapter 8.

returned. Kirkland admitted: "I don't know where he went to; he rode out, but I don't know how long he was away."[57]

Essentially, there is no record of James Henry having been seen between his departure after dinner on the 27th, and the discovery of his body in his bed on the morning of the 28th. In a great landowner, with a numerous family and many employees, this is surprising. It may also be significant that Kirkland spoke of "Adlestrop, where the coffin was deposited," rather than "where Mr Leigh was buried." For his part, contrary to the view of observers such as Phoebe Russell, Dr Wake, after speaking with Julia-Judith, considered that no inquest was necessary. This was apparently because Kirkland had told him that James Henry had been ill on the earlier journey between Doncaster and Rotherham on the 21st.[58]

Lord Saye and Sele, nephew by marriage of the deceased, was then called to answer questions. As well as succeeding to the title of Saye and Sele in 1847, the Reverend Frederick Twisleton-Wykeham-Fiennes was rector of Adlestrop between 1825 and 1852. He was therefore well placed to assist in the putative burial of his uncle in 1823. Some years after Griffin's trial, Twisleton-Wykeham-Fiennes was to marry, as his second wife, his cousin, Chandos' daughter Caroline.[59] Clearly, he was very close to the affairs of his Stoneleigh aunt and uncle. His 1849 evidence appeared a little mixed up.

> "I wished to have pleasant recollections of my uncle, and did not go in after he was found dead."

On the other hand, Saye and Sele claimed to have been present at Dr Wake's examination of the body.

---

57. *Report* (1849), p. 27, column 1.
58. *Report* (1849), p. 26, column 2.
59. Biographical information by Eldred Frederick Godson, http://www.geni.com/people/Ven-Frederick-Twisleton-later-Twisleton-Wykeham-Fiennes-10th-Baron-Saye-Sele/6000000008136107307 (Accessed 5 January 2016).

"The mouth might have been open. I did not observe anything else about the mouth. I am positive I saw nothing else. There was a small effusion of blood under the nose."[60]

And, finally:

"My Lord, I saw my uncle dead."[61]

From this internally contradictory evidence, which emphasised what Lord Saye and Sele did *not* see, it was (doubtless intentionally) difficult to draw anything conclusive. Once again, Chandos Leigh himself was not on the scene; according to Saye and Sele, Chandos and Margarette had been at Adlestrop.[62]

Dr Wake himself was not, in March 1849, in a fit state to give evidence. His wife, Martha Wake, was called. Griffin and another, unnamed man, had at some earlier period interviewed her, with the unnamed man being quite offensive:

"A stranger with Mr Griffin at the time had insulted [Mrs Wake] by saying that 'the light would shine out — and the truth be known,' inferring that Dr Wake would be punished for what she had [told] them. [Mrs Wake] considered he was very abusive and told a great many untruths, and it was therefore that she was offended."

She told Griffin that he (not his friend) could visit again, but he had indicated that he was satisfied with her information.[63]

The evidence of Kirkland and Lord Saye and Sele was, then, vague and equivocal. The evidence of Sarah Smallbone, transmitted through Mary Draper and others, was, by contrast, very specific. Further, in alleging that Kirkland had received £50 for his part in the fake interment, Smallbone's evidence compromised that of Kirkland. As with other aspects of

---

60. *Report* (1849), p. 27, column 1.
61. *Report* (1849), p. 27, column 1.
62. *Report* (1849), p. 27, column 1.
63. *Report* (1849), p. 27, column 2.

this case, it is instructive to follow the money. Fifty pounds was a fortune to a working person. Adam Murray, in his *Agricultural Report for Warwickshire*, tells that, in Warwickshire in 1813:

> "*Hired farm-servants*. The wages given to ploughmen and waggoners, boys, &c. differ in different parts of the county; but in general, they run from 12, 14, 16, and some as high as 20 guineas per year, and their board."[64]

Fifty guineas, then, was two-and-a-half times the maximum amount that a skilled servant could usually expect to earn, in addition to his or her board, in a year.

The possibility remains that Sarah Smallbone either imagined, or pretended, that she was given a large amount of money as payment. But there seems no reason for her to have done so. Kirkland had every incentive, both legal and financial, to conceal his role and present false evidence. Smallbone, on the other hand, had nothing, except some emotional relief, to gain by confessing hers. It appears likely, then, that Smallbone was telling the truth about the bizarre concoction of a fake burial for James Henry Leigh.

An unlikely source, the official history of Parliament, confirms that there was sufficient motive on the part of others, including Julia-Judith and Chandos, to collude in James Henry's disappearance.

> "[As MP for Winchester, James Henry] was intended as a stopgap for his only son Chandos Leigh, a rake and versifier who frequented Holland House, but it was [James Henry] Leigh himself who came in at the 1820 general election."[65]

Chandos, as we have seen, took no official part in public life, possibly because too many questions would have been asked about his activities since leaving Harrow School. Instead, his father served in the seat,

---

64. Murray (1813), p. 169.
65. Philip Salmon/David R. Fisher, "Leigh, James Henry (1761–1823), of Adlestrop, Glos. and Stoneleigh Abbey, Warws,'"in D.R. Fisher (ed.), *The History of Parliament: The House of Commons 1820–1832* (2009), digitised at http://www.historyofparliamentonline.org/volume/1820–1832/member/leigh-james-1765–1823 (Accessed 5 January 2016).

without distinction, until his retirement. In November 1822, James Henry's retirement from his seat was announced at a dinner given by Richard Temple Grenville, Lord Buckingham and Chandos (1776–1839), the man who had taken the title which, growing up, James Henry had probably expected to inherit. Adding further insult, Temple Grenville, his political master, insisted that James Henry vacate the seat of Winchester for the father-in-law of James Henry's daughter Caroline, to take effect for the start of the 1823 session. This was Sir Edward Hyde East (1764–1847). Many years later, as brother-in-law and supporter of Chandos Leigh, Edward Hyde East's son, James Buller East, was present in court both in May 1848, to hear the charges against Chandos, and in March 1849, to hear Griffin prosecuted for libel. In 1823, without a seat in Parliament, and with Chandos' family growing, there must have seemed to be little role remaining for James Henry Leigh.

While James Henry had featured in the reported suppression of the Christopher stone, he was not alleged to have taken a role in the murders at the bridge or in the abbey grounds in the period 1812–1814. We have seen that it was widely believed that it was James Henry Leigh's horror at the reports of the murder of John Leigh, which induced him, in October 1823, to abandon his wife, his family, and the Stoneleigh estate.

His successor for Winchester, Edward Hyde East, who became intimate enough with the Leighs to consider Adlestrop (according to the always refreshingly blunt history of Parliament) "one of his bolt holes," had had a chequered career. Appointed in 1813 as a judge in Bengal, India, he was said to have presided over the 1819 case of his own son-in-law, James William Croft, who had seduced and left pregnant the daughter of a family friend. Croft had apparently urged the girl to fake insanity and suicide as a cover for her disappearance. Croft was "moderately fined and banished."[66] It may be that Edward Hyde East, who suggested the course of a faked death to his son-in-law's victim, recommended a similar strategem in 1823 to his Adlestrop friends, James Henry and Julia-Judith Leigh.

---

66. Philip Salmon/Howard Spencer, "East, Sir Edward Hyde (1764–1847), of 12 Stratford Place, Mdx," http://www.historyofparliamentonline.org/volume/1820-1832/member/east-sir-edward-1764-1847 (Accessed 5 January 2016).

In another strange parallel, Edward Hyde East was, in January 1847, to be discovered dead in his bed by his butler, who had found the room locked. The circumstances were surprising enough to merit an inquest, although the jury in the end agreed with the consulting doctor that the cause of death had been "sanguineous apoplexy, induced solely from natural causes."[67] It is curious that two consecutive MPs for Winchester were said to have died in exactly the same bizarre and unexplained manner.

To return to 1823, the disappearance from the scene of James Henry Leigh solved a number of problems. Chandos Leigh, "rake and versifier," and by now father of a family, succeeded to the wealth of the Stoneleigh estate. Temple Grenville, Lord Buckingham and Chandos, and his wife the Duchess (daughter of James Henry's erstwhile guardian the late Duke of Chandos), who was said to control the seat of Winchester, got Hyde East a seat in Parliament.[68] Caroline Leigh East and her husband James Buller East now had a father/father-in-law who enjoyed the benefits of Parliamentary status. Last but definitely not least, Julia-Judith got rid of a husband who may have been causing difficulties through the belated development of scruples. At a time when George Leigh's claim on the Stoneleigh estate was gathering momentum, the last thing she needed was a conscience in the family.

---

67. H. J. Spencer, "East, Sir Edward Hyde, First Baronet (1764–1847)," *Oxford Dictionary of National Biography*, Oxford University Press, 2004; online edn, Jan 2008 http://www.oxforddnb.com/view/article/8408 (Accessed 5 Jan 2016).
68. East "was returned unopposed on the interest of the 1st duke of Buckingham, who [denied] that Winchester was really controlled by his wife:" http://www.historyofparliamentonline.org/volume/1820–1832/member/east-sir-edward-1764–1847 (Accessed 5 January 2016).

The Missing Monument Murders

CHAPTER THIRTEEN

The White Powder

"[Sarah Smallbone] said some person came for a jug of ale, and the Hon. Julia Leigh gave her a powder to put in the beer, and he died when he got to his work."

Elizabeth James, 1849[1]

One reported death from Stoneleigh in this period remains to be mentioned. This is that of the "black man," named as John Thomas, who came with Thomas Hill Mortimer from London and arranged for the bridge conspirators, chief among them George Shaw, to swear that they would undertake the murders of the masons.[2] Shaw's account was the most detailed. He told William Faxon that

"…a black man had been brought down to Stoneleigh to swear the murderers to do the deeds: he was brought down by Mortimer or Hill."[3]

The fact that Faxon was unfamiliar with the exact form of Thomas Hill Mortimer's name indicates how distant from the seats of Stoneleigh power the bone-collector of Ashow was. It may, however, confirm the substance of his evidence: Faxon did not elaborate on what he had heard from Shaw, because he did not know enough to do so. Faxon reported that Wilcox had said that John Thomas himself was then killed, and buried in the section of Stoneleigh Abbey known as Fountain Court.[4]

---

1. *Report* (1849), p. 21, column 1.
2. Evidence of John Wilcox: Griffin (1848), p. 54; Shaw quoted in William Faxon evidence: *Report* (1849), p. 22, column 2.
3. Faxon in *Report* (1849), p. 22, column 2.
4. *Report* (1849), p. 22, column 2.

The Fountain Court is the name for a section of the abbey which has been identified as part of the medieval Cistercian fabric.[5]

At Griffin's trial, a labourer named William Jeffs claimed to have dug up a human skull in the Fountain Court, finding the teeth and nostrils in perfect condition. He had intended to take the skull home, but it had been taken away. Jeffs did not say when he had found the skull, or by whom it was taken from him.[6] Despite Jeffs' noting the good condition of the skull's features (perhaps suggesting that it had belonged to a person recently deceased), it is important to remember — a fact we often overlook — that until the development of carbon dating in the twentieth century, there was no reliable way of dating organic artefacts or human remains. An investigator in the 1840s, even supposing he or she had no motive other than an impartial desire to learn the truth, had no reliable way of telling whether an excavated skull was that of a medieval monk, or a murder victim of 30 years prior. The absence of any means of dating allowed Whitehurst, Chandos Leigh's lawyer, to dismiss the finding of any human remains at Stoneleigh, as the monks had been buried in the grounds during previous centuries:

> "Upon [the evidence] which referred to the finding of bones or skulls in the Fountain Court, at Stoneleigh, [Whitehurst] remarked that such a circumstance was by no means remarkable, inasmuch as it was impossible to excavate two yards in that place without some such discovery. The fact was that Stoneleigh Abbey had been a monastery, and this Fountain Court had been the burial place of the monks in olden times."[7]

Thus was the allegation of the burial of John Thomas written off, without any further attempt at investigation.

While it might seem as if John Thomas' race might narrow down his identity, this is not necessarily the case. It has been estimated that the black population of London in the later eighteenth century may have

---

5. Richard K. Morris, "From Monastery to Country House: An Architectural History of Stoneleigh Abbey, 1156–c. 1660," in Bearman (ed.) 2004, pp. 15–61. Figure 2, p. 16, shows an isometric projection created by Guy Silk in 1957.
6. *Report* (1849), p. 24, column 2.
7. *Report* (1849), pp. 7, column 2, and 8, column 1.

amounted to between 5,000 and 10,000, including, after the American War of Independence, a sizeable loyalist community which included black members.[8] In addition, the commonness of the man's name, if it actually was "John Thomas," makes identification next to impossible.

The killing of the four unnamed masons who had worked on the bins should also receive more attention than it did in Griffin's trial. Sarah Smallbone had claimed that Julia-Judith had given her a substance to put in the food served to the men. John Wilcox claimed that if he had eaten the same beef, he would also have died. The powder was, in all probability, arsenic. Arsenic was everywhere in the nineteenth century. It was most commonly used on farms as a poison for rats and other vermin, but arsenic compounds were present in paints, wallpaper fabrics, soap, toys, and medications.[9] It was also used as a sheep dip and crop insecticide.[10]

During the same time as the bridge at Stoneleigh was under construction, a famous poisoning case was being tried in London. This was that of Eliza Fenning. In June 1815, Fenning was hanged after being found guilty at the Old Bailey of attempting to poison her employer, Orlibar Turner, and his son and daughter-in-law. Fenning worked as a cook in their house, and served some dumplings, with steak, to the family. All three, as well as Fenning herself, became ill (although none died from the effects). The allegation was that she had put arsenic in the dumpling dough. Fenning protested her innocence, but evidence was presented by a surgeon, John Marshall, that he had been able to decant arsenic from rinsings from the dish used to serve the dumplings. Without much more consideration, Fenning was found guilty and sentenced to death.[11]

Even by the primitive standards of the time, this investigation appeared, to many observers, to have been seriously flawed. Anyone could have accessed the arsenic and done whatever they liked with it; it had been

---

8. Clive Emsley, Tim Hitchcock and Robert Shoemaker, "Communities—Black communities," Old Bailey Proceedings Online (www.oldbaileyonline.org, version 7.0, 5 January 2016).
9. Sandra Hempel, *The Inheritor's Powder: A Cautionary Tale of Poison, Betrayal and Greed* (Phoenix, 2013, Kindle version), p. 25 = Kindle 363; used by Young John Bodle "to treat the itch (scabies)," p. 155 (= Kindle 1948).
10. Hempel, p. 95 (= Kindle 1209).
11. The classic account is in *The Newgate Calendar* (n.d. but early 19th-century; Wordsworth Classics, Ware, 1997), pp. 320–325.

sitting in a drawer marked "Arsenic, deadly poison."[12] The surgeon was mistaken in alleging that it was arsenic which produced a black residue on a knife.[13] There was no reliable test for determining the presence of arsenic in human remains or other substances. In addition, the symptoms of arsenic poisoning were very similar to those of diseases such as cholera, and there was next to no diagnosis except the observation of symptoms. As Robert Christison (1797–1882), pioneering Scottish toxicologist, put it:

> "The entire success of a criminal poisoning depends on the process imitating the effects of a natural disease."[14]

This meant that a would-be arsenic poisoner, prior to 1820, was either going to be lucky and get away with it; or be very unlucky, like Eliza Fenning, and be hanged.

By the time of Griffin's libel trial in 1849, the situation was very different. In the 1830s, English chemist James Marsh refined testing of substances for arsenic, extracting a poisonous gaseous form of the element from a suspect substance.[15] This test, with some refinements, remained standard through the nineteenth century. In 1839, the leading French toxicologist Mathieu Orfila extracted quantities of arsenic from the liver, spleen, kidneys, heart and muscles of a human corpse.[16] His testing was famously used in the 1840 trial of Marie Lafarge for the murder of her husband.

Despite the increasing ability of chemists to detect arsenic, and the increasing reliance of the courts on their advice, the prevalence of deliberate arsenic poisoning in the England of the 1840s was astonishing. In 1845, Sarah Freeman was executed for having poisoned her child, mother, husband and brother. The body of her child, whose death had been ascribed to natural causes, was exhumed after her brother's death,

---

12. *Newgate Calendar*, p. 320.
13. Hempel (2013), p. 134 (= Kindle 1688).
14. Quoted in Hempel (2013), p. 63 (= Kindle 809).
15. Marsh testing in Bodle case: Hempel (2013), p. 136 (= Kindle 1708).
16. Hempel (2013), p. 43 (= Kindle 560–565).

and found to contain traces of arsenic.[17] In the mid-1840s, there were "the Norfolk poisonings." Jonathan Balls apparently poisoned at least three of his grandchildren, his wife, and himself; the disinterred remains indicated arsenic.[18] The Home Secretary (George Grey, whom we have already met in *Chapter 11*) sent a London chemist to investigate; arsenic was found in the remains of several of Balls' family members, including a child who had been buried for ten years.[19] The late-1840s saw what was described as an "epidemic" of poisoning in Essex: Sarah Chesham (known as "Sally Arsenic") was acquitted of killing her children in 1847, but in 1849, after her husband died of a painful illness, arsenic was found in his body: Sarah Chesham was found guilty and executed.[20] Chesham had apparently recruited at least one other female into the practice: Mary May was convicted in 1848 of the murder of her brother, apparently to receive his burial-club benefit. In her turn, Mary May appeared to have inducted Hannah Ham into the sisterhood. Ham was having an affair, and on the sudden death of her husband in the spring of 1847, she faced trial in 1849 for his murder. The juries of Essex seemed reluctant to convict, and Hannah Ham was found not guilty.[21]

This, then, was the fevered background against which Sarah Smallbone and John Wilcox told Mary Draper about the Stoneleigh poisonings. Four masons were said to have been poisoned with beef.

> **Mary Draper:** Willcox told me four men had died eating beef and mutton, which had been poisoned, and they all died at the table… I went down and asked [Smallbone], and she said it was John Willcox who did it. He said the drink these men had was poisoned. I did not ask the names of the four men… He did not say why they had been poisoned; they had been at work in the cellar, making up some bins.[22]

---

17. James C. Whorton, *The Arsenic Century: How Victorian Britain Was Poisoned at Home, Work, and Play* (Oxford University Press, 2010), p. 47 (= Kindle 931–939).
18. Whorton (2010), p. 45 (= Kindle 903).
19. Whorton (2010), p. 46 (= Kindle 926). Newspaper account in "British Extracts," (from *Bell's Messenger*), "Wholesale Poisoning in Norfolk," *The Maitland Mercury and Hunter River General Advertiser*, 18 November 1846, p. 3.
20. Whorton (2010), p. 39 (= Kindle 814–823).
21. Whorton (2010), pp. 35–38 (= Kindle 755–797).
22. *Report* (1849), p. 18, column 2.

Wilcox had told Faxon a similar story:

> **Faxon:** Wilcox told me he had poisoned 4 men at the Abbey; he took them a bit of beef, a bit of mutton, and some ale. He went in the butler's pantry and helped himself, and then went back to the men. He saw they looked very drooping, so he locked the door and never saw them again.[23]

Another man was said to have been poisoned with a drink. Mary Draper said that Smallbone

> "…said Mrs Leigh gave her the poison, and told her to put it in [a man's] drink and stir it up with a spoon. She did not know the man's name; he was taken to Warwick."[24]

Smallbone had also told this to Elizabeth James.

> "[**Elizabeth James: Smallbone**] said some person came for a jug of ale, and the Hon. Julia Leigh gave her a powder to put in the beer, and he died when he got to his work."[25]

Griffin had been a little more specific in his necessarily brief and circumspect 1848 summary of the allegations:

> "*Another man, name known*, not a Scotchman, nor a tramp, poisoned by Mrs Smallbone, at the instigation of another female, who gave her a poison, a white powder, to put into beer, and told her to stir it with a spoon. This man died as soon as he got to his work, and an inquest was held, and the verdict, 'apoplexy.' [Source] Mrs Smallbone's confession."[26]

Faxon had more to add:

---

23. *Report* (1849), p. 22, column 2.
24. *Report* (1849), p. 19, column 1.
25. *Report* (1849), p. 21, column 1
26. Griffin (1848), pp. 64–65.

> "**Faxon**: [Wilcox] said one man escaped into the privy, that Mr [Chandos] Leigh went to Wilcox and said 'Jack, which way is he gone?' Wilcox pointed after him, and his Lordship followed, telling Wilcox to make haste after him. Chandos followed him into the privy and cut his throat."[27]

Another version came from Joseph Lee, a friend of John Wilcox's, with Wilcox himself, again, the ultimate source:

> "[Wilcox] told me he stood by while Mrs Julia Leigh, the housekeeper, and several other persons, mixed some poison in some ale. They gave it into his hand and ordered him to give it to the men who were at supper in the kitchen. He took it to them and they drank it. Four of them died instantly; the fifth vomited it up, and "crope" [sc. crept] to "the petty" and then his young master, Chandos, asked him where he was, and Wilcox told him. Lord Leigh ordered him to follow him, and he bade Wilcox hold the man across his knee whilst Lord Leigh cut his throat with a pen-knife."[28]

It was entirely possible that the four men could have died "instantly," or at least very soon. Death from arsenic poisoning could take place almost immediately, or it could take some hours or even days. Within ten minutes, immediate symptoms include stomach cramps, nausea, vomiting, and watery or bloody diarrhea, so it is entirely plausible that victim number five rushed to the privy or "petty" (the outdoor toilet).[29] Desperate thirst follows, with vomiting the only result. Finally, the strain of system breakdown on the heart causes collapse.[30] If the allegations by Smallbone and Wilcox were true, Julia-Judith must have counted on being one of the lucky poisoners of her time. She did, according to their evidence, take the precaution of employing other people to place the poison in the beer or food, rather than doing it with her own hands. In the much more arsenic-aware environment of 1847, and with Julia-Judith safely deceased, Smallbone may well have felt that she herself would be the one to pay the penalty if murder were established.

---

27. *Report* (1849), p. 22, column 2.
28. *Report* (1849), p. 24, column 1.
29. Symptoms: Hempel (2013), p. 36 (= Kindle 480); timing of death: p. 38 (= Kindle 497).
30. Hempel (2013) p. 38 (= Kindle 497).

There were also suggestions that three other men, possibly Scots workmen, had been poisoned, one named Walker or Walkerley. No particular light was shed on these during Griffin's libel trial, although one interesting witness appeared. This was Jane Goode, "upwards of 100-years-of-age:"

> "I was 100 on the 1st of February last [1849]. I have lived at Stoneleigh nearly 80 years. A man of the name of Walkerley lodged at my house there. He died at my house; he had been ill some time before he died. Mr Hyde, surgeon, Kenilworth, attended him; during the last week of his life I attended and gave him his last food."

She was asked if she had poisoned him:

> "The witness with surprise, 'Oh! No; mercy on you, never, Sir! (Laughter) The man was ill a week, and had every thing he desired. His wife came to the house before he was buried. At that time it was never said or hinted by any one that he died of poison."[31]

Jeacock, the parish clerk, latest in a line of retainers whose evidence had, since the 1820s, decidedly been in favour of the Leigh family, testified that he had never heard of any murders at Stoneleigh. Further,

> "He knew Walkerly and Gilmore very well. There was a headstone to the former in Stoneleigh church-yard."[32]

In his 1848 book, Griffin — as we have seen, a man familiar with the latest scientific discoveries — called for chemical analysis of any remains exhumed from Stoneleigh Abbey. He argued that investigations, properly and honestly conducted, could be seen as supporting Chandos' position, or (as Griffin put it) as "witnesses" for him. Griffin lists four of these "witnesses," then:

---

31. Griffin (1848), p. 78; *Report* (1849), p. 27, column 2.
32. *Report* (1849), p. 30, column 1.

> "Fifthly, *an analysis publicly conducted* [italics in original] by independent chemists of the stomachs of the two Scotchmen Walker or Walkley [sic] who died at Goode's, and another who died at Claridge's and of all the bodies that may be found in the bridge or in certain other places."[33]

One of the peculiarities of arsenic as a poison is that it can destroy, as well as the functioning of human and animal organs, the micro-organisms which would generally cause their putrefaction after death. While not a universal effect, this meant that in some nineteenth-century cases, a corpse which indicated the presence of arsenic was better preserved than one in which death had occurred through normal causes.[34] In addition, as testing improved, and arsenic was able to be detected more readily in remains, bodies exhumed up to ten years after death could, as shown in the Norfolk case, indicate poisoning. In calling for testing of remains which, should they be located, would have been more than 30 years dead, Griffin was probably stretching the capabilities of current science. The call was tactical rather than realistic.

A curious sidelight is that the one chemical analysis which did take place was of the remains of Richard Barnett. He died not long after the murder hearing in May 1848, probably in July. The popular press reported Barnett's death as due to alcohol poisoning.

> "The examining surgeon at the inquest said he found the whole internal coating of the stomach much inflamed, but he found nothing to satisfy him that poison had been used. He had firmed [sic, sc. formed] the opinion that the effects were attributable to drink, and that the deceased had been an habitual drinker. The verdict of the jury was, that death had resulted from inflammation, produced by intoxicating liquors."[35]

Griffin was reported to have discussed the death in his public lectures:

---

33. Griffin (1848), p. 78.
34. Whorton (2010) p. 69 (= Kindle 1259).
35. Report in *The Tablet*, 22 July 1848, p. 15. Thanks to R. J. Stove for this reference.

> "[Griffin] stated during his lecture that he, as well as the public generally, entertained strong suspicions that the man Barnett, who died very soon after he had made his extraordinary statements in May last, had not met with his death fairly—that Lord Leigh, by his wealth, possessed sufficient means of stopping the mouth of any one who was likely to be a dangerous witness against him. The contents of Barnett's stomach, he said, had been forwarded to a chemist to be analysed, but the person who analysed them had not been called to speak to the presence or absence of poison, and the investigation before the Coroner was irregularly conducted."[36]

Such an unsatisfactory inquest was not unusual. The increasing pressure on chemists to give evidence in criminal cases meant that some were reluctant to commit themselves; and local authorities were often unwilling to make available sufficient funds for thorough coronial investigation.[37] In the absence of any investigation, the response of the Leigh legal team and family supporters to all the allegations was similar: as Griffin had pointed out in his book, it consisted mainly of ridicule, where not of evasion. Perhaps surprisingly, at Griffin's trial for libel, the Leigh case exhibited numerous errors of fact, possibly because it was not believed to be important enough to get details right.

In opening the case against Griffin on 31 March 1849, Chandos' chief counsel, Mr Whitehurst QC, outlined the background of the Leigh peerage case. He had either been given incorrect information by Chandos (or by Thomas Hill Mortimer), or the research conducted by his own team (consisting of a second QC, Mr Humfrey, plus two additional lawyers, Mr Miller and Mr Mellor) had been careless. He outlined Chandos' immediate ancestry as follows:

> "[The late] Mary Leigh, knowing that the present Lord Leigh's family were the elder branch of the same family as her late brother and herself, made a will in which she left the property in question to the Rev. Thomas Leigh,

---

36. Statement at Griffin's trial, probably (though unclear) by H. D. Cooper, shorthand writer: *Report* (1849), p. 10, column 2.
37. Whorton (2010), p. 41 (= Kindle 838–846).

who was the grandfather of the present Lord Leigh, then Mr Chandos Leigh, for his life."[38]

The Reverend Thomas was not the grandfather of Chandos, but his great-uncle. In attempting to depict a closer relationship than actually existed, it may be that Whitehurst was trying to strengthen Chandos' standing. Whitehurst went on to misrepresent the year of the Reverend Thomas' death.

"In 1812 the Rev. Thomas Leigh died…"[39]

The Reverend Thomas died in June 1813. This error, however, also, may have served the function of making James Henry Leigh's accession to the estate earlier than it actually was. Further mistakes, or calculated misrepresentations, followed. In giving the history of the Christopher stone, Whitehurst quoted the claimant George Leigh as having asserted that Christopher's son Roger had married Constance Clent.[40] This was not the case; George Leigh and his agents never asserted this, as it would have made no sense in the context of the claim. One final error was made in the opening remarks. Whitehurst claimed that the last Lord Leigh, Edward, had died in 1788; he actually died in 1786.[41] The vast bulk of Whitehurst's statement, however, consisted of rhetorical complaint about Griffin's actions. As opposed to complaint, the arguments made against Griffin's claims were few, but one argument Whitehurst offered is particularly striking.

> "By a new, and [Whitehurst] did not hesitate to say, a most mischievous law, passed in 1843 by the legislature, and introduced by a former member of the bar, a defendant was allowed to plead the truth of the libel he had published. Before 1843, if a man published a libel he could not plead the truth of the facts as a justification. That was a wise law, for it said if a party had a claim or charge to make let him do so in a legal manner: a stranger,

---

38. *Report* (1849), p. 4, column 2.
39. *Report* (1849), p. 5, column 1.
40. *Report* (1849), p. 5, column 1.
41. *Report* (1849), p. 8, column 1.

like Mr Griffin, who had nothing to do with Lord Leigh, had no right to libel a man and say 'I will prove its truth,' and run that man to great expenses. The old law said if you libel a man we will punish you for it."[42]

Whitehurst was objecting to the new system of "truth as a defence against libel." In 1843, the Libel Act brought in the important innovation that it provided libel defendants with a defence that the alleged libel was true, and that the defendant had published it in the public interest.[43] Until this time, courts had generally only had to determine if the defendant had, in fact, written, published, or spoken the libel. This meant that, prior to the 1843 law,

> "…throughout the early nineteenth century, criminal libel charges [against whistleblowers and publishers] were thus regularly used to allow an individual to preserve potentially embarrassing or scandalous secrets."[44]

It is typical of Charles Griffin, who wished to take advantage of the latest scientific advances, that he also hoped to be afforded the new protections supposedly offered by the legislation of 1843. It is also curious that Chandos' counsel would deplore the 1843 changes. Claiming that the truth of the allegations by Barnett and Wilcox was irrelevant to whether Griffin had libelled Chandos or not, was a strange way of protecting Chandos. On this view, presumably, Whitehurst did not see himself as called upon to protest Chandos' innocence of the crimes alleged: he was called upon to maintain that the very existence of the allegations, true or untrue, required his client to defend himself by charging Griffin with libel. Yet the fact that Chandos felt obliged to bring a libel action went a long way to suggesting that some of the allegations were true. Charging a writer with libel was tantamount to an admission of the truth of at least some of the misdeeds alleged. That this was the case had been acknowledged during debate on the 1843 law.

---

42. *Report* (1849), p. 7, columns 1–2.
43. Sean Latham, *The Art of Scandal: Modernism, Libel law, and the* Roman à Clef (Oxford University Press, 2009), p. 76.
44. Latham (2009), p. 76.

"Ironically, the considerable protections afforded a plaintiff [complaining about libel]… meant, as one member of Parliament noted in 1843, that 'the prosecution by indictment [that is, criminal libel] is practically an admission of the truth of the libel.'"[45]

Clearly, Chandos and his legal team would have preferred to have been operating under the pre-1843 regime, where all that had to be established was that Griffin had published the information in question. Instead, in the post-1843 environment, they were obliged to contend with a fresh airing of the allegations, in considerable detail, as Griffin attempted to establish their truth as the basis for his defence. Perhaps even more curiously, Whitehurst attacked not only Griffin's "truth" defence, but his implied "public good" one. Whitehurst maintained that even if the truth of the allegations about Chandos had been established, it might not have been in the public interest for them to be aired.

"…If [a murder] charge were true, if a man had committed murder, and if it could be shown, it did not necessarily follow that it was 'for the public good' to publish that crime, unless it could also be shown that such publication was for the public good…"[46]

Today's readers find it hard to understand how it could be claimed that *any* proven murder charge should be suppressed on public interest grounds, but Whitehurst considered that his audience would accept this position. Yet again, however, such a position served, if nothing else, to undermine Chandos' situation in relation to the allegations, rather than to strengthen it.

In terms of positive information to support Chandos' case, his team had little to offer. Chandos himself took the stand and was questioned. His answers gave very little away.

> **Griffin:** [W]as your Lordship there [at Stoneleigh] at the commencement of the erection of the bridge?

---

45. Latham (2009), p. 76.
46. *Report* (1849), p. 8, column 1.

The Missing Monument Murders

> **Chandos:** No, I was not there; that was in June or July, 1812, as near as I can recollect; I cannot charge my memory as to the exact time…
> **Griffin:** Did your Lordship see it before the Rev. Thomas Leigh's death?
> **Chandos:** Yes; if it was commenced in 1812, and I was there, I must have seen it.
> **Griffin:** Did your Lordship go to it, to see the progress of it?
> **Chandos:** No; I might have done so, but I took no interest in it.[47]

In an 1816 essay, Chandos had referred to the bridge in terms of greater involvement:

> "I build a magnificent bridge to gratify my vanity; yet, in after-times I shall hear nothing of it; perchance nothing of this, of any world!"[48]

On the stand in 1849, Chandos claimed not to remember George Shaw, Matthew Billinges, or Forbes. He did, however, admit to remembering John Wilcox.

> **Griffin:** Does your Lordship recollect John Wilcox?
> **Chandos:** I recollect John Wilcox being at Stoneleigh. I think he was Steward's room boy, but I am not quite certain, in my father's time, and I believe he was employed to fetch letters from the post office.[49]

Shortly, the cross-examination returned to the bridge.

> **Mr Humfrey, for Chandos:** Did your Lordship never go to the bridge when the works were going on?
> **Chandos:** I cannot say I was not; I think I was there in 1813, when the bridge was nearly completed; when the key-stone of the arch was put in; and that was in the summer, I think.
> **Humfrey:** And your Lordship never saw any blood there? (Roars of laughter.)

---

47. *Report* (1849), p. 13, column 1.
48. "On a Future State," *Fragments of Essays* (London: G. Sidney, 1816), pp. 10–11.
49. *Report* (1849), p. 13, column 1.

Chandos: Bless you! No.⁵⁰

Griffin, addressing the jury, made a statement in his own defence.

"[Griffin] did not think the History of England, and scarcely of the world, could afford a parallel to the extraordinary circumstances that took place four or five and thirty years ago at Stoneleigh, and the disclosures that have recently been made respecting them. If they should turn out to be true, and he had a right to suppose they possibly might be, till they were fully and thoroughly investigated, till every particle of evidence was brought forward that could bear upon the case… It was not his duty there to prove that all the facts of this case were true; it was his case to prove that the suspicions he had referred to in his book existed in the public mind."⁵¹

Griffin objected to the conduct of Chandos' son-in-law Charles Adderley, who had been on the bench at the time when Richard Barnett's original statement had been under consideration. Griffin noted that neither the Home Secretary, Warwickshire magistrates, nor the coroner, had organized any investigation, and that thus they had failed in their duties.⁵² Furthermore, Griffin argued, it would have been straightforward to have opened the sealed vault in Stoneleigh church, to examine the coffin plates. This would have established whether further searches were necessary.⁵³ The question of the coffin plates was, as Griffin argued, one of the central matters at issue, and would have been relatively easy to investigate. Understandably, it had taken a back seat behind matters such as the alleged throat-cuttings, burials and poisonings, but in fact it would have provided an indication about whether those killings had or had not taken place.

---

50. *Report* (1849), p. 13, column 2.
51. *Report* (1849), p. 13, column 2.
52. *Report* (1849), p. 14, column 1.
53. *Report* (1849), p. 14, column 2.

The Missing Monument Murders

CHAPTER FOURTEEN

Coffin Plates

"A pick axe and candle would in less than half an hour reveal if Barnett's evidence be right as to the nine coffin plates, and a pound or two cover the expence [sic], which I will cheerfully pay myself, and for once in my life become a gambler, and wager a few pounds on the event, to go to a charity if I am right."

Charles Griffin, 1848[1]

For a phenomenon which has been pretty well universal for hundreds of years, the coffin plate is an archaeological and genealogical resource which has been surprisingly seldom discussed. In its simplest form, it is a metal plate which bears information about the deceased, notably his or her name and often dates of birth and death, to be attached to the outside of the casket.

The reason for having such a thing is clear: once a person is deceased and their body inside a coffin, it is important to have a clearly visible, and durable, way for the coffin to be identified with its occupant. In fact, today in Australia it is a legal requirement for coffins to bear "a name plate or inscription stating the family name and at least one other name of the deceased" (South Australia Cremation Regulations 2001).[2]

Ironically, in view of the fact that the very point of the plate is that it should stay with the deceased for the purpose of identification, the separation of plates from their dedicated coffins has been a long-standing practice. Unlike a stone memorial, a small piece of metal is easily

---
1. Griffin (1848), p. 84.
2. Section 9, Coffins, 1f. Australian Funeral Directors Association, *Funeral Industry Coffins, Caskets and other Receptacles Guidelines* (September 2008), http://afda.org.au/app/webroot/media/member/Coffins%20Guidelines%20Sep%202008.pdf (Accessed 11 January 2016).

detached and carried. Some enthusiasts who collect, display, and trade historic plates through media sites such as Pinterest or Ebay seem to be under the erroneous impression that plates were never attached to a coffin, but were prepared for survivors as a keepsake.[3] It may be more comfortable to believe this than to accept that these items have been despoiled from someone's grave.

The coffin plates of the famous, or infamous, dead have been particularly liable to removal. The plate from the inner coffin of Oliver Cromwell was removed within a very few years of his death in 1658, remained in the keeping of various families for centuries, and was offered for auction by Sotheby's in 2014.[4]

In the 1848 hearing, Richard Barnett stated that in 1811, he had removed nine plates from the coffins in the family vault in Stoneleigh village church. He claimed that this was in the presence of "Mr Leigh" (perhaps Chandos rather than James Henry), Julia-Judith, George Jones (the elder), James Roberts, "Mr Harris of the Red-house," and Jonathan Soden.[5] Mr Harris will have been William Harris, a churchwarden at that time, who later gave a statement confirming his recollection of the Christopher stone.[6]

At Griffin's 1849 libel trial, several witnesses confirmed the removal of coffin plates from the Stoneleigh vault. A plasterer named Robert Eden testified that he had heard about the removal of coffin plates from the old vault.

> "He had also heard from the masons about the removal of coffin plates: they were to let the late Mr Jones know when they had taken them off, and he

---

3. "They were never on the actual coffins, instead they were created as a memento for the family to take home with them": Olive Tree Genealogy, https://www.pinterest.com/lorinems/coffin-plates/ (Accessed 21 September 2015).
4. Vincent Dowd, "How Oliver Cromwell's Coffin Plate Ended Up for Auction," http://www.bbc.com/news/entertainment-arts-30378146 8 December 2014, (Accessed 11 January 2016). The plate fetched £74,500, more than six times the pre-auction estimate: Daniel Mansfield, "Historic death plate buried with Oliver Cromwell fetches more than £70,000 at auction," http://www.elystandard.co.uk/news/historic_death_plate_buried_with_oliver_cromwell_fetches_more_than_70_000_at_auction_1_3895811 (Accessed 11 January 2016).
5. Griffin (1848), p. 51.
6. Harris deposition dated 13 January 1820: Leigh (1834), vol. I, p. 324, note. In *Report* (1849), Harris is described as of the Red Horse (presumably Inn, and presumed no longer extant), not 'Red-house', p. 11, column 1.

was to inform Lady [sic] Leigh; and they went into the vault after. It was said that some had been taken away, but he had not heard what quantity."[7]

Elizabeth James reported that Sarah Smallbone, too, had implicated Julia-Judith in the coffin plate removal.

"[Smallbone] said the coffin plates had been taken off and given to my lady, and she had taken them home in the carriage; they were taken to the abutments of the bridge and enclosed there."[8]

Joseph Lee, Stoneleigh labourer and friend of John Wilcox, stated that he had gone into the old church vault with school friends, prior to its final sealing up.

"I counted 24 coffins,—saw many coffin plates, and saw Christopher Leigh's coffin plate,—a man named Finch being occupied in taking a copy of it. They dined that day at 11 o'clock, and Finch could not copy it. When we went back after dinner Mrs Darby and Mrs Julia Leigh came out of the vault. Mrs Julia Leigh had got a breast-plate in her hand. I accompanied Robert Finch to finish his copy, and the plate was gone off the coffin."[9]

A stonemason named George Naylor, who had known George Shaw, testified that before his death, Shaw had told him (Naylor) about his role in the bridge deaths, as well as

"…the removal of the monuments buried in the park, as well as the placing of the coffin plates in the abutments of the bridge."[10]

Drawings and records of the coffins and coffin plate legends in the old vault, possibly by the mysterious Mr Warde (see *Chapter 6*), survive in a document in the Leigh papers.[11] The inclusion of Mary Leigh's coffin

---

7. *Report* (1849), p. 15, column 2.
8. *Report* (1849), p. 21, column 2.
9. *Report* (1849), p. 24, column 1.
10. *Report* (1849), p. 25, column 1.
11. SBTRO DR 18/3/50/1, photocopy kindly provided by SBTRO, 2015.

dates the drawing and transcription to between 1806 and the alleged removal of the plates in 1811. This would fit with a date around 1808 as suggested by Mr Warde, who in 1828 wrote to Chandos that his brother had made copies "twenty years" previously.[12]

It would appear that, somehow or other, Griffin also possessed a copy of this transcription. He wrote in his 1848 book:

> "I possess copies of every legible inscription (I believe) that was in the vault previous to Barnett's sacrilegious intrusion, and drawings of some of the plates."[13]

The drawing seems to show a total of 22 or 23 coffins, some of infants or children as they are much smaller than the others. However, the attached text states that there were 26 coffins in the vault. The drawing shows that the identifying coffin plates are still in place.

The transcriber has included coffin and coffin plate inscriptions from the following family members. The first set is on the left side of the chamber, looking in; the second set, going up to 15, on the right.

Left hand group:
1. Edward Lord Leigh, died 9 March 1737 (aged 53)
2. Mary dowager Lady Leigh, died 6 September 1742 (aged 56)
3. Ann Leigh, died 5 August 1728 (aged 15)
4. Unidentified, except for letters "M. L."
5. Similar but with text "Obit. May 5 AD 1713" inscribed in lead
6. Edward Leigh Esq. eldest son of Edward Lord Leigh. Died 3 August 1737 (aged 28)
7. An unidentified coffin below another
8. Unidentified, bearing only an escutcheon with the Leigh arms
9. Unidentified, below number 10
10. Thomas Lord Leigh, died 12 November 1710 (aged 50)
11. Lady Eleanor, wife of Thomas Lord Leigh, died 23 July 1705[14]

---

12. SBTRO DR 18/17/53/4, 7 February 1828.
13. Griffin (1848), p. 84.
14. It is unclear whether Lady Eleanor's coffin is actually number 11, or number 12.

Right hand group:
1. Edward Lord Leigh, born 1 March 1742/3, died 26 May 1786
2. Mary Leigh, born 4 May 1736, died 3 July 1806
3. Lady Leigh, died 5 April 1769 (aged 51)
4. Thomas Lord Leigh, died 30 November 1749 (aged 36)
5. Maria Rebecca Lady Leigh, died 7 December 1746 (aged 32)
6. Child, Thomas Leigh, second son of Thomas Lord Leigh, died 7 December 1741 (aged 2)
7. Child, Thomas Leigh, son of Thomas Lord Leigh and Maria Rebecca Leigh, died 12 October 1738
8. Unidentified
9. Lead inscription on coffin: "Here lyeth the body of the lady Altham wife to the Right Honourable ye Lord Altham Second Son to the Earl of Anglesey and Daughter to the Honourable Charles Leigh Esq and Ann Leigh his lady SHE DEPARTED this life ye 4th day of June aged 24 years March 30th 1684."
10. Unidentified, underneath number 11
11. "Christopher Leigh Esq. 4th Sonne of the late Thomas Lord Leigh & the late Lady Mary his Wife deceased Sept: 15: Anno Dom: 1672."
12. Large lead coffin, no inscription
13. Large lead coffin, no inscription
14. Child: "Thos. Fil. Nat. Max. Th. D. Leigh de Stoneleigh et DELEA No:RAE [sic, sc. Eleanorae] VX[oris]: OB. IVN: 17. AD 1685. Aet. 3" ("Thomas eldest son of Thomas Lord Leigh of Stoneleigh and Eleanor his [second] wife, died 17 June 1685, aged 3")
15. Child: Arabella Leigh. 1696.

The transcriber has appended the following notes:

"Observe those Coffins that are plain are all lead only the others are covered with Black Velvet richly Ornamented with Silver. Except the late Lord Leigh's which is cover'd with Crimson Velvet. There are 26 Coffins in the vault. Edw: Lord Leigh [Number 1, left group, died 1737] was one of the largest Men in the Kingdom his Coffin is 7 feet 3 inches in length, in Breadth 2 feet 10 inches, in height 1 foot 8 inches."[15]

This transcription supplies important evidence in support of the claim by Joseph Lee that Christopher Leigh's plate had, at least at one time, existed in the vault. The question arises as to why Julia-Judith allegedly ordered the removal of the coffin plates of Christopher Leigh and eight others. After all, the existence of Christopher Leigh, and his dates of baptism and death, had never been in question. What point could there be in removing the direct evidence of his burial?

The answer must be that this removal of Christopher's coffin plate reinforced and supported the removal of his memorial stone from the south wall of the church, and the destruction of records at the abbey. At Griffin's trial, Ann Burford, who had been head still-room maid at the abbey between 1819 until the end of 1821 or start of 1822, gave evidence as follows.

> "Once the Hon. Mrs Leigh told me to follow her with a candle into a back room, which I did, and there were some papers in the grate which had been torn up, and she told me to set fire to them, which I did. There was a gentleman in the room, and he gave Lady [sic] Leigh some papers, which she tore up, gave to me, and I put them in the fire. Lady Leigh locked the door while I was there. I told Mrs Leigh in the still-room afterwards that I thought I had done wrong by burning those papers; she said 'pooh, pooh, still-room maid; they were rubbish we wanted to get rid of, that were of no consequence.' In a day or two afterwards, Lady Leigh brought Master Colville into the still-room to me, and she made me a present of a guinea to go to Warwick to purchase a little present for myself."[16]

Any information about Christopher was potentially evidence about his putative descendants. In 1811, after all, Julia-Judith and James Henry had not yet succeeded to the estate: they were vulnerable to a claim along the lines of James Leigh Perrot's or Colonel Smith Leigh's, and even more

---

15. SBTRO DR 18/3/50/1, photocopy kindly provided by SBTRO, 2015.
16. *Report* (1849), p. 21, column 1.

so to a claim based upon Christopher. A thorough suppression of every detail relating to Christopher must have seemed the safest approach.

But Barnett claimed that he had removed nine coffin plates, which presumably did not include Christopher's, which (if Joseph Lee's evidence was correct), Julia-Judith had personally removed. This must have been a high proportion of those visible at the time: the stacking of coffins (the transcriber's drawing shows that several were in stacks of two or three, some with an additional small coffin on top) meant that several coffins had no visible identification.

Again, this wholesale removal must have been in order to suppress any potential information which might lead to claims. Any Leigh who had reached a marriageable age at death might be thought to have left heirs. For example, left-hand coffin number 6, Edward (d. 1737), only months after his father (Edward the third Lord, d. 1737, left-hand coffin number 1), died aged 28.[17] A man of this age might normally have been expected to leave an heir or heirs. As it happened, and has been noted in an earlier chapter, a surprisingly high number of Leigh inheritors died unmarried and/or without surviving children; but in 1811, Julia-Judith must have thought that the chance of would-be heirs emerging was high.

Griffin reported that as well as the removal of coffin plates, a child's coffin was removed from the vault and "deeply buried in open ground." He claimed a living witness existed for this information.[18] This was not, however, corroborated or clarified at Griffin's 1849 trial. The drawings show two small coffins stacked on top of right-hand side number 12 (unidentified), which in turn stands on top of number 11 (Christopher Leigh's). It is possible that one of these was removed because its proximity to Christopher Leigh's suggested that he might have had (as in John Ilett's informal observations, which he later denied under oath) "children who died in infancy."[19]

As Griffin suggested in 1848, opening the sealed vault would not be difficult or expensive as the headnote to this chapter indicates.[20] For

---

17. Table 1, in Bearman (ed., 2004), p. 130, has a death date of 1738 for Edward the Third Lord Leigh. The burial data clearly indicates a death date of 9 March 1737.
18. Griffin (1848), p. 64.
19. Ilett as quoted by Thomas Smith, in Leigh (1834), vol. II, p. 5, note.
20. Griffin (1848), p. 84.

once, he assumed a light-hearted tone, affecting to relish the prospect of a Gothic adventure. He was well aware, however, the significance of the vault was not only about an attempt to suppress Leigh family information through the removal of coffin plates and/or the child's coffin. The state of the coffins in the vault would show whether or not Barnett's evidence could, in general, be believed. If the coffin plates were seen to have been removed, this would corroborate Barnett's wider revelations. Unprejudiced observers would consider that if Barnett were to be proven correct about the vault, there was good reason to believe his evidence about the murders at the bridge.

Of course, the Leigh family was also aware that the state of the vault would be a pointer to the state of other matters. Such was the importance of the vault that it was entirely omitted from the statements of Chandos' legal team, both in 1848 and in 1849. The strategy must have been to ignore it, and hope that it would go away.

Whitehurst did, in his opening statement, mention the coffin plates in a would-be parody of Griffin's position. He wished to suggest that a search of the bridge and/or abbey might reveal relevant objects planted by would-be claimants and their supporters.

> "The idea of finding bodies in the abutments of the bridge was perfectly ridiculous; but [Whitehurst] had his suspicions whether they might not find bodies, coffin plates, or monuments in the adjacent ground, carried there, doubtless, by parties who only wanted leave to search, and then as 'those who hide can find,' the same parties would turn up something they had buried before, and cry out, 'Oh! Here's the proof; here's part of a monument; here are coffin plates, skulls, bones, and everything else which they desired to pick up.'"[21]

What Whitehurst avoided mentioning was that examination of the church vault would reveal if relevant items were *absent*, not *present*. It was unlikely, or indeed (if reports about their burial were correct), next

---

21. *Report* (1849), p. 6, column 2.

to impossible that stolen coffin plates could be planted back in the vault in time for inspection.

In 1848 or 1849, there was no legal authority which was willing to enforce the opening and inspection of the vault, over which the Leigh family had effective power. In summing up for the jury the case against Griffin, the judge, Chief Justice Wilde, remarked that Griffin's demands for investigation of the bridge and the vault had been surprising.

> "The request to pull down the bridge and open the vault was a very unusual one indeed, and one which it was surprising any man could have suggested, who had ever heard the sound of the word law, much more an attorney."[22]

Even today, it would appear (from guidelines issued for the use of archaeologists) that the management of family vaults in English churches requires considerable tact and diplomacy. Their dual (and vaguely defined) status as the "property" both of the church and of the relevant family or families is part of the issue here.

> "Parishes or the owners of private land and chapels often see their curation of such material as a 'sacred trust.'"[23]

On the other hand, burial vaults represent a highly valuable resource for archaeologists and historians—or, as in Griffin's case, the putative forensic investigators *avant la lettre* who, he hoped, would take the initiative. Even the "neglect and disuse of vaults," or in the Leigh case their probable despoliation, is a feature of their cultural importance.[24] Here as in other ways, Griffin was ahead of his time in identifying clues towards tracing the actual history of Stoneleigh events. For his contemporaries such as Justice Wilde, Griffin's commitment to the pursuit of the truth was more than unusual: it was extraordinary.

---

22. *Report* (1849), p. 33, column 1.
23. J. Elders, V. Harding, J. Litten, A. Miles, N. Powers, C. Roberts, J. Schofield, J. Sidell, B. Sloane, B. White, "Archaeology and Burial Vaults: A Guidance Note for Churches," Association of Diocesan and Cathedral Archaeologists Guidance Note 2, produced in consultation with the Advisory Panel of the Archaeology of Burials in England (APABE), July 2010, p. 5.
24. Elders *et al* (2010), p. 7.

The vault, then, was intimately connected with the key point at issue in 1848 and 1849, and indeed now, in this book. This is whether Richard Barnett, George Shaw and Sarah Smallbone, not to mention (at certain periods) John Wilcox and William Faxon, told the truth in the statements they had made; or whether they had concocted, or separately developed, a bizarre and horrific fantasy, either at the time of the alleged events or before reporting them years later.

The events these people had narrated were very difficult to believe. But was it *more* difficult to believe that they had spoken falsely in narrating them? The credibility of these witnesses was, and is, the key issue.

As Shaw and Smallbone were both dead by 1848 (and since Shaw's statement was effectively lost, and Smallbone never made one), and as Wilcox was selective in the evidence to which he was prepared to swear, the living witnesses relevant to the legal enquiry were Barnett and Faxon.

Whether a witness has previously had a conviction is, and has historically been, one factor in assessing the extent of his or her credibility.[25] At abortive proceedings against Chandos in March 1848, Chandos' team attempted to discredit Barnett as a witness on the basis that he had been tried for theft and served six months imprisonment. Barnett claimed that he was falsely imprisoned and that someone else had committed the crime.[26] Even after Barnett's death, this remained a way in which Chandos' lawyer, Whitehurst, impugned his evidence.[27]

The impression given by Barnett himself, however, was that his evidence was credible. Another criterion for assessing credibility has been the intellectual capacity or recall of the witness.[28] It was probably in addressing this matter that Mary Draper considered that Barnett "was in as sound a state of health as a man could possibly be; he was perfectly reconciled to tell what he knew about it."[29]

---

25. See, e.g., "Credibility," Judicial Commission of New South Wales, Evidence Act 1995, 3.7 and subsequent divisions. http://www.judcom.nsw.gov.au/publications/benchbks/civil/credibility.html#p4-1200 (Accessed 11 January 2016).
26. Griffin (1848), pp. 51–52.
27. *Report*, p. 6, column 1.
28. "Credibility,'" Judicial Commission of New South Wales, Evidence Act 1995, 3.7 and subsequent divisions. http://www.judcom.nsw.gov.au/publications/benchbks/civil/credibility.html#p4-1200 (Accessed 11 January 2016).
29. *Report* (1849), p. 18, column 1.

A man named Candy who had worked with Richard Barnett, and heard his stories, described him as follows.

> "[Barnett was] a curious, listless, restless man…[who, Candy thought at first] was labouring under some delusion at the time he first talked of these affairs. [Candy] had entered several memoranda as to his conversation with Barnett, and his opinions on his statements. He imagined if the statements were true Lady [sic] Leigh must have been a second Lady Macbeth; and in his memorandum book, in reference to this matter he had quoted Shakespeare, who wrote, 'Murder, though it hath no tongue, will out, with most miraculous organ.'"[30]

Candy's statement was greeted with laughter by the court.

Griffin had noted in 1848 that, on signing his deposition, Barnett had said to the clerk taking his statement:

> "I'll lay my life down, sir, if they are not found."

Griffin went on, aware that the credibility of Barnett would prove to be the key issue:

> "Many persons are much impressed with the truthfulness of this spontaneous ebullition of Barnett…"[31]

So much for the credibility, in *absolute* terms, of Barnett. Assessment requires, however, consideration of the *relative* likelihood that Barnett was telling truths, or telling untruths, about events at the vault and the bridge.

If Barnett's testimony was false, it is important to consider on what grounds it may have been made. There are several varieties of false testimony, some voluntarily given, some less voluntarily, or involuntarily.

False confession is certainly a forensic and psychological phenomenon, which has in modern times received a considerable amount of attention. Reviews of DNA evidence in numerous cases have resulted in the eventual

---

30. *Report* (1849), p. 24, column 2.
31. Griffin (1848), p. 58.

exoneration of convicted persons, including in some cases where a false confession had been given and previously believed.[32]

It is difficult to establish what proportion of confessions are falsely made. A comprehensive 2009 study notes that there are four ways in which a confession may be demonstrated to be have been false:

1. When it can be established that the suspect confessed to a crime which did not occur;
2. When the crime occurred, and it can be established that the suspect could physically not have been able to commit the crime, e.g. he/she was proven to be elsewhere at the time;
3. When the crime occurred, but another person was demonstrated to have perpetrated it; or
4. When scientific evidence, in recent years commonly DNA evidence, conclusively establishes the suspect's innocence.[33]

This study goes on to identify police misclassification, coercion, and contamination of suspect accounts as the major causes of false confessions. It claims that vulnerable suspects, such as the young, the addicted, and the mentally unstable, are particularly likely to respond to police interrogation with a false confession, sometimes in the hope of receiving leniency or the fear of harsher treatment.[34]

Barnett confessed to having committed the thefts from the Stoneleigh vault, and having been a witness (admittedly at some remove, and without being an eyewitness) to the murders at the bridge. For the moment, let us focus on the vault theft as the subject of his direct confession, bearing in mind that its veracity, or otherwise, will have a bearing on his other evidence.

Clearly, no police coercion was involved in Barnett's confession. There were, as we have seen, effectively no police active in rural Warwickshire in 1848, let alone detectives keen to investigate the vault. Rather, the whole weight of official authority lay with the church and the Leighs,

---

32. Richard A. Leo, "False Confessions: Causes, Consequences, and Implications," in *Journal of American Academy of Psychiatry and the Law*, 37:332–43, 2009, p. 332.
33. Leo (2009), p. 333.
34. Leo (2009), pp. 335–336.

who (according to Barnett), so far from opposing his crime, actually prompted and supervised his commission of the theft.

Barnett's confession cannot be shown to have been false under any of the four scenarios listed above. There was no investigation. Therefore, it was never established that the crime did not occur (1). It was not shown that Barnett had an alibi (2). No other person was shown to have committed the theft (3). Obviously, scientific evidence was never sought or applied to bring about any finding of innocence (4). Barnett's confession, therefore, does not fall into any of these categories of demonstrated falsity.

It should also be noted that in addition to false confessions which may be more or less the result of coercion, there is a category of entirely voluntary false confessions. In the twentieth and twenty-first centuries, these have generally occurred in response to widely publicised crimes, such as the Lindbergh kidnapping in the 1930s and the Black Dahlia murder in the 1940s. Numerous people who come forward with confessions to these crimes may be subject to psychiatric disorders. Others may wish to protect others from suspicion, or to get revenge on another person.[35]

Whether Barnett's confession fell into any of these categories needs to be examined. While some hearers of Barnett's stories thought him deluded (e.g. Candy), others found him as lucid as could be (e.g. Draper). It is, however, certainly possible that he suffered from a psychiatric disorder.

There is no reason to think that Barnett was trying to protect anyone else from suspicion of the vault theft. Again, with no investigation, there were effectively no suspects until he nominated himself.

The matter of revenge is a little more complex. In claiming that the Leigh family watched him rob the vault, Barnett was certainly attempting to share the blame. On his own account, he first formally brought forward all his evidence to William Prowting Roberts in order to assist in a claim on the Stoneleigh estate, probably that by James Leigh or John Leigh (I) in the early 1840s.

> "I didn't say anything [for many years] about seeing the two men murdered, because I didn't think it worth my while. I knew I was fighting against a big

---
35. Leo (2009), p. 338.

one. I mean, by the big one, Lord Leigh. I am doing the best I can towards fighting him now. I divulged the matter to Mr Roberts because the parties were trying for it. By 'trying for it' I mean the estate. It was to help them forward in a claim to the estate."[36]

After Barnett's death, at Griffin's 1849 trial, Whitehurst claimed that all the evidence from Barnett, Wilcox, Smallbone, Shaw and others consisted of

"... incredible, foolish statements, as either the invention of low, vulgar minds, for the purpose of getting money from the claimants [such as James Leigh or John Leigh], or as the more wicked productions and concoctions of baser persons, and for more malicious purposes."[37]

He rhetorically asked

"... if it were at all justifiable, because a raving mad woman [Smallbone], or wicked drunken men, like Wilcox or Barnett, (about whose death [Whitehurst] still had suspicions,) told a parcel of lies for the purpose of gaining money, an attorney like Mr Griffin was to re-assert them, with his own remarks, and publish them to the world?"[38]

Whitehurst, then, treated Barnett's evidence as false and having been made simply in order to make financial gain.

Yet Barnett made no financial gain from confessing to the vault theft. He stated in evidence: "I received no money but what I worked for."

In addition: "I paid my own expenses to Manchester [to see William Prowting Roberts]."[39] Whitehurst did not provide actual evidence of Barnett having received any payments, so it would appear that the allegation that Barnett gave false testimony for financial gain may be discounted.

There is a final category of false testimony, or — depending on one's point of view — there may be. This is the controversial recovered or false

---

36. Barnett evidence in *Report* (1849), p. 11, column 1.
37. *Report* (1849), p. 32, column 1.
38. *Report* (1849), p. 32, column 1.
39. *Report* (1849), p. 12, column 2; (Manchester fare) column 1.

memory syndrome. It is a situation in which a person may be convinced that they have experienced a traumatic event, which either did not happen, or which did happen but in which they were not, actually, involved.

Psychologists have been able to establish that the phenomenon occurs, using studies where testers have suggested false events as having happened earlier in the lives of the test volunteers. The volunteers appeared to create false memories of accidents, emergency department visits, and so on, after suggestion by the researchers.[40]

As noted, this is an area fraught with controversy. If recollections by people of past traumas can be presented as mistaken or artificially created, it has been argued, this is *carte blanche* for perpetrators of child sexual abuse or other criminal acts against children.[41] On the other hand, equally, if such "memories" can be false, then innocent people could be charged with serious offences on the basis of untrue claims.

It can be observed, however, that where false memories have been shown to have been created (e.g. in the research setting), there has been a strong social imperative at work. In a research experiment, the volunteer is likely to be responsive, on a subconscious as well as conscious level, to the apparent demands or requirements of the researchers.[42] This implied direction is also likely to operate in the context of a patient seeking assistance from a therapist.[43]

There was certainly no social imperative operating upon Barnett which would suggest to him that he had been involved in traumatic events. In fact, the opposite was at work: a reluctance even to hear, let alone to believe, his recollections. John Toone, who worked with Barnett at times, would sometimes walk away because he did not want to hear Barnett's stories once again.[44]

---

40. Ira E. Hayman, Jr, and Elizabeth F. Loftus, "Some People Recover Memories of Childhood Trauma that Never Really Happened," in Paul S. Applebaum, Lisa A. Uyehara, and Mark R. Elin (eds.), *Trauma and Memory: Clinical and Legal Controversies* (Oxford University Press, 1997), 3–24, pp. 6–8.
41. See, e.g. South Eastern Centre Against Sexual Assault and Family Violence (SECASA), Melbourne, Victoria, "False Memory Syndrome for Workers," http://www.secasa.com.au/pages/false-memory-syndrome/ "[FMS] not only denies the reality of survivors' experience but also puts therapists at risk of legal action" (Accessed 11 January 2016).
42. Hayman and Loftus (1997), p. 9.
43. Hayman and Loftus (1997), pp. 11–12.
44. *Report* (1849), p. 17, column 1.

It could be argued that the social agitation of the 1840s provided just such a social imperative for creating a false account, but it could equally be argued that the politically charged environment gave encouragement to Barnett to tell the truth for the first time. While the possibility remains that Barnett was psychiatrically disturbed, it is unlikely that William Prowting Roberts, an experienced lawyer of uncontested integrity, would have pursued the charges against Chandos Leigh in May 1848 unless he had had confidence in the testimony of Barnett.

CHAPTER FIFTEEN

The Book Transaction

'Jack, which way is he gone?'

Chandos Leigh to John Wilcox (reportedly, c. 1815)[1]

The role of John Wilcox was central to the entire story. He was the one surviving person, apart from Chandos Leigh, who had been witness to events from 1812 through to 1849.

As the post-boy in that early period, Wilcox claimed to have witnessed the bringing of the Christopher stone, disguised, into Stoneleigh Abbey, and its concealment in the cellar. He claimed to have been present at the bridge on the fateful night when Billinges and Forbes were killed, and to have witnessed their murder by Julia-Judith, Chandos, George Jones Snr, and William Wood.

It was from his dramatic account that we learned that Chandos, after cutting the throat of one of the victims, collapsed and had to be pulled away from the abutment. Wilcox stated under oath, then retracted, the allegation that he had picked up Chandos' glove, which was stained with blood, and kept it for some time.

Wilcox, along with Smallbone, was a key witness to the poisonings allegedly orchestrated by Julia-Judith. He claimed to have been involved in poisoning food served to several of the stonemasons, who subsequently died. It was he who alleged that poisoning victim number five struggled to get to the privy, where his throat was cut by Chandos, urging Wilcox to follow and assist.

---

1. *Report* (1849), p. 22, column 2.

Wilcox made a statement containing some of these sensational allegations in 1848, as it was produced at the abortive proceedings against Chandos Leigh. Wilcox then repudiated the statement, claiming that he had not been sober when he made it. Because Wilcox rejected his own testimony, its status is problematic.

However, there may be some evidence about Wilcox from the Leigh papers. Norma Hampson, in her article "The Poet and the Paternalist" (in the 2004 volume on Stoneleigh edited by Robert Bearman), cites correspondence dealing with Chandos' expenses incurred on the account of a certain bookseller called Wilkes.[2] Given that John Wilcox's name appears in some contexts (notably in giving evidence in May 1829) as "Wilcooks,"[3] it is quite possible that this supposed bookseller was actually he, with "Wilkes" another version of his surname, and that the demands related to blackmail payments on the basis of the bloodstained glove.

There is certainly some evidence that code was being used in correspondence about the matter. In March 1830, Thomas Hill Mortimer wrote from Albany to Chandos at Stoneleigh. On the outside of the letter was written, unusually, "March 5th 1830. Letter about Wilkes bookseller."

> "I cannot help troubling you with a few lines lest that dirty fellow Wilkes should pester you with his importunities. He has been calling upon me two or three times a week, on endeavouring to persuade me that he was hardly dealt by in regard to the book transaction, now upwards of 12 years ago, and to write to you in his favour.
>
> I told him, in the first interview I had with him after the receipt of your packet containing the record correspondence, that the Business was settled either with him or some person on his behalf in the year 1818. That the agreement between you and him for the purchase, was returned to me at the time it had. I had it now in my possession cancelled.
>
> He pretended total ignorance of having received my money, and having referred to his solicitor who I of course took his receipts for the foregoing

---

2. Hampson (2004), pp. 180, 187.
3. Leigh (1834), vol. II, pp. 193ff.

The Book Transaction

payments, but the Bills & Receipts which I paid on your account were, on that occasion collected and delivered to Mistress Leigh your Dear Niece.

I remain Dear Sir
Your most devoted obliged humble Svt.
Thos Will [sic: sc. Hill] Mortimer

His request that you would return the said papers he sent you a short time since, I suspect, would have been with a view, in case he could no further improve on your liberality, to attempt to force some additional contribution, by threat of noticing in print the terms of the original agreement which he might have imagined might annoy you & by your judicious consignments of them to ———-? he is disappointed—but rightly deserves the ——————-? I have attached to him."[4]

(The words expressed by dashes were presumably indecipherable by the transcriber.)

It is very unlikely that a bookseller whose bills had been unpaid in the period 1812–1818 should still have been pursuing Chandos Leigh in 1830. It was more or less routine for Regency aristocrats to fail to pay their bills. As the authorities on Byron and Newstead Abbey put it:

"Byron, like his great-uncle before him, and along with many of his contemporary aristocrats, was happy enough to live with debt…"[5]

So, undoubtedly, was Chandos. Therefore, the matter referred to is likely to have been, in actuality, something both more obscure and more serious. Most of the Leigh letters are not accompanied by a helpful direction about their contents. In labelling this letter as about "Wilkes bookseller," Mortimer (or subsequent archivists) may have been attempting to give it a disguise.

---

4. SBTRO DR 18/17/55/5, as transcribed by Garry Strachan (October 2014, provided to author).
5. J. V. Beckett and Sheila Aley, *Byron and Newstead: The Aristocrat and the Abbey* (Newark and London: University of Delaware Press, 2001), p. 168.

Apart from the guarded and circuitous language which Mortimer uses in the letter, there is certainly code in his expression "Mistress Leigh your Dear Niece." A niece of Chandos Leigh whose name was "Mistress Leigh" (a surprisingly archaic formulation, rather than Miss Leigh) would have had to have been either born a Miss Leigh, or married a nephew of Chandos who was a Mr Leigh. Yet Chandos had no brothers to have issue a Miss Leigh as his niece, or a Mr Leigh as his nephew.

Chandos had four younger sisters. Two (Julia and Caroline) married, but both died without issue. His sister Mary had married, in 1817, Frederick Colvile, and had children. His youngest sister Augusta married, in 1827, Grenville Berkeley, and had children.[6] So any niece of Chandos' would be a Miss Colvile or a Miss Berkeley, not a Miss Leigh. Any such niece, in any event, will have been a child in 1830, not of an age to act as Chandos' or Hill Mortimer's agent (even supposing that women were regularly used in this manner, which was not the case).

So Hill Mortimer was referring to someone other than a niece of Chandos, and almost certainly a male. "Mistress Leigh" may be code for Chandos' brother-in-law Frederick Colvile. There is some evidence that Colvile was an intimate of Julia-Judith. In 1849, Ann Burford, still-room maid at Stoneleigh in the period 1819–1822, reported that it was in the company of "Master Colville" that Julia-Judith made her a present of a guinea, after requiring her (in a locked room) to burn several papers.[7] These may even have been the papers to which Mortimer refers in this letter, i.e. documents relating to Wilkes/Wilcox's claims against Chandos.

If my theory is correct, the termination of proceedings to which Mortimer refers, "in the year 1818," will have involved Wilcox handing over the bloodstained glove. Without this physical evidence, Wilcox's position was subsequently weak, and Hill Mortimer and Chandos could defy him to pursue them further. It is clear, however, that he persisted in making demands for money.

It is not clear when Wilcox had made the statement which was produced at the hearing in 1848, only to be dismissed at the hearing proper. The sequence of events may have been that Wilcox made the statement,

---

6. *Burke's Peerage and Baronetage*, n.d. but c. 1981, p. 1575.
7. *Report* (1849), p. 21, column 1.

then (prior to the hearing) used its existence as a way of re-opening threats to Chandos, only to be silenced by a counter-threat of libel. By May 1848, not only was Wilcox no longer in a position to blackmail Chandos, but in fact the reverse was the case: Wilcox was now at risk of being prosecuted for libel or extortion.

That Wilcox continued, however, to seek payments was acknowledged in passing by Chandos' lawyer, Whitehurst, in summing up the case against Griffin in March 1849. The non-appearance of Wilcox to give evidence in support of Griffin was noted with glee by Whitehurst.

> "The reason was clear: Wilcox might make his money by giving rumour to these abominable lies, but he knew that transportation was no joke, and if he swore to them in a witness box he would be prosecuted like Barnett, and would have suffered, too, like him, had he not died or been purposely kept out of the way."[8]

(Whitehurst's statement here, incidentally, suggests — which was nowhere else admitted by the Leigh team — that Barnett had suffered some kind of retribution after giving his evidence in 1848.)

Wilcox's position had always been equivocal. He was the only witness of whom it could convincingly be said that he was seeking purely his own financial gain. On the other hand, his evidence was so explosive, and (if all his reported remarks are included) so voluminous, that it cannot be set aside in considering the events overall.

Like Barnett, Wilcox was very young when he allegedly witnessed the suppression of the monument and the bridge murders. In the summer of 1812, Chandos was 20, Barnett 15 or 16, and Wilcox probably no older than 14 (a youth older than this is unlikely to have been called "the postboy"). There is something about Wilcox's account of the privy murder which suggests a kind of friendship or intimacy. In Wilcox's reported version via the evidence of Faxon, Chandos called to him "Jack, which way is [poisoning victim number five] gone?"[9] The use of the nickname Jack, rather than the impersonal surname or even position name ("steward,"

---

8. *Report* (1849), p. 32, column 1.
9. *Report* (1849), p. 22, column 2.

"still-room maid") generally used to address servants, suggests a personal relationship, and there is an easy expectation of compliance.[10]

One of the few facts which Chandos, on the witness stand in 1849, admitted, was remembering Wilcox: while denying everything else, he felt unable to deny this. It is not beyond the bounds of possibility that, like his life model Byron, Chandos, in early adulthood, cultivated homosexual intimacy with younger males. At Cambridge in 1805, Byron became passionately attached to John Edleston, a choirboy at Trinity Chapel.[11] Chandos was not at Oxford, where such adventures might more readily have taken place, but at Stoneleigh; the available youths were of a lower class. On such a view, there might be even more ground for Wilcox to attempt to blackmail Chandos in later years.

While Wilcox's self-serving motives meant that his evidence was fatally compromised, the evidence of the use of code in the Leigh papers may support a history of blackmail, the poor man's libel action. Chandos' payments to Wilcox—which Whitehurst's reference confirms—were strong evidence that Chandos wished to hide their shared history.

Because the statement made by George Shaw was not admitted at the trial of Chandos Leigh in 1848, it did not appear in Griffin's book or in the newspaper reports of his libel trial in 1849. For this reason, it has effectively been suppressed. Nonetheless, its content was more or less revealed at Griffin's trial. Shaw claimed that he personally had removed monuments from Stoneleigh church; that he sold remnants of these and bought alcohol; and that he swore an oath (under the supervision of the black man John Thomas) to bring about the deaths of Billinges and Forbes at the bridge. This version highlights the men's initial reluctance to kill Billinges, because he had a wife and children.

There seems no reason to doubt that Shaw made a statement to these effects. In so far as the account confirms those of Barnett and Wilcox, there seems reason to believe its substance. The fact that Shaw admitted to criminal involvement is no reason to discredit his evidence, any more than a confession by any criminal need be doubted. The same analysis

---

10. Ann Burford's account indicates that Julia-Judith addressed her as "still-room maid."
11. Leslie A. Marchand, *Byron: A Portrait* (London: Omega, 1976), p. 38.

as applied in the previous chapter to Barnett's account could be applied here, in attempting to assess whether Shaw's confession was false.

Sarah Smallbone, for her part, never made a signed statement, being in poor health and in fear of going to trial herself. Nonetheless, a significant quantity of evidence was obtained from her confidantes Mary Draper and Elizabeth James. She claimed to have witnessed some murders ordered by Julia-Judith, and to have taken part in others. Similarly, of course, assessment on the lines set out in the previous chapter cannot establish that her confessions were false. There is no reason to doubt that Smallbone was telling the truth.

As Chandos Leigh's team pointed out, Smallbone was seriously unwell in her final year. The Leigh team brought forward Obadiah Ayton, a Kenilworth surgeon, to confirm this, and to imply that her judgment was affected by alcohol.

> "She became paralysed in her left side, and was, in consequence, confined to her bed. She was naturally weak-minded—was very ignorant and illiterate. She had an idiotic cry, and would be in tears frequently...at one time she took a great deal of rum, but latterly she had not the means."[12]

No other attempt was made to rebut the evidence of Smallbone.

Finally, there is the evidence of William Faxon, overlooked in 1848 and aired to the mirth of the court in 1849. Faxon did not claim to have witnessed the murders, but did allege that he saw (and touched) evidence of blood on the site, the following day. He also claimed to have witnessed the bringing of covered objects to the bridge site, and their burial there. Faxon also alleged that he spoke with William Billinges and asked after Joseph, and that Billinges alleged that Joseph Billinges had been killed by a falling stone.[13]

Being separate from the evidence of Barnett, Wilcox, Shaw, and Smallbone, that of Faxon is this much more valuable. No attempt was made to rebut his evidence in 1849. Because his evidence was lengthy and rambling (and, no doubt, because as an elderly bone-collector, he was

---

12. *Report* (1849), p. 30, column 1.
13. *Report* (1849), p. 22, column 1.

of very low caste), Chandos Leigh's supporters greeted his evidence with ridicule, but no actual counter-evidence.

This brings us to the matter of what persuaded the courts in both 1848 and 1849 that there was no substance to the allegations about the bridge murders. Today's readers of Norma Hampson's account would conclude that an exhaustive assessment must have taken place.

> "Under cross-examination the thirty-four-year-old charge was found to be a complete fabrication and Chandos was acquitted. Demands to have the bridge excavated were refused on the grounds that, if nothing were found, the accusers would not be satisfied until the entire Abbey was excavated."[14]

In fact, however, as we have seen, Chandos faced no cross-examination in 1848 (George Jones junior claimed that it would "degrade his noble client").[15] No investigation was undertaken of the Stoneleigh vault, the bridge, or any site at the abbey: Hampson omits to point out that there was no forensic analysis, or that there was effectively no police or detective activity in Warwickshire in 1848. Shaw's statement and Smallbone's evidence were not admitted. Hampson accepts at face value the unsupported assertion of George Jones junior (the son, let us not forget, of one of the men accused of direct involvement in the bridge murders) that any excavation which did not yield results would lead to further demands.

Hampson also fails to inform her readers that no less a lawyer than William Prowting Roberts considered that charges against Chandos were appropriate. The charges were not "found to be a complete fabrication" at all. They were simply ignored, in the abrupt decision to discharge Chandos. The 1848 decision, then, was made purely on class grounds: that the evidence of a man such as Barnett could not be allowed to impugn one such as Chandos Leigh. So much for the magistrates' decision-making in 1848.

In Griffin's libel trial in 1849, while ostensibly Griffin now had the advantage of the "truth and public good" provisions of the 1843 legislation, in practice it appeared that the jury was operating under the

---

14. Hampson (2004), p. 185.
15. Griffin (1848), p. 58.

pre-1843 framework. In the post-1843 setting, however, Chandos' team had at least to make a pretence of contesting the truth of the allegations.

They did this through bringing forward several men who claimed to have worked on the bridge in the period 1812–1815, and not to have heard anything about any murders. As described in an earlier chapter, stonemason Alexander Hay was produced. (Barnett had claimed that 'Aleck Haywood' and 'John Haywood' were present on the night of the murders.[16])

> "I left London the 31st of August, 1812, and on arrival at Stoneleigh began my work there. My brother, John Hay, and some others were also employed with me…There were no Billinges employed on my side of the river [Stoneleigh side]… There were no stones laid without my seeing them. There was no stone laid at night; it would not have been done without my knowledge. There was no other work than pumping done at night. I never heard of a William Forbes working there. No man was killed by the falling of a stone. There was no accident at the bridge at all; if there had been a sore finger I should have heard of it."[17]

Clearly, this is a variant of our old friend the O'Farrell argument, deployed with regularity in earlier years by Thomas Hill Mortimer: if X had occurred I would have known about it; I did not know about it; therefore X did not occur. If Barnett and Shaw were correct in alleging that the men present on the night had been offered money to conceal the events, this would account for Hay/Haywood's failure to have noticed any "accident."

The other key witness brought forward was none other than stonemason William Wood, who had been named by Shaw and Wilcox as having personally assisted in cutting the throats of the bridge victims.

> "I worked at Stoneleigh Bridge in March, 1815; it was then all finished with the exception of the wing walls. I never assisted in killing any men on the bridge. (Laughter.)"

---

16. Griffin (1848), p. 51.
17. *Report* (1849), p. 28, column 2.

[Or did you assist in killing anybody else?]

"Never in my life. The first work I did was to assist in taking down part of the bridge, because the crown was too high… I heard of one Thomas Ramsay being hurt in 1815, by falling amongst some rubbish and spraining his wrist… With that exception, I never heard of any one being hurt, or of any one being murdered throughout. I never assisted to carry down on a truck any monument to deposit in the abutment, by night or day, nor did I ever see any coffin plates except in the vault… There was no man of the name of Proud or Forbes."[18]

Clearly Wood delivered his evidence in a jocular manner. The additional detail about Thomas Ramsay spraining his wrist seems a satire, designed to make light of the allegations. Wood did confirm, however, Barnett's claim that the course of stones (following the murders) required paring off.

Leigh's team also brought forward John Maryatt, a Kenilworth labourer, who said that he would have heard of any rumour of murder if it had occurred. A similar thing was stated by a sawyer called John Lines.[19]

Robert Jeacock, the next witness, took it on himself to deny that anything such as had been alleged had occurred. He did not state his qualifications for knowing this, but he was undoubtedly a relative of the parish clerk Job Jeacock, who then appeared.

Job Jeacock had long ago, in the 1828–29 case, declared that neither he nor his father had any recollection of the Christopher stone. Yet Jeacock had during the years 1805 to 1812 been resident in Coventry, not a regular attender at Stoneleigh church.[20] He was also the person who had been careless enough to tell Mary Iorns that he "had determined to stick to it that there never was such a monument."[21]

On this occasion in 1849, Job Jeacock (now 58) added to the "minor injuries" list.

---

18. *Report* (1849), p. 29, column 1.
19. *Report* (1849), p. 30, column 1.
20. Robert Jeacock: *Report*, p, 30, column 1. Job Jeacock deposition: Leigh (1834), vol. II, pp. 304–306; p. 305, note, re absence in Coventry.
21. Leigh (1834), vol. II, p. 127, note.

The Book Transaction

"In the year 1819, a man was buried [at Stoneleigh] who had died from a cut of the finger, received whilst dressing sheep, and there had been no death from accident, in his recollection, before or since. [Jeacock] remembered that some few days after the man was buried seeing that the ground had been disturbed, and he took out the coffin again to see whether the body was there, and it was quite safe. His impression was that the body had been disturbed for the purpose of being taken away for dissection, but was found in a too decomposed state. At no other period had he observed that the churchyard had been disturbed, and if it had he most certainly should have detected it. He had never heard of any murders having been committed at Stoneleigh till very recently, and he knew Walkerly and Gilmore very well."[22]

This bizarre evidence by Jeacock raises far more questions than it answers. As we have seen, arsenic was in widespread use as a sheep treatment, so the anonymous man cited by Jeacock might, indeed, have been poisoned. Jeacock also, unwittingly, confirmed that there appeared to have been disturbance of burials at Stoneleigh. Was it common that village graves were raided for dissection materials? Perhaps conscious that he was revealing too much, Jeacock quickly reverted to the O'Farrell defence.

In another striking reprise of 1828, the Leigh team also brought forward Jonathan Soden, who had been a key witness against the Christopher stone at that earlier time (in direct contradiction of numerous members of his own family). This time, he said:

"He was employed at the bridge in the years 1813 and 1814, and had never murdered any one there or at the Abbey; neither had he heard of any men being missed."[23]

When examined in detail, this counter-evidence produced by the Leigh team is glaring in its inadequacy. The main witnesses were Alexander Hay, claiming to be the person named by Barnett as Haywood, who (if Barnett and Shaw were correct) had almost certainly been paid for his

---

22. *Report* (1849), p. 30, column 1.
23. *Report* (1849), p. 30, column 1.

silence about the night; and William Wood, who was in 1848 charged, along with Chandos, with the bridge murders, but against whom charges were dropped so that his evidence could assist Chandos.[24] In the event, neither Wood nor Chandos was cross-examined at the 1848 hearing. If Hay/Haywood had been paid off, the same must have been true of Wood.[25] Their evidence was compromised by that of Barnett and Shaw.

The supplementary witnesses, Job Jeacock and Jonathan Soden, had nothing to contribute but their ongoing loyalty to the Leigh family. We recall that Causton had recorded that, some time after the 1828 hearings, Jonathan Soden admitted in conversation that he was convinced that the Christopher stone must, after all, have existed.[26] Yet having denied its existence under oath, Soden was committed to being a Leigh witness, as it appeared, ever afterwards.

It was not to be expected, however, that the jury, which consisted of merchants and other worthies of Edgbaston and Leamington, would be familiar with the entire Stoneleigh story from 1806 through 1828 to 1829.[27] Most observers would have no idea that Jeacock and Soden were simply paid-off hacks from an earlier Leigh legal case. They would also have to have been paying a good deal of attention to realise that Wood's evidence was seriously compromised.

The final evidence brought forward was curious. None other than Thomas Hill Mortimer himself, in a late cameo appearance, produced it. There is some evidence from later in this year, in no less a source than the correspondence of Benjamin Disraeli, that Mortimer, by this time, did not have a particularly good reputation.[28] It may be that it had been considered best to keep him out of the Leigh prosecution until now.

The document which Mortimer was wheeled out to display was the copy of the register of St Martin in the Fields, from August 1670, which indicated that Christopher Leigh, "a bachelor," and Constance Clent

---

24. Griffin (1848), pp. 51, 57.
25. Griffin (1848), p. 53.
26. Leigh (1834), vol. II, p. 39, note.
27. List of jurors at *Report* (1849), p. 3.
28. M. G. Wiebe, J. B. Conacher, John Matthews (eds.), *Benjamin Disraeli: Letters 1848-1851* (The Disraeli Project, University of Toronto Press, 1993, Volume 5), letters number 1925, Disraeli to Lord Granby, 23 November 1849; and 1926, same to same, 29 November 1849, pp. 258–259.

intended to be married.²⁹ While, as noted in an earlier chapter, this document put paid to the theory of a first marriage of Christopher Leigh, it had no direct relevance to the issue at hand: whether Griffin had libelled Chandos Leigh.

As early as 1832, Causton had concluded that while the Christopher stone had very probably existed, it had not been a reliable document, and might well have been a forgery. Griffin, in 1848, had come more or less to the same conclusion, preferring however to call its information "an error."³⁰ Yet here was Hill Mortimer, producing the bachelorhood of Christopher Leigh as the clinching confirmation of Griffin having libelled Chandos.

Presumably the basis for its production was to indicate that Chandos had no need to have engaged in fraud, let alone worse crimes, because any claim based upon Christopher Leigh was in error. Yet Mortimer had not, for whatever reason, produced this document at any point between 1811 and 1829, when it might have been decisive—and might, in fact, have prevented further crimes and frauds from being committed during the period. Following this, Griffin made his final statement.

> "He called on the Jury to accompany their verdict with a declaration that an enquiry ought to take place as to these matters... 'If I should be found guilty, (everything is possible in this world), I shall resign myself to my fate with a thorough conviction in my own breast that I have done my duty, privately and publicly, in everything that relates to this matter; and I shall go into prison without a sigh or without a trouble in my breast, except for those that I leave behind me. I feel confident that Justice will be done the public: this is my object.'"³¹

Whitehurst responded, his derisive tone contrasting strongly with the seriousness of Griffin's.

---

29. *Report*, p. 30, column 2.
30. Griffin (1848), p. 44.
31. *Report*, p. 31, column 1.

"The tale of Mrs Smallbone, as to the making the grave with Lady [sic] Leigh for 'poor Sprawson,' reminded him of the nursery story of 'Cock Robin'—'Who'll dig the grave?—I, said the Owl, I'll dig the grave!' (laughter)."[32]

Reverting to a pre-1843 mood, Whitehurst homed in on Griffin.

"The defendant had represented Lord Leigh in the worst of characters, had compared him with the worst of criminals, and had even threatened, that whatever was the result of this trial, he would persevere in this course of conduct; and yet pretended that he had no malice against Lord Leigh! It was absurd, and [Whitehurst] trusted that the law would protect his Lordship, and prevent the repetition of this atrocious crime."[33]

The judge, Chief Justice Thomas Wilde, summed up. Wilde (1782–1855) would, in 1850, be raised to the peerage, at the same time as being appointed Lord Chancellor; like Henry Brougham and Thomas Denman, he had established himself as a Whig lawyer and politician.[34] Wilde considered that the matters raised by Griffin and Barnett were absurd, and that therefore the truth criterion had not been fulfilled.

"With respect to Barnett's testimony... it looked more like a fairy tale laid before the magistrates, rather than the deliberate statements of one who had never divulged these matters, as his own deposition stated, until he thought, 30 years after their rumoured occurrence, that they might help the new claimant to gain the estate."

On the public interest criterion, Wilde was also sceptical.

"The jury would judge whether it was for the public benefit to allege all the charges that could be picked up against an individual from every idle

---

32. *Report*, p. 32, column 1.
33. *Report*, p. 32, column 2.
34. J. M. Rigg, "Wilde, Thomas, First Baron Truro (1782-1855)," rev. T. G. Watkin, *Oxford Dictionary of National Biography*, Oxford University Press, 2004; online edn, Sept 2011 http://www.oxforddnb.com/view/article/29401 (Accessed 19 Feb 2016).

> gossip ... [Griffin's] book was a libel in point of law, and there was no legal justification for its publication; and if they thought it had a tendency to hold the prosecutor [Chandos] up to hatred and contempt, they would find the defendant guilty, because if they were of that opinion, it became an act intentionally done, and therefore maliciously done."[35]

The jury "almost instantly" gave a verdict of guilty. Griffin asked if they thought he had published the libel knowing it to be false, and they found him guilty of this too.[36]

Initially, Wilde set bail for Griffin to reappear at the court of the Queen's Bench in London for sentencing. Bail was set at £300, with an additional £250 for Griffin's appearance in London. Griffin complained that he could not find fresh providers of bail.[37]

The following day, an affidavit by George Jones Jnr, for Chandos Leigh, was read which alleged that Griffin was preparing to leave for America, "for the purpose of eluding justice." Griffin strongly denied this.[38]

Prior to sentencing, Wilde went on to make remarks suggesting that Griffin's tale was implausible.

> "[Griffin] had so heaped together the charge of murder upon murder—which, in a single instance, might possibly have borne the resemblance of truth, that the whole became ridiculous and absurd, and showed at once some bad motive by which it had been moved."[39]

Wilde sentenced Griffin to gaol for two years, then a good behaviour bond (£500 from himself, and £250 each from two other persons) for five years. "The defendant was immediately taken into the custody of the governor of the Gaol, and conducted to prison."[40]

---

35. J. M. Rigg, "'Wilde, Thomas, First Baron Truro (1782-1855)," rev. T. G. Watkin, *Oxford Dictionary of National Biography*, Oxford University Press, 2004; online edn, Sept 2011 http://www.oxforddnb.com/view/article/29401 (Accessed 11 Jan 2016). Wilde judgment: *Report* (1849), p. 33, columns 1–2.
36. *Report* (1849), p. 33, column 2.
37. *Report* (1849), p. 34, column 1.
38. *Report* (1849), p. 34, column 1.
39. *Report* (1849), p. 34, column 2.
40. *Report* (1849), p. 35, column 2.

The Missing Monument Murders

CHAPTER SIXTEEN

A Soul for the Structure

"At Stoneleigh Park, the seat of the Leigh family in Warwickshire, the story is maintained that one or more human victims lie buried under the foundations..."

Iona and Peter Opie, 1951[1]

We know that Charles Griffin survived his gaol term and lived for many years. A photograph of him appears on the website of the Leamington Spa Museum and Gallery. It shows a man in his sixties, with long untidy hair and beard, holding what appears to be an election poster (the only legible words are "Electors" and his own name). His face appears to show great intensity and indignation. We do not know if Charles Griffin was preparing to stand for election himself, or challenging the campaign of another candidate. Griffin was born in about 1805, so from his age in the portrait, it may have been taken in the context of the 1865 or 1868 general election.

Griffin also appears in the 1871 census. He was 66-years-old, living in Leamington, widowed; still, by occupation, "attorney and solicitor." With him lived his sons, Charles (28) and Horace (17), and his sister-in-law Maria Crotty (59).[2] It is probably this Charles Griffin who died in 1874, and was buried, on 9 February of that year, where he had lived, at Leamington.[3]

---

1. Iona and Peter Opie (eds.), *The Oxford Dictionary of Nursery Rhymes* (first published OUP 1951; Bath: The Softback Preview by arrangement with Oxford University Press, 1992), p. 276.
2. "England and Wales Census, 1871", database with images, *FamilySearch* (https://familysearch.org/ark:/61903/1:1:V5BC-J7L (Accessed 11 January 2016), Charles Griffin, 1871.
3. "England Deaths and Burials, 1538–1991," database, *FamilySearch* (https://familysearch.org/ark:/61903/1:1:J83F-93L (Accessed 11 January 2016), Charles Griffin, 09 Feb 1874; citing, reference pn 42; FHL microfilm 1,067,482.

By contrast, Chandos Leigh was dead 18 months after his successful prosecution of Charles Griffin. Chandos died on 27 September 1850, in the Star Hotel in Bonn, Germany.[4] The account in the Leigh papers, reproduced by Hampson, is that Chandos had gone to Germany to seek treatment for the partial paralysis which he suffered: a complaint attributed by Jane Rhodes to Chandos' "past excesses."[5] The term "excess" was widely used with an implication of exceeding the bounds of "decency," which is to say sexual restraint. In addition, partial paralysis is one of the symptoms of advanced syphilis.[6] It could be that Chandos had fled England after the public airing of all the evidence in Griffin's trial. He died at the age of 58.

It appears that the Leigh family took steps to suppress the information brought forward in 1848 and 1849. The US Library of Congress copy of Charles Griffin's book bears the unusual manuscript annotation on the flyleaf:

"Suppressed and bought up by the (Leigh) family."[7]

The received biography of Chandos was written for the *Dictionary of National Biography* (Volume XI, 1909) probably in the 1880s, by Edward Walford, a Warwickshire antiquarian and journalist. Walford died in 1897, so this gives a date *ante quem* for his version of events. The reader of this article will not learn that Chandos was charged with murder in 1848. It focuses on Chandos' noble forebears, his poetry and tracts, his friendship with Byron, and his liberal politics.[8] Walford gives as one of

---

4. Michael Lawrence Rhodes, "Chandos Leigh, 1st Baron Leigh," http://www.geni.com/people/Chandos-Leigh/6000000012990477840 (Accessed 12 January 2016).
5. Hampson (2004), p. 185. Cites (for Chandos' death) SBTRO DR 671/221; (for Jane Rhodes' opinion) DR 18/23/17: p. 279, notes 25 and 26.
6. Excess: "(4) Extravagant violation of law, decency, or morality... Chiefly *pl*[ural]. Now with mixture of sense 5 ...(5) The overstepping the limits of moderation...[includes examples from Mrs Radcliffe, 'All excess is vicious,' *Myst. Udolpho* ii, 1794; 'eastern Luxury's excess, *The Bengallee*, 1829]' *OED*, vol. I, 1971, p. 916. Syphilis: 'Symptoms of the late stage of syphilis include...paralysis (not [being] able to move certain parts of your body):' "*Syphilis — CDC fact sheet*, http://www.cdc.gov/std/syphilis/stdfact-syphilis.htm (Accessed 12 January 2016).
7. Marion J. Kaminkow (ed.), *Genealogies in the Library of Congress*, vol. II K-Z (Genealogical Publishing Co. Inc., 1972 and 2001), p. 83, item number 10343.
8. Edward Walford, "Leigh, Chandos, First Baron Leigh of the Present Creation (1791–1850)," *DNB* (ed. Sidney Lee), vol. XI (London: Smith, Elder, and Co., 1909), pp. 870–871. Walford

his sources (after Burke's *Peerage* and other standard works) "Personal information," which in all probability means the Leigh family.

Chandos' granddaughter, Mary Cordelia Leigh (1866–1956), wrote a booklet-length article, "Stoneleigh Abbey, from its Foundation to the Present Time" (apparently first published in the *Pall Mall Magazine*, 1896).⁹ According to this work, no events of note apparently occurred at Stoneleigh after the early eighteenth century. No mad fifth Lord Edward; no worthy Mrs Mary Leigh; no Reverend Thomas: and certainly no Julia-Judith, or Chandos (let alone a George Leigh, a Barnett, a Wilcox, or a Griffin). Nearly two hundred years of Stoneleigh history was ignored.

Yet some hints percolated to the outside world, even during the nineteenth century. As early as 1871, an article in *Nature* made a jocose reference to the case. It was cited in the 1890s, for his own reasons, by a writer in a masonic journal.

> "In *Nature*, under date June 15, 1871, we find: 'It is not many years since the present Lord Leigh was accused of having built an obnoxious person—one account, if we remember right, said eight obnoxious persons—into the foundation of a bridge at Stoneleigh.'"¹⁰

There was already confusion about the dating. In 1871, "the present Lord Leigh" was Chandos' son, William Henry Leigh (1824–1905), who was never accused of anything. In addition, the motives were now strangely muddled.

The 1871 article was a review of a book which purported to put forward an explanation for apparently unaccountable traditions. The theory was that these were survivals of earlier, less sophisticated cultures, in a similar

---

dates: obituary, "Edward Walford (1823–1897)," *The Times* 22 November 1897, issue 35367, p. 6.
9. Mary Cordelia Leigh, in Lord Frederic Hamilton (ed.), *Pall Mall Magazine* vol. X, September-December 1896. Poorly scanned version at https://archive.org/stream/pallmallmagazine10lond/pallmallmagazine10lond_djvu.txt (Accessed 12 January 2016. No date given in printed facsimile version, *Stoneleigh Abbey, From Its Foundation to the Present Time* (Hardpress Classics Series, n.d. but about 2013). Mary Cordelia biography: Sheila Woolf, "Cordelia Leigh," http://www.leamingtonhistory.co.uk/cordelia-leigh/ (Accessed 12 January 2016).
10. Anonymous, "Builders' Rites and Customs," *The Masonic Trowel*, n.d. but from internal evidence probably 1890s, certainly prior to death of Queen Victoria in 1901, http://www.themasonictrowel.com/books/lexicon_of_freemasonry_by_Albert_Mackey/files/BMAP1/bmac-15.htm (Accessed 12 January 2016).

way as certain anatomical features of species were now, in the work of writers such as Darwin, being seen as vestigial survivals.

While dismissing the charge ("Of course so preposterous a charge carried on its face its own sufficient refutation"), the 1871 writer, followed by the 1890s writer, linked the Stoneleigh case with traditional accounts of foundation sacrifice. This was believed to be the ancient practice whereby humans, animals, or symbolic objects were buried, or placed, in stone structures, presumably in order to propitiate the relevant powers, and ensure the building's stability.[11]

Mortimer Collins (1827–1876), a miscellaneous writer, referred to the case in a work published, after his death, in 1879.

> "[Chandos'] title to the estate was at one time questioned; and an inventive attorney produced a most marvellous case against him, accusing him and Lady [sic] Leigh of pulling down one side of Stoneleigh Church, to get rid of some genealogical testimony furnished by the monuments, and of causing a huge stone to be dropped on some men who were engaged in building a bridge across the river Sow [sic], it being important to suppress their evidence. I forget how many murders this lawyer (who very justly suffered imprisonment) charged against one of the gentlest and most amiable of men."[12]

Unlike other writers, Collins seems to have recalled the actual features of the case, from personal knowledge at the time (erring only in naming the river as the Sowe, not the Avon).

By the end of the century, the Stoneleigh case had taken its place among "mysteries of great families." The Reverend Thomas Thiselton Dyer (1848–1923), a popular non-fiction writer, published in 1895 a book called *Strange Pages from Family Papers* ("Chapter 1: Fatal Curses,

---

11. "Primitive Culture," *Nature* (Nature Publishing Group, 15 June 1871), vol 4, no. 85, 117–119, p. 118 (extract reprinted by permission from Macmillan Publishers Ltd: *Nature* Nature Publishing Group, 15 June 1871; license number 3818560174396 dated 29 February 2016).
12. Tom Taylor and Mortimer Collins, *Pen Sketches by a Vanished Hand from the Papers of the Late Mortimer Collins*, 2 vols, http://babel.hathitrust.org/cgi/pt?id=mdp.39015068342321;view=1up;seq=221 (Accessed 12 January 2016 (orig. publ. 1879)), vol. I, pp. 191–192.

Chapter 2: The Screaming Skull"). This interesting work included an account of the events of 1848.

> "In the year 1848, the Warwick magistrates investigated a most extraordinary and preposterous charge of murder against Lord Leigh, his deceased mother, and persons employed by them, in the course of which inquiry one of the accusers professed to have been in possession of a secret connected with the matter for a number of years. The accusation seems to have arisen from the attempt of certain parties to seize Stoneleigh Abbey on pretence that it rightfully belonged to them, and not to Lord Leigh."[13]

After briefly re-telling the evidence of Barnett, as reported in newspapers of the time, Thiselton Dyer concluded:

> "The whole story, however, was a deliberate and wilful fabrication, the facts were contradicted and circumstantially refuted, and of course so worthless a charge was dismissed by the Bench."[14]

Thiselton Dyer probably assumed, without examining the evidence himself, that it was "circumstantially refuted" at the time. If he had done the research himself, he would have known that it certainly had not been.

By the early decades of the twentieth century, the case had passed into the realm of folklore. Max Sylvius Handman (1885–1939), born in Romania, became a professor of sociology and economics in the USA.[15] He wrote an article, "Human Foundation Sacrifices in Balkan Ballads," which appeared in a 1923 collection edited by the journalist and southwestern activist J Frank Dobie, *Coffee in the Gourd*. This placed the Stoneleigh case firmly in the region of legend.

---

13. Thiselton Dyer (1895), Kindle version (Project Gutenberg, 2005) location 1719–1723.
14. Thiselton Dyer (1895 and 2005), location 1735.
15. Dates and information from obituary, "In Memoriam Max Sylvius Handman," John R. Durbin, University of Texas at Austin index of memorial resolutions and biographical sketches, http://www.utexas.edu/faculty/council/2000-2001/memorials/AMR/Handman/handman.html (Accessed 12 January 2016).

"Fifty years ago Lord Leigh was accused of having sacrificed a human being in order to ensure the security of Stoneleigh Bridge."[16]

Handman went on to discuss reported cases in Romanian and other European folklore of "foundation sacrifice." Unfortunately, Handman gave no reference for his citation of the Stoneleigh case, so we do not know what oral or printed tradition was extant at this time. It would appear that the only way in which he, or his source, could account for the report of a killing associated with the bridge, would be in the context of foundation sacrifice, however bizarre this might seem for the nineteenth century.

On the face of it, perhaps this had entered Chandos' thinking too. Some Romantic poets championed the role of the druids in British classical recorded history, and prehistory, as that was understood at the very outset of archaeological inquiry.

Chandos did, in fact, refer in one of his later poems to the druids. He describes a grove of trees,

> "Each fit to canopy a throne
> Of royal priest — the druid's stone."[17]

Chandos appended explanatory notes which quoted the role of the oak tree in Celtic culture, as described by Thomas Moore in his *History of Ireland* ("just published"), and in "Henry's *History of* England."[18] The eighteenth-century poet James Thomson had identified the druids as an archetype of British liberty, and they continued to hold a special place in Whig ideology.[19] So far, so congenial for Chandos and his public *persona*.

---

16. Handman (1923), reproduced at http://www.sacred-texts.com/ame/cig/cig06.htm (Accessed 12 January 2016).
17. "A Park Scene," in C. Leigh, *Fifth Epistle to a Friend in Town, Warwickshire, and Other Poems* (London: Richard Bentley, 1835), p. 23.
18. Leigh (1835), p. 24.
19. William Levine, "Collins, Thomson, and the Whig Progress of Liberty," *Studies in English Literature, 1500–1900*, vol. 34, no. 3, Restoration and Eighteenth Century (Summer, 1994), pp. 553–577, p. 555.

Yet the human sacrifice known, to every reader of Caesar and Tacitus, to have been a feature of ancient British society, represented a problem for this progressive ideological position.

> "Even as Romanticism, eager to see the Celtic priesthood [of druids] as champions of liberty for their resistance to Roman imperialism, spread the myth of the noble Druids, their apologists frequently found themselves in the uncomfortable position of having to explain away or otherwise account for the obvious conclusion that the stone circles provided the loci for unspeakable rites."[20]

It was not to be seriously thought that Chandos would perform a human sacrifice of his own in order to establish his credentials as a modern druid. Nonetheless, we should note that even new English bridges of the eighteenth and nineteenth centuries were subject to a strange ritual, rationalised as a survival of ancient sacrifices.

Before work began on Blackfriars Bridge in 1760, money, plate, and a personal medal were placed within the foundations. As late as May 1825, to mark the start of work on Hammersmith Bridge, the first suspension bridge erected across the Thames, a ceremony was held in which Augustus Frederick, the Duke of Sussex, performed a Masonic rite. This involved the fixing of an engraved brass plate that praised the builders and the designer, and the placing of gold coins and a silver trowel in one of the coffer dams. As this was put in place the Duke completed the ritual by making a further offering and saying:

> "I have poured the corn, the oil and the wine, emblems of wealth, plenty and comfort. So may the bridge tend to communicate prosperity and wealth."[21]

The nineteenth-century Freemasons themselves, it has to be said, struggled to explain the survival of these vestigial procedures. In the same

---

20. Matthew Schneider, "Wrung by sweet enforcement": Druid Stones and the Problem of Sacrifice in British Romanticism,' *Anthropoetics* II no. 2, January 1997, p. 4. http://www.anthropoetics.ucla.edu/Ap0202/keats.htm (Accessed 12 January 2016).
21. Chris Roberts, *Cross River Traffic: A History of London's Bridges* (London: Granta, 2005). Blackfriars: p.53; Hammersmith: p. 92.

1890s article which had recalled the 1871 mention of the Stoneleigh case, the anonymous author went on to account for the tradition as a barely understood, subconscious echo of animal and human sacrifice.

> "Our forefathers, ages ago, buried a living human sacrifice in the same place to ensure the stability of the structure: their sons substituted an animal: their sons again a mere effigy or other symbol: and we, their children, still immure a substitute, coins bearing the effigy, impressed upon the noblest of metals, the pure red gold, of the one person to whom we all are most loyal, and whom we all most love, our gracious Queen.
>
> I do not assert that one in a hundred is conscious of what he is doing: if you ask him, he will give some different reason: but the fact remains that unconsciously, we are following the customs of our fathers, and symbolically providing a soul for the structure. 'Men continue to do what their fathers did before them, though the reasons on which their fathers acted have been long forgotten.'"[22]

It is known that Chandos' son, William Henry the second Lord Leigh (1824–1905) was an active Freemason, being the first Grand Master of the Mark Grand Lodge.[23] Freemasonry appealed to a wide spectrum of Romantic writers, whether or not they were personally involved.[24] In all likelihood, Chandos may have been a mason. But even as a mason, or a druid, it is highly unlikely that either of these fantasy *personae* afforded the reason for the alleged killings at the bridge.

The real reasons were far more mundane, involving (as Collins had written in the 1870s) evidence about the Stoneleigh succession. Presumably Leigh family members were happier to have the "foundation sacrifice" story circulated than any version which approached a plausible reality.

---

22. "Brother Speth," quoted in Anonymous, "Builders' Rites and Customs," *The Masonic Trowel*, n.d. but from internal evidence probably 1890s, http://www.themasonictrowel.com/books/lexicon_of_freemasonry_by_Albert_Mackey/files/BMAP1/bmac-15.htm (Accessed 12 January 2016).
23. Andrew Prescott, "Well Marked? Approaches to the History of Mark Masonry," *Pietre-stones, Review of Freemasonry* (n.d. but from internal evidence after 2003), http://www.freemasons-freemasonry.com/prescott01.html (Accessed 12 January 2016).
24. Jennifer N. Wunder, *Keats, Hermeticism and the Secret Societies* (Aldershot: Ashgate, 2008), p. 47.

It would be surprising if they were entirely happy with one version which was known to be extant in the twentieth century. Here, the Stoneleigh bridge was linked with the foundation-sacrifice account of a well known nursery rhyme, "London Bridge is Falling Down." No lesser authorities than Iona and Peter Opie wrote in their magisterial *Oxford Dictionary of Nursery Rhymes* (1951):

> "At Stoneleigh Park, the seat of the Leigh family in Warwickshire, the story is maintained that one or more human victims lie buried under the foundations, and attempts have been made to connect the name of Leigh with the refrain 'Dance over my Lady Lea'... And London Bridge itself is not without a tainted reputation, for there is in the capital a tradition that the stones of this great bridge, too, were once bespattered with the blood of little children."[25]

As it happens, there is no archaeological evidence to this effect for London Bridge. We have already noted the vagueness of the Freemason fraternity about the reasons for the rituals associated with new bridges. The lurid expressions about children's blood apparently came from the nineteenth century folklorist Alice Gomme.[26]

As for Stoneleigh, the Opies did not provide any source for the tradition, but their status as the ultimate authority on nursery rhyme lore must have added its own weight. Despite the apparent unlikelihood of the Leighs themselves having propagated this version, the Opies' language ("At Stoneleigh Park... the story is maintained") may suggest that they received the "tradition" directly from the family associated with the park. The omission of the bridge, and the vague implication that the "victims" lay instead under the park or abbey itself, may also point to this.

Following the Opies, but reviving the bridge, Paul G Brewster, a folklorist specialising in children's games, wrote in 1971:

---

25. Iona and Peter Opie (eds.), *The Oxford Dictionary of Nursery Rhymes* (first published OUP 1951; Bath: The Softback Preview by arrangement with Oxford University Press, 1992), p. 276.
26. John Clark, "London Bridge: Foundation Sacrifices Revisited," academia.edu, https://www.academia.edu/9826479/London_Bridge_foundation_sacrifices_revisited (Uploaded 18 December 2014; accessed 13 October 2015), p. 3.

> "Many conjectures have been made as to the origin and the age of our [London Bridge is Falling Down] game. Because of the fact that in some British versions there appears the refrain
>
> Dance over my Lady Lea!
>
> [T]here has been an attempt to connect this name with the family Leigh (seat Stoneleigh). There is a tradition that human victims were immured in the foundations of a bridge in Stoneleigh Park."[27]

Brewster, unfortunately, gave no source for this "attempt" or "tradition." Brewster went on:

> "Those [not named] who accept this theory point out also that Sir Thomas Leigh was Lord Mayor of London in 1558."[28]

Note that with the reference to Sir Thomas, medieval or, at latest, Tudor events are implied. Yet the thesis is actually no closer to reality. However attractive it might be to have Julia-Judith (never, actually, Lady Leigh, but often called so) immortalised in association with a sinister custom, this connection is pure fantasy.

If the Stoneleigh tradition was discussed in any detail, in any work between 1971 and the Bearman volume of 2004 (mentioned in *Chapter 4*), I am not aware of it. An ambitious 1987 book called *Press Freedoms: A Descriptive Calendar of Concepts, Interpretations, Events, and Court Actions, From 4000 BC to the Present*, by Louis Edward Ingelhart, includes a brief mention under the year 1849:

> "Charles Griffin was sentenced to two years for libel against the Leigh family in his book *Stoneleigh Abbey thirty-four years ago*."[29]

---

27. Paul G. Brewster, "The Foundation Sacrifice Motif in Legend, Folksong, Game and Dance," *Zeitschrift für Ethnologie*, Bd. 96, H. 1 (1971), 71–89, p. 84.
28. Brewster (1971), p. 84.
29. Louis Edward Ingelhart, *Press Freedoms: A Descriptive Calendar of Concepts, Interpretations, Events, and Court Actions, From 4000 BC to the Present* (New York, Westport, London: Greenwood Press, 1987), pp. 196–197.

It is interesting, and perhaps a sign of the times, that Griffin's punishment, rather than the "foundation sacrifice" or other elements, had become the focus of such notice as there was.

The 2004 collection, *Stoneleigh Abbey: The House, Its Owners, Its Lands* (edited by Shakespeare scholar Robert Bearman) presented papers given at a 1999 conference at Stoneleigh. Bearman introduced the volume.

> "The Leigh family, though elevated to the peerage in the early seventeenth century, produced no figures of national importance: only one, Chandos Lord Leigh, has managed to secure a modest foothold in the *Dictionary of National Biography*... [After 1806] the estates... passed to the descendants of [the first Sir] Thomas' eldest son, who had settled at Adlestrop in Gloucestershire. Their story... is outside the scope of this study, but they were clearly a gifted and talented family (one was the mother of Jane Austen) and their accession to the family estates ushered in a golden period in the Leigh story."[30]

In describing the post-1806 order as a "golden period," Bearman, like the Leigh family of the nineteenth century, was glossing over much that was unpleasant. As we have seen, the half-century after 1806 was punctuated with allegations of fraud, village discord, legal wrangling both within and without the Leigh family, and blackmail, culminating in a murder charge and a libel trial.

Two chapters in the volume make reference to the cases. In Chapter 5, Mairi Macdonald summarises events from 1828 through to 1849 with little editorial comment.[31] In the following chapter, Norma Hampson, as we have seen, makes a summary reference which strongly suggests that the charges were only dismissed after investigation.[32]

In 2010, an updated article on Chandos Leigh was published in the now online *Dictionary of National Biography*. The author is David Hill Radcliffe, literary historian at Virginia Tech and author of the very useful Spenserians web pages. Radcliffe has at least adverted to the

---

30. Bearman (2004), Preface to Bearman (ed.) 2004, p. 7.
31. Macdonald (2004), p. 158.
32. Hampson (2004), p. 185.

murder charges, but suggests, oddly, that their genesis was in political disagreements.

> "Chandos Leigh championed free trade and liberal policies not always popular at home in Warwickshire. He certainly had enemies. In 1844 his title was challenged by other descendants of Sir Thomas Leigh and over thirty rioters forcibly entered Stoneleigh Abbey in search of evidence… [after the murder charge] the bridge was left intact and the charges dismissed as fabulous, but not before a parade of witnesses had testified to poisonings, mysterious disappearances, and irregular doings among the family retainers."[33]

Radcliffe, for reasons unclear, has chosen to adopt a jocular tone similar to that which characterised the Leigh legal team's attitude in 1848 and 1849. My view, in writing this book, has been that it is time to examine the evidence in detail, treat it with the seriousness it deserved, and set out what actually occurred between 1806 and 1849.

One of the features of the Stoneleigh events has been their capacity to engage observers who, without originally intending it, were drawn into playing a role once they recognised that something extraordinary, and probably fraudulent, had taken place. Henry Kent Causton, in all probability, never intended to become the analyst of the 1828 and 1829 cases. Yet this is what happened, after he became a friend and creditor of the claimant George Leigh, and listened to all the evidence from the people, great and small, of Stoneleigh.

Lionel Place, Warwickshire landowner and friend of the Reverend James Roberts and Captain Francis Mason, became an actor in events once he witnessed his friend's strange turnaround about the existence of the Christopher stone.

Most importantly, Charles Griffin, local lawyer and amateur scientist, first of all took part as the attorney acting for some of the men who broke into Stoneleigh Abbey. But then, on hearing, reading and considering

---

33. David Hill Radcliffe, "Leigh, Chandos, First Baron Leigh (1791—1850)," *Oxford Dictionary of National Biography*, Oxford University Press, 2004; online edn, Sept 2010 http://www.oxforddnb.com/view/article/16375 (Accessed 12 Jan 2016). Spenserians: "Spenser and the Tradition: English Poetry 1579–1830," http://spenserians.cath.vt.edu/ (Accessed 12 January 2016).

the evidence of Barnett, Shaw and Smallbone, he decided to take matters further. Griffin was the third man who, almost against his will, found himself unable to ignore or pass over what had taken place.

Griffin's judgment, and sense of justice, directed him to call for a proper forensic investigation. This is all that he was guilty of. The non-existence of police investigative structures at the time, and above all, the strongly entrenched legal presumption against any interference in the affairs of a great landowner, meant that his calls failed utterly, and he himself suffered a gaol sentence as a result.

Chief Justice Wilde, in closing the case against Griffin, pointed out that the number of the alleged killings told against their plausibility. In effect, Wilde found the allegations "absurd," that is, unlikely and implausible, as he said a "fairy tale." Such an interpretation was also made, expediently, by members of the extended Leigh support base, such as Chandos' son-in-law, the prominent evangelical MP, C B Adderley. Following Chandos' court appearance in May 1848, Adderley wrote to the *Leamington Spa Courier*.

> "Sir,—The gravity with which you reported the allegations of wholesale murders at Stoneleigh thirty four years ago, in your last Monday's number, induces me to correct your version a little, lest you should be supposed a real believer in Jack the Giant Killer, and cause uneasiness in nurseries, or more seriously pander to the vicious appetites of vulgar minds..."[34]

Adderley went on to ridicule the murder allegations, and suggest that Barnett would subsequently suffer transportation. In adducing the fairy tale as a model, perhaps Adderley was suggesting the first of the "nursery-rhyme/foundation sacrifice" accounts to which, as we have seen, the Leigh family was later willing to accord status.

Importantly, that Adderley was able to dismiss the allegations as mere fairy tale is partly because the concept of the serial killer, as a feature of real life rather than legend, was not one which, in 1848, had found currency. Although, as we saw, this was at the very period when several

---

34. Quoted in Griffin (1848), p. 59.

people, having poisoned numbers of victims with arsenic, could have been named as Britain's first serial killer, neither the concept nor the term had entered most people's consciousness. (Mary Ann Cotton, who was hanged in 1873, has been named as Britain's first female serial killer.[35])

But, as Griffin pointed out, it was more plausible to believe that the allegations were true, than to believe that they were false. Let Griffin, in full flight in his "libellous" work, have the last word here.

> "I am now doing [my part], and I trust effectually, in endeavouring to elicit all the information I can, for 'I do believe' in much that has been asserted — sacrilege — fraudulent suppression of evidence — murder — perjury by wholesale — a mock funeral — I do not think it absurd so to believe, for history is full of such things. 'I do *not* believe' in death-bed confessions of crimes *never committed.* 'I do *not* believe' in three ignorant persons, at a hundred miles distance from each other, forging the *same* tale of horrid crimes in which they were engaged thirty-four years ago, and two of them going to their final account with a lie on their lips, 'damning themselves to everlasting fame.' I do *not* believe history ever recorded *such* confessions, were there never such to record. With the facts before me, it would be absurd, indeed, if my belief were other than it is."[36]

I agree with Griffin. The case for investigation — by now archaeological rather than forensic — remains strong. As Griffin recommended, it would be relatively easy to open the Stoneleigh church vault. If the Leigh family coffin plates are in place as in the 1808 drawings, then no further investigation need take place. If they are missing, this would confirm, in essence, the evidence of Richard Barnett.

One final vignette is appropriate. A 2008 visitor to Stoneleigh took a walk beside the river Avon, near the bridge, and had an unsettling experience.

---

35. David Wilson, *Mary Ann Cotton: Britain's First Female Serial Killer* (Sherfield on Loddon: Waterside Press, 2013).
36. Griffin (1848), p., 68. His text actually has "there we<r>e never such to record," but it is probable that the first two words were transposed during typesetting, and I have reversed their order in quoting the passage.

"I was at the edge of the river Avon, in a field at Stoneleigh Abbey—enjoying the view when I became aware of a lady watching me from the other side of the river. I got the feeling she wasn't pleased with me being there as she had quite a cross expression on her face. I noticed she was dressed in a tweed outfit (similar to those worn by people hunting). I felt uneasy as I wasn't sure if I was on private land and that this lady may well be the land owner.

I decided as she was still watching me to cross over the bridge just ten feet away and apologise to her—to my great surprise as I got to the end of the bridge and looked left to where the lady had been stood moments before there was nobody there. I was absolutely terrified and I ran away as fast as I could. I have no idea who the lady was but she certainly gave me the impression I wasn't meant to be where I was!"[37]

The visitor's name was Zara Griffin. I do believe in serial killers; I don't believe in ghosts: yet it is very tempting to think that Julia-Judith (probably too early for tweed), or Mary Cordelia Leigh, came back to frighten a Griffin away from the haunted shades of the bridge at Stoneleigh.

---

37. Zara Griffin, March 2008, quoted in comment on website "Mysterious Britain," noting that account first appeared on a BBC page, "Weird Warwickshire" and linking to that page: http://www.mysteriousbritain.co.uk/england/warwickshire/hauntings/stoneleigh-abbey.html (Accessed 12 January 2016).

The Missing Monument Murders

Afterword

Many of the bizarre events detailed in this book are believed to have occurred—if I have convinced you that they occurred at all—in the extended family, and during the lifetime, of Jane Austen (who died in July 1817). It is well known that Austen, particularly in her work *Northanger Abbey*, downplayed the likelihood of strange, cruel, and Gothic deeds taking place in the England of her time. She had the character Henry Tilney pour cold water on Catherine Morland's surmises that his father, General Tilney, had done away with his wife.

> "Dear Miss Morland, consider the dreadful nature of the suspicions you have entertained. What have you been judging from? Remember the country and the age in which we live. Remember that we are English, that we are Christians. Consult your own understanding, your own sense of the probable, your own observation of what is passing around you—Does our education prepare us for such atrocities? Do our laws connive at them? Could they be perpetrated without being known, in a country like this, where social and literary intercourse is on such a footing; where every man is surrounded by a neighbourhood of voluntary spies, and where roads and newspapers lay everything open?"[1]

Austen was revising this work in the final part of her life. We know that she thought that James Henry Leigh and Julia-Judith Leigh were, in her words, "worthless".[2] Could it be that she had heard hints of horrific events at Stoneleigh Abbey? Charles Griffin pointed out that there were rumours circulating among working people at the time.[3] Was Austen

---

1. Austen, *Northanger Abbey, Lady Susan, The Watsons, Sanditon* (Oxford: Oxford World's Classics, 2003), p. 145.
2. Letter 86, 3–6 July 1813: Le Faye (2011), p. 225.
3. Griffin (1848), p. 69.

trying to convince herself that such things as murder could not, after all, have taken place?

There were, however, motives even within Austen's immediate family at work to keep any secrets. James Leigh Perrot and his wife Jane were the beneficiaries of a great deal of money from the Stoneleigh branch of the family. It was entirely in their interest to see, hear, and speak no evil about the Stoneleigh Leighs. The Austens, until James Leigh Perrot's death in March 1817, had confidently expected to benefit from his bequests. It was both easier, and more expedient, for everyone, to reject any rumour as simply ill-informed gossip. To raise questions, as Charles Griffin found out more than 30 years later, was to risk one's professional career and personal liberty.

Family Tree

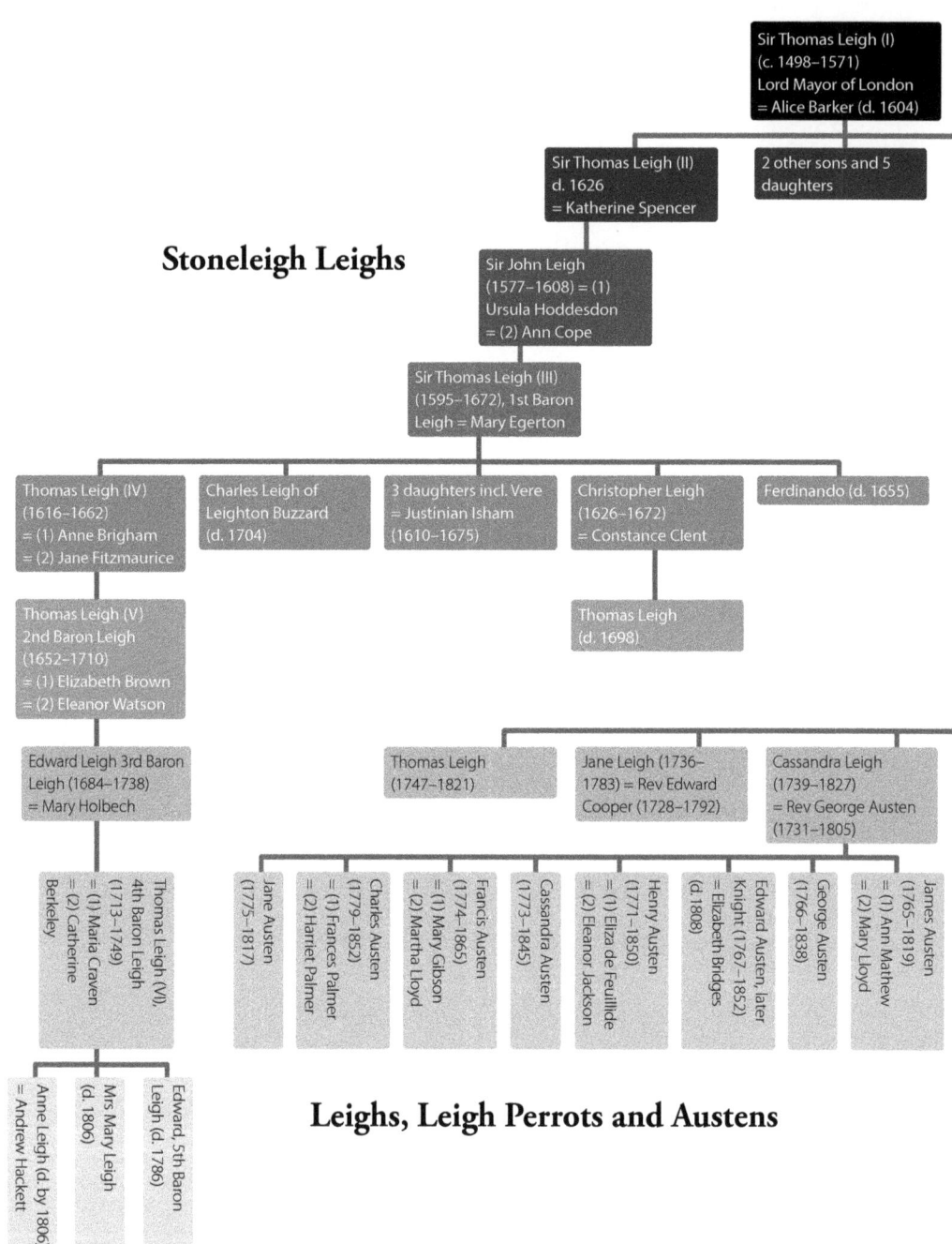

The above family tree is based on a range of sources, including the trees in Deirdre Le Faye's *A Chronology of Jane Austen and Her Family 1600-2000* (Cambridge University Press, 2013), and standard works on the peerage. Some sources claim that Sir Thomas Leigh (III) died in 1671 but 1672 appears to be the consensus and has been used throughout this work.

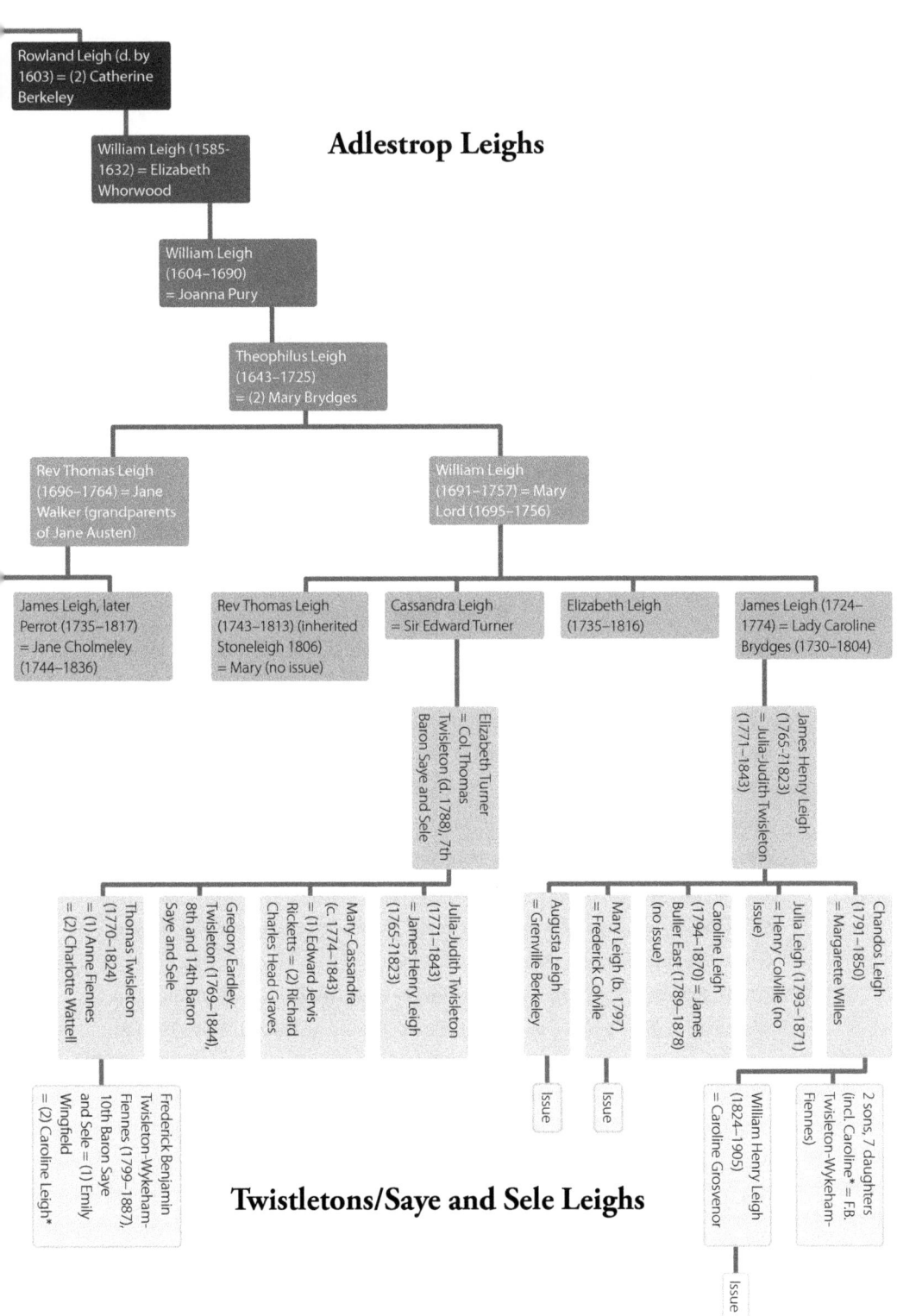

Select Bibliography

Standard reference works include:

FamilySearch https://familysearch.org

History of Parliament Online http://www.historyofparliamentonline.org

Leigh family papers held on behalf of National Archives at Shakespeare's Birthplace Trust Record Office, Stratford-upon-Avon (SBTRO) http://discovery.nationalarchives.gov.uk/details/a?_ref=188

Oxford Dictionary of National Biography Online http://www.oxforddnb.com (subscription or institutional log-in required)

The Gentleman's Magazine

Works cited

Anonymous. "Builders' Rites and Customs," *The Masonic Trowel*, n.d. but from internal evidence probably 1890s, certainly prior to death of Queen Victoria in 1901, http://www.themasonictrowel.com/books/lexicon_of_freemasonry_by_Albert_Mackey/files/BMAP1/bmac-15.htm (Accessed 12 January 2016)

Anonymous. *Report of the Trial for libel (The Queen, on the prosecution of the right honourable Lord Leigh, v. Charles Griffin) in calumniously alleging murders to have been committed at Stoneleigh Abbey, thirty-four years ago. Tried at the Warwickshire Lent assizes, 1849, before Chief Justice Sir Thomas Wilde, Knight. From the type of the* Warwick Advertiser *of Saturday, April 7th, 1849; with corrections and additions* (Henry Sharpe, Warwick, 1849)

Anonymous. Review of E. Cresy, *A Practical Treatise on Bridge Building* (London: John Williams), in *The Civil Engineer and Architect's Journal*, Volume II, May 1839, pp. 189–190

Anonymous. "Primitive Culture," *Nature* (Nature Publishing Group, 15 June 1871), volume 4, no. 85, 117–119 (extract reprinted by permission from Macmillan Publishers Ltd: *Nature* Nature Publishing Group, 15 June 1871; licence number 3818560174396 dated 29 February 2016)

Anonymous. Review, "Art. IX, *Leigh's Poems*, Lindsell, 1818," *The British Critic*, Volumes 9–10, 1818

Anonymous. *The Book of English Trades, and Library of the Useful Arts* (London: J. Souter for Richard Phillips, 1818)

Apperley, Charles James. *Nimrod's Hunting Tours, Interspersed with characteristic anecdotes, sayings, and doings of sporting men, including notices of the principal crack riders of England* (London: M. A. Pittman, 1835)

Austen, Caroline (with introduction by Deirdre Le Faye). *Reminiscences of Caroline Austen* (The Jane Austen Society, 1986)

Austen, Jane. James Kinsley and John Davie (eds.), with an introduction and notes by Claudia L. Johnson. *Northanger Abbey, Lady Susan, The Watsons, Sanditon* (Oxford: Oxford World's Classics, 2003)

Baker, William. *Critical Companion to Jane Austen: A Literary Reference to Her Life and Work* (Facts on File Inc.: New York, 2008)

Bearman, Robert (ed.) *Stoneleigh Abbey: The House, Its Owners, Its lands* (Stoneleigh Abbey Limited, 2004)

Beatty, Bernard. "A2 at Albany: Byron in 1814," *The Byron Journal*, volume 39, issue 1, 2011, 1–10

Beckett, John, with Sheila Adey. *Byron and Newstead* (Newark: University of Delaware Press, 2002)

Beltz, George Frederick. *A Review of the Chandos Peerage Case, Adjudicated 1803, and of the pretensions of Sir Samuel Egerton Brydges, baronet, to designate himself per legem terrae Baron Chandos of Sudeley* (n.d. but from internal evidence c. 1834)

Bentley, David. *English Criminal Justice in the Nineteenth Century* (London: Hambledon Press, 1998)

Black, Maggie and Le Faye, Deirdre. *The Jane Austen Cookbook* (London: The British Museum Press, 1995)

Boucher, Cyril T. G. *John Rennie 1761–1821: The Life and Work of a Great Engineer* (Manchester: Manchester University Press, 1963)

Brewster, Paul G. "The Foundation Sacrifice Motif in Legend, Folksong, Game and Dance," *Zeitschrift für Ethnologie*, Bd. 96, H. 1 (1971), 71–89

Brougham, Henry (but at the time anonymous). "Art. II, *Hours of Idleness: A Series of Poems, Original and Translated*. By George Gordon, Lord Byron, a Minor," *The Edinburgh Review, or Critical Journal*, Vol. XI, October 1807-January 1808, 285–289

Brydges, Sir [Samuel] Egerton (ed.) "Twisleton, Lord Say and Sele," in *Collins's Peerage of England: Genealogical, Biographical, and Historical. Greatly Augmented, and Continued to the Present Time, by Sir Egerton Brydges, K. J.* In nine volumes. Vol. VII (London: F.C. and J. Rivington (etc.), 1812)

Burke, John. *Burke's Peerage and Baronetage*, 105th edn, 2nd impression (prob. 1981)

Burke, John. *A Genealogical and Heraldic History of the Commoners of Great Britain and Ireland*, vol. III (London, 1836)

Burke, John. *A General and Heraldic Dictionary of the Peerage and Baronetage of the British Empire*, fourth edn, vol. II (London, 1833)

Burke, John. *A General and Heraldic Dictionary of the Peerages of England, Ireland and Scotland, Extinct, Dormant, and in Abeyance* (London: Henry Colburn and Richard Bentley, 1831)

Byron, Lord George Gordon. *Byron's Letters and Journals: "Wedlock's the Devil"* (ed. Leslie A. Marchand) (Harvard University Press, 1975)

Byron, Lord George Gordon. *The Poetical Works of Lord Byron* (Geoffrey Cumberlege, Oxford University Press, edn of July 1904 reset in 1945, reprinted 1950)

Causton, John S. "The Causton Family in the Printing Trade in London, Including a Brief History of Sir Joseph Causton and Sons Ltd., Printers, Publishers and Stationers," http://homepage.ntlworld.com/john.causton/Causton-Printers.htm (Accessed 4 March 2016)

Challinor, Raymond. "Roberts, William Prowting (1806–1871)," *Oxford Dictionary of National Biography*, Oxford University Press, 2004; online edn, Jan 2008. http://www.oxforddnb.com/view/article/23781 (Accessed 9 Dec 2015)

Child-Villiers, Margaret Elizabeth Leigh, Countess of Jersey, *Fifty-one Years of Victorian Life* (London: John Murray, 1922)

Chrimes, Mike. "Jones Family (fl. 1770–1835)," in Skempton *et al.* (eds., 2002), 378–379

Clark, John. "London Bridge: Foundation Sacrifices Revisited," academia.edu, https://www.academia.edu/9826479/London_Bridge_foundation_sacrifices_revisited, uploaded 18 December 2014, accessed 13 October 2015

Collins, Irene. *Jane Austen: The Parson's Daughter* (London: The Hambledon Press, 1998)

Coultan, Mark. "The $3000 Drop O'Farrell Couldn't Recall," *The Australian* 16 April 2014, p. 6

Courtney, W. P. "Repton, Humphry (1752–1818)," *Dictionary of National Biography* (ed. S. Lee), vol. XVI, 1909, 914–916

Cowie, Leonard W. "Parr, Samuel (1747–1825)," *Oxford Dictionary of National Biography*, Oxford University Press, 2004, http://www.oxforddnb.com/view/article/21402

Critchley, T. A. *A History of Police in England and Wales* (London: Constable, 1978)

Crossling, John. "History of Warwick Pubs," http://www.hunimex.com/warwick/pubs/g_inns.html (Accessed 15 December 2015)

Cross-Rudkin, P. S. M. "Rennie, John, FRS, FRSE (1761–1821)," in A.W. Skempton et al. (eds.), *A Biographical Dictionary of Civil Engineers in Great Britain and Ireland, Volume 1: 1500–1830* (London: Thomas Telford Publishing on behalf of the Institution of Civil Engineers, 2002), 554–569

Daniels, Stephen. "Repton, Humphry (1752–1818)," *Oxford Dictionary of National Biography*, Oxford University Press, 2004; online edn, Jan 2012 http://www.oxforddnb.com/view/article/23387 (Accessed 9 Dec 2015)

Debrett, John. *The Baronetage of England*, fourth edn, vol. II (London, 1819)

Duckworth, Alistair M. "Mansfield Park and Estate Improvements: Jane Austen's Grounds of Being," *Nineteenth-Century Fiction*, vol. 26, no. 1 (June 1971), 25–48

Dyer, the Reverend Thomas Thiselton. *Strange Pages from Family Papers* (1895), Kindle version (Project Gutenberg, 2005)

Elders, J., V. Harding, J. Litten, A. Miles, N. Powers, C. Roberts, J. Schofield, J. Sidell, B. Sloane, B. White, "Archaeology and Burial Vaults: A Guidance Note for Churches," Association of Diocesan and Cathedral Archaeologists Guidance Note 2, produced in consultation with the Advisory Panel of the Archaeology of Burials in England (APABE), July 2010

Emsley, Clive (ed.) *The Newgate Calendar*, introduction by Clive Emsley (Ware: Wordsworth Classics of World Literature, 1997)

Emsley, Clive, Tim Hitchcock and Robert Shoemaker, "Communities — Black Communities," Old Bailey Proceedings Online www.oldbaileyonline.org (version 7.0, 5 January 2016)

Field, William. *Memoirs of the Life, Writings, and Opinions of the Rev. Samuel Parr, LLD* (London: Henry Colburn, 1828). Reproduced at http://lordbyron.cath.lib.vt.edu/monograph.php?doc=SaParr.1828&select=II8 (Accessed 1 December 2015)

Frank, Christopher. *Master and Servant Law: Chartists, Trade Unions, Radical Lawyers and the Magistracy in England, 1840–1865* (Farnham: Ashgate, 2010)

Fryer, Hazel. "The Park and Gardens at Stoneleigh Abbey," in Bearman (ed. 2004), 243–261

Gomme, Andor. "Abbey Into Palace: A Lesser Wilton?" in Bearman (ed. 2004), 82–115

Griffin, Charles Esq., M. L. E. S., "Why Do Electrised Bodies Recede from Each Other?" in *The Annals of Electricity, Magnetism, and Chemistry; and Guardian of Experimental Science*, vol. VIII, January 1842, 1–17

Griffin, Charles, Solicitor. *Stoneleigh Abbey, Thirty-four Years Ago, Containing a short history of the claims to the peerage and estates, and a catalogue of the confessed and suspected crimes, &c. &c. &c.* [sic.] (Birmingham: R. J. Salter, 1848)

Griffin, Charles. "Abstract of a Paper on the Homogeneous Attraction of Electricity, by C. Griffin, Esq., Leamington," in *Transactions and Proceedings of the London Electrical Society from 1837 to 1840* (London: Smith, Elder and Co., 1841), 148

Hampson, Norma. "The Poet and the Paternalist," in Bearman (ed. 2004), 179–196

Handman, Max Sylvius. "Human Foundation Sacrifices in Balkan Ballads," in J. Frank Dobie (ed.), *Coffee in the Gourd* (1923), reproduced at http://www.sacred-texts.com/ame/cig/cig06.htm (Accessed 12 January 2016)

Hare, Robert. "This Charming Psychopath: How to Spot Social Predators Before They Attack," 10 December 2012, https://www.psychologytoday.com/articles/199401/charming-psychopath (Accessed 4 March 2016)

Harringman, Brian, Alan Harmer, and Julie Harmer (née Fardon), *The Fardons of Gloucestershire, England* (online book, dated 6 September 2007, material copyright 2015 Alan Harmer)

Hayman, Jr, Ira E. and Elizabeth F. Loftus, "Some People Recover Memories of Childhood Trauma that Never Really Happened," in Paul S. Applebaum, Lisa A. Uyehara, and Mark R. Elin (eds.), *Trauma and Memory: Clinical and Legal Controversies* (Oxford University Press, 1997), 3–24, 6–8

Hempel, Sandra. *The Inheritor's Powder: A Cautionary Tale of Poison, Betrayal and Greed* (Phoenix, 2013, Kindle version)

Hilton, Boyd. *The Age of Atonement: The Influence of Evangelicalism on Social and Economic Thought 1795–1865* (Oxford: Clarendon Press, 1988)

Hunt, Leigh. *The Autobiography of Leigh Hunt* (London: Smith, Elder and Co., 1860)

Huxley, Victoria. *Jane Austen and Adlestrop: Her Other family* (Windrush Publishing: Moreton-in-the-Marsh, Gloucestershire, 2013)

Ingelhart, Louis Edward. *Press Freedoms: A Descriptive Calendar of Concepts, Interpretations, Events, and Court Actions, from 4000 BC to the Present* (New York, Westport, London: Greenwood Press, 1987)

Judicial Commission of New South Wales. "Credibility," Evidence Act 1995, 3.7 and subsequent divisions. http://www.judcom.nsw.gov.au/publications/benchbks/civil/credibility.html#p4-1200 (Accessed 11 January 2016)

Kaminkow (ed.), Marion J. *Genealogies in the Library of Congress,* vol. II K-Z (Genealogical Publishing Co. Inc., 1972 and 2001)

King, Gaye. "The Jane Austen Connection," in Bearman (ed. 2004), 163–177

Latham, Sean. *The Art of Scandal: Modernism, Libel Law, and the* Roman à Clef (Oxford University Press, 2009)

Le Faye, Deirdre (ed.). *Jane Austen's Letters* (4th edition, Oxford University Press, 2011)

Le Faye, Deirdre. *A Chronology of Jane Austen and Her Family 1600-2000* (Cambridge University Press, 2013)

Leigh, Chandos. "On a Future State," *Fragments of Essays* (London: G. Sidney, 1816)

Leigh, Chandos. *Poems of Chandos Leigh* (second edn., with additions) (London: W. Lindsell, 1818)

Leigh, Chandos. *Tracts, Written in the Years 1823 & 1828* (Warwick: John Merridew, 1832)

Leigh, Chandos. *Walks in the Country* (London: Edward Moxon, 1844)

Leigh, George. *The Leigh Peerage: Being a full and complete history of the claim of George Leigh, Esq. to the dormant title of Baron Leigh, of Stoneley, in the county of Warwick: comprising a report of the evidence taken before the Lords' committee for Privileges, with notes, analytical and explanatory: and certain additional evidence, forming the ultimatum to this very mysterious case. In two volumes* (Henry Kent Causton, jun.: London, 2nd edn, 1834)

Leigh, Mary Cordelia. "Stoneleigh Abbey, from its Foundation to the Present Time," in Lord Frederic Hamilton (ed.), *Pall Mall Magazine* vol. X, September-December 1896. Poorly scanned version at https://archive.org/stream/pallmallmagazine10lond/pallmallmagazine10lond_djvu.txt (Accessed 12 January 2016). Facsimile version, *Stoneleigh Abbey, from Its Foundation to the Present Time* (Hardpress Classics Series, n.d. but about 2013)

Leo, Richard A. "False Confessions: Causes, Consequences, and Implications," in *Journal of American Academy of Psychiatry and the Law,* 37:332–43, 2009

Linebaugh, Peter. *The London Hanged: Crime and Civil Society in the Eighteenth Century* (London: Verso, 2006)

Lloyd's Weekly London Newspaper, 27 October 1844: http://www.leighrayment.com/peers/peersL2.htm (Accessed 7 December 2015)

Lobban, Michael. "Brougham, Henry Peter, First Baron Brougham and Vaux (1778–1868)," *Oxford Dictionary of National Biography*, Oxford University Press, 2004; online edn, Jan 2008. http://www.oxforddnb.com/view/article/3581 (Accessed 8 Dec 2015)

Macdonald, Mairi. "'Not Unmarked by Some Eccentricities': The Leigh Family of Stoneleigh Abbey," in Bearman (ed. 2004), 131–162

Marchand, Leslie A. *Byron: A Portrait* (London: Futura Publications, 1976)

Marshall, John. *Royal Naval Biography; Or, memoirs of the services of all the flag-officers, superannuated rear-admirals, retired-captains, post-captains, and commanders, whose names appeared on the Admiralty List of Sea-Officers at the commencement of the year 1823, or who have been since promoted; etc.* Supplement: Part I. (London: printed for Longman, Rees, Orme, Brown, and Green, Paternoster Row, 1827)

Martin, A. W. "Parkes, Sir Henry (1815–1896)," *Australian Dictionary of Biography* vol. 5 (Melbourne: Melbourne University Press, 1974), online version http://adb.anu.edu.au/biography/parkes-sir-henry-4366 (Accessed 4 March 2016)

Morris, Bob. "History of Criminal Investigation," in Tim Newburn, Tom Williamson and Alan Wright (eds.), *Handbook of Criminal Investigation* (Cullompton, Devon/Portland, Oregon: Willan Publishing, 2007), 15–40

Morris, Richard K. "From Monastery to Country House: An Architectural History of Stoneleigh Abbey, 1156-c. 1660," in Bearman (ed. 2004), 15–61

Munsche, P. B. *Gentlemen and Poachers: The English Game Laws 1671–1831* (Cambridge University Press, 1981)

Murphy, G. Martin. "Thomas, Vaughan (1775–1858)," Oxford DNB online, http://www.oxforddnb.com.wwwproxy0.library.unsw.edu.au/view/article/27241?docPos=2 (Accessed 20 February 2016)

Murray, Adam. *[A] General View of the Agriculture of the County of Warwick: With observations on the means of its improvement, drawn up for the consideration of the Board of Agriculture and Internal Improvement* (London: B. Mcmillan, 1813)

Opie, Iona and Peter (eds.) *The Oxford Dictionary of Nursery Rhymes* (first published Oxford University Press 1951; Bath: Softback preview by arrangement with OUP, 1992)

Parkes, Joseph. *A History of the Court of Chancery; With practical remarks, on the recent Commission, report, and evidence, and on the means of improving the administration of justice in the English courts of equity* (London: Longman, Rees, Orme, Brown, and Green, 1828)

Peacock, Thomas Love. *Headlong Hall* (London: Dent, Everyman's Library, 1969)

Port, M. H./David R. Fisher, "Leigh, Robert Holt (1762–1843), of Whitley, Wigan, and Hindley Hall, Aspull, Lancs." http://www.historyofparliamentonline.org/volume/1790-1820/member/leigh-robert-holt-1762-1843 (Accessed 2 December 2015)

Prescott, Andrew. "Well Marked? Approaches to the History of Mark Masonry," *Pietre-stones, Review of Freemasonry* (n.d. but from internal evidence after 2003), http://www.freemasons-freemasonry.com/prescott01.html (Accessed 12 January 2016)

Pustilnik, Lev A. and Gregory Yom Din. "Influence of Solar Activity on [the] State of [the] Wheat Market in Medieval England," 2003, http://arxiv.org/ftp/astro-ph/papers/0312/0312244.pdf (Accessed 8 December 2015)

Radcliffe, David Hill. "Leigh, Chandos, First Baron Leigh (1791–1850)," *Oxford Dictionary of National Biography*, Oxford University Press, 2004, online edn, Sept 2010 http://www.oxforddnb.com/view/article/16375 (Accessed 12 Jan 2016)

Radcliffe, David Hill. "Spenser and the Tradition: English Poetry 1579–1830" http://spenserians.cath.vt.edu (Accessed 12 January 2016)

Reynolds, Elaine A. *Before the Bobbies: The Night Watch and Police Reform in Metropolitan London, 1720–1830* (Stanford: Stanford University Press, 1998)

Rigg, J. M. "Wilde, Thomas, First Baron Truro (1782–1855)." rev. T. G. Watkin, *Oxford Dictionary of National Biography*, Oxford University Press, 2004; online edn, Sept 2011 http://www.oxforddnb.com/view/article/29401 (Accessed 19 Feb 2016)

Roberts, Chris. *Cross River Traffic: A History of London's Bridges* (London: Granta, 2005)

Rule, John. *Albion's People: English Society 1714–1815* (London and New York: Longmans, 1992)

Saint, Andrew. "Rennie, John (1761–1821)," *Oxford Dictionary of National Biography*, Oxford University Press, 2004; online edn, Sept 2013 http://www.oxforddnb.com/view/article/23376 (Accessed 9 Dec 2015)

Salmon, Philip/David R. Fisher. "Leigh, James Henry (1765–1823), of Adlestrop, Glos, and Stoneleigh Abbey, Warws," in D. R. Fisher (ed.), *The History of Parliament: The House of Commons 1820–1832* (Cambridge University Press, 2009), digitised as http://www.historyofparliamentonline.org/volume/1790-1820/member/leigh-james-henry-1765-1823 (Accessed 5 January 2016)

Salmon, Philip/Howard Spencer. "East, Sir Edward Hyde (1764–1847), of 12 Stratford Place, Mdx," http://www.historyofparliamentonline.org/volume/1820-1832/member/east-sir-edward-1764-1847 (Accessed 5 January 2016)

Schneider, Matthew. "'Wrung by Sweet Enforcement': Druid Stones and the Problem of Sacrifice in British Romanticism," *Anthropoetics*, II no. 2, January 1997 http://www.anthropoetics.ucla.edu/Ap0202/keats.htm (Accessed 12 January 2016)

Skempton, A. W. *Civil Engineers and Engineering in Britain, 1600–1830* (Aldershot: Variorum Ashgate, 1996)

Smith, David Frederick. "Grey, Sir George, Second Baronet (1799–1882)," Oxford *Dictionary of National Biography*, Oxford University Press, 2004; online edn., Jan 2008 http://www.oxforddnb.com/view/article/11533 (Accessed 9 Dec 2015)

Smith, Francis. *An Historical and Descriptive Guide to Leamington Spa, With a brief account of Warwick, Kenilworth, Guy's Cliff, Grove Park, Stoneleigh, Baginton, Offchurch, etc.* (Leamington, London: Southam, 7th edition, 1827)

Smith, William. *A New and Compendious History of the County of Warwick, From the Earliest Period to the Present Time, etc.* (Birmingham: W. Emans, 1830)

Smith, Reverend Sydney. "English Public Schools," review of *Remarks on the System of Education in Public Schools* (apparently published anonymously; London: Hatchard, 1809), in *Essays Social and Political* (first and second series in one volume) (London: Ward, Lock and Co., n.d. but from internal evidence early twentieth century)

Smith, the Reverend Sydney. "Review of *Three Letters on the Game Laws*," in Smith, *Essays Social and Political* (n.d.), 368–380

South Eastern Centre Against Sexual Assault and Family Violence (SECASA) Melbourne, Victoria. "False Memory Syndrome for Workers," http://www.secasa.com.au/pages/false-memory-syndrome/

Southern, Henry and Nicholas Harris Nicolas (eds.) *The Retrospective Review, And historical and antiquarian magazine,* second series, vol. I, 1827, 505–511

Spence, Jon. *A Century of Wills from Jane Austen's Family 1705–1806* (Sydney: Jane Austen Society of Australia, 2001)

Spence, Jon. *Becoming Jane Austen: A Life* (London and New York: Hambledon Continuum, third ed, 2007)

Spencer, H. J. "East, Sir Edward Hyde, First baronet (1764–1847)," *Oxford Dictionary of National Biography*, Oxford University Press, 2004; online edn, Jan 2008 http://www.oxforddnb.com/view/article/8408 (Accessed 5 Jan 2016)

Stoneleigh Historical Society. "The Swan Inn," revised 2015, http://issuu.com/stoneleighhistorysociety/docs/swan_revised_2015_for_website/3?e=9414998/13481082 (Accessed 24 November 2015)

Taylor, David. *Policing the Victorian Town: The Development of the Police in Middlesbrough c. 1840–1914* (Basingstoke: Palgrave Macmillan, 2002)

Taylor, Tom, and Mortimer Collins. *Pen Sketches by a Vanished Hand from the Papers of the Late Mortimer Collins* (1879), 2 volumes, http://babel.hathitrust.org/cgi/pt?id=mdp.39015068342321;view=1up;seq=221 (Accessed 12 January 2016)

Thorne, R. G. "Leigh, James Henry (1765–1823), of Adlestrop, Glos. and Stoneleigh Abbey, Warws," http://www.historyofparliamentonline.org/volume/1790-1820/member/leigh-james-henry-1765-1823 (Accessed 4 March 2016)

Tyack, Geoffrey. "Stoneleigh Abbey in the Nineteenth Century," in Bearman (ed. 2004), 116–130

Vague, Tom. "The Madness of King George and the Great London Riots of 1780," http://www.housmans.com/kingmob.pdf (Accessed 18 November 2015)

Walford, Edward. "Leigh, Chandos, First Baron Leigh of the Present Creation (1791–1850)," *Dictionary of National Biography* (ed. Sidney Lee), vol. XI (London: Smith, Elder and Co., 1909), 870–871

Watkins, Andrew. "The Medieval Abbey: Its Lands and its Tenants," in Bearman (ed. 2004), 198–213

West, William. *The History, Topography and Directory of Warwickshire (etc.)* (Birmingham: R. Wrightson, 1830)

Whorton, James C. *The Arsenic Century: How Victorian Britain Was Poisoned at Home, Work, and Play* (Oxford University Press, 2010, Kindle version)

Wiebe, M. G., J. B. Conacher, John Matthews (eds.). *Benjamin Disraeli: Letters 1848–1851* (The Disraeli Project, University of Toronto Press, 1993, vol. 5)

Wilson, David. *Mary Ann Cotton: Britain's First Female Serial Killer* (Sherfield on Loddon: Waterside Press, 2013)

Wilson, Harriette. *Harriette Wilson's Memoirs* (selected and edited with an introduction by Lesley Blanch) (first published by Joseph Stockdale in 1825; London: Century Publishing, 1985)

Wiltshire, John. "Exploring *Mansfield Park*: in the footsteps of Fanny Price," *Persuasions* 28 (June 2006), 81–100

Wunder, Jennifer N. *Keats, Hermeticism and the Secret Societies* (Aldershot: Ashgate, 2008)

Young, G. M. and W. D. Handcock (eds.). *English Historical Documents*, vol. XII (1) 1833–1874 (London: Eyre and Spottiswoode, 1956)

Zuccato, Edoardo. *Petrarch in Romantic England* (Basingstoke and New York: Palgrave Macmillan, 2008).

Index

A

Abinger, Lord *xvi*, *68*
accusations *ix*, *20*, *51–55*, *179*, *193*
Adam, William *xv*, *68*, *85*, *193*
Adderley, Charles *255*, *301*
Adlestrop *ix*, *22*, *31*, *115*, *227*, *233*
   Adlestrop House *163*
   burials at *221*
Adlington *159*
advertisements *59*, *177*
agents *162*
   estate agent *xviii*
   Leigh family agent *x*
Agricultural Report for Warwickshire
   xviii, *32*, *66*, *237*
Albany *66*, *128*
Albion Mills *189*
Alcott, John *xiii*, *89*
allegations. See *accusations*
American War of Independence *42*
annuity *31*, *124*
apoplexy *233*, *239*, *246*
Apperley, Charles James *131*
aristocracy *123*
   failure to pay bills *275*
   rising against *207*
arsenic *243*, *283*, *302*
   symptoms of arsenic poisoning *247*

Ash, Dr John *25–27*
Ashow *73*, *81*, *211*, *241*
   Church of the Assumption of Our Lady *223*
assault by James Leigh *170*
Assizes
   Derbyshire Assizes *208*
   Warwick Assizes *170*, *180*
   York Assizes *39*
Astrop House *163*
Atherton Stower *146*
atonement *138*, *178*
Attorney-General *xv*, *57*, *150*
Austen, Caroline *32*, *158*
Austen, Cassandra (daughter of Cassandra Leigh Austen) *158*
Austen, Cassandra Leigh (mother of Jane Austen) *xvi*, *19*, *21*
Austen, Francis *92*
Austen, James *92*
Austen, Jane (main references) *xvi*, *19*, *30*, *38*, *43*, *130*, *158*, *183*, *234*, *305*
   Jane Austen Society of Australia *v*, *22*
Austen-Leigh, Emma *158*
Austen, Reverend George *92*
authorship *xiv*, *xviii*, *22*
   Chandos Leigh *115–120*, *130*
Avon (River Avon) *45*, *192*

Ayton, Obadiah *279*

B
bad blood *85*
Baddams, John *89*
bailiff *xiii, 33, 162*
baker
   Baylis Edward *73*
   "brewer and baker" *21*
Balls, Jonathan *245*
bankruptcy
   Robert Leigh *153*
Banks, Mr *149*
Barnett, Richard *x, xi, 20, 131, 172, 193–200, 208, 249, 258–272, 302*
Bath *28, 43*
   Assembly Rooms *183*
bath house *185*
Baylis, Edward *xi, 221*
   baker *73*
Bearman, Robert *79, 274, 299*
Beckley, Oxfordshire *145*
belfry *83, 99*
Bengal *238*
Berkeley, Grenville *276*
Bertram, Sir Thomas *22*
Bicknell, Mark *231, 234*
Billinge(s), Joseph *ix, 217, 279*
Billinge(s), Matthew *xvii, 20, 174, 198*
Billinge(s), William *xvii, 203, 203–218, 279*
Billington, John *222*
Birmingham *27, 63, 96, 179, 189, 204*
Blackfriars Bridge *189, 295*
blackmail *xi, xviii, 126, 274, 299*
   poor man's libel *278*
black man *212, 241*
Blackrod, Lancashire *xiv, 49, 160*
blacksmith *146, 195*
Blissett, William *ix, 131, 174, 181, 221, 225*
blood *199, 254, 279*
   blood money *175*
   bloodstains *273, 276*
Bodkin, W H *208*
bone-collector *xii, 211, 241, 279*
Boulton, Matthew *189*
Bradshaigh, Sir Roger *153, 159*
Brandon, Charles *23*
Bretherton *159*
Brewster, Paul G *297*
bridge *x–xvii, 20, 45, 145, 173–178, 183–202, 291*
   abutments *174, 197, 213, 259*
   arches *188, 197*
   costs *196*
   foundations *131*
   rites and rituals *295*
Broadwell *31*
Brougham, Henry *xv, 65, 121, 128, 171, 286*
Broughton Castle *33, 42*
Brown, Capability *184*
Bryan, Thomas *70*
Brydges, Lady Anne Eliza *165*
Brydges, Samuel Egerton *45*
Buckingham, Lord *238*
Burford, Ann *xi, 201, 262, 276*
burials *213, 221–225, 237, 242, 255*
   disturbance of burials *283*
   summary burial *230*

Burke, John *160*
Butler, George *117*
Byrom, Henry *155*
Byron, Lord *xviii, 46, 116, 196, 275–279, 290*

C

calumnies *60, 209*
Cambridge *278*
canals *189*
Candy *267*
Canley *146*
Canning, George *128, 158*
carbon dating *242*
catacombs *145, 227*
Catholic emancipation *164*
Cato Street Conspiracy *59*
Causton, Henry Kent *xviii, 57, 57–58, 102, 141, 142–152, 176, 284, 300*
celebrity *xv, xviii, 183*
cellars *73, 145, 221*
   wine cellars *72, 75, 145, 194*
Chancery *47, 50*
Chandos
   Dukedom of Chandos *45*
   Duke of Chandos *165*
   Marquess of Chandos *166*
Chartists *204, 207*
Chawton *34, 55*
chemists *244, 249*
Chesham, Sarah *245*
Cheshire *48, 54*
Chester *159*
cholera *244*
Christ Church, Oxford *120*
Christison, Robert *244*
Christopher stone *ix, xi, 61, 154, 273, 283*
   denial of existence *81*
   witnesses to *56, 61–80*
church repairs *61*
Chute, William *93*
Cistercian *242*
class *37, 61, 80*
   idle/productive classes *167*
   middle-class *63*
cleaner *78*
Clent, Constance *53, 148, 251, 284*
clergy
   power to give jobs *31*
   sycophantic clergymen *45*
Cochran, Peter *127*
Cockshutt, Josias *38*
code *132, 274, 276, 278*
coercion *268*
coffins *261*
   child's coffin *263*
   coffin plates *45, 173, 255–256, 282*
   Cromwell, Oliver *258*
College of Heralds *24*
Collins, Mortimer *292*
Colvile, Frederick *276*
Combermere *54, 151*
   Combermere Abbey *151*
   Cottons of Combermere *54*
concealment *194*
confessions *xi, 173, 210, 220*
   deathbed confessons *210*
   false confession *267*
confusion
   sowing confusion *226*

Index

connections *120*
conscience *239*
conviction *161*
Cooke, Reverend Theophilus Leigh *145*
cooks *xi*, *173*, *220*, *243*
Copley, Sir John Singleton *xv*, *59*, *150*
Cotton, Mary Ann *302*
Cotton, Penelope *54*, *62*, *151*
Cotton, Sir George *151*
Cotton, Sir Robert *151*
County and Borough Police Act 1856 *205*
County Police Act 1839 *205*
Coventry *179*, *231*
Cox, Reverend Thomas *146*
credibility *266*
crime
  crime prevention *204*
  "crimes" *138*
Croft, James William *238*
Cromwell, Oliver
  see coffin plates *258*
cruelty *119*
Cubbington *93*
cunning *119*

D

Darley, Richard *xiii*, *64*, *67*, *81*, *162*
Dashwood, Fanny *31*
Dashwood, Mr *21*
Day, John *227*
death's head *141–160*
De Bourgh, Lady Catherine *45*
debt *275*
defunct peerage *168*

delusion *269*
Denman, Thomas *xv*, *65*, *141*, *167*, *208*, *286*
depositions *59*, *73*, *144*, *161*, *194*
depression *43*, *140*
detection *204*, *206*
Dingley, Daniel *ix*, *181*, *221*, *224*
Dingley, John *224*
disappearance *161*, *164*, *213*, *229*, *300*
discord *299*
Disraeli, Benjamin *284*
dissection *283*
dissent *117*
dissipation *122*
DNA evidence *267*
Draper, Mary *xi*, *180*, *210*, *219*, *266*, *279*
Draper, William *219*
Druids *294*
Drury, Joseph *117*
Drury Lane *126*
Dry, John *84*
Dudley, Duchess *147*
Dudley, Sir Robert *156*
Dunbar High School *189*
Duntisborne Rouse *92*
Dyer, Reverend Thomas Thiselton *292*

E

East, James Buller *238*
eccentricity *28*, *79*, *164*
Eden, Robert *258*
emigration *111*
employees *xi*
engineers *44*, *191*
  gas engineer *146*

ensigns *56*
escutcheons *65*
essays *165*
Europe *163, 167*
evasion *250*
eviction *xii, 89, 112*
evidence *46, 141*
  contamination of *268*
  false evidence *237*
evil *185*
excavation *180*
expired/extinct titles *166–168*
extortion *277*
extravagance *163*

F

fabrication *142, 149, 280, 293*
falsity
  false memory syndrome *270*
family
  destruction of records *51*
  family tree *152, 310*
Farden/Fardon, James *225*
Faulkes, Benjamin *77*
Faxon, William *xii, 180, 198, 203, 211, 241, 266, 279*
fear *20, 63, 90, 173, 268, 279*
Fenning, Eliza *243*
Ferdinand II *156*
Fiennes, Richard *38*
Fillongley *27, 98*
fines and recoveries *55*
flattery *133, 145*
Fletchampstead Hall *51*
Foote, Maria *126*

Forbes, William (?) *ix, 174, 198, 281*
forgery *155*
foul play *223*
foundation sacrifice *292*
Fountain Court *212, 241*
Fox, Charles James *132, 204*
fraud *299, 302*
Freeman, Sarah *244*
Freemasons *295, 297*
free trade *164*
French Revolution *36*
funeral
  fake/mock funeral *x, 219, 302*

G

game *31, 227*
  gamekeeper *131, 225*
Garter King at Arms *24*
gatehouse *187*
genealogy *160*
Geneva *163*
Gentleman's Magazine *25, 39, 149*
  obituary of James Henry Leigh *232*
Germany *290*
Gifford, Sir Robert *57*
Gilmore *248*
Gloucestershire *22, 92*
gold-seeking *50*
Gomme, Alice *297*
Goode, Jane *248*
Gordon Riots *36*
Goren & Price *109*
gossip *114, 125, 306*
Great Bookham *145*
greed *114, 168*

Green Dragon Inn 220
greenhouse 224, 225
Green, Sarah 226
Gregory, Colonel 229
Grenville, Richard Temple 165
Grey, George xv, 203, 245
Griffin, Charles xi, 170, 195, 203, 250, 257, 289, 300, 305
Griffin, Zara 303
guilt 138, 178
Gumley/Gumbley, Hannah xii, 66, 110

H

Hackett, Anne 47
Haigh 148
Halford Bridge 233
Hallam, Joseph 86
Hallam, Mary 87
Ham, Hannah 245
Hammersmith Bridge 295
Hampshire 34, 92
Hampson 290
Hampson, Norma 80, 150, 274, 280, 299
handbills 58
Handley, George 84
Handman, Max Sylvius 293
Hands, Richard 83
hanging 224, 243
Harley Street 39, 115
Harris, William 84, 258
Harrow School xviii, 46, 116, 162, 237
hatred 119
Hatton 132, 136
Hay, Alec 226
Hay, Alexander 281, 283

Hay (Hayward/Haywood), John x, 131, 225, 226
Hazlitt, William 130
Heard, Sir Isaac 24
Heath, Benjamin 116
heirs 29
Henry VIII 23
heralds 152
High Sheriff 101, 120
Hill, Joseph x, 24
Hill Mortimer, Thomas x, 46, 57, 104, 128, 144, 162, 212, 241, 274
   evidence of 284
Hill Radcliffe, David 299
Hiorns/Iorns/Irons, Mary 282
Hobhouse, Henry 57
Hobhouse, John Cam 128
Holland House 128
Holy Alliance 134
Home Secretary xv, 57, 203, 245, 255
homosexuality 278
Hood, Lord 91, 103, 111
household 115
House of Lords xv, 19, 39
   Privileges Committee 56, 141
Howe, Humphrey 147
Howlett, Thomas 146
Humfrey, Mr, QC 250
hunting 131
Hunt, Isaac 42
Hunt, James Henry Leigh xviii
Hunt, Leigh 42, 130
Hyde East, Sir Edward 238
Hyde, Mr 248
hypocrisy 165, 166

I

identification
  bodies of *257*
identity *217*
Ilett, John *xiii, 71, 175, 263*
illegitimacy *157*
ill-feeling *33*
imprisonment *xv, 112, 170, 287*
Ingelhart, Louis Edward *298*
inheritance *21–34, 47, 165, 170*
injury
  minor injuries *282*
inquest *xiv, 222, 229, 232, 250*
insanity *164*
inscription *19, 45, 61, 82, 107*
insolvency *49*
insurrection *116*
integrity *272*
investigation *59, 110, 148, 206, 242, 248, 301*
Iorns/Irons/Hiorns, Mary *xii, 78*
iron founders *195*
Isham, Sir Justinian *77*
itinerant workers *178*

J

James, Elizabeth *224, 241, 259, 279*
Jeacock, Job *xiii, 154, 248, 282*
Jeacock, Robert *282*
Jeffs, William *242*
Jervis, John *190*
Jones, Charles *192*
Jones, George Jnr (solicitor) *xv, 169, 209, 213, 219, 287*

Jones, George Snr *x, xiii, 51, 162, 192, 229, 273*
Jones, Inigo *188*
Judd, William *146*
jurisdiction *60*
jury *284*

K

Kelly, Fitzroy *xv, 65*
Kenilworth *xi, 68, 212, 219*
King George IV *194*
King, James *183*
King's Bench *56*
King William IV *168*
Kinman, Ann *226*
Kirkland, Samuel *x, 229, 233*
Knight, Edward Austen *34*

L

Lafarge, Marie *244*
Lamb, Charles *130*
Lamport Hall *77*
Lancashire *48, 159*
  "Lancashire stone" *45*
landowners *206, 301*
landscape designer *183*
land steward *81*
Lapworth, Mrs *222*
Law, Nancy *228*
lawyers *20, 85, 207, 208, 242, 279, 286*
  radical lawyers *207*
Leamington Spa *169, 179, 199, 220, 231*
  Museum and Gallery *289*
Lee, John *67, 84*
Lee, Joseph *259, 262*

Index

Lee, Nathaniel *151*
legend *20, 293*
Legh, Ursula *155*
Leigh
   "worthless" Leighs *305*
Leigh, Alexander *153*
Leigh Austen, Cassandra. See *Austen, Cassandra Leigh (mother of Jane Austen)*
Leigh, Chandos *x, xvi, 19, 33, 46, 55, 101, 115–140, 141, 161, 203, 237, 273–288, 290, 299*
   Dictionary of National Biography 290
   "excesses" *290*
   murder charge against *266*
   trial of *274*
Leigh, Christopher *xvi, 19, 49, 259, 261, 284*
   coffin plate *262*
   family line outlined *52*
Leigh East, Caroline *239*
Leigh, Edmund *156*
Leigh, Edward (Fifth Baron, Lord) *xvi, 23*
   insanity *164*
Leigh, Elizabeth *32*
Leigh family papers *80, 108, 195, 223, 229, 259, 274, 310*
Leigh, Ferdinand *156*
Leigh, George *xiv, 49, 53, 141, 300*
Leigh, James Henry *x, xvi, 29, 33, 133*
   compared to Mr Rushworth *185*
   mock funeral *219–239*
Leigh, James (rioter) *xvi, 169–170*

Leigh, John (I) (claimant) *ix, x, xiv, 181, 221, 269–270*
   alleged murder of *234, 234–238*
Leigh, John (II) (rioter) *xiv, 169*
Leigh, Julia-Judith *ix, x, xvi, 20, 33, 35–46, 143, 224, 262, 273*
   compared to Maria Bertram *185*
   death of *169*
Leigh, Mary *xvii, 22, 24, 47, 116*
   coffin plate *259*
Leigh, Mary Cordelia *291, 303*
Leigh Perrot, James *xiv, 29, 48, 306*
Leigh Perrot, Jane *xiv*
Leigh, Reverend Thomas *19–20, 67, 86, 143, 183, 250–256*
Leigh, Robert Holt *xvii, 158*
Leigh, Roger *xvii, 49, 148, 155*
Leigh, Sir Thomas (I) *23, 52, 156, 298*
Leigh, Sir Thomas (II) *93, 156*
Leigh, Sir Thomas (III) (First Baron, Lord) *54*
Leigh, Thomas (rioter) *169*
Leighton Buzzard *53*
Leigh, Vere *77*
Leigh, William *157, 291*
letters patent *168*
libel *xv, 19, 173, 219, 251, 277*
   Libel Act 1843 *252*
   libel trial *258*
   truth and public good *280*
Lillington *225*
Lines, John *282*
literature *46*
"Littlebrain, Lord" *186*
Liverpool *114, 155, 213*

London 28, 163, 204
  London Bridge 200
  London Docks 190
  London Electrical Society 171
Lord Chancellor xv, xvi, 50, 149, 286
Lord Chief Justice xv, 65
Lord Mayor of London 23, 298
Lyndhurst, Lord xv

M

Macdonald, Mairi 79, 299
machinery 195
magistrates 169, 173, 203–218, 227, 255, 293
maids xi, 201, 262, 276
management 161
Manchester 155, 179, 208
  Manchester Corn Exchange 179
  Manchester Guardian 214
Manning, A 151
Mansfield, Lord 210
Mansfield Park 21, 30, 40, 42, 52, 183
marriage 22, 151
  marriage registers 99
  social advancement through 185
Marshall, John 243
Marsh, James 244
Maryatt, John 282
Mason, Captain Francis xiii, 103
Mason, Francis 300
Masonic rites 295
masons. See *stonemasons*
Mason, William 174
May, Mary 245
Mellor, Mr 250
memorial stone 53, 56

memory
  recovered memory 270
mental health 24, 140, 164
Merridew, John 165
Metropolitan Police Act 204
Milbanke, Annabella 128
Milestone, Mr 186
Miller, Mr 250
misconduct 49
misogyny 129
misrepresentations 251
money xi
  follow the money 237
monument 162
  destruction of monuments 46
Moore, Thomas 294
Morland, Catherine 305
motivation 114
Mozley, Mr 155
Munro, Alexandra 174
murder ix, 19, 46, 173, 228, 273
  charge of murder xi, 173
  conspiracy to murder x
Murray, Adam xviii, 51

N

Napoleonic Wars 103
Nature
  article citing the case 291
Naylor, George 213, 259
Neve, Peter le 151
Newdigate, Sir Roger 27
Newstead Abbey 126
night-watchmen 205
"Nimrod" 131, 226

Northamptonshire *77, 163*
Northanger Abbey *19, 23, 38, 130, 183, 305*

O

oaths *278*
O'Farrell, Barry *82*
    O'Farrell approach *83, 146, 281, 283*
Old Bailey *243*
Opie, Iona and Peter *289, 297*
Orfila, Mathieu *244*
Oriel College *28*
Overton *92*
Oxford/Oxfordshire *24, 92, 120, 145*

P

paid-off hacks *284*
Palfrey, Jasper *xii, 66, 84*
Palmer, John *184*
Paris *163*
parish
    parish committee *84, 97, 162*
    parish records *45*
Parkes, Thomas *89*
Parks Ann (née Whitmore) *xii*
Parliament *166, 207*
    Parliamentary reform *164*
Parr, Reverend Samuel *xviii, 132*
passion *119*
past
    recollections of past trauma *271*
Peacock, Thomas Love *186*
pedigree *151, 157*
Peel, Robert *57, 204*
Penn, William *28*
perjury *302*

Perks, Ann *63*
Perks, John *xii, 44, 62, 146, 188*
Perks, Richard *xii, 64, 85, 162*
Perrot, Thomas *30*
Persuasion *103*
philanthropy *96*
Phillips, Sarah *216*
Piccadilly *128*
Place, Lionel *xii, 100, 101, 300*
plausibility *301*
plumbers *62*
plunge pool *185*
plurality *92*
poaching *226*
poetry *xvi, 46, 161, 178, 290*
    "Warwickshire's greatest poet" *178*
poisoning *xi, 20, 181, 219, 241–256, 255, 273, 300, 302*
    alcohol poisoning *249*
    "poisoning the wells" *149*
police *204, 280, 301*
politics
    political disagreement *300*
    politicians *xv, 286*
Pollock, William Frederick (?) *xv, 208–211*
poor relief *78*
portraits *77, 175*
post-boy *xi, 71, 175, 273*
prayer book *49*
Price, Fanny *43*
Pride and Prejudice *21, 63*
prosecution *175, 206*
    private prosecution *206*
"protection" *123*

Proud, Thomas *ix*, *20*, *174*
psychology *271*
public
"public good" *253*
public interest *286*
public school *119*
publicity *48*
publishers *252*

Q
Queen's Bench *208*, *287*
Queen Victoria *168*

R
radicalism *xviii*
Ramsay, Thomas *282*
reckless spending *46*
records
destruction of *xi*, *262*
parish records *54*
Red Book *187*
religion *37*
Rennie, John *x*, *xviii*, *20*, *45*, *188*
rents *111*
repairs *81*, *97*, *162*
Repton, Humphry *183*, *188*
Retrospective Review *151*
revenge *269*
reward *114*
Rhodes, Jane *xviii*, *112*, *123*, *290*
Ricketts, Edward Jervis *190*
ridicule *250*
riot *170*, *203*, *205*, *300*
rivalry *47–60*
Roberts, Gregory *xii*, *113*, *141*

Roberts, Henry *108*
Roberts, Mrs *98*
Roberts, Reverend James *xii*, *xiv*, *84*, *96*, *300*
Roberts, William Prowting *xv*, *207*, *208*, *269*, *272*, *280*
Robinson, Reverend William *112*
Robison, Professor John *197*
Romanticism *295*
Romilly, Sir Samuel *47*
Royal Commission *205*
Russell, Lord John *204*
Russell, Pheobe *231*
Rylance, William *49*

S
"Sally Arsenic" *245*
Saye and Sele, Lord and Lady *33*, *35*, *146*, *233*
Scarlett, Sir James *xvi*, *58*, *68*, *142*, *167*
science *171*, *204*, *248*
Scots workmen *248*
secrecy *252*
sworn to secrecy *xi*, *212*, *241*
security *22*
"Senex" *25*
Sense and Sensibility *21*, *31*
serial killers *301*, *303*
servants *20*, *45*, *61*
sex worker *xviii*, *123*
Shaftesbury, Earl of *149*
Shaw, George *x*, *xi*, *20*, *161*, *173*, *203*, *241*, *259*, *266*
Sheerness *215*
Sherborne St John *93*

Shirley, Elizabeth *79*
shooting *225*
shoplifting *30*
Shuttleworth, Philip *135*
silence
  buying silence *195*
Skeffington, Lumley *126*
Smallbone, Richard *220*
Smallbone, Sarah *xi*, *20*, *173*, *219*, *241*, *243*, *259*, *266*, *279*
  death of *203*
Smith, Charles *188*
Smith, John *47*
Smith, Joseph (workman) *ix*, *174*, *227*
Smith, Reverend Sydney *xviii*, *119*
Smith, Sydney *132*, *227*
Soden, Jonathan *xiv*, *90*, *258*, *283*
Soden, William *67*
solicitors *x*, *xv*, *169*
Sotherton *21*, *26*
Southern, Henry *153*
Spa Fields Rioters *59*
speculation *231*
Spenser, Edmund *126*
Sprawson, John *ix*, *181*, *221*, *223*
Stareton *226*
statute of limitations *56*
Stevenson, Robert *190*
Steventon, Hampshire *92*
steward *169*
  stewardship *xviii*
Stewart, Dugald *136*
St Martin in the Fields *284*
Stone, Henry *77*
Stoneleigh *ix*

Stoneleigh Abbey Thirty-four Years Ago *176*
Stoneleigh Abbey *x*, *xviii*, *19*, *161*
  attempt to seize *293*
  invasion of *169*
  management of assets *45*
  Stoneleigh Abbey bridge *183–202*
  Stoneleigh Abbey Preservation Trust Limited *77*
  Stoneleigh village church *ix*, *xi*, *xvi*, *19*, *52*, *53*, *258*
  plans and drawings *82*
  Stoneleigh church vault *258*, *280*, *302*
stonemasons *x*, *20*, *89*, *145*, *172*, *197*, *258*, *281*
  death of four masons *245*
  poisoning of *273*
strangulation *181*
Stratford-upon-Avon *225*
suicide *39*, *87*
  suicidal thoughts *140*
summary dismissal *178*
suppression *xiii*, *49*, *161*, *210*, *238*, *253*, *277*, *290*
  suppression of evidence *263*, *302*
Surrey *145*
suspects
  vulnerable suspects *268*
suspicion *119*
Swan Inn *86*
swearing *169*, *212*, *241*, *278*

T

tanner *xiv*, *49*
Taylor, Andrew *49*

Temple Grenville, Richard *238*
Temple Guiting *226*
tenants *45, 82, 89, 233*
   ejectment *56, 66*
testimony *xi, 20*
theatre *41, 233*
theology *137*
Thomas, John *x, 175, 181, 241–256, 278*
Thomas, Reverend Vaughan *xiv, 92*
Thompson, John *221*
Thomson, James *294*
throat-cutting *180, 255, 273, 281*
Tilney, Henry *305*
timber *51*
tithes *92, 95*
Toone, John *219, 231, 271*
Tossill Farm *112*
toxicology *244*
tradesmen *20, 61, 146*
transcripts *58, 80, 150*
transportation *227, 277, 301*
truth *251*
   libel case in *286*
tunnelling *192*
Turner, John *226, 227*
Turner, Orlibar *243*
Twisleton, Colonel Thomas *xvii, 35, 39, 43, 140*
Twisleton-Wykeham-Fiennes, Frederick *233*
Twycross, Edward Thornton *146*
tyranny *119*

U

usher *73*

V

valet *233*
vanity *254*
Vaudrey, Reverend Gilbert *54*
vaults *73, 228, 255, 257–272*
verse *121*
vested interest *306*
victims *177*
   alleged victims listed *181*
vigilante justice *227*
violence
   institutionalised violence *119*
"visitations" *152*

W

wagons *69*
Wake, Dr *xiv, 232*
Wake, Martha *236*
Walford, Edward *290*
Walker or Walkerley (workman) *248*
Walker, William *86, 88*
Walks in the Country *168*
Warde, Mr J *108, 259*
warrant *169*
warrener *83*
Warwick/Warwickshire *xviii, 19, 48, 93, 101, 220, 268, 300*
   Warwick County Record Office *222, 230*
Watergall *51*
Waterloo Bridge *190, 191*
Watt, James *189*
wealth *23, 166, 186, 250*
   rich and stupid client *186*
Webb, Mr *229*

Webster, John *62*
Weddington *xii*
    Weddington Castle *101*
Westminster Bridge *63*, *114*
wheelwrights *195*
Whigs *xv*, *xviii*, *115*, *132*, *165*, *204*, *286*
    druids and *294*
whistleblowers *252*
Whitehead, John *65*
Whitehead, Joseph *87*
Whitehurst, Mr, QC *180*, *232*, *242*, *250*, *277*
whitewashing *162*
Whitmore, Ann. See *Perks, Ann*
Wigan *xiv*, *xvii*, *49*, *58*, *148*
Wilcox (or Wilcooks), John *xi*, *20*, *71*, *153*, *174*, *175*, *211*, *220*, *243*, *254*, *259*, *266*, *273*
Wilde, Chief Justice Thomas *xvi*, *265*, *286*, *301*
Wildershaw *156*
Wilkes (bookseller) *274*
Wilkes, John *37*
will *28*, *45*, *50*, *56*, *250*
Willes, Margarette *163*, *164*
Willes, Reverend William Shippen *163*
Wilson, Harriette *66*, *123*
Winchester *165*, *166*, *238*
Windham, William *184*
wine cellar. See *cellars*
Wishaw *112*
witnesses *xi*, *61*, *177*
    credibility *266*
    intimidation *110*
    persuasion of *105*
    previous conviction *266*
Witts, Reverend F E *227*
women *170*
    novel-reading *130*
Wood, Billy/William *xi*, *173*, *174*, *211*, *222*, *273*, *281*, *284*
Wood, Mr (of Manchester) *155*
workhouse *86*
Wrenbury *54*
Wyatt, Samuel *189*

Y

Yarnton *92*
Yates, Sarah *158*
York *39*

Helena Normanton and the Opening of the Bar to Women
by Judith Bourne

The first comprehensive account of Helena Normanton's historic fight to join the Bar and for it to be opened up to women. It will appeal to women's groups, feminists and all those concerned with women's place in the world. Set in the early-20th century at a key time in women's emancipation it raises issues that still resonate.

The book describes how a childhood aspiration to join an Inn of Court—forged when visiting a solicitor with her perplexed mother—led to Helena's determination to open the then exclusively male Bar of England and Wales to women. It tells how—largely lost to history—the press were quick to pigeon-hole, harass and publish stories about her, leading to disciplinary proceedings concerning the barrister's cardinal sin of self-publicising. Once qualified and enmeshed in a world of men, she faced a constant struggle to establish herself against a backdrop of prejudice, misogyny and discrimination.

Helena Normanton was an unusually talented and a prolific writer for national magazines, a leading feminist in an era of profound change and a speaker who would entrance audiences at home and abroad (she toured the USA). Every step of her progress seems to have courted controversy yet she also found supporters and admirers amongst the grandest names of the day.

Paperback & eBook | ISBN 978-1-909976-32-0 | 2016 | 320 pages

www.WatersidePress.co.uk

Sir William Garrow: His Life, Times and Fight for Justice
by John Hostettler and Richard Braby
With a Foreword by Geoffrey Robertson QC

A comprehensive account of lawyer William Garrow's life, career, family and connections. Garrow was born in Middlesex in 1760 and called to the Bar in 1783. He was the dominant figure at the Old Bailey from 1783 to 1793 as depicted in the award-winning BBC series *Garrow's Law*. Later he became an MP, Solicitor-General, Attorney-General and finally a judge and lawmaker within the Common Law Tradition. *Sir William Garrow* is a generous work in which well-known legal historian and biographer John Hostettler and family story-teller Richard Braby (a descendant of Garrow) combine their skills and experience to produce a gem of a book.

'A law book yes, but boring no, a delight to read': *Internet Law Book Reviews*

'A blockbuster of a book': *Phillip Taylor MBE of Richmond Green Chambers*

'[Hostettler and Braby's] definitive biography … is informative, entertaining and a really good read, and in the process rescues Garrow from undeserved obscurity': *Littlehampton Gazette*

Paperback & eBook | ISBN 978-1-904380-69-6 | 2011 | 352 pages

www.WatersidePress.co.uk

www.ingramcontent.com/pod-product-compliance
Ingram Content Group UK Ltd.
Pitfield, Milton Keynes, MK11 3LW, UK
UKHW022226080825
461673UK00008B/299